発信型英語

10000語レベル
スーパー
ボキャブラリー
ビルディング

The Secret of Supereffective Vocabulary Building

植田一三 [著] *Ueda Ichizo*

ベレ出版

プロローグ

　皆さんお元気ですか。英語の勉強は順調でしょうか？　本書の母体となる第1弾を出版してから8年以上の歳月が流れましたが、お陰様で、数多くの読者に絶賛されるベストセラーとなり、ボキャブラリー不足に悩む日本人の語彙力UPに多大な貢献ができたことを非常に喜んでいます。

　しかし第1弾は、フレーズ化も少なく、レベル別分類も無く、CDも別売であったために、どちらかと言えば、認識語彙・表現力をUPさせる要素が強く、また収録された膨大な語彙を覚えるのが困難であった読者の方も多かったのではなかろうかと思われます。

　そこで本書である第2弾は、まず一般語彙力UPでは、タイム、エコノミスト、CNNがエンジョイでき、英検準1級・1級を始めとする英語の各種資格検定試験に合格できるように、最も重要な語彙を厳選し、頻度別に編集しています。また、語彙のフレーズ化とそのコロケーション（語と語の結びつき）のカテゴリーの頻度を明示し、必ずきっちりと覚えられるように努力しました。これによって語感が養われ、それぞれの語が非常に運用語彙になりやすいと思います。さらに、音素の解説や紛らわしい語トレーニングや語呂合わせなどによってとっつきの悪いハイレベルな語彙をできるだけ覚えやすくなるように配慮しました。

　分野別語彙力UPでは、英語の資格検定試験すべてにパスできるように、分野別と同時に検定試験別に分類し、目標設定や目的意識が明確になるようにしています。またできる限りフレーズにすることによって、皆さんの運用語彙・表現力のパワーがミルミルUPできるようになっています。さらに各種資格検定試験突破のコツや、語彙力UP

の図表や略語や、TOEIC満点突破のための多義語など、非常にためになるコラムを満載しています。そして、この分野別語彙では何よりも、日本のことは何でも英語で発信できるように、日本事象必須語彙・表現を厳選している点が第1弾との大きな違いです。

さらに第1弾とは大きく異なり、本書に収録された語彙・表現すべてを3枚のCDに収めてあり、特に分野別語彙では、英語と日本語の対訳の両方の音声が録音されているので、通勤・通学の電車の中でも効果的にボキャブラリービルディングができるようになっています（効果的な語彙補強を目指す人は、このCDを一般語彙も分野別語彙も必ずシャドーイングしながら聞いてください）。

この本＆CDをマスターすれば、皆さんの語彙・表現力はきっと生まれ変わることでしょう。そして、各種資格検定試験にもどんどんとパスしていくと信じています。

最後にこの壮大な3ヵ年プロジェクトである本書の製作にあたり、多大な協力をしてくれたASC（アクエアリーズ）英検1級講座講師の佐藤博一氏（サイエンス語彙担当）、工業英検1級講座客員講師の上田満彦氏（サイエンス化学語彙担当）、ASC通訳ガイド講座講師の田中達也氏（日本事象語彙担当）、JAIKA通訳士の迫田喜久子氏（政治経済語彙担当）、木澤晴美氏（一般社会語彙担当）、ASC英検1級講座講師の柴田哲氏（一般語彙＆校正担当）、上田敏子氏（一般語彙＆校正担当）、堺研二氏（一般語彙担当）、田中秀樹氏（一般語彙＆全体校正担当）、および出版社のスタッフと本書執筆の母体となった参考文献の著者の方々には、心から感謝の意を表したいと思います。

それから何よりも、いつも私とスタッフの努力の結晶である著書を愛読してくださる読者の皆さんには心からお礼申し上げます。

それでは皆さん、明日に向かって英語の道を

Let's enjoy the process!　（陽は必ず昇る！）

CONTENTS

発信型英語10000語レベルスーパーボキャブラリービルディング

プロローグ

第1章　語彙力アップの勉強法と実力診断テスト

1-1　語彙・表現力ＵＰの秘訣とは!?　14
　　■効果的語彙力増強の10の法則　14

1-2　実力診断テスト　22
　　1. 英検1級突破語彙問題（5問）　22
　　2. 通訳ガイド試験突破日本事象語彙問題（5問）　23
　　3. TOEIC満点突破語彙問題（5問）　23
　　4. 工業英検・ミシガン英検1級突破語彙問題（5問）　24
　　5. iBT TOEFL115点突破学問分野別語彙問題（5問）　25
　　6. 国連英検特Ａ突破時事英語問題（5問）　26

第2章　一般語彙力パワーＵＰコロケーション

2-1　第1日　一般語彙力パワーＵＰ形容詞編 基礎レベルPart1　32
　　● 音素の力でボキャブラリーＵＰ〔1〕　39

2−2　第2日　一般語彙力パワーＵＰ形容詞編 基礎レベル**Part2**　43
　　　● 音素の力でボキャブラリーＵＰ〔2〕　50

2−3　第3日　一般語彙力パワーＵＰ形容詞編 必須レベル**Part1**　54
　　　● 音素の力でボキャブラリーＵＰ〔3〕　60

2−4　第4日　一般語彙力パワーＵＰ形容詞編 必須レベル**Part2**　66
　　　● 音素の力でボキャブラリーＵＰ〔4〕　73

2−5　第5日　一般語彙力パワーＵＰ形容詞編 必須レベル**Part3**　77
　　　● 音素の力でボキャブラリーＵＰ〔5〕　84

2−6　第6日　一般語彙力パワーＵＰ形容詞編 完成レベル**Part1**　88
　　　● 音素の力でボキャブラリーＵＰ〔6〕　95

2−7　第7日　一般語彙力パワーＵＰ形容詞編 完成レベル**Part2**　100
　　　● 音素の力でボキャブラリーＵＰ〔7〕　106

2−8　第8日　一般語彙力パワーＵＰ動詞編 基礎レベル　110
　　　● 音素の力でボキャブラリーＵＰ〔8〕　116

2−9　第9日　一般語彙力パワーＵＰ動詞編 必須レベル**Part1**　123
　　　● 音素の力でボキャブラリーＵＰ〔9〕　128

2−10　第10日一般動詞力パワーＵＰ動詞編 必須レベル**Part2**　135
　　　● 音素の力でボキャブラリーＵＰ〔10〕　142

2−11　第11日一般語彙力パワーＵＰ動詞編 完成レベル　146
　　　● 音素の力でボキャブラリーＵＰ〔11〕　152

2−12　第12日一般語彙力パワーＵＰ名詞編 必須レベル　157
　　　● 音素の力でボキャブラリーＵＰ〔12〕　164

第3章　分野別語彙力パワーＵＰ文系語彙

3−1　第13日　政治語彙に強くなる　172
　　　□ 政治関係語彙に強くなる　172

- ☐ 選挙関係語彙に強くなる　177
- ● タイム・エコノミストエンジョイ必須句動詞マスター！①　179
- ☐ 外交関係語彙に強くなる　182
- ● タイム・エコノミストエンジョイ必須句動詞！マスター！②　184

3-2　第14日　経済・ビジネスの語彙に強くなるPart1（経済・金融関係）　189

- ☐ 財政・景気語彙に強くなる　189
- ☐ 貿易・国際経済語彙に強くなる　193
- ☐ 投資関係語彙に強くなる　195
- ☐ 企業活動・会計その他の語彙に強くなる　197
- ● TOEIC満点突破：意外な意味に要注意！　①　199

3-3　第15日　経済・ビジネスの語彙に強くなるPart2（ビジネス・オフィス関係）　200

- ☐ 会社・職場　最重要語彙表現をマスター！①　200
- ☐ 会社・職場　最重要語彙表現をマスター！②　204
- ☐ 商業・経営・ビジネス　最重要語彙表現をマスター　206
- ☐ 商業・経営・ビジネス　重要語彙表現をマスター！　209
- ☐ 産業　重要語彙表現をマスター！　210
- ● TOEIC満点突破：意外な意味に要注意！②　213

3-4　第16日　教育語彙に強くなる　214

- ☐ 学問分野の語彙に強くなる　214
- ☐ 学校・クラス・試験の語彙に強くなる　215
- ☐ 言語・コミュニケーションの語彙に強くなる　218
- ☐ 教育全般の語彙に強くなる　219

3-5　第17日　一般社会語彙に強くなる　221

- □ 結婚・家庭・ライフスタイルの語彙に強くなる　221
- □ 専門職の語彙に強くなる　223
- □ 宗教・イデオロギーの語彙に強くなる　224
- □ 格差社会の語彙に強くなる　226
- □ 文化・歴史・風俗の語彙に強くなる　227
- ● TOEIC満点突破：意外な意味に要注意！③　230

3-6　**第18日　スポーツ・アート語彙に強くなる**　231
- □ スポーツの語彙に強くなる　231
- □ アート・レジャーの語彙に強くなる　233

3-7　**第19日　乗り物・交通・旅行語彙に強くなる**　237
- □ 乗り物の語彙に強くなる　237
- □ 交通の語彙に強くなる　238
- □ 旅行の語彙に強くなる　239

3-8　**第20日　日用品語彙に強くなる**　241
- □ 日用品・家庭用品の語彙に強くなる　241
- □ 家・建物の語彙に強くなる　244

第4章　日本のことは英語で何でも発信できる日本事象語彙

4-1　**第21日　日本のことは英語で何でも発信できる通訳ガイド必須日本事象語彙（食生活編）**
- □ 日本の食べ物に関する語彙に強くなる　248
- □ 日本の料理分野の語彙に強くなる　255
- □ 食関連分野の語彙に強くなる　261
- □ 動物に関する語彙に強くなる　263
- □ 鳥に関する語彙に強くなる　265

- □ 魚介に関する語彙に強くなる　266
- □ 昆虫に関する語彙に強くなる　268
- □ 植物に関する語彙に強くなる　270

4−2　第22日　日本のことは英語で何でも発信できる
通訳ガイド必須日本事象語彙（伝統文化・風物編）　272

- □ 伝統芸術分野の語彙に強くなる　272
- □ 宗教に関する語彙に強くなる　276
- □ 日本人の心を表す語彙に強くなる　282
- □ 文学に関する語彙に強くなる　283
- □ 日本の行事に関する語彙に強くなる　286

4−3　第23日　日本のことは英語で何でも発信できる
通訳ガイド必須日本事象語彙（風物・娯楽編）　290

- □ 風物に関する語彙に強くなる（家の中編）　290
- □ 風物に関する語彙に強くなる（家の外編）　292
- □ 風物に関する語彙に強くなる（服）　294
- □ 風物に関する語彙に強くなる（その他）　294
- □ 伝統スポーツに関する語彙に強くなる　295
- □ 遊びに関する語彙に強くなる　298
- □ 観光に関する語彙に強くなる　299

第5章　分野別語彙力パワーUP理系語彙

5−1　第24日　物理語彙に強くなる　304

- □ 物理一般語彙に強くなる　305

（1）力　305　（2）振動、回転、速度　306　（3）流体　306
（4）熱　307　（5）光　308　（6）原子、量子　309

5−2　第25日　電気語彙に強くなる　311

□ エレクトロニクス関連語彙表現に強くなる　311
　　（1）電子物理　311　（2）部品、材料　313　（3）回路　314
　　（4）計測、試験　316
　　　□ 通信・コンピュータ関連語彙表現に強くなる　318
　　（1）通信　318　（2）コンピュータ　320
　　　□ 電力関連語彙表現に強くなる　327

5-3　**第26日　機械語彙に強くなる**　330
　　　□ 機械一般用語関連語彙表現に強くなる　330
　　（1）寸法、形状、力　330　（2）振動、回転、速度　333
　　（3）流体　333　（4）熱　334　（5）光　334
　　　□ 機械装置関連語彙表現に強くなる　335
　　（1）動力伝達装置　335　（2）振動、回転、速度　337
　　（3）流体装置　337　（4）熱器具、装置　338
　　（5）工具、加工、工作、製造、建設機械　339
　　（6）部品、材料　340

5-4　**第27日　化学語彙に強くなる**
　　　□ 化学一般語彙に強くなる　343
　　　□ 化合物に関する語彙に強くなる　345
　　（1）無機化合物　345　（2）有機化合物　345
　　　□その他の語彙に強くなる　347

5-5　**第28日　数学語彙に強くなる**　353

5-6　**第29日　スペースサイエンス語彙に強くなる**　360
　　　□ 天文学語彙に強くなる　360

5-7　**第30日　環境語彙に強くなる**　363
　　　□ エコロジーの語彙に強くなる　363
　　　□ 気象に関する語彙に強くなる　366
　　　□ 地形に関する語彙に強くなる　369

5-8　第31日　医学語彙に強くなる　373
　　□ 医療に関する語彙に強くなる　373
　　□ 病気に関する語彙に強くなる　379
　　□ 人体に関する語彙に強くなる　387

● 英語索引　390
● 日本事象語彙の日本語索引　422
● 参考文献　430

第1章

語彙力アップの勉強法と実力診断テスト

1-1
語彙・表現力UPの秘訣とは!?

　語彙力をUPさせるには、何よりもまず、様々な英語の語彙・表現が非常に好きであるということです。これは私の英検1級対策指導25年以上の経験から言えることですが、語彙の豊富な人々すべてに共通している点です。好きであると、どんどん英単語を吸収していきますが、嫌いだと表現はどんどん逃げていきます。ですから英単語・表現を覚えるには、苦手意識を持ち、逃げ腰になるのはもっての外で、今は好きでなくても、まず「ボキャブラリーが大好き、私は語彙が豊富である」と何回も唱えて自己暗示にかける必要があります。さてそれでは次に、効果的な語彙力UPの方法を具体的に述べていきましょう。

効果的語彙力増強の10の法則

1. 五感をすべて用いて語彙を身につける。

2. 英英辞典を引いて語感を養う。

3. 英単語はフレーズで覚える。

4. 語根・音素の知識を身につける。

5. 語彙の豊富な英文（放送）をインプットする。

6. 英単語の多義性・比喩的意味などに注意する。

7. 類語とのニュアンス・用法の違いを知る。

8. 英語の検定試験を受ける。

9. 覚えた英単語を会話や作文で意図的に使う。

10. 様々な英語の辞典を読む。

　まず1．の「五感をすべて用いて語彙を身につける。」というのはボキャビルの基本です。そのためには「音読」したり、「シャドウイング」したり、「フラッシュカード」を作ったり、「自分の声で語彙表現を吹き込んだり」して、「耳で聞く」、「口で話す」、「手で書く」、「目で読む」という4つの行為が必要です。大脳生理学によると、聴覚記憶というのは長く残るので、効率よく英語の語彙を覚えるためには、必ず耳で聞きながら声に出さなければなりません。音読とシャドウイングでは視覚情報が加わる分、前者の方が、記憶効率が良いと言えますが、間違った発音やイントネーションで覚えてしまう危険があるし、リスニング力を同時にUPできるというメリットもあるので、初級・中級者の場合は、特に後者をお勧めします。しかし、同時に「音読」も大切で、英語を始めた頃の私は、自分の声がヘッドホンから聞こえてくる「キオークマン」という装置を用い、それをつけた時は「変

身！」と自分の世界にこもり、8時間以上かけてニューズウィークや英字新聞をカバーツーカバー音読するのが日課でしたが、その時に語彙力が加速的にUPしました。また電子辞書が普及してから、ペーパー辞書を引いていた時と違って、英語学習者の英単語の記憶が悪くなったように思いますが、それはすぐに引けて、下線も入れず、また語彙のノートを作る人が減ったからでしょう。便利になった反面を打開するためにも、英英辞典の定義と例文を音読するように心がけましょう。

次に重要なのは英英辞典を引くということです。これは英語の語感を養い発信力をUPさせるために欠かせないことです。例えば"friend"という語を、英和辞典を引いている人は「友達」と理解するでしょうが、英英辞典（ロングマン）では、"someone who you like very much and like to spend time with"となっています。このfriendという単語は中国語の「パンユ」に相当するとも言え、日本語の「友達」よりも関係が深く、「親友」に近い感じがお分かりいただけるでしょう。また、"tactful"は英和辞典では「機転の利く、如才ない」となっていますが、英英辞典では（コビルド）"careful not to say or do something which would hurt other people's feelings would offend or upset them"、（ロングマン）"careful not to cause offense or upset people"となっており、日本語の「機転が利く」とはかけ離れており、「如才ない」の意味の一部しか表していません。前者は、英語の"resourceful（=good at finding ways of dealing with practical problems)"の方が近いと思います。このように、英単語とそれに相当する日本語とでは意味の広がり（semantic field）が異なる場合がほとんどで、attitude、integrity、proudをそれぞれ「態度」、「高潔」、「誇って」と訳してみても、それら

の単語の一面しか反映しておらず、sophisticated、experience、qualificationにしても、それぞれ日本語の「洗練された、自信のある」、「経験」、「資格」と、意味の幅がずれていることが分かるでしょう。

　次に、できるだけ「フレーズ」で覚えるようにしましょう。語彙には認識語彙（passive［recognition］vocabulary）と、運用語彙（active［working］vocabulary）があって、受験英語では前者を増やす傾向があるようですが英語のコミュニケーション能力を高めるには、後者を増やす努力（発信型ボキャブラリービルディング）をする必要があります。そのために必要なのが、どんどん英語のフレーズをInputすることです。それらを覚えることによって、その表現が運用できるようになるのです。そういった意味で英検1級を始めとする英語の資格検定対策勉強で大学入試対策のようなやり方をして、運用語彙が非常に少ないのは誠に残念なことです。そこで本書は、全体にわたって（特に一般語彙セクションでは）、フレーズで効率的に覚えられるように多大な配慮をしました。

　第4の「語根・音素の知識」の重要性は言うまでもないでしょう。日本語の場合に漢字を見れば大体の意味の見当がつくように、英語でも語根や音素から意味が推測できるようになっています。本書では第2章の各パートのコラムで「音素の知識でスーパーボキャブラリーパワーUP」を紹介しています。

　第5も言うまでもないことでしょう。具体的には「実践ビジネス英語（NHKラジオ）」、「CNN Express（朝日出版社）」、茅ヶ崎マンスリー、CNN News、タイム、ニューズウィーク、エコノミスト（購読すれば全テキストや音声が無料でダウンロードできてお得）などが

あります。それらは堅い語彙からやわらかい語彙に至るまで実に豊富な語彙、イディオムで書かれて（話されて）いて、1万語水準以上の単語や口語表現を覚えるのに最適です。また様々なジャンルの洋画の英語字幕ビデオを見ながら英語をInputするのもいいでしょう。理想的には、最低「実践ビジネス英語」、「CNN Express」、タイム（ニューズウィーク）を週に1記事（1回目は辞書を引かずに読み、2回目は引いて読む）、洋画（英語字幕）を週に1本見て、生きた教材を通して語彙力UPをしていただきたいものです。

　次に、英単語を的確に運用するには、そのコアミーニングや多義性に常に目を向ける必要があります。ほとんどの英単語は多くの意味を持っており、コアの意味から連想ゲームのように意味が広がっていきます。特に、一見簡単に見えるgeneral wordsは実態がつかみにくいので要注意です。例えば、stationも「駅」だけでなく、「発着所、署、持ち場、停泊所」の意味があり、calendarも日本語の「カレンダー」よりも意味が広く、「日程表、年間行事」の意味があります。また、一見コアの意味だけで用いられているように思える場合でも、他の意味も引きずっていますので、英単語はホリスティックに捉える必要があります。

　次に、日本人が英語のスピーキングやライティングをする時に一番厄介な問題の1つが、適語の選び及び類語の使い分けです。日本語と英語の意味の幅（semantic field）が異なるために、英和辞典や単語集を用いて「翻訳型の学習法」で主にメインの意味を覚えることにより語彙補強をしてきたほとんどの日本人は、文脈に合った適語の選びや類語の使い分けが正しくできていないのが現状です。事実、フォーマルな語を使うべきライティングやパブリックな発言でインフォーマルな語を使ってしまったり、くだけた会話で、ニュースで使わ

れるような堅い語彙を使ってしまったりすることも多いです。またポジティブな意味を持つ語と思って使うと、ネガティブな意味合いの語であるためひんしゅくを買ってしまったりすることも多いわけです。実際、英検1級に合格している英語の教員でさえも、problem、explain、develop、contribute、say、know、treat、introduce、reviewなどの基本単語を正しく使いこなせていない場合が多いようです。単語がwritten English（いわゆる「漢字英語」）かspoken English（いわゆる「ひらがな英語」）か、つまりフォーマル度が即座に分かったり、appreciative（誉めて）かderogatory（けなして）か、euphemistic（婉曲的）かhyperbolic（誇張的）かなどを覚える必要があります。また文脈によって、literal meaning（文字通りの意味）かfigurative meaning（比喩的意味）か変わってきますので、それらも両方覚えなくてはなりません。

　次に、私の経験と観察によると、ボキャブラリービルディングのモチベーションは英検1級、通訳ガイド、国連英検特Aなどのような英語の検定試験を受ける時にすごく高まります。そこで、英語の各種検定試験はパスするためばかりでなく、英語の勉強、特に語彙補強のモチベーションを高めるためにも受けるのが効果的です。英検1級だと１万語水準以上の語彙を、国連英検特Aの場合はその上にさらにタイムやエコノミストでよく使われる高度な時事英語＆イディオムを覚えないと歯が立ちません。皆さんも、どんどん英語の各種資格検定試験にチャレンジしましょう！

　9.はいわゆるOutputの機会を増やすことで、その方法としてはネイティブスピーカーと会話したり、英語のDiscussionやDebateに参加したり、英文ライティングや日英トランスレーションにチャレン

ジしたりすることなどが挙げられますが、特にお勧めなのが英語でE-mail通信したり、英文記事を読んでその感想文を書いたり、英検1級2次対策のためのarticleを書いたりすることです。そしてその時は英英辞典を引きながら、斬れる表現を用いて達意で視覚に訴えるような英語を書こうと努力することです。よく英語のInputや語彙補強の努力をしないで英語でchattingやdiscussionをしている人がよくいますが、そういった人たちは何年たっても平易な英語や日本的な発想（Japanese frame of reference）の英語しかしゃべれず、タイムや洋画のユーモアやレトリックについていけない場合が多いようです。また、重要なのは"risk takers"になれということです。こんな語彙・表現を会話で使っていいのだろうかと常に迷いながら無難な道を歩んでいると、運用語彙など増えるはずがありません。本当に運用語彙を増やしたければ、ネイティブとの会話で無理に使って、その反応を見ながら語彙補強するぐらいの「度胸」がいります。

最後に「英語の辞典を読む」ことに関してですが、これもボキャブラリービルディングには絶大な威力を発揮します。特に英語の勉強を生涯の趣味（intellectual pursuit）としてエンジョイされる方はぜひチャレンジしてみてください。そこでこの本を書くにあたって、参考文献として巻末に挙げている辞典の中で、特にお勧めのものについて触れておきます。

☆**最新日米口語辞典** – 私の英語を"生まれ変わらせた"英語道の達人、松本道弘氏の力作。この辞典をマスター後、タイムや洋画がすごく分かりやすくなった（私の場合は、例文すべてを約300時間（1カ月）かかってノートに写し、それをすべてテープに録音し、ネイティブスピーカーとの会話の中でリアクションを見ながら数年がかりでほぼすべてを覚えた）。少し古くなっている表現もあるが8割ぐらいは今で

も使える。この本を読破すれば、あなたの英語は生まれ変わる！

☆World Almanac for Kids － 350ページの子供用の百科辞典で、様々な分野の語彙を絵や写真を見ながら覚えられるので非常に効果的！

☆アメリカ口語辞典—日米口語辞典が日本語の発想を英語の発想にTranslateするための学習書とすれば、この辞典は英米人の原点である聖書やシェークスピアの発想を学び、現代のアメリカンイディオムを根本から学ぶのに必読の書！

☆現代用語の基礎知識—様々の分野の背景知識と語彙力を同時にInputすることは英字誌をエンジョイするのに"must"！

☆トレンド英語日本図解辞典—英語の発信力は、英語圏の事物を英語で何でも言える能力と、日本の事物を英語で何でも説明できる能力の2つから成るが、この本は後者の力をUPさせるのに最適の書！

　さて皆さん、いかがだったでしょうか。皆さんの語彙補強のアプローチは、今まで述べてきた10項目のうちどれぐらいが当てはまっているか点をつけてみてください。10点満点で5点以下の人は、語彙力UPの方法に非常に問題があると言えるので、すぐにアプローチを改善しましょう。よく年を取って英単語を覚えられないという人がいますが、記憶力が衰えても、最初に述べた自己暗示と10の原則を守れば大幅に改善できると信じています。それでは皆さん、明日に向かってボキャブラリービルディング！

Let's enjoy the process!（陽は必ず昇る！）

1-2
実力診断テスト

史上最強「資格7冠突破語彙テスト」にチャレンジ！

　これは現在の語彙テストの中で最もバランスの取れたハイレベルのもので、全部で30問、構成は1. 英検1級突破語彙（8千～1万語レベル語彙2問、1万～1.5万語レベル2問、句動詞1問の計5問）。 2. 通訳ガイド試験突破日本事象語彙（5問） 3. TOEIC満点突破語彙（多義語問題とビジネス専門語彙の計5問） 4. 工業英検・ミシガン英検1級突破語彙（5問） 5. iBT TOEFL115点突破学問分野別語彙（5問） 6. 国連英検特A突破時事英語問題（5問）となっています。

それでは皆さん、用意はいいですか？　制限時間は20分です。

1. 英検1級突破語彙問題（5問）

1. The pianist acknowledged the young upstart's (　　) on the keyboard.（8千語水準）
   1. prowess　2. prominence　3. proximity　4. proclivity
2. The lesser-known fortress was totally (　　) to any surprise attack.（8千語水準）

1. revolting   2. impervious   3. irrelevant   4. monolithic
3. Intoxicated by the (　　) of his fans, the movie star waved happily to the crowds.（1.2万語水準）
   1. dexterity   2. humility   3. adulation   4. supremacy
4. Relaxation in a natural setting can have a (　　) effect on one's physical as well as mental.（1.2万語水準）
   1. lucrative   2. malign   3. salutary   4. fiscal
5. You must (　　) Henry and tell him you never want to see him again.（中級レベル）
   1. fall for   2. knock off   3. level with   4. impose on

2．通訳ガイド試験突破日本事象語彙問題（5問）

1. 鵜飼　　　　（　　　　　　　　）
2. 桐ダンス　　（　　　　　　　　）
3. ぎっくり腰　（　　　　　　　　）
4. 義理チョコ　（　　　　　　　　）
5. 回送列車　　（　　　　　　　　）

3．TOEIC満点突破語彙問題（5問）

1. We should (　　) the family's request to keep the details strictly confidential.
   (A) place   (B) initiate   (C) honor   (D) juggle
2. If anything should happen, it's my responsibility and I am ready to (　　) my resignation letter.
   (A) tender   (B) propose   (C) generate   (D) file

3. Mike was given a 50-day (　　) period to pay the overdue bill amounting to $5,000.
　(A) cancellation　(B) grace　(C) credit　(D) default
4. A: How much is the taxi fare from the airport to the hotel?
　B: It's a (　　) fare of $50.
　(A) flat　(B) total　(C) regular　(D) base
5. We need at least $100,000 in (　　) money to buy the property to open a beauty parlor.
　(A) hand　(B) initial　(C) seed　(D) hush

4．工業英検・ミシガン英検1級突破語彙問題（5問）

1. (e　　) separates water into oxygen and hydrogen.
　（水を電気分解すると、酸素と水素に分離する）
2. The (v　　) of a liquid increases as the temperature is lowered.
　（液体の粘性は、温度が減少するにつれて増加する）
3. Sulfuric acid has a (s　　) of 1.84, almost as twice heavy as water.
　（硫酸は水のほぼ2倍の重さで、比重は1.84である）
4. (r　　) is a chemical change involving a loss of oxygen, an acquisition of hydrogen, a decrease in valence of a metal, or an acquisition of electrons.
　（還元とは、酸素の喪失、水素の獲得、金属原子化の減少、あるいは、電子の獲得を伴う化学変化である）
5. (n　　) is created by warming a mixture of potassium nitrate and concentrated sulphuric acid.（硝酸は、硝酸カリウムと濃硫酸との混合を温めて生成される）

5. iBT TOEFL115点突破学問分野別語彙問題（5問）

1. An auxiliary language used between groups of people who speak different languages. English is the world's most common one, followed by French.
   (1. pidgin   2. creole   3. lingua franca   4. cognate)

2. The 20th century art movement which developed between the two world wars and explored the world of fantasy, dreams and the subconscious. The canvasses employ such illogical and bizarre juxtapositions as a railway engine emerging from a fireplace.
   (1. cubism   2. fauvism   3. impressionism   4. surrealism)

3. A lump of rock or metal in orbit around the sun which varies in diameter from about 1,000km to a few centimeters. It is believed to be debris left over from the formation of the inner planet of the solar system.
   (1. nebula   2. supernova   3. quasar   4. asteroid)

4. This is a type of animal that carries its babies in a pocket of skin on its body. It was found only in Australia, North and South America, New Guinea and South-east.
   (1. rodent   2. marsupial   3. mollusk   4. primate)

5. A non-flowering plant which lacks chlorophyll and cannot manufacture its own food, depending entirely on other living organic matter for sustenance.
   (1. algae   2. fungus   3. parasite   4. cytoplasm)

6. 国連英検特A突破時事英語問題（5問）
（過去問題より出題）

（※ 1、2番は選択問題、3〜5番は文法の間違い探し）

1. Increasingly, they have a choice. With India's nascent high-tech industry expanding, a small but growing (　) of its best and brightest graduates is staying home to start careers, rather than hustling to the United States. India's braindrain is beginning to (　) off.

    A. portion – taper　　　B. segment – dwindle
    C. quota – crescendo　　D. amount – slacken

    （2000年第2回特A国連英検問題）

2. Kokubunji City Mayor wants authorities to delay the launch of the system, which was (　) by a law enacted three years ago. Critics also worry that the new system could serve as a (　) to a slew of personal data stored at different locations and make it easier for hackers to make mischief.

    （2002年第2回特A国連英検問題）

    A. warranted – toehold　　B. mandated – stepping-stone
    C. sanctioned – passageway　D. injuncted – bridge

3. Reform is inevitable, as Mr. Schroeder understands. (A) When push comes to shove, one can count on the new chancellor (B) to be a pragmatist. His government will (C) come around to discover what everybody else, including Britain's reformed Labour Party, (D) has already learned.

    （1999年第1回特A国連英検問題）

4. After the IBM computer Deep Blue (A) unseated humanity,

at least temporarily, (B) the finest playing chess entity on planet, Garry Kasparov, explained: "I lost my fighting spirit." (C) The unexpectedly swift denouncement to the bitterly fought contest, after just 19 moves in the sixth and final game, (D) came as a surprise.

（1997年第2回特A国連英検問題）

5. Nintendo Corp.'s newest video-game machine, (A) a long-awaited 64-bit player (B) that the company has been billed as state-of-the-art, (C) went on sale in 20,000 Japanese stores Sunday. Jun Ueda, a student, said he had waited in line all night (D) to be sure he got one.

（1997年第1回特A国連英検問題）

解　答

1．英検1級突破語彙問題（5問）

1. (1) prowess「優れた技術」
2. (2) impervious「影響されない、傷つかない」
3. (3) adulation「賞賛、お世辞」
4. (3) salutary「有益な、ためになる」
5. (3) level with「（人）に率直に打ち明ける」

2．通訳ガイド試験突破日本事象語彙問題（5問）

1. 鵜飼　（cormorant fishing これは常識！）
2. 桐ダンス　（chest of drawers made of paulownia ちょっと難しい！）
3. ぎっくり腰　（acute lower back pain, sprained lower back）

4. 義理チョコ（chocolate given out of courtesy　直訳して"moral obligation"を使うのは不適）
  5. 回送列車（out-of-service train, deadhead train）

3．TOEIC満点突破語彙問題（5問）
  1. 正解（C）"honor"は「要請に応じる、約束を守る」
  2. 正解（A）"tender"は「提出する」
  3. 正解（B）"grace period"は「猶予期間」
  4. 正解（A）"flat fare"は「一律料金」
  5. 正解（C）"seed money"は「元手、資本金」

4．工業英検・ミシガン英検1級突破語彙問題（5問）
  1. Electrolysis
  2. viscosity
  3. specific gravity
  4. Reduction
  5. Nitric acid

5．iBT TOEFL115点突破学問分野別語彙問題（5問）
  1. (3) lingua franca「共通語、国際語」
  2. (4) surrealism「超現実主義」
  3. (4) asteroid「小惑星」
  4. (2) marsupial「有袋類、有袋動物」
  5. (2) fungus「真菌、菌（類）」

6．国連英検特A突破時事英語問題（5問）
  1. (A) taper off（次第に減る）は必須熟語

2. (B) 制度に危険性があるという文脈を読み取ること
3. (C) come around to ～（～に同意する）の形で、toは名詞を目的語に取る
4. (B) chess playing　英文の読みの語呂の問題
5. (B) bill A as B（AをBと宣伝する）なので、受身を能動態にすること

　自分のスコアを下の6つの棒に記入して線を結んでください。形のゆがみで自分の苦手が分かるので、この本を勉強して弱点を克服してください。

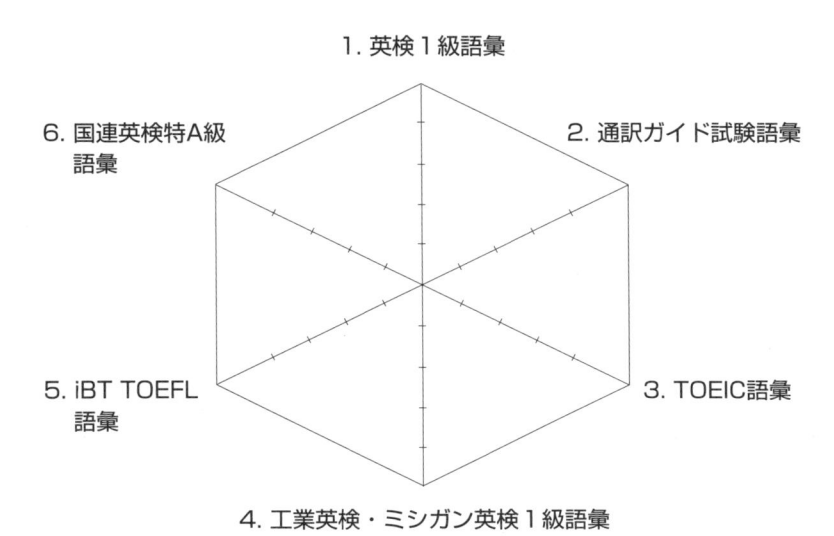

1. 英検1級語彙
2. 通訳ガイド試験語彙
3. TOEIC語彙
4. 工業英検・ミシガン英検1級語彙
5. iBT TOEFL語彙
6. 国連英検特A級語彙

（評価）
30点：資格試験を超越した英語の達人レベル
27〜29点：7冠突破レベル－非常にバランスの取れた優れた語彙力
　　　　　の持ち主！
24〜26点：5冠突破レベル－英語のプロの語彙力の域！
21〜23点：4冠突破レベル－素晴らしい、もう一息頑張りましょう！
18〜20点：3冠突破レベル－語彙力は、英語学習者の中ではかなり
　　　　　ある方
15〜17点：1冠突破レベル－一応英語のプロとしての素地はあると
　　　　　言える
14点以下：語彙力が非常に弱いので、効果的なボキャブラリービル
　　　　　ディングに励みましょう！

　さて皆さん、いかがでしたか、非常にチャレンジングでしたか？　どのセクションが難しかったでしょうか？　このテストで9割以上取れた人は苦手分野のない、広範囲にわたる語彙力UPをしている英語の実力者だと言えます。英語のプロを目指す人は8割以上取れるように頑張りましょう。また正答数が5割に満たない人は非常に語彙力が弱いと言えるので、語彙補強に力を入れて英語の勉強に励みましょう。それでは明日に向かってボキャブラリービルディング！
Let's enjoy the process!（陽は必ず昇る！）

第2章

一般語彙力パワーUP
コロケーション

2-1　第1日

一般語彙力パワー UP
形容詞編　基礎レベル Part1

　第1日～第12日の12日間は一般語彙力パワー UP 大特訓です。ここでのボキャブラリーは、あらゆる資格試験に出題される、覚えておくべき必須の927の単語を抽出し、その単語と非常に相性が良く結びつきの良いコロケーションを通じて加速的にボキャブラリービルディングを行います。この語彙をマスターすれば、タイム、ニューズウィーク、エコノミストなどに代表される英文雑誌を、辞書を引くことなく読めるようになれます。また、英検1級を始めとする各種資格検定試験にパスしやすくなります。特に、英検1級の穴埋め語彙問題などは、コロケーションを知っていれば「瞬速」で解くことができます。さらに、コラムでは音素の力でボキャブラリーパワー UP を始めとし、様々なものを enjoy するようになっています。それでは皆さん、まず第1日目は「形容詞編　基礎レベル Part1（6千～8千語水準）」です。

　本章では、特に覚えるべき最も重要なコロケーション3つの音声をCDに収録しておりますが、他のコロケーションも重要ですのでぜひ覚えるようにしましょう。

☐ **accéssible** to (the public, audience, the disabled, wheelchairs)(〜に利用しやすい・〜に分かりやすい)	「一般大衆・障害者」と結びつきやすい
☐ **afféctus** (speech, manner, way of walking)(気取った)	「態度」と結びつく
☐ **ágile** (mind, brain, motion)(鋭敏な・機敏な)	「頭脳・動作」と結びつく
☐ **alárming** (speed, rate, increase, decline, situation)(驚くべき)	「速さ・割合・増減」と結びつきやすい
☐ **ambíguous** (statement, message, attitude)(あいまいな)	「発言・態度」と主に結びつく
☐ **ámiable** (mood, manner, disposition)(愛想の良い)	「態度・性格」と主に結びつく
☐ **árdent** (supporter, fan, advocate, admirer)(熱烈な)	「支持者」と結びつく
☐ **atténtive** (care, hospitality, service)(よく気がつく・親切な)	「お世話・おもてなし」と結びつく
☐ **auspícious** (sign, start, debut, event, occasion)(幸先の良い)	「始まり・出来事」と主に結びつく
☐ **austére** (budget, fiscal policies, beauty, design)(厳しい・緊縮の・簡素な)	「政策・デザイン」と結びつきやすい

II 一般語彙力パワーUPコロケーション

☐ **authéntic** (work, painting, information, document)(本物の・正真正銘の)	「作品・情報」と主に結びつく
☐ **báckward** (countries, areas, children, culture)(発展の遅れた・覚えの悪い)	「地域・子供」と主に結びつく
☐ **bland** (statement, comment, performance, foods, diet)(精彩がない・味気ない)	「発言・実績・食べ物」と結びつきやすい
☐ **bleak** (future, prospect, landscape, outlook, vision)(見通しの暗い・荒涼とした)	「見通し・風景」と主に結びつく
☐ **brisk** (walk, business, weather, trade, breeze)(活発な・活況な・さわやかな)	「動作・取引・天気」と結びつきやすい
☐ **cándid** (opinion, advice, answer)(率直な)	「意見」と結びつく
☐ **cáptivàting** (smile, personality, story, book)(魅惑的な・人の心をとらえる)	「性格・話」と結びつきやすい
☐ **cárdinal** (issues, questions, principles, rules, law)(基本的な・主要な)	「問題・規則」と結びつく
☐ **catchy** (name, melody, slogan, song)(覚えやすい)	「名前・メロディー・スローガン」と結びつきやすい

☐ **cohérent** (explanation, argument, theory, policy, strategy)(首尾一貫した・論理的な)	「説明・理論」と主に結びつく
☐ **cómparable** (figures, data, size, costs)(匹敵する・同程度の)	「数値・データ」と結びつきやすい
☐ **complácent** (attitude, feeling, smile, laugh)(自己満足した)	「態度・感情」と主に結びつく

英検1級最重要頻出単語 その1

　語彙を増やすには、語彙問題のレベルの高さで知られる英検1級合格を目指して勉強するのが非常に効果的です。そこで、ここでは皆さんがその対策勉強をしやすいように、過去20年間の英検1級語彙問題の選択肢として4回以上用いられ、かつ出題もされた最頻出語彙をいくつか挙げておきましょう。

【過去4回以上使われた最頻出語彙】

abate, abortion, **abrasive**, adept, adjourn, allege, **amenable**, **animosity**, anonymous, augment, avert, benevolent, blatant, censure, coerce, commend, **complaisant**, contentious, dearth, deference, delegate, **demeanor**, deride, destitute, deter, detrimental, dexterous, dispel, disperse, **dissipate**

☐ **compúlsive** (gambler, smoker, shopper, drug user, bargain hunter)（病みつきの）	「常習者」と結びつく
☐ **concéivable** (risk, change, scenario, emergency)（想像できる）	「リスク・事態」と主に結びつく
☐ **córdial** (atmosphere, relationship, friendship, greeting)（心からの・思いやりのある）	「雰囲気・人間関係」と主に結びつく
☐ **crisp** (vegetable, salad, morning, air, weather)（新鮮な・さわやかな・心地良い）	「食べ物・天候」と主に結びつく
☐ **cróoked** (business, deal, river)（不正な・湾曲した）	「取引・自然」と結びつきやすい
☐ **dáring** (deed, adventure, attempt, project)（大胆不敵な・大胆な）	「行い・試み」と主に結びつく
☐ **deadly** (disease, weapon, attack, virus)（致死の・致命的な）	「病気・武器」と主に結びつく
☐ **decéased** (person, patient, family member)（亡くなった・死去した）	「人・家族」と結びつく
☐ **decísive** (action, victory, moment, factor, influence, results)（決定的な）	「活動・結果・影響」と結びつきやすい
☐ **demánding** (job, task, work schedule)（要求の厳しい）	「仕事」と結びつく

☐ **despícable** (crime, attack, lie, cruelty, killing)(卑劣な・卑しむべき)	「犯罪・悪行」と結びつく
☐ **detáched** (house, home, attitude, manner, view)(分離した・客観的な)	「家屋・態度」と主に結びつく
☐ **dísmal** (failure, defeat, performance, achievement, record)(惨めな・陰気な)	「失敗・パフォーマンス」と主に結びつく
☐ **displáced** (families, workers, people)(故郷のない・追放された)	「家族・労働者・人」と結びつきやすい
☐ **dreary** (life, landscape, prospect)(わびしい・荒涼とした)	「生活・見通し」と結びつきやすい
☐ **drowsy** (lecture, voice, silence, air)(眠気を誘う)	「声・雰囲気」と結びつきやすい
☐ **dúbious** (claim, business, practices, activities)(怪しげな・疑わしい)	「正当性・活動」と結びつきやすい
☐ **dúplicate** (copy, document, key, software)(複製の)	「書類・製品」と結びつきやすい
☐ **enchánting** (garden, house, view, picture)(魅惑的な・うっとりするような)	「場所・景色」と主に結びつく
☐ **ènigmátic** (character, smile, remark, figure)(謎の・不可解な)	「性格・態度」と主に結びつく

II 一般語彙力パワーUPコロケーション

☐ **énterprìsing** (company, firm, business people, merchant)(積極的な・企業心に富む)	「企業・ビジネスマン」と結びつく
☐ **errátic** (behavior, movement, nature)(風変わりな・行き当たりばったりの)	「行動・性質」と主に結びつく
☐ **evásive** (action, answer, reply)(責任逃れの・言い逃れの・ごまかしの)	「行為・返答」と主に結びつく
☐ **exclúsive** (club, coverage, contract, deal, right)(独占の・排他的な)	「組織・取引・権利」と結びつく
☐ **explícit** (account, instruction, agreement, consensus, guidance)(明快な)	「説明・同意」と主に結びつく
☐ **exqúisite** (design, beauty, embroidery, jewelry, cuisine)(精巧な・絶妙な)	「デザイン・作品」と主に結びつく
☐ **fanátic** (believer, fan, organization)(熱狂的な・狂信的な)	「信奉者・組織」と結びつく
☐ **féasible** (plan, project, approach, excuse)(実行可能な)	「計画・手法」と主に結びつく
☐ **fórmidable** (task, challenge, enemy, force)(手ごわい・恐るべき)	「課題・敵」と主に結びつく
☐ **frívolous** (behavior, conduct, activity)(つまらない・浅はかな)	「行為」と結びつく

□ **gigántic** (building, house, error, fraud)(巨大な)	「建物・誤り」と結びつきやすい
□ **glámorous** (woman, actress, job, career)(魅力に満ちた)	「女性・仕事」と主に結びつく

音素の力でボキャブラリーUP〔1〕

sp **spr**	スパーッと飛び出すエネルギー spa（スパー）と温泉わき出る

spasm　　（けいれん、発作）スパズム！と発作起こる
spawn　　（卵（を産む）、結果）スポーン！と卵を産む
sperm　　（精液、精子）スパーム！と精子飛び出る
spew　　　（どっと吐き出す、噴出する）スピューと吐き出す
splurge　　（誇示（する）、乱費（する））スプラージ！と金を乱費する

spook　　　（おばけ、驚かす）スプーク！とおばけ飛び出る
sporadic　　（散発的な、点在する）スポラディック！と突如起きる散発的

spur　　　（拍車（をかける）、刺激）スパーッと拍車をかける
spurn　　（はねつける、拒絶する）スパーン！とはねつける
sprout　　（芽、芽を吹く、芽生える）スプラウー！と芽を吹く

☐ **glóssy** (magazine, photo, hair, skin) （光沢のある・つやのある）	「紙面・髪・肌」と主に結びつく
☐ **gregárious** (women, animals, plants, life)（社交的な・群生の）	「人・動植物」と主に結びつく
☐ **gróundless** (accusation, rumor, anxiety, report)（根拠のない）	「非難・噂・不安」と結びつきやすい
☐ **gúllible** (customers, buyers, admirers, tourists)（だまされやすい）	「客・崇拝者」と結びつく
☐ **háunting** (images, memories, pictures, music)（忘れられない）	「イメージ・記憶」と主に結びつく
☐ **házardous** (waste, chemicals, materials)（危険な・有害な）	「汚染［化学］物質」と主に結びつく
☐ **héretic** (beliefs, views, thoughts)（異端の・異教の）	「信条・主義」と結びつく
☐ **illégible** (handwriting, manuscript, signature, memo)（判読できない）	「筆跡・サイン」と結びつく
☐ **immúne** to (disease, attacks, criticism, damages)（〜に免疫のある・〜を免れた）	「病気・攻撃」と主に結びつく
☐ **impérative** (command, need, duty)（緊急の・命令的な）	「命令・必要性」と主に結びつく

☐ **ímpudent** (attitude, remark, gaze) （生意気な・厚かましい）	「態度」と結びつく
☐ **incéssant** (need, noise, attack, demands, activity)（絶え間ない）	「必要性・活動」と結びつきやすい
☐ **indébted** (country, company, person) （負債がある）	「国・会社・人」と結びつく
☐ **indígnant** (complaints, voices, crowd, supporter)（憤慨した）	「不満・群衆」と主に結びつく
☐ **índolent** (life, worker, disease, tumor) （怠惰な・無痛性の）	「生活・病気」と主に結びつく
☐ **indúlgent** (attitude, lifestyle, parents) （寛大な・甘い）	「態度・人」と主に結びつく
☐ **ingénious** (idea, device, design, solution)（巧妙な・独創性のある）	「アイデア・機械装置」と主に結びつく
☐ **instantáneous** (response, decision, solution, access)（即座の・瞬間の）	「反応・対応」と主に結びつく
☐ **íntegral** (aspect, element, component) （不可欠な）	「側面・要素」と主に結びつく
☐ **intélligible** (account, explanation, message, expression) （分かりやすい・明瞭な）	「説明・表現」と主に結びつく

II 一般語彙力パワーUPコロケーション

■ 復習テスト

Choose the best answer from the 10 words below for each blank.

1. (　) (failure, defeat, performance, achievement, record)
2. (　) (explanation, argument, theory, policy, strategy)
3. (　) (walk, business, weather, trade, breeze)
4. (　) (character, smile, remark, figure)
5. (　) (supporter, admirer, advocate, fan)
6. (　) (accusation, rumor, anxiety, report)
7. (　) (future, prospect, landscape, outlook, vision)
8. (　) (plan, project, approach, excuse)
9. (　) (task, challenge, enemy, force)
10. (　) (sign, start, debut, event, occasion)

> A. ardent　B. auspicious　C. bleak　D. brisk　E. coherent
> F. dismal　G. enigmatic　H. feasible　I. formidable
> J. groundless

■ 解　答

1. F　2. E　3. D　4. G　5. A　6. J　7. C　8. H　9. I　10. B

　皆さん、お疲れ様でした。以上で第1日の「形容詞編 基礎レベル Part1」は終了です。次回は「形容詞編 基礎レベル Part2」です。それでは、明日に向かってボキャブラリービルディング！

Let's enjoy the process!（陽は必ず昇る！）

2-2　第2日
一般語彙力パワーUP
形容詞編　基礎レベル Part2

　第2日目は、「形容詞編 基礎レベルPart2（6千～8千語水準）」です。それでは、皆さんの語彙力をぐーんとパワーUPしていただきましょう！

□ **intóxicàted** (driver, frenzy, yelling)（酔った）	「運転手・騒ぎ」と主に結びつく
□ **íntricate** (pattern, design, work, system)（複雑な）	「形態・作品」と結びつきやすい
□ **intrínsic** (value, nature, power, quality)（固有の・本質的な）	「価値・性質」と結びつきやすい
□ **irrélevant** (information, question, answer, matter)（無関係な・的外れの）	「情報・応答」と主に結びつく
□ **lávish** (lifestyle, spending, hospitality)（ぜいたくな・浪費の・惜しみない）	「生活・消費・歓待」と主に結びつく

☐ **língering** (doubts, fears, memories, hope, suspicion)(長引く)	「感情」と主に結びつく
☐ **lóoming** (crisis, threat, disaster)(迫りくる)	「危機」と主に結びつく
☐ **magnánimous** (deed, gesture, attitude)(寛大な)	「行い・態度」と主に結びつく
☐ **márital** (relationship, problem, conflict)(夫婦の・結婚の)	「関係・問題」と主に結びつく
☐ **méager** (salary, income, hope, profits)(わずかな)	「収入」と主に結びつく
☐ **methódical** (manner, approach, style, campaign)(秩序立った・几帳面な)	「手法」と主に結びつく
☐ **metículous** (planning, attention, care, research)(細心の)	「計画・注意・研究」と主に結びつく
☐ **míserly** (spending, tip, allowance)(しみったれた・けちな)	「消費・報酬」と主に結びつく
☐ **mìsléading** (information, report, statement, answer, conduct)(誤解を招きそうな)	「情報・行い」と結びつく
☐ **mònuméntal** (achievement, blunder, failure)(記念碑的な・途方もない)	「偉業・失敗」と結びつきやすい

☐ **muggy** (heat, weather, summer, air)（蒸し暑い）	「天候・季節」と主に結びつく
☐ **négligible** (amount, mistake, damage, risk)（取るに足りない・ごくわずかな）	「量・誤り・被害」と結びつきやすい
☐ **nimble** (movement, fingers, footwork)（素早い）	「動作」と結びつく
☐ **nosy** (media, reporter, neighbors)（詮索好きな）	「メディア・隣人」と結びつきやすい
☐ **obscéne** (calls, pictures, publications)（わいせつな）	「行為・表現」と主に結びつく
☐ **obscúre** (reason, origin, author, artist, works)（不明瞭な・無名の）	「理由・起源・芸術」と結びつきやすい
☐ **òbsoléte** (technology, computer, design, building)（時代遅れの）	「科学技術・機械装置・デザイン」と結びつきやすい
☐ **óminous** (sign, warning, signal, news)（不吉な）	「前触れ・知らせ」と主に結びつく
☐ **òutrágeous** (crime, demand, price, remark, costume)（言語道断の）	「行為・要求・価格」と結びつきやすい
☐ **òverdúe** (payment, bill, interest, wages)（延滞の・未払いの）	「支払い」と主に結びつく

II 一般語彙力パワーUPコロケーション

☐ **percéptive** (observation, insight, comment)（鋭敏な・洞察力のある）	「洞察・観察」と主に結びつく
☐ **permíssive** (society, parents, attitude, law, legislation)（寛容な・許容の）	「社会・態度・法律」と結びつきやすい

語呂合わせで覚える英検1級単語 その1

英語の勉強は長期戦なので、どうしても英単語が覚えにくい人は、語彙補強を楽しくするために、語呂合わせを利用するのも一案です。

☐ **adroit**（あー驚いた機敏な奴！）
☐ **affinity**（あーひねても 大好き彼のこと！）
☐ **aggravate**（あっぐらぐらベットで病気の悪化！）
☐ **agile**（あじゃーいるいる機敏なハエ！）
☐ **annihilate**（全滅させ 穴へ入れい！ と命ず）
☐ **atrocious**（おっとろしや 残酷な人！）
☐ **aversion**（お婆じゃんじゃん増えて大嫌い！）
☐ **brusque**（ブラ透けている無愛想な女）
☐ **cajole**（お世辞過剰でたぶらかす）
☐ **carnage**（カーネじゃー 大殺戮の原因は）
☐ **chubby**（茶瓶のようにぽちゃっとした体）
☐ **coalition**（これ、しゃんと連合作れ！）
☐ **coax**（ここーくすぐってあやそうぜ）
☐ **collusion**（肩こるーじゃん 共謀は）
☐ **colossal**（殺されるほど膨大な借金）

☐ **perpétual** (motion, struggle, conflict, challenge)（永久の・万年の）	「運動・争い」と結びつきやすい
☐ **pértinent** (issues, information, questions)（的を射た・関連した）	「問題・情報」と主に結びつく
☐ **pervásive** (influence, problem, power)（行き渡る・蔓延した）	「影響・問題」と主に結びつく
☐ **pláusible** (explanation, excuse, reason, claim)（もっともらしい・巧みな）	「説明・理由」と主に結びつく
☐ **predóminant** (influence, opinion, power)（支配的な・圧倒的に多い）	「影響・力」と主に結びつく
☐ **prestígious** (award, prize, university, company, hotel)（名声のある・一流の）	「賞・組織」と結びつく
☐ **presúmptuous** (attitude, behavior, demand)（ずうずうしい）	「態度・要求」と主に結びつく
☐ **preténtious** (attitude, behavior, manner)（これ見よがしの・思い上がった）	「態度」と結びつく
☐ **prospéctive** (candidate, customer, client, employee)（見込みのある・予想される）	「候補者・客」と主に結びつく
☐ **protrácted** (negotiation, illness, war)（長引いた・長期化する）	「交渉・病気・戦争」と結びつきやすい

II 一般語彙力パワーUPコロケーション

☐ **prúdent** (management, conduct, opinion, manner)(慎重な・懸命な)	「行為・態度」と結びつきやすい
☐ **quaint** (village, town, custom, house)(古風な・趣のある)	「地域・習慣」と主に結びつく
☐ **rash** (decision, action, promise, challenge)(軽率な)	「決定・行動」と主に結びつく
☐ **rèassúring** (advice, message, smile)(安心させる)	「言葉・態度」と主に結びつく
☐ **resóurceful** (leader, executive, politician)(機知に富む)	「リーダー」と結びつく
☐ **rígorous** (training, check, test, standards)(厳しい)	「検査・基準」と主に結びつく
☐ **robúst** (economy, business, growth)(活気のある・堅調な)	「経済」と主に結びつく
☐ **rúthless** (dictator, criminal, brutality)(冷酷な・無慈悲な)	「独裁［犯罪］者・行為」と結びつきやすい
☐ **scórnful** (look, laugh, remark, attitude)(軽蔑するような)	「態度」と結びつく
☐ **sécular** (world, society, government)(世俗の・非宗教的な)	「世界・政府」と結びつきやすい

☐ **shabby** (appearance, clothes, treatment, performance)(みすぼらしい・粗末な)	「身なり・待遇」と主に結びつく
☐ **sínister** (plot, conspiracy, figure, image)(不吉な・邪悪な)	「企み・姿」と主に結びつく
☐ **sloppy** (management, handling, clothes, dress)(ずさんな・だらしない)	「経営・服装」と主に結びつく
☐ **sly** (smile, grin, look)(ずる賢い・茶目っ気のある)	「表情」と結びつく
☐ **sómber** (face, voice, cloud, mood, atmosphere)(陰気な)	「表情・雰囲気」と結びつきやすい
☐ **stággering** (success, achievement, performance, amount, number)(驚異的な・膨大な)	「業績・数値」と結びつきやすい
☐ **stale** (food, air, odor, smell)(新鮮でない)	「食べ物・におい」と主に結びつく
☐ **strénuous** (efforts, activity, exercise, work)(激しい・活発な)	「努力・活動」と主に結びつく

Ⅱ 一般語彙力パワーUPコロケーション

音素の力でボキャブラリーUP〔2〕

shr シュルシュルと縮むよ、鋭いよ！本当に君は **shrewd**（シュルど）いよ

shrewd　（抜け目ない、鋭い）シュルどーい！
shriek　（悲鳴（を上げる）、かん高い声（で言う））
　　　　シュリーク！と鋭い声を出す
shrill　（かん高い（声を出す））シュリル！と鋭い声を出す
shrivel　（しぼむ，しなびる）シュリブルブル！としぼんじゃう
shrug　（（肩）をすくめる）シュラッグ！と肩をすくめる
shrimp　エビ縮んで（小エビ）になる
shred　縮んで（断片・破片）になる

☐ **stuffy** (room, nose, atmosphere) （息苦しい・詰まった）	「部屋・鼻」と結びつきやすい
☐ **stúnning** (performance, success, achievement, view, scenery, beauty) （驚くべき・目の覚めるような）	「業績・眺め」と結びつきやすい
☐ **suscéptible to** (damage, disease, attack, pressure)（〜の影響を受けやすい）	「被害・病気・攻撃」と結びつきやすい

☐ **tácit** (understanding, agreement, acceptance, approval)（暗黙の）	「同意・理解」と結びつく
☐ **tédious** (job, chore, task)（退屈な）	「仕事」と結びつく
☐ **tèmperaméntal** (nature, character, disposition)（気まぐれな・気分屋の）	「性格」と主に結びつく
☐ **tenácious** (efforts, strength, resistance, opposition)（粘り強い）	「力・抵抗」と主に結びつく
☐ **tránsient** (popularity, fashion, life, pleasure)（一時的な・はかない）	「人気・人生」と主に結びつく
☐ **trífling** (matter, affair, amount, sum, charge)（些細な・わずかな）	「出来事・金額」と主に結びつく
☐ **unpáralleled** (achievement, record, growth, prosperity)（比類なき）	「業績・繁栄」と主に結びつく
☐ **unprécedented** (scale, level, move, step)（前例のない）	「規模・措置」と主に結びつく
☐ **véhement** (opposition, objection, criticism, attack)（熱心な・猛烈な）	「抗議・批判」と主に結びつく
☐ **vénerable** (saint, priest, tradition, institution)（由緒ある・伝統を誇る）	「聖人・伝統」と結びつきやすい

☐ **víle** (odor, smell, crime, attack, rumor) （汚い・ひどい）	「におい・悪行」と主に結びつく
☐ **vúlgar** (tongue, language, words) （下品な・俗悪な）	「言葉」と主に結びつく
☐ **wícked** (grin, smile, crime, deed) （邪悪な）	「表情・行い」と主に結びつく

■ 復習テスト

Choose the best answer from the 10 words below for each blank.
1. (　) (job, chore, task)
2. (　) (training, check, test, standards)
3. (　) (odor, smell, crime, attack, rumor)
4. (　) (planning, attention, care, research)
5. (　) (efforts, strength, resistance, opposition)
6. (　) (management, handling, clothes, dress)
7. (　) (technology, computer, design, building)
8. (　) (understanding, agreement, acceptance, approval)
9. (　) (award, prize, university, company, hotel)
10. (　) (crisis, threat, disaster)

A. looming   B. meticulous   C. obsolete   D. prestigious
E. rigorous   F. sloppy   G. tacit   H. tedious   I. tenacious
J. vile

■ 解　答
1. H　2. E　3. J　4. B　5. I　6. F　7. C　8. G　9. D　10. A

　皆さん、お疲れ様でした。以上で第2日の「形容詞編 基礎レベル Part2」は終了です。次回は「形容詞編 必須レベル Part1」です。それでは、明日に向かってボキャブラリービルディング！
Let's enjoy the process!（陽は必ず昇る！）

2-3　第3日
一般語彙力パワーUP
形容詞編　必須レベル Part1

　第3日目は、必須レベル（8千～1.2万水準）の一般語彙力パワーUPにチャレンジしていただきましょう。このレベルの単語が分かってくると、洋書やタイム、ニューズウィーク、エコノミストなども辞書なしで読めるようになってくるので、英文リーディングが非常に楽になってきます。それでは第3日目の「形容詞編 必須レベルPart1」を最後まで頑張りましょう!!

□ **abbréviàted** (word, name, version, time, plan)（短縮された・略された）	「語句・形式」と主に結びつく
□ **àcrimónious** (debate, dispute, exchange, argument, lawsuit)（激しい・辛らつな）	「議論」と結びつく
□ **ádamant** (opposition, refusal, attitude, position)（断固とした・頑固な）	「反対・態度」と主に結びつく
□ **adróit** (handling, maneuvering, management)（巧みな）	「取り扱い」と結びつく

☐ **áffable** (demeanor, character, personality, nature)（愛想の良い）	「態度・性格」と結びつく
☐ **àltruístic** (love, action, behavior)（利他的な）	「態度・行為」と主に結びつく
☐ **ámicable** (settlement, agreement, relationships)（友好的な）	「関係・取り決め」と主に結びつく
☐ **ántiquàted** (ideas, method, system, view)（時代遅れの・旧式の）	「考え・方法」と主に結びつく
☐ **àpathétic** (attitude, behavior, audience)（冷淡な・無関心な）	「態度」と主に結びつく
☐ **appálling** (crime, cruelty, incident)（恐ろしい・衝撃的な）	「惨事」と結びつく
☐ **archáic** (rules, word, smile)（古風な・時代遅れの）	「規則・言語・表情」と結びつきやすい
☐ **ascétic** (practice, training, monk, life)（禁欲的な）	「修行・生活」と主に結びつく
☐ **astúte** (management, observation, investment, businesspeople)（目先の利く・抜け目ない）	「経営手腕・観察」と結びつきやすい
☐ **atrócious** (crime, offense, brutality)（凶悪の・残虐な）	「犯罪・残虐」と結びつく

II 一般語彙力パワーUPコロケーション

☐ **audácious** (attack, demand, attempt)（大胆不敵な）	「攻撃・要求・試み」と結びつきやすい
☐ **authóritàtive** (statement, voice, advice)（権威ある・正式な）	「声明」と結びつきやすい
☐ **àutocrátic** (rule, leadership, government)（独裁的な・横暴な）	「支配・政府」と結びつく
☐ **àvarícious** (person, nature, disposition)（欲深い・貪欲な）	「人・性格」と結びつく
☐ **bálmy** (weather, climate, wind, breeze)（さわやかな）	「天候」と結びつく
☐ **banál** (question, joke, remark, story)（平凡な・つまらない）	「発言」と結びつく
☐ **bizárre** (taste, behavior, situation)（奇妙な・異様な）	「趣味・振る舞い・状況」と結びつきやすい
☐ **bríttle** (bone, ceramic, glass)（もろい・壊れやすい）	「壊れやすいもの」と主に結びつく
☐ **búoyant** (economy, business, market)（上り調子の・回復力のある）	「経済」と主に結びつく
☐ **búrgeoning** (industry, market, business)（急成長する・新興の）	「産業」と主に結びつく

☐ **cállous** (attitude, behavior, disregard) （無神経な・冷淡な）	「態度」と結びつく
☐ **càtegórical** (denial, statement, answer)（絶対的な・明確な・断定的な）	「主張」と結びつく
☐ **clandéstine** (meeting, activity, operation, affair)（秘密の・人目につかない）	「会議・活動」と主に結びつく

英検1級最重要頻出単語 その2

その1と同様、太字の語彙はハイレベルな未知語であるかもしれません。英検1級の語彙問題は、選択肢の意味が文脈なしで理解できないといけないので、1、2ともに8割ぐらいは分かるように語彙補強に励みましょう（太字はハイレベルな語）。

【過去4回以上使われた最頻出語彙】

dividend, **divulge,** elude, emanate, embody, entice, eradicate, **exhort,** forgery, impede, implore, **inept,** intervene, lucrative, marginal, muster, oblivious, plight, **precipitate, preclude,** procure, **rampage,** reminisce, **rout,** seclude, tenacious, viable

---

☐ **colóssal** (statue, figure, stone) （巨大な・壮大な）	「像」と主に結びつく

☐ **commúnal** (facility, property, harmony, violence)（共同の・公共の）	「施設・状況」と主に結びつく
☐ **compélling** (reason, evidence, argument, story)（説得力のある）	「理由・証拠」と主に結びつく
☐ **còndescénding** (attitude, look, laugh)（へりくだった・人を見下すような）	「態度」と結びつく
☐ **condúcive** to (growth, success, development) （〜の助けとna る・〜に貢献する）	「成長・成功」と主に結びつく
☐ **conténtious** (issue, matter, area) （議論を起こす）	「問題・地域」と主に結びつく
☐ **crass** (remark, statement, attempt, action)（粗野な・下品な）	「言動」と主に結びつく
☐ **crúmpled** (paper, clothes, suit) （しわくちゃの）	「紙・服」と主に結びつく
☐ **curt** (statement, message, answer) （素っ気ない・短い）	「言葉」と主に結びつく
☐ **dainty** (hands, feet, cup) （きゃしゃな・繊細な）	「肢体・装飾物」と結びつきやすい
☐ **dáunting** (challenge, task, prospect) （おじけづかせる）	「課題・展望」と主に結びつく

☐ **defórmed** (baby, child, body) （奇形の）	「人体」と結びつきやすい
☐ **deft** (handling, footwork, movement) （器用な・手際の良い）	「取り扱い・動作」と結びつきやすい
☐ **defúnct** (company, government, practice, law)（現存しない・廃止された）	「組織・慣習」と主に結びつく
☐ **dejécted** (look, face, troops) （落胆した・意気消沈した）	「表情・人（集団）」と主に結びつく
☐ **derógatory** (remarks, comment, name)（軽蔑的な）	「発言・言葉」と結びつく
☐ **devóut** (Christian, pilgrims, faith, follower)（敬虔な・信心深い）	「信者・信仰」と結びつく
☐ **déxterous** (pianist, fingers, hands, movement)（器用な・機敏な・巧妙な）	「職人・手の動作」と結びつく
☐ **diláted** (pupils, blood vessels, arteries)（広がった・拡張した）	「身体の器官」と結びつく
☐ **díre** (straits, need, poverty) （急を要する・ひどい）	「窮状・必要性」と主に結びつく
☐ **dispáraging** (remarks, comments, statement)（中傷的な）	「発言」と結びつく

II 一般語彙力パワーUPコロケーション

□ **dispássionate** (analysis, assessment, voice, view)（公平な・冷静な）	「分析・意見」と結びつきやすい

音素の力でボキャブラリーUP〔3〕

gl　光、光る　**glory** は栄光の光

glimmer　（ちらちら光る、かすかに光る）
glisten　（ぴかぴか光る）
glint　　（きらきら光る）
gloat　　（ほくほく［満足］している）嬉しそうな人は光っているから
glare　　（ぎらぎら光る）
glow　　（白熱（して輝く）、冷光（を放つ））
gloss　　（光沢，つや（を出す））
glaze　　（うわ薬をかける）とぴかぴか光る
glimpse　光を当てて（ちらりと光る、かすかな光）

☐ **drówsy** (eyes, voice, driving) （眠そうな）P.37の補足	「目・声・運転」と結びつきやすい
☐ **eláted** (face, smile, feeling, mood) （大喜びで）	「表情・感情」と主に結びつく
☐ **emáciàted** (body, face, appearance) （やせ衰えた・やつれた）	「体・姿」と結びつく
☐ **embédded** in (system, framework, culture)（埋め込まれた・組み込まれた）	「体制・文化」と結びつきやすい
☐ **èmbryónic** (development, stage, period)（初期の・胎児の）	「発達・段階」と主に結びつく
☐ **empáthic** (understanding, reading, response)（共感的な・親身の）	「理解・対応」と結びつきやすい
☐ **endéaring** (smile, gesture, character) （親しみやすい・愛情のこもった）	「しぐさ・性格」と主に結びつく
☐ **ensúing** (battle, conflict, controversy) （後に続く・結果として起こる）	「争い」と結びつきやすい
☐ **entícing** (dishes, smell, incentives, perks)（魅惑的な）	「料理・特典」と結びつきやすい
☐ **équitable** (share, distribution, allocation)（公平な・公正な）	「分配」と主に結びつく

II　一般語彙力パワーUPコロケーション

☐ **érudìte** (professor, scholar, knowledge, study)(博学な)	「博学者・知識」と結びつきやすい
☐ **èsotéric** (Buddhism, practices, rites)(難解な・秘伝的な)	「宗教・儀式」と主に結びつく
☐ **estránged** (couple, husband, wife)(疎遠になった・別居している)	「カップル・夫婦」と結びつきやすい
☐ **exálted** (position, status, spirit, love)(気高い)	「地位・精神」と結びつきやすい
☐ **exásperàted** (look, voice, cry)(いら立った)	「態度」と主に結びつく
☐ **excrúciàting** (pain, agony, ordeal)(耐え難いほどの)	「苦痛」と結びつく
☐ **exórbitant** (price, demand, fee)(法外な)	「価格・要求」と結びつく
☐ **fáltering** (economy, market, steps)(よろめく・低迷している)	「経済・足取り」と結びつきやすい
☐ **fár-fétched** (idea, dream, story)(ありそうもない)	「考え・話」と主に結びつく
☐ **fár-réaching** (influence, impact, program, plan)(広範囲にわたる・遠大な)	「影響・計画」と主に結びつく

☐ **fastídious** (care, attention, cleanliness, appetite)（細心の・好みにうるさい）	「注意・性癖」と結びつきやすい
☐ **ferócious** (attack, fighting, battle, competition)（激しい）	「攻撃・争い」と結びつく
☐ **férvent** (supporter, believer, advocate)（熱心な・熱意のある）	「支持者・信者」と結びつく
☐ **fíckle** (market, consumer, weather, wind)（気まぐれな）	「経済・天候」と結びつきやすい
☐ **flágrant** (violation, breach, error)（極悪の・はなはだしい）	「犯罪・誤り」と結びつく
☐ **flambóyant** (costumes, clothes, personality, character)（派手な）	「衣装・性格」と主に結びつく

■ 復習テスト

Choose the best answer from the 10 words below for each blank.

1. (　) (pain, agony, ordeal)
2. (　) (debate, dispute, exchange, argument, lawsuit)
3. (　) (crime, offense, brutality)
4. (　) (supporter, believer, advocate)
5. (　) (price, demand, fee)
6. (　) (company, government, practice, law)
7. (　) (economy, business, market)
8. (　) (Buddhism, practices, rites)
9. (　) (denial, statement, answer)
10. (　) (challenge, task, prospect)

A. acrimonious　B. atrocious　C. buoyant　D. categorical
E. daunting　F. defunct　G. esoteric　H. excruciating
I. exorbitant　J. fervent

■ 解　答

1. H　2. A　3. B　4. J　5. I　6. F　7. C　8. G　9. D　10. E

皆さん、お疲れ様でした。以上で第3日の一般語彙力パワーUP「形容詞編 必須レベル Part1」は終了です。次回は「形容詞編 必須レベル Part2」です。それでは、明日に向かってボキャブラリービルディング！
Let's enjoy the process!（陽は必ず昇る！）

アルファベットの意味を知る！ その1

　英単語を覚える時に、アルファベットの語感を持つことは非常に役立つことが多いので、ぜひ知っておきましょう！

A：ウアーッと広がり〜に向かう（add, expand, demand, land）
B：バンと叩いて壊れる（batter, break, blow, bomb, blast）
C：くっと中へ閉じ込め固定する（contain, close, confine, choke, charm）
D：どんどん下へ落ちて離れていく（down, drop, drip, dump）
E：2つの物がどんどん伸びて引っつく（extend, meet, echo, even, exert）
F：フアーッと舞い上がる（fly, fire, float, flame, flare, flirt）
G：グイッと引き寄せる（get, grab, grip, graze, greed, gist）
H：力を加えて高く上げるフレー！胴上げのイメージ
　（honor, hail, howl, heave, hoist, heap, hectic, hype）
I：ぴったり合って細長くなる（両手を引っつけたイメージ）
　（fit, initiate, inlet, inside, slit, instinct, institute, intricate）
J：圧力を加えるとジューッと飛び出す（jet, juice, jut, jubilant, jab, jitter）
K：味方を守り、敵を突き飛ばす（keep, kick, knife, kind, kindle）
L：力が緩んで広がる（long, lax, loose, lust, slack, late）
M：どんどん増えて固まる（mountain, mammoth, mold, magma, maximum）

2-4 第4日
一般語彙力パワーUP
形容詞編 必須レベル Part2

　第4日目は、「形容詞編 必須レベルPart2（8千〜1.2万語水準）」です。それでは、皆さんの語彙力をぐーんとパワーUPしていただきましょう!!

☐ **flashy**(clothes, dress, jewelry)（派手な）	「服装・装飾品」と主に結びつく
☐ **flimsy**(excuse, evidence, clothing, material)（薄っぺらい）	「主張・素材」と主に結びつく
☐ **fortúitous**(discovery, happening, meeting)（偶然の）	「発見・出来事」と主に結びつく
☐ **fráctious**(politics, nation, baby, animal)（対立が絶えない・気難しい）	「政治・動物」と結びつきやすい
☐ **frántic**(search, effort, attempt, activity)（必死の・死に物狂いの）	「捜索・試み」と結びつく

☐ **fraught** with (dangers, problems, difficulties)(〜に満ちた)	「危険・困難」と結びつきやすい
☐ **fúll-flédged** (member, war, service)(一人前の・本格的な)	「職業・規模」と主に結びつく
☐ **gaunt** (face, body, figure)(やせこけた)	「顔・体」と主に結びつく
☐ **giddy** (height, excitement, sensation)(目がくらむ・有頂天の)	「高所・興奮」と主に結びつく
☐ **glib** (tongue, answer, salesperson, politician)(口先だけの・口のうまい)	「言葉・発話者」と結びつく
☐ **gráphic** (design, artist, image, description)(図形の・生き生きした)	「デザイン・イメージ」と主に結びつく
☐ **grúeling** (task, training, race, battle, schedule)(厳しい・必死の)	「仕事・争い」と主に結びつく
☐ **hággard** (face, look, appearance)(やつれた)	「表情・姿」と結びつく
☐ **hapházard** (approach, manner, fashion, sampling)(でたらめの・偶然の)	「手法」と主に結びつく
☐ **hazy** (idea, memory, dream)(かすみがかかった・漠然とした)	「考え・記憶」と結びつきやすい

Ⅱ 一般語彙パワーUPコロケーション

☐ **héctic**(schedule, lifestyle, pace) （あわただしい）	「ライフスタイル」と主に結びつく
☐ **hefty**(fine, price, pay, tax) （多額の・圧倒的な）	「お金・支払い」と結びつく
☐ **hilárious**(joke, comedy, story, tale) （こっけいな）	「冗談・話」と主に結びつく
☐ **horréndous**(crime, accident, experience, injuries)（身の毛もよだつ・恐ろしい）	「犯罪・事件」と主に結びつく
☐ **húmdrùm**(job, life, routine) （平凡な・退屈な）	「仕事・生活」と結びつく
☐ **immáculate**(condition, appearance, collection)（清潔な・欠点のない）	「状態・収集物」と主に結びつく
☐ **ímminent**(danger, threat, crisis) （切迫した）	「危険」と主に結びつく
☐ **impéccable**(service, performance, taste, credentials)（非の打ち所のない）	「パフォーマンス・経歴」と結びつきやすい
☐ **impénding**(death, crisis, danger) （差し迫った・今にも起こりそうな）	「危険」と主に結びつく
☐ **impérvious** to (heat [water], pain, criticism)（～を通さない・～に鈍感で）	「熱［水］・痛み・批判」と結びつきやすい

□ **incípient** (disease, sign, stage) （始まりの・初期の）	「病気・兆候」と主に結びつく
□ **indélible** (image, impression, stain, ink)（消えない）	「印象・染み」と結びつく
□ **índigent** (artist, child, population) （貧しい）	「人」と結びつく
□ **inépt** (management, handling, government, bureaucrats) （不適切な・能力に欠ける）	「管理・組織」と主に結びつく
□ **ingénuous** (mind, nature, smile) （無邪気な・純真な）	「性格」と主に結びつく
□ **ingráined** (habit, prejudice, behavior, attitude)（根深い・深く染み込んだ）	「習慣・行動」と結びつく

語呂合わせで覚える英検1級単語 その2

- □ **daunt**（どーんと 気力をくじいちゃう！）
- □ **detest**（なんでテストよ大嫌い！）
- □ **dilate**（早く出れ！と道を広げる）
- □ **dire**（不吉な ダイヤは犯罪の元）
- □ **disperse**（何ですぱーすぱ煙撒き散らす！）
- □ **elude**（警察いるーど速く逃げろ！）
- □ **embezzle**（いいんべずるずるお金を横領）

- ☐ **eschew**（イエス、チューしてもセックス避ける）
- ☐ **faux pas**（失敗するとはアホーパー！）
- ☐ **fervent**（ふぁーばんばんと燃え盛る）
- ☐ **fiasco**（ふぃあー！すこぶる大失敗！）
- ☐ **fickle**（ふぃくるくる変わる気まぐれな）
- ☐ **fissure**（フィーシャーシャー水漏れ裂け目から）
- ☐ **flounder**（もがいてもがいてふらふらんだー！）
- ☐ **foment**（ほめんと 扇動するのは難しい）
- ☐ **farce**（ふぁーすごい茶番だぜ）

☐ **inqúisitive** (mind, spirit, bystanders, reporters)（探求好きな・せんさく好きな）	「気性・人」と主に結びつく
☐ **insátiable** (appetite, greed, desire, avarice)（貪欲な）	「欲望」と結びつく
☐ **inscrútable** (face, mask, countenance)（不可解な・深遠な）	「顔・表情」と結びつく
☐ **insídious** (disease, threat, problem)（潜行性の・陰湿な）	「病気・脅威」と結びつきやすい
☐ **insínuàting** (remark, voice, manner)（ほのめかした）	「言葉・態度」と結びつく
☐ **insípid** (performance, joke, taste)（面白みのない・味気ない）	「パフォーマンス・味覚」と結びつきやすい

☐ **ìnsurmóuntable** (obstacle, problem, difficulties)（乗り越えられない）	「障害」と結びつく
☐ **intráctable** (problem, pain, conflict)（手に負えない・治りにくい）	「問題・痛み」と主に結びつく
☐ **invíncible** (army, force, spirit)（無敵の・ゆるぎない）	「軍隊・精神」と主に結びつく
☐ **ìrrefútable** (evidence, proof, argument)（反ばくできない）	「証拠・主張」と主に結びつく
☐ **irrévocable** (contract, decision, damage, loss)（取り消し不能の）	「契約・決定・損害」と結びつきやすい
☐ **jóvial** (mood, atmosphere, crowd)（陽気な）	「雰囲気・人」と主に結びつく
☐ **júbilant** (crowd, supporters, celebration, festivities)（喜びに満ちた・歓喜の）	「群衆・祭り」と主に結びつく
☐ **lácklùster** (economy, performance, trading)（活気のない・精彩を欠いた）	「経済・パフォーマンス」と結びつきやすい
☐ **láudable** (goal, attempt, objective)（称賛に値する）	「目標・試み」と主に結びつく
☐ **lénient** (treatment, sentence, attitude)（寛大な・甘い）	「処置・態度」と主に結びつく

☐ **lewd**(conduct, act, expression) （みだらな）	「行為・表現」と主に結びつく
☐ **listless**(face, feeling, performance) （無気力な）	「表情・パフォーマンス」と結びつく
☐ **lúcid**(explanation, argument, statement) （明快な）	「主張・説明」と結びつきやすい
☐ **lúcrative** (job, business, deal, contract) （もうかる）	「ビジネス・契約」と結びつく
☐ **lúdicrous**(idea, price, situation) （こっけいな・ばかげた）	「考え・価格・状況」と結びつきやすい
☐ **lúkewárm** (response, reaction, support, interest)（生ぬるい・気のない）	「反応・支持・興味」と結びつきやすい
☐ **luxúriant**(growth, grass, hair) （豊かな・青々と茂った）	「成長・植物」と結びつきやすい
☐ **malévolent**(evil, spirit, ghost) （悪意のある）	「悪・霊」と結びつく

音素の力でボキャブラリー UP〔4〕

squ キューと押しつぶすエネルギー！ **squeeze** と締めつけられて苦しいよう〜！

- squabble （口論（する）、小ぜり合い）してお互いを締めつける
- squalid （不潔な、むさ苦しい、下劣な）押しつぶされたむさ苦しい部屋
- squander （浪費する、散財する）浪費して家計が締めつけられる
- squirm 締められ（身をよじる、もがく）
- squash （押し［踏み］つぶす、押し［詰め］込む）
- squeak （キーキーきしむ、ギャーギャー泣く）
- squeal （キーキー［ギャーギャー］と言う）
- squawk 絞めつけられて（ガーガー鳴き、ブーブー言う）
- squelch （押しつぶして）ぺちゃんこにする
- squirt ギュッと絞ると（噴出、ほとばしる）

☐ **mèdiócre** (performance, life, school grade)（平凡な・月並な）	「パフォーマンス」と主に結びつく
☐ **ménial** (job, task, work, chore)（退屈で・単調な）	「仕事」と結びつく

一般語彙力パワーUPコロケーション

II

☐ **mércenàry** (army, force, troops) （報酬目当ての）	「軍隊」と主に結びつく
☐ **mórbid** (love, curiosity, fascination, fear, imagination)（病的な）	「感情・興味・想像」と主に結びつく
☐ **mundáne** (affairs, tasks, chores) （平凡な・ありふれた）	「出来事・仕事」と結びつく
☐ **mýstic** (power, rites, lake) （神秘的な）	「力・儀式・自然」と結びつきやすい
☐ **obnóxious** (attitude, behavior, character)（不快な）	「態度・性格」と結びつく
☐ **opínionàted** (comment, remarks, guide)（頑固な・独断的な）	「発言」と主に結びつく
☐ **òpportúne** (moment, time, occasion) （適当な・好都合の・時宜を得た）	「時節」と結びつく
☐ **osténsible** (purpose, aim, reason) （見せかけの）	「目的・理由」と主に結びつく
☐ **òstentátious** (wealth, lifestyle, display) （派手な）	「富・態度」と主に結びつく
☐ **óvercàst** (sky, weather, day) （曇った・陰鬱な）	「天気」と主に結びつく

☐ **págan**(religion, rites, worship) （異教の）	「宗教・儀式」と主に結びつく
☐ **páltry**(salary, wage, budget) （わずかな）	「給料・予算」と主に結びつく
☐ **páramòunt** (importance, concern, leader, chief)（最重要の・最高の）	「重要性・関心事・リーダー」と主に結びつく
☐ **paróchial** (interests, views, attitude) （偏狭な）	「態度・見方」と主に結びつく
☐ **pátronìzing**(attitude, manner, remarks) （横柄な・恩着せがましい）	「態度」と結びつく
☐ **pedántic** (speech, lecture, writing style)（学者ぶった）	「発言・文体」と主に結びつく
☐ **pénitent**(sinner, thief, offender) （後悔した）	「罪人」と結びつく
☐ **pént-úp**(frustration, anger, demand) （うっ積した）	「感情・需要」と結びつく
☐ **perémptory** (command, demand, instruction)（有無を言わせぬ）	「命令・要求」と結びつく

■ 復習テスト

Choose the best answer from the 10 words below for each blank.

1. (　) (disease, sign, stage)
2. (　) (task, training, race, battle, schedule)
3. (　) (joke, comedy, story, tale)
4. (　) (attitude, manner, remarks)
5. (　) (moment, time, occasion)
6. (　) (explanation, argument, statement)
7. (　) (death, crisis, danger)
8. (　) (job, business, deal, contract)
9. (　) (management, handling, government, bureaucrats)
10. (　) (appetite, greed, desire, avarice)

A. grueling   B. hilarious   C. impending   D. incipient
E. inept   F. insatiable   G. lucid   H. lucrative   I. opportune
J. patronizing

■ 解　答
1. D   2. A   3. B   4. J   5. I   6. G   7. C   8. H   9. E   10. F

皆さん、お疲れ様でした。以上で第4日の「形容詞編 必須レベル Part2」は終了です。次回は「形容詞編 必須レベル Part3」です。それでは、明日に向かってボキャブラリービルディング！

Let's enjoy the process!（陽は必ず昇る！）

2-5　第5日

一般語彙力パワー UP
形容詞編　必須レベル Part3

　第5日目は、「形容詞編 必須レベルPart3（8千〜1.2万語水準）」です。それでは、皆さんの語彙力をぐーんとパワー UP していただきましょう!!

☐ **perfúnctory**(attitude, manner, glance, look)（おざなりの・熱意のない）	「態度・振る舞い」と主に結びつく
☐ **pithy**(comment, remark, summary, sentence)（的を射た・簡潔な）	「発言・文章」と結びつく
☐ **pívotal**(role, event, moment)（極めて重要な）	「役割・出来事」と結びつきやすい
☐ **plácid**(nature, lake, stream)（穏やかな）	「性格・自然」と主に結びつく
☐ **póignant** (memories, love story, grief, sorrow)（胸を刺すような・心を打つ）	「記憶・悲しみ」と主に結びつく

☐ **precárious** (position, situation, condition)（不安定な）	「立場・状況」と主に結びつく
☐ **precócious** (children, talent, development)（早熟な）	「才能・発育」と主に結びつく
☐ **prepósterous** (idea, notion, claim)（ばかげた）	「考え・主張」と結びつきやすい
☐ **prístine** (condition, forest, wilderness)（手つかずの・自然のままの）	「状態・自然」と主に結びつく
☐ **pródigal** (son, life, expenditure)（浪費する）	「息子・生活・支出」と結びつきやすい
☐ **prodígious** (capacity, quantity, amount)（莫大な）	「量」と結びつく
☐ **profáne** (act, language, literature, music)（俗悪な・世俗的な）	「行為・芸術」と結びつきやすい
☐ **profúse** (apologies [thanks], decoration, bleeding)（あふれるばかりの）	「謝辞・装飾・体液」と結びつきやすい
☐ **prolífic** (writer, composer, bird)（多産の・多作の）	「創作家・動物」と結びつきやすい
☐ **prophétic** (word, vision, voice)（予言的な）	「言葉・先見の明」と主に結びつく

☐ **rádiant** (smile, energy, light, heat) （光を放つ・きらきら輝く）	「エネルギー」と結びつきやすい
☐ **rávishing** (beauty, looks, scenery) （魅惑的な・うっとりさせる）	「美貌・光景」と主に結びつく
☐ **recéptive** (audience, mood, mind) （理解力［包容力］のある）	「観衆・ムード」と結びつきやすい
☐ **reclúsive** (state, artist, writer) （孤立した・人目を避けた）	「国家・人」と主に結びつく
☐ **reléntless** (attack, pursuit, pressure, heat)（容赦ない）	「攻撃・圧力」と結びつきやすい
☐ **remórseful** (tears, eyes, apology) （後悔の）	「態度・言葉」と主に結びつく

英検1級重要頻出単語 その1

　今度は過去20年間にわたって選択肢として3回以上用いられ、かつ問題の解答にも使用された頻出語彙を挙げておきましょう。20年間を通して見ると、同じ語彙が出題される確率は20%ぐらいですが、解答以外の選択肢が語彙問題に出題される確率はその2～3倍と高くなります。そこで、こういったリストが重要となってくるわけです。

> **【過去3回以上使われた頻出語彙】**
>
> **absolve**, acquit, adherent, **adroit**, adverse, affable, **affront**, alienate, alleviate, allude, altruism, articulate, bask, belittle, circumvent, **clandestine**, clout, **commensurate**, compatible, condone, conjecture, **consummate**, contemplate, **contingency**, convergence

☐ **remúnerative** (business, work, employment)（採算の取れる）	「経済活動」と主に結びつく
☐ **repúgnant** (odor, smell, crime, behavior)（不快な）	「におい・行為」と主に結びつく
☐ **resílient** (economy, business, material)（回復力のある・弾力性のある）	「経済・物質」と結びつきやすい
☐ **réticent** (child, student, attitude)（寡黙な）	「人・態度」と結びつく
☐ **rífe** with (corruption, conflicts, problems)（〜がはびこって）	「悪事・問題」と主に結びつく
☐ **rústic** (scenery, atmosphere, cottage, house)（田舎の・ひなびた）	「景色・建物」と結びつきやすい
☐ **sálient** (features, points, characteristics)（主要な）	「特徴・要点」と主に結びつく

☐ **sánguine** (view, disposition, complexion, temper)（楽天的な・血色の良い）	「物の見方・性格・顔色」と結びつきやすい
☐ **sardónic** (smile, grin, humor, joke, laugh)（冷笑的な）	「笑い・ジョーク」と主に結びつく
☐ **scórching** (heat, sun, summer)（焼けつくような）	「熱・太陽」と主に結びつく
☐ **scrúpulous** (attention, accuracy, fairness)（几帳面な・綿密な）	「注意・正確さ・公正さ」と結びつきやすい
☐ **sédentàry** (lifestyle, job, worker)（座ることの多い）	「生活・仕事」と主に結びつく
☐ **sénsual** (pleasure, intercourse, experience)（官能的な）	「肉体的な感覚」と主に結びつく
☐ **sízzling** (summer, meat, love affair)（非常に暑い・ジュージューいう）	「暑い気候・食物」と主に結びつく
☐ **slóvenly** (appearance, manner, habits)（だらしない）	「身なり・態度」と主に結びつく
☐ **sórdid** (crime, affair, story)（卑劣な）	「犯罪・事件」と主に結びつく
☐ **spárse** (population, crowd, hair)（わずかな）	「群集」と結びつきやすい

II 一般語彙力パワーUPコロケーション

☐ **sporádic** (fighting, shooting, violence) （散発的な・時々起こる）	「戦闘・暴力」と主に結びつく
☐ **squálid** (slums, district, apartment) （むさくるしい）	「居住・地区」と結びつきやすい
☐ **staunch** (supporter, advocate, opposition)（筋金入りの）	「支持者・反対者」と主に結びつく
☐ **stríngent** (rule, regulation, requirement)（厳しい）	「規則・要求」と結びつく
☐ **súmptuous** (meal, dinner, palace, collection)（豪華な・ぜいたくな）	「食事・装飾」と主に結びつく
☐ **táinted** (blood, food, money) （汚れた・腐った）	「血や食物などの生物・お金」と結びつきやすい
☐ **tántalìzing** (smell, taste, flavor) （食欲・興味をかき立てる）	「香り・味」などと結びつく
☐ **tántamòunt** to (terrorism, torture, failure)（～に等しい）	「悪事・失敗」と結びつきやすい
☐ **télling** (comment, evidence, example, blow)（有力な・手ごたえのある）	「意見・証拠・一撃」と結びつきやすい
☐ **ténuous** (relationship, position, connection)（薄い・浅はかな）	「関係・立場」と結びつきやすい

☐ **térse** (statement, reply, comment) （簡潔な）	「発言」と主に結びつく
☐ **thorny** (issue, problem, question) （厄介な）	「問題」と結びつく
☐ **tícklish** (problem, situation, issue, question)（慎重を要する）	「問題・状況」と結びつく
☐ **torrid** (heat, summer, love affair) （灼熱の・熱烈な）	「熱・暑さ」と主に結びつく
☐ **translúcent** (plastic, glass, screen, film)（半透明の）	「薄い物質」と主に結びつく
☐ **ultérior** (motive, purpose, object) （潜在した・隠された）	「動機・目的」と主に結びつく
☐ **ùnassúming** (manner, appearance, personality)（控えめな・実直な）	「態度・性格」と主に結びつく
☐ **undáunted** by (failure, obstacles, setbacks)（〜にひるまずに）	「失敗・障害」と結びつく
☐ **véngeful** (enemy, spite, malice) （執念深い・復しゅうに燃える）	「敵・悪意」と結びつく

Ⅱ 一般語彙力パワーＵＰコロケーション

音素の力でボキャブラリーUP〔5〕

sl する する、ずるずる、つるつる、のろのろ、ぺらぺら薄〜いよ！つるっと

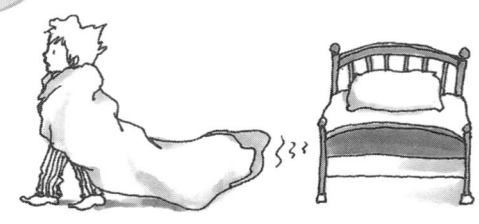

slipshod （だらしない、ずさんな）
sleazy （薄っぺらな、安っぽい、だらしのない）
sleek （なめらかな、しゃれた身なりの、口先のうまい）
slither （ずるずる滑る（こと）、滑るようにして進む）
sloppy （だらしのない、びしょびしょの、水っぽい）
slovenly （だらしない、ずさんな）
sluggish （怠惰な、のろい、緩慢な，不振の）
slumber （うとうとする、まどろみ）ずるずる〜とうたた寝する
slick （つるつる滑る、なめらかな、口先のうまい）
slant （傾斜（する）、偏向、観点）傾斜をずるずる滑り落ちる

□ **vénomous** (snake, attack, criticism) （有毒な・悪意に満ちた）	「蛇・攻撃」と主に結びつく
□ **verbóse** (speech, explanation, letter) （冗長な）	「話・文体」と結びつく

☐ **véxing** (problem, question, issue, situation)（いらいらさせる）	「問題」と主に結びつく
☐ **víbrant** (economy, business, color, voice)（活力のある・鮮やかな）	「ビジネス・色・声」と結びつきやすい
☐ **vígilant** (attention, guard, watch)（慎重な）	「注意・警戒」と結びつきやすい
☐ **vísionàry** (leader, artist, works)（先見の明のある・空想にふける・幻想の）	「指導者・芸術」と結びつきやすい
☐ **vivácious** (girl, lady, personality)（陽気な・生き生きした）	「女性・性格」と主に結びつく
☐ **volúptuous** (body, figure, mouth)（グラマーな・肉感的な）	「肉体」と結びつく
☐ **vorácious** (appetite, reader, consumer)（貪欲な・猛烈な）	「欲求（者）」と主に結びつく
☐ **wáning** (popularity, moon, influence, confidence, prestige)（衰えていく・欠けていく）	「人気・月・影響」と結びつきやすい
☐ **wary** (eyes, look, expression)（警戒している・用心深い）	「目つき・表情」と主に結びつく
☐ **wáyward** (behavior, child, wind)（わがままな・不規則な）	「態度・風向き」と主に結びつく

II 一般語彙力パワーUPコロケーション

☐ **whímsical** (idea, fancy, creation) （気まぐれな）	「考え・創作」と主に結びつく
☐ **wíthering** (look, attack, criticism) （ひるませるような・しおれさせる）	「目つき・攻撃・批判」と結びつきやすい
☐ **wóeful** (cry, song, failure) （悲惨な・悲痛な）	「泣き声・歌・失敗」と結びつきやすい

■ 復習テスト

Choose the best answer from the 10 words below for each blank.

1. （　） (heat, sun, summer)
2. （　） (memories, love story, grief, sorrow)
3. （　） (smile, energy, light, heat)
4. （　） (body, figure, mouth)
5. （　） (rule, regulation, requirement)
6. （　） (attack, pursuit, pressure, heat)
7. （　） (idea, fancy, creation)
8. （　） (issue, problem, question)
9. （　） (speech, explanation, letter)
10. （　） (attention, accuracy, fairness)

A. poignant　B. radiant　C. relentless　D. scorching
E. scrupulous　F. stringent　G. thorny　H. verbose
I. voluptuous　J. whimsical

■ 解　答
1. D　2. A　3. B　4. I　5. F　6. C　7. J　8. G　9. H　10. E

　皆さん、お疲れ様でした。以上で第5日の「形容詞編 必須レベル Part3」は終了です。次回は「形容詞編 完成レベル Part 1」です。それでは、明日に向かってボキャブラリービルディング！

Let's enjoy the process!（陽は必ず昇る！）

2-6　第6日
一般語彙力パワー UP
形容詞編　完成レベル Part 1

　第6日目は「完成レベル」で主に1万〜1.5万語水準というハイレベルな語彙を集めています。この水準が分かってくると、洋書や英字紙を読んでいても、一般語彙では知らない語がほとんどなくなってきます。それでは「形容詞編 完成レベル Part 1」を気合を入れて頑張りましょう！

☐ **aménable** to (treatment, advice, guidance, control)（従順に従う）	「管理・指示」と主に結びつく
☐ **arcáne** (rules, language, knowledge)（難解な）	「規則・言葉・知識」と結びつきやすい
☐ **árduous** (task, work, journey)（骨の折れる・困難な）	「仕事・旅」と主に結びつく
☐ **árid** (land, desert, climate)（乾燥した・不毛の）	「地形・気候」と結びつく
☐ **assíduous** (study, efforts, research)（勤勉な・根気強い）	「勉強・努力」と主に結びつく

☐ **beléaguered** (city, country, government, politician)（包囲された・窮地に立たされた）	「場所・組織」と結びつきやすい
☐ **bígoted** (attitude, remarks, opinion)（頑固な・頭の固い）	「態度・言葉」と主に結びつく
☐ **blátant** (discrimination, racism, lie, violation)（露骨な）	「差別・不正」と結びつく
☐ **bóisterous** (crowd, party, laughter)（騒々しい）	「群集」と主に結びつく
☐ **bóorish** (behavior, attitude, conduct)（粗野な）	「態度」と結びつく
☐ **brázen** (lie, attack, attempt, face)（厚かましい・ずうずうしい）	「嘘・振る舞い」と主に結びつく
☐ **brúsque** (answer, reply, question, manner)（ぶっきらぼうな）	「応答」と主に結びつく
☐ **canny** (politician, marketing, investment)（慎重な・抜け目のない）	「政治・ビジネス」と結びつきやすい
☐ **cógent** (reason, argument, case)（説得力のある）	「理由・主張」と結びつく
☐ **comménsurate** with (ability, experience, skill)（～に釣り合った）	「能力・経験」と主に結びつく

II 一般語彙力パワーUPコロケーション

☐ **consúmmate** (skill, performance, professional)（完璧な・熟練した）	「芸・技」と主に結びつく
☐ **cópious** (amounts, quantities, notes, index)（豊富な）	「量・メモ」と結びつきやすい
☐ **córpulent** (body, figure, belly)（肥満した）	「体」と結びつく
☐ **coy** (smile, look, glance, voice)（内気な）	「しぐさ」と主に結びつく
☐ **crafty** (business, idea, strategy, politician)（ずる賢い）	「ビジネス・考え」と結びつきやすい
☐ **crýptic** (message, remarks, clues, comment, question)（不可解な・謎めいた）	「言葉・発言」と主に結びつく
☐ **cúrsory** (look, glance, inspection, examination)（大ざっぱな）	「目の動き・調査」と主に結びつく
☐ **decrépit** (house, machinery, old age)（老朽化した・弱った）	「建物・機械・高齢者」と結びつきやすい
☐ **demúre** (wife, lady, smile, look)（慎み深い・控えめな）	「女性・しぐさ」と結びつく
☐ **deránged** (killer, gunman, fan, group)（錯乱した・狂った・乱れた）	「殺人者・集団」と主に結びつく

☐ **dérelict** (land, building, house) （遺棄された）	「土地・家屋」と結びつきやすい
☐ **dévious** (route, method, plan) （遠回りの・不正な）	「道・方法・計画」と結びつきやすい
☐ **diabólical** (plan, plot, scheme) （極悪非道な・悪魔のような）	「計画」と主に結びつく
☐ **didáctic** (lecture, instruction, literature) （教訓的な・説教的な）	「講義・文学作品」と結びつきやすい
☐ **díffident** (voice, smile, personality) （遠慮がちな）	「態度・性格」と主に結びつく
☐ **dilápidàted** (building, house, condition) （ぼろぼろの）	「建物・状態」と主に結びつく

語呂合わせで覚える英検1級単語 その3

☐ **gaffe** （えらいへましてギャフん！）
☐ **gaunt** （ゴーンと やせこけやつれたよ）
☐ **haggard** （歯がーどれもガタガタやつれた男）
☐ **hamper** （はんぱーだ邪魔だよ！）
☐ **importune** （インポチュー（ン）して SEX せがむ）
☐ **inaugurate** （いーいのー？ぐれてタバコ始めても）
☐ **insurgence** （いんさーじゃんじゃ反乱起こせ！）
☐ **jeopardy** （行くぜパーティ 危険な乱交）

- ☐ laconic（ほらここに来る人そっけない）
- ☐ lethargy（おれさじー投げたよ脱力感）
- ☐ loathe（切ろうずんずん長髪大嫌い）
- ☐ maim（目むくまでとことん傷つける）
- ☐ malady（こまるでい社会の弊害）
- ☐ massacre（まさかー 大虐殺するとは！）
- ☐ novice（伸びすぎたラーメン作りは素人だ）
- ☐ orgy（おーじいさんどんちゃん騒ぎだ）

☐ **dimínutive**(size, form, figure, body)（小さい）	「形・体つき」と結びつきやすい
☐ **disgrúntled**(workers, customers, voters)（不機嫌な）	「労働者・客・有権者」と結びつきやすい
☐ **dracónian**(law, measures, penalty, rules)（極めて厳しい）	「規則・罰則」と主に結びつく
☐ **ebúllient**(character, personality, mood)（活気にあふれた）	「性格・雰囲気」と主に結びつく
☐ **édifying**(speech, sermon, book, story)（啓発する・ためになる）	「話」と結びつきやすい
☐ **éerie**(silence, glow, feeling, experience)（不気味な）	「雰囲気・感覚」と結びつきやすい

☐ **egrégious** (error, mistake, blunder, abuse, violation)(甚だしい・言語道断な)	「へま・悪行」と結びつく
☐ **engáging** (smile, manner, personality)(人を引きつける)	「態度・性格」と主に結びつく
☐ **ephémeral** (dream, beauty, life)(はかない・つかの間の)	「夢・美しさ・人生」と結びつきやすい
☐ **exácting** (standards, demands, requirement)(厳しい・骨の折れる)	「基準・要求」と主に結びつく
☐ **exhílaràting** (feeling, experience, news)(うきうきさせる)	「感情・経験」と主に結びつく
☐ **éxtant** (text, manuscript, document)(現存の)	「文書」と主に結びつく
☐ **exúberant** (energy, personality, mood)(あふれるばかりの・熱狂的な)	「活気・性格」と主に結びつく
☐ **flédgling** (actress, company, democracy, industry)(未熟な・駆け出しの)	「職業・組織」と主に結びつく
☐ **flíppant** (attitude, comment, remarks)(軽々しい)	「態度・発言」と結びつきやすい
☐ **fúrtive** (movements, glances, affair)(人目を忍んだ)	「動作・行為」と結びつきやすい

☐ **gárbled** (words, message, sound, speech)（文字化けしている・不明瞭な）	「文字・音」と主に結びつく
☐ **gárish** (color, clothes, neon) （派手な）	「色・服装」と結びつきやすい
☐ **gárrulous** (woman, boss, colleague) （おしゃべりな・口数の多い）	「人」と結びつく
☐ **grándiòse** (scheme, plan, idea) （仰々しい）	「計画・アイデア」と結びつきやすい
☐ **gratúitous** (violence, insult, assumption, promise)（根拠のない・不当な）	「暴力・侮辱・仮定」と結びつきやすい
☐ **gróuchy** (boss, eldery, worker) （不機嫌な）	「人」と結びつく
☐ **grúesome** (death, murder, killing, incident)（身の毛のよだつ）	「殺人・事件」と結びつきやすい
☐ **hálcyon** (days, era, period) （平穏な）	「時代」と結びつく
☐ **hállowed** (ground, halls, tradition) （神聖な）	「場所・建物・伝統」と結びつきやすい

> 音素の力でボキャブラリーUP〔6〕

| st |
| str |

細長く張った　str - 緊張のエネルギー **stress**（ストレス）たまるよ、緊張して

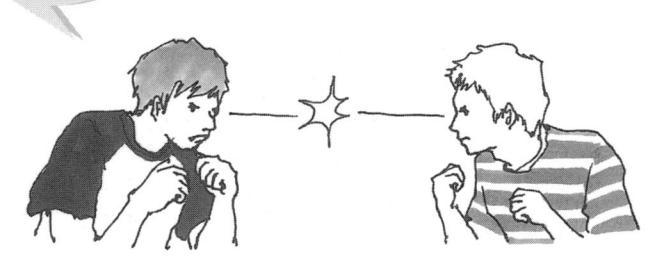

stifle (窒息する、抑圧［抑制］する) スタイフルと抑圧、窒息する

straggle (それる、はぐれる、落後する、散在する)「l」がついてだらけてしまったが「はぐれて困った緊張感」

strenuous (精力的な、激しい、奮闘的な) ストレニュアス！と激しく奮闘緊迫感

stringent (厳しい、切迫した、金詰まりの) ストリンジャンと厳しい切迫感

stern (厳しい、いかめしい) スターン！と顔がこわばる

strife (争い、けんか) ストライフ！と争い緊張高まる

streak (筋、層、気味) ストリークと細長い筋

sturdy (たくましい、丈夫な、不屈の) スターディ！筋肉張ってたくましい

☐ **hárrowing** (experience, story, scenes, ordeal)(痛ましい)	「体験・話」と結びつきやすい
☐ **héinous** (crime, offence, attack)(凶悪な・悪質な)	「犯罪・攻撃」と結びつく
☐ **ìdiosyncrátic** (behavior, reaction, personality)(特異な・風変わりな)	「行動・反応・性格」と主に結びつく
☐ **idýllic** (surroundings, countryside, life)(田園の・牧歌的な)	「環境・生活」と主に結びつく
☐ **ignóble** (action, savage, death)(卑しむべき・不名誉な)	「行為」と主に結びつく
☐ **illústrious** (career, history, company, name)(輝かしい・傑出した)	「経歴・組織」と結びつきやすい
☐ **impássioned** (plea, appeal, speech)(熱烈な)	「訴え・演説」と結びつく
☐ **impérious** (attitude, gesture, glance, look)(横柄な)	「態度・しぐさ」と結びつく
☐ **imprégnable** (castle, defense, fortress)(難攻不落の)	「要塞・守り」と主に結びつく
☐ **ìnadvértent** (error, disclosure, oversight)(不注意な)	「誤り・過失」と結びつきやすい

☐ **incapácitàted** by (illness, injury, accident)（再起不能になる） incapacitated body の用途を含む	「病気・事故」と結びつく
☐ **incísive** (argument, criticism, critique)（鋭い）	「論評」と主に結びつく
☐ **ìncórrigible** (liar, criminal, drinker, smoker)（手に負えない）	「ネガティブな人物」と主に結びつく
☐ **ìndispósed** with a (cold, headache, stomachache)（〜で気分がすぐれない）	「病気」と結びつく
☐ **inéxorable** (progress, process, rise, fate, force)（不変の）	「進展・運命・力」と結びつきやすい
☐ **ìnfinitésimal** (area, distance, quantity)（非常に小さい）	「面積・距離・量」と結びつきやすい
☐ **ingrátiàting** (smile, voice, charm)（魅惑的な・取り入るような）	「しぐさ」と主に結びつく
☐ **inímical** to (growth, values, interests)（敵意のある・反している）	「成長・価値」と結びつきやすい
☐ **iníquitous** (act, plot, practice)（不正の・邪悪な）	「行為・企み」と主に結びつく
☐ **inórdinate** (amount, number, fear) 〜（法外な・過度の）	「量・数・恐れ」と結びつきやすい

☐ **intrépid**(adventure, explorer, traveler)(勇敢な)	「冒険家」と結びつきやすい

■ 復習テスト

Choose the best answer from the 10 words below for each blank.

1. ( ) (dream, beauty, life)
2. ( ) (message, remarks, clues, comment, question)
3. ( ) (task, work, journey)
4. ( ) (death, murder, killing, incident)
5. ( ) (error, mistake, blunder, abuse, violation)
6. ( ) (reason, argument, case)
7. ( ) (experience, story, scenes, ordeal)
8. ( ) (attitude, comment, remarks)
9. ( ) (law, measures, penalty, rules)
10. ( ) (lie, attack, attempt, face)

> A. arduous B. brazen C. cogent D. cryptic E. draconian
> F. egregious G. ephemeral H. flippant I. gruesome
> J. harrowing

■ 解 答
1. G 2. D 3. A 4. I 5. F 6. C 7. J 8. H 9. E 10. B

　皆さん、お疲れ様でした。以上で第6日の「形容詞編 完成レベル Part1」は終了です。次回は「形容詞編 完成レベル Part2」です。それでは、明日に向かってボキャブラリービルディング！

Let's enjoy the process!（陽は必ず昇る！）

難関英検1級合格必勝法！

　合格を確実にするには、まず語彙問題とエッセイライティング問題のスコアを足して40点を安定して取ることを目指してください。これは半年ぐらいの集中トレーニングで比較的到達しやすい目標で、短期的努力が最も報われやすいものです。これによって、残りのリーディング問題とリスニング問題の正解率が7割、つまり60点中42点（リーディングで18点、リスニングで24点）であっても大体の合格点である80点を2点上回るスコアで合格することができます。エッセイライティングと、2次試験は密接に関連しており、ライティングのスコアと処理スピードが低いと2次試験が通りにくいので特に力を入れてください。

　そしてここで重要になってくるのが問題を解く「スピードトレーニング」です。英検の語彙問題はほとんどがコロケーションで解ける問題なので、語彙の豊富な人なら2〜3分でやって楽に満点が取れるレベルのものです。ですから普段から真面目にボキャブラリービルディングをして、本番では語彙問題とライティング問題を必ず35分以内に処理できるようにトレーニングしましょう。また、語彙とライティングセクションを35分で処理することは、リーディング問題得点 UP とリスニング問題先読み "focused listening" によるスコア UP につながり、とても重要です。そこで、まず語彙とライティング問題を35分以内で解いた後、穴埋め問題には2題で絶対15分以上かけないという、いわゆる「ラップタイム」というものを作りましょう。次に、内容一致問題3題をできれば40分、最悪でも45分で解き、必ず5〜10分間、リスニング問題の選択肢を先読みし、問題や解答を予測しておくのと、リスニング問題で集中力を発揮して得点を自分の能力の Max に高められるように頭を休めておきましょう。

II 一般語彙力パワーUPコロケーション

2-7　第7日
一般語彙力パワーUP
形容詞編　完成レベル Part2

　第7日目は、「形容詞編 完成レベルPart2（1万～1.5万語水準）」です。それでは、皆さんの語彙力をぐーんとパワーUPしていただきましょう!!

☐ **ìntrospéctive**（mind, nature, personality）（内省的な）	「気性・性格」と主に結びつく
☐ **iráte**（customer, client, message, voice）（激怒した）	「客・意見」と主に結びつく
☐ **jáded**（appetite, eyes, attitude）（疲れきった・うんざりした）	「食欲・態度」と主に結びつく
☐ **knotty**（issue, question, problem）（複雑な）	「問題」と結びつく
☐ **lacónic**（speech, comment, remarks, account）（簡潔な）	「スピーチ・発言」と結びつく

☐ **loquácious** (lady, man, mood) （多弁な・おしゃべりな）	「人」と結びつく
☐ **lúrid** (crime, sex, tale) （身の毛のよだつような・けばけばしい）	「犯罪・セックス」と結びつきやすい
☐ **lush** (forest, garden, meadow) （青々と茂った）	「森林・牧草地などの緑」と結びつく
☐ **macábre** (killing, murder, death) （身の毛のよだつ）	「殺人・死」と結びつきやすい
☐ **moot** (issue, point, question) （未解決の・議論の余地のある）	「問題」と主に結びつく
☐ **murky** (waters, world, past) （濁った・不透明な）	「水・世界・過去」と結びつきやすい
☐ **nébulous** (concept, idea, figure) （不明瞭な）	「考え・姿」と主に結びつく
☐ **nefárious** (activity, purpose, scheme) （非道な）	「行為・目的」と結びつきやすい
☐ **nònchalánt** (attitude, behavior, shrug) （無関心な）	「態度・振る舞い」と主に結びつく
☐ **nóxious** (fume, chemical, animal) （有害な）	「化学物質・動物」と結びつきやすい

II 一般語彙力パワーUPコロケーション

☐ **obtrúsive** (behavior, color, lighting) （押しつけがましい・目障りな）	「行為・色彩」と結びつきやすい
☐ **offícious** (interference, nuisance, lie) （おせっかいな）	「干渉・嘘」と主に結びつく
☐ **ónerous** (duty, task, responsibility, contract)（煩わしい）	「仕事・責任」と主に結びつく
☐ **ornáte** (carving, furniture, language, interior)（飾り立てた）	「装飾品・文体」と主に結びつく
☐ **pejórative** (word, term, statement) （軽蔑的な）	「言葉・発言」と結びつく
☐ **pernícious** (effect, influence, disease) （有害な）	「影響・病気」と結びつきやすい
☐ **pláintive** (cry, melody, voice, sound) （悲しげな）	「叫び・メロディー」と主に結びつく
☐ **polémic** (literature, discourse, essay) （論争の・論争好きな）	「文学・論文」と結びつく
☐ **precípitous** (slope, decline, fall, drop)（険しい・崖のような・急激な）	「傾斜・減少」と主に結びつく
☐ **propítious** (time, moment, start, sign)（幸先の良い・好都合な）	「時節」と結びつく

☐ **prosáic** (writing, expression, life) （散文体の・平凡な）	「文体・生活」に結びつきやすい
☐ **pugnácious** (character, disposition, mood)（好戦的な）	「性格・ムード」と結びつきやすい
☐ **púngent** (smell, odor, criticism) （辛らつな・鼻につんとくる）	「におい・批評」と結びつきやすい

英検1級重要頻出単語 その2

　太字で示されたようなハイレベルな単語を覚える場合は、品詞を変えてでも必ずフレーズにする必要があります。それを何度も音読して自分のものにしてしまいましょう。

【過去3回以上使われた頻出語彙】

copious, **covert**, demise, denounce, depreciation, detention, discharge, discretion, disseminate, dissolution, distortion, efficacy, embed, emergent, emulate, engross, enunciate, evict, exclusion, exodus, **exponential**, fabricate, feign

---

☐ **quixótic** (adventure, attempt, project, plan)（非現実的な）	「冒険・試み・計画」と結びつきやすい
☐ **rédolent** of the (smell, late 70s, good old days)（〜のにおいのする・〜を偲ばせる）	「におい・時代」と主に結びつく
☐ **refráctory** (child, disease, brick)（手に負えない・耐火性の）	「子供・病気」と結びつきやすい
☐ **repléte** with (dangers, technical jargon, errors)（〜でいっぱいの）	「情報・間違い」と結びつきやすい
☐ **repúlsive** (smell, odor, force)（ひどく不快な・反発する）	「におい・力」と結びつきやすい
☐ **respléndent** (jewelry, dress, color)（まばゆい）	「装身具・色」と結びつきやすい
☐ **salácious** (gossip, story, material)（わいせつな）	「話題・資料」と結びつきやすい
☐ **sálutàry** (effect, lesson, experience)（有益な）	「効果・教訓」と主に結びつく
☐ **shaggy** (hair, beard, beast)（けむくじゃらの・毛羽立った）	「毛・動物」と結びつきやすい
☐ **sham** (marriage, battle, election)（見せかけの・偽装の・模擬の）	「結婚・戦争・選挙」と結びつきやすい

☐ **sleek** (design, shape, elegance) （光沢のある・口先のうまい）	「デザイン」と主に結びつく
☐ **snug** (bar, room, house) （居心地の良い）	「施設・家」と結びつきやすい
☐ **spécious** (argument, claim, reasoning) （見掛け倒しの）	「主張・理由」と主に結びつく
☐ **squéamish** about (worms, blood, needle) （すぐに気分が悪くなる・吐き気を催す）	「虫・血など不快にさせるもの」と結びつきやすい
☐ **standóffish** (attitude, relationship, manner)（よそよそしい）	「態度・関係」と主に結びつく
☐ **strídent** (criticism, opposition, demands, voice)（耳障りな・執拗な）	「批判・要求」と主に結びつく
☐ **stupéndous** (success, work, performance, efforts) （素晴らしい・並外れた）	「成功・成果・努力」と結びつきやすい
☐ **submíssive** (wife, women, attitude, behavior)（従順な）	「女性・態度」と結びつきやすい
☐ **succínct** (summary, description, explanation, introduction) （簡潔な・簡明な）	「言葉・説明」と結びつく

II 一般語彙力パワーUPコロケーション

□ **súpple**（body, skin, leather, texture）（柔軟な・しなやかな）	「体・布」と主に結びつく

音素の力でボキャブラリーUP〔7〕

scr

scr ごしごしすって抵抗のエネルギー！
必死で抵抗 scream（キャーと叫ぶ）

scrape　（ひっかく、こする、すりむく）
scrawl　（なぐり書き（する）、落書き（する））
screech　（金切り声で叫ぶ）scream より耳障りな叫び
scribble　（なぐり書き（する）、落書き（する））
scrimp　（節約する）切り詰めるのは我慢して欲望に抵抗
scrub　（ゴシゴシ磨く、こすって取り除く）
scrutiny　（綿密な調査［検査］）こすって綿密な検査する

□ **sùrreptítious**（visit, look, glance, efforts）（人目を忍ぶような・秘密の）	「訪問・目つき」と結びつきやすい
□ **swéltering**（heat, summer, sun, temperature）（うだるように暑い）	「暑さ」と主に結びつく

☐ **táttered** (clothes, reputation, relationships)（ボロボロの・ずたずたの）	「衣服・名声・関係」と結びつきやすい
☐ **télltàle** (sign, mark, symptom, smell)（証拠となる・隠しおおせない）	「サイン・兆候」と結びつきやすい
☐ **tépid** (water, response, support, applause)（ぬるい・熱意に欠ける）	「水・反応・支持」と結びつきやすい
☐ **títillàting** (story, tale, experience, entertainment)（刺激的な・興奮させる）	「話・体験」と主に結びつく
☐ **títular** (head, king, leader, bishop)（名ばかりの）	「地位・役職」と結びつく
☐ **tríte** (remarks, dialogue, cliché, statement)（平凡な・陳腐な）	「発言・言葉」と結びつく
☐ **ùnabáshed** (curiosity, enthusiasm, racist, materialism)（臆面もない・恥ずかしがらない）	「好奇心・主義者」と主に結びつく
☐ **ùncánny** (ability, talent, insight)（神秘的な・人並み外れて鋭い）	「能力・洞察力」と結びつく
☐ **uncóuth** (behavior, manner, language)（無骨な・がさつな）	「態度・言葉」と主に結びつく
☐ **úndulàting** (countryside, hill, landscape)（起伏する・波打つ）	「地形」と結びつく

II 一般語彙力パワーUPコロケーション

☐ **unténable** (theory, reason, position, view)（支持できない・受け入れ難い）	「理論・理由・立場」と結びつきやすい
☐ **vénal** (politician, practice, motive)（腐敗した・金で動く）	「政治家・慣習・動機」と結びつきやすい
☐ **verbátim** (record, report, transcript, translation, account)（逐語的な）	「記録・翻訳」と結びつく
☐ **véritable** (treasure, goldmine, paradise)（正真正銘の）	「財宝・楽園」と結びつきやすい
☐ **vindíctive** (spirit, feeling, enemy, attack)（復しゅう心のある・悪意に満ちた）	「感情・敵・攻撃」と結びつきやすい
☐ **vírile** (power, strength, courage)（男らしい・力強い）	「力・勇気」と結びつきやすい
☐ **vírulent** (disease, opposition, criticism, hostility)（悪性の・敵意に満ちた）	「病気・反抗」と結びつきやすい
☐ **vocíferous** (opposition, complaints, critic, crowd)（さかんな・騒々しい）	「反対・不平」と主に結びつく
☐ **wánton** (killing, destruction, violence, vandalism)（抑制できない・勝手気ままな）	「破壊行為」と結びつきやすい
☐ **wístful** (smile, look, eyes, mood)（切ない気持ちの・もの欲しそうな）	「表情・しぐさ」と主に結びつく

☐ **wry** (smile, look, humor, remarks) （意地悪な・しかめっ面の・皮肉な）	「表情・言葉」と主に結びつく

■ 復習テスト
Choose the best answer from the 10 words below for each blank.

1. (　) (adventure, attempt, project, plan)
2. (　) (fume, chemical, animal)
3. (　) (marriage, battle, election)
4. (　) (effect, influence, disease)
5. (　) (crime, sex, tale)
6. (　) (summary, description, explanation, introduction)
7. (　) (time, moment, start, sign)
8. (　) (issue, point, question)
9. (　) (opposition, complaints, critic, crowd)
10. (　) (ability, talent, insight)

A. lurid　B. moot　C. noxious　D. pernicious
E. propitious　F. quixotic　G. sham　H. succinct
I. uncanny　J. vociferous

■ 解　答
1. F　2. C　3. G　4. D　5. A　6. H　7. E　8. B　9. J　10. I

　皆さん、お疲れ様でした。以上で第7日の「形容詞編 完成レベル Part2」は終了です。次回は「動詞編 基礎レベル」です。それでは、明日に向かってボキャブラリービルディング！

Let's enjoy the process!（陽は必ず昇る！）

2-8 第8日
一般語彙力パワーUP
動詞編 基礎レベル

　第8日目からは一般語彙力パワーUPの動詞編です。ここではタイム、ニューズウィーク、エコノミストやCNNなどをエンジョイし、また、英検1級をはじめとする各種資格検定にパスするためのハイレベルな重要動詞316個のコロケーションを音読しながら一気に運用レベル語彙まで高めていただきましょう。それでは、まずは「動詞編 基礎レベル（6千～8千語水準）」からです。

☐ **àggravàte** the (problem, crisis, situation, condition)（悪化させる）	「問題・状況」と主に結びつく
☐ **állocàte** (funds, money, budget) for the project（割り当てる・配分する）	「お金」と結びつく
☐ **allót** (shares, equity, tasks, assignments, time) to someone（割り当てる）	「金融・仕事・時間」と結びつきやすい
☐ **allúde** to sb's (failure, resignation, problem)（ほのめかす）	「言及しにくいこと」と主に結びつく

☐ **amáss** (a fortune, wealth, money)（蓄える・蓄積する）	「お金」と結びつく
☐ **assímilàte** (information, ideas, immigrants)（吸収する・理解する）	「情報・移民」と結びつきやすい
☐ **augmént** (income, salary, forces, personnel)（増やす・増強する）	「収入・人員」と主に結びつく
☐ **avért** the (crisis, danger, disaster, catastrophe, defeat)（避ける）	「危険」と結びつく
☐ be **cénsured** for one's (misconduct, failure, opinion)（～で非難される）	「行為・言動」と結びつく
☐ **cáter** to sb's (needs, demand, interests)（～を満たす）	「要求・需要」と結びつく
☐ **chérish** one's (memory, idea, dream)（～を大切にする）	「思い出・アイデア・夢」と結びつきやすい
☐ **collábboràte** on a (project, research, work)（協力する・合作する）	「計画・研究・作品」と結びつきやすい
☐ **compíle** a (document, report, dictionary)（編纂する）	「文書・辞書」と結びつく
☐ **compóund** the (problem, difficulty, crime, interest) （(事態を) 悪化させる・(利子を) 生む）	「問題・犯罪・利子」と結びつきやすい

☐ **concéde** one's (demand, error, fact, defeat)(譲歩する・真実［敗北］を認める)	「要求・真実・敗北」と結びつきやすい
☐ **confórm** to the (standards, requirements, rules, demands)(〜に従う)	「基準・要求・規則」と主に結びつく
☐ **contríve** a (plot, scheme, device)(企む・考案する)	「計画・装置」と主に結びつく
☐ **crípple** the (economy, industry, government)(損なわせる)	「経済・組織」と結びつきやすい
☐ **crúmbling** (building, relationship, economy, empire)(崩れかけの)	「建物・関係・制度」と結びつきやすい
☐ **curtáil** the (expenditure, spending, production, cost)(削減する)	「費用・活動」と主に結びつく
☐ **degéneràte** into (chaos, disorder, violence, recession)(悪化して〜になる)	「無秩序・混乱」と結びつく
☐ **denóunce** (terrorism, violence, sb's failure)(非難する)	「暴力・失敗」と結びつきやすい
☐ **depíct** the (scenes, event, reality, history)(〜を描く)	「場面・出来事」と結びつきやすい
☐ **déviàte** from the (standards, values, rules, route)(〜から外れる)	「基準・規則」と主に結びつく

☐ **diffúse** the (idea, information, light, tension, feeling)（発散する・拡散する）	「情報・光・感情」と結びつきやすい
☐ **dispél** the (image, doubt, fear, rumor)（払いのける）	「イメージ・疑い・恐れ」と結びつきやすい

語呂合わせで覚える英検1級単語 その4

☐ **oust**（アウ！ストライクで打者追い出す）
☐ **paucity**（ぽおー（と）してないでお金不足してるのだから）
☐ **penchant**（好きなペンチャント使ってよ！）
☐ **pernicious**（頭をパーにしやすい有害な物質）
☐ **pithy**（ぴしっと引き締まった表現だ！）
☐ **portent**（ポテンと倒れる不吉な兆し）
☐ **predicament**（たっぷりでかめん 食べて下痢の 窮地！）
☐ **quandary**（苦境で何も食わんだりー！）
☐ **rampant**（ランパンはいた痴漢がはびこる）
☐ **redundant**（しりだんだんと余分な贅肉）
☐ **remnant**（いい品全部売れ無念と 残り物に嘆く）
☐ **remorse**（頭剃りもーす 自責の念）
☐ **rift**（しりふと触るお尻の裂け目）
☐ **rubble**（トラブル起きて瓦礫の山）
☐ **sardonic**（去るどにくたらしい小ばかにしたやつ）
☐ **scorch**（スコッチウイスキーのど焼ける）

☐ **dispérse** the (crowds, demonstrators, protesters)(追い払う)	「群集」と結びつく
☐ **disrúpt** the (activity, operation, process)(妨げる・妨害する)	「活動・プロセス」と主に結びつく
☐ **dissólve** the (parliament, congress, partnership)(解散する・解消する)	「議会・関係」と主に結びつく
☐ **distórt** the (image, fact, truth, market)(ゆがめる・歪曲する)	「イメージ・現実」と結びつきやすい
☐ **distráct** one's (attention, mind, thought)((人)の気を散らす)	「注意・気持ち」と結びつきやすい
☐ **divért** (attention, money, funds, resources)(そらす・迂回する)	「注意・お金」と主に結びつく
☐ **dwíndling** (support, resources, supply)(弱まる・減少する)	「支援・資源」と主に結びつく
☐ **embráce** the (concept, notion, principle)(受け入れる・信奉する)	「概念・原則」と結びつきやすい
☐ **endórse** a (plan, proposal, bill, policy)(承認する)	「計画・法案」と結びつきやすい
☐ **eróde** one's (confidence, freedom, power)(損なう・むしばむ)	「信頼・自由・権力」と結びつきやすい

☐ **eváde** (tax, payment, responsibility, arrest)（逃れる・回避する）	「支払い・責任」と結びつきやすい
☐ **explóit** (resources, opportunity, workers)（有効に使う・悪用する・搾取する）	「資源・機会」と結びつきやすい
☐ **fábricàted** (evidence, data, confession, house)（捏造された・でっち上げの）	「証拠・情報」と結びつきやすい
☐ **fórge** a(an) (alliance, relationship, signature)（結ぶ・偽造する）	「同盟・関係」と結びつきやすい
☐ **fret** about one's (mistake, future, health)（心配する・いら立つ）	「心配事」と結びつく
☐ **góbble** up (food, drinks, profits)（ガツガツ食べる・食いつぶす）	「飲食物・利益」と主に結びつく
☐ **grópe** for (keys, words, solutions, answers)（手探りする・模索する）	「物・言葉」と結びつきやすい
☐ **grúdge** (one's time [money], sb's success)（出し惜しむ・ねたむ）	「時間・金・成功」と結びつきやすい
☐ **grúmble** about the (pay, food, low income)（不平を言う）	「不満の原因」と結びつく
☐ **hámper** the (progress, development, efforts)（妨げる・阻む）	「発展・努力」と結びつきやすい

☐ **hérald** the (arrival, beginning, end, start) of space age（〜の到来を告げる）	「開始・終了」と結びつく

音素の力でボキャブラリーUP〔8〕

dr だらだら、ずるずる、引きずって
だらだら、ずるずる **dream**
夢うつつ

drawl 　　だらだらと（ものうげに話す）
dreary 　　（わびしい）人生だらだら生きる
drowsy 　　だらだら、ずるずる（うとうと眠いよ）
drudgery （骨折り仕事）ずるずる長引く骨折り仕事
draggle 　（ずるずる引きずって汚す［ぬらす］）
drivel 　　だらだらと（くだらないことを言う）
drool 　　だらだらと（よだれをたらす）
droop 　　だらりと（たれる［しおれる］）

☐ **impéde** the (economic growth, development, recovery)（妨げる）	「成長・発展」と主に結びつく
☐ **ímprovìse** a (speech, song, poem)（即興でする）	「スピーチ・曲」と主に結びつく

☐ **incórporàte** (technology, information, companies)（組み込む・法人格にする）	「テクノロジー・会社」と結びつきやすい
☐ **indúce** (sleep, relaxation, labor)（誘発する）	「身体症状・感情」と主に結びつく
☐ be **inféstted** with (insects, cockroaches, rats)（～がはびこっている）	「虫・ネズミ」と主に結びつく
☐ **inflíct** (damage, harm, injury, suffering) on someone（与える・負わせる）	「危害」と結びつく
☐ **inhíbit** the (growth, progress, development, one's impulse [desire])（抑制する・妨げる）	「成長・進展」と主に結びつく
☐ **íntegràte** the (technology, business, market, information, data)（統合する）	「テクノロジー・ビジネス・情報」と結びつきやすい
☐ **intímidàte** the (opponents, enemies, women)（脅す）	「敵・弱者」と結びつきやすい
☐ **intrúde** into sb's (property, territory, privacy)（侵入する）	「所有地・領域」と結びつきやすい
☐ **lurk** in the (shadows, night, corner)（潜む）	「影・夜・角」と結びつきやすい

II 一般語彙力パワーUPコロケーション

☐ **manípulàte** the (data, prices, market, information)(操作する)	「情報・市場」と結びつきやすい
☐ **méddle** in (politics, internal affairs, business)(～に干渉する)	「政治・ビジネス」と結びつきやすい
☐ **míngle** with (celebrities, crowds, strangers, guests)(入り交じる)	「群衆」と主に結びつく
☐ **mispláce** the (key, wallet, file, document)(置き忘れる)	「所持品」と結びつきやすい
☐ **néutralìze** (acid, poison, effect, influence, opposition)(中和する・効力をなくす)	「薬物・効力」と結びつきやすい
☐ **núrture** a (spirit, dream, child, relationship)(育む・養育する・助成する)	「精神・子供・関係」と結びつきやすい
☐ be **obséssed** with the (idea, notion, money, sex, woman)(～に取りつかれる)	「考え・欲望」と主に結びつく
☐ **òutgrów** one's (problem, habit, clothes)((成長して)問題がなくなる・役に立たなくなる)	「問題・習慣・衣服」と主に結びつく
☐ **òutwéigh** the (advantage, disadvantage, benefit, risk)(～より重要である・勝る)	「長所・短所」と主に結びつく

☐ òverthrów the (government, theory, regime, power)（転覆させる）	「政府・理論」と主に結びつく
☐ procláim one's (innocence, independence, support)（宣言する）	「無実・独立・支持」と結びつきやすい
☐ procúre (equipment, weapons, acceptance)（入手する・獲得する）	「物資・承諾」と主に結びつく
☐ públicize the (fact, event, issue, problem)（公表する）	「事実・出来事・問題」と結びつきやすい
☐ recéding (hairline, memory, coastline)（後退していく）	「引く［消える］もの」と結びつきやすい
☐ reíteràte one's (support, commitment, opinion, position)（繰り返して言う）	「支援・立場」と主に結びつく
☐ rélish the (food, time, opportunity, chance)（楽しむ・味わう）	「食べ物・時間［機会］」と結びつきやすい
☐ rénder a (decision, judgement, report, service) （（判決）を下す・提出する・提供する）	「判決・レポート・サービス」と結びつきやすい
☐ repént one's (sin, crime, deed) （後悔する・懺悔する）	「悪行・罪」と結びつく

II 一般語彙力パワーUPコロケーション

☐ **représs** (one's feeling [desire], the rebellion)(抑制する・制圧する)	「感情・反対者」と結びつきやすい
☐ **retárd** the (development, progress, reaction, process)(遅らせる・妨害する)	「発達・反応」と主に結びつく
☐ **roam** the (street, forest, countryside)(徘徊する・歩き回る)	「通り・場所」と結びつきやすい
☐ **scrub** (floors, one's eyes [skin])(ゴシゴシ磨く・こする)	「床・人体」と主に結びつく
☐ **scrútinìze** the (document, information, content)(調べる・検査する)	「文書・情報」と結びつきやすい
☐ **sedúce** (women, customers, voters)(誘惑する・そそのかす)	「女性・客・有権者」と結びつきやすい
☐ **shun** (responsibility, confrontation, temptation, publicity)(避ける・遠ざける)	「責任・望まない事柄」と結びつきやすい
☐ **soothe** sb's (anger, nerves, pain, temper)(和らげる・なだめる)	「怒り・痛み」と主に結びつく
☐ **stífle** (creativity, yawns, sb's protest [growth])(抑制する・鎮圧する)	「創造性・あくび・抗議」と結びつきやすい
☐ **subdúe** (the rebels [crowd], one's fear [desire])(抑制する)	「群集・感情」と主に結びつく

☐ The (violence, storm, wind, inflation) **abáted.** (〜が和らぐ・おさまる)	「勢いや激しさ・嵐」と主に結びつく
☐ **ùndermíne** sb's (efforts, confidence, health, credibility)（損なう）	「努力・信頼・健康」と結びつきやすい
☐ **whine** about (unfairness, taxes, racism)（泣き言を言う・めそめそする）	「不満の種」と結びつきやすい
☐ **withhóld** (information, payment, consent, support)（差し控える）	「情報・支払い」と結びつきやすい
☐ **withstánd** the (earthquakes, attack, pressure, heat)（抵抗する・耐える）	「災害・攻撃」と結びつきやすい

■ 復習テスト

Choose the best answer from the 10 words below for each blank.
1. (　) (one's feeling [desire], dissidents)
2. (　) the (government, theory, regime, power)
3. (　) a (an)(alliance, relationship, signature)
4. (　) the (expenditure, spending, production, activities)
5. (　) the (economic growth, development, recovery)
6. (　) the (image, doubt, fear, rumor)
7. (　) the (problem, crisis, situation, condition)
8. (　) the (data, prices, market, information)
9. (　) one's (confidence, freedom, power)
10. (　) the (crisis, danger, disaster, catastrophe, defeat)

> A. aggravate   B. avert   C. curtail   D. dispel   E. erode
> F. forge   G. impede   H. manipulate   I. overthrow
> J. repress

■解　答
1. J   2. I   3. F   4. C   5. G   6. D   7. A   8. H   9. E   10. B

　皆さん、お疲れ様でした。以上で第8日の「動詞編 基礎レベル」は終了です。次回は「動詞編 必須レベル Part1」です。それでは、明日に向かってボキャブラリービルディング！
Let's enjoy the process!（陽は必ず昇る！）

2-9　第9日
一般語彙力パワーUP
動詞編　必須レベル Part 1

第9日目は8千～1.2万語水準の一般語彙力パワーUPの動詞です。これら必須レベルの単語はほとんどが英文雑誌でよく使われるものばかりなので、気合を入れてボキャブラリービルディングに励みましょう！

☐ **alláy** one's (fear, concern, suspicion, anxiety, doubts)（和らげる・静める）	「不安・疑い」と主に結びつく
☐ **allévìate** (poverty, suffering, fears, food shortage)（～を軽減する・和らげる）	「貧困・苦難・不安」と結びつきやすい
☐ **ámputàte** sb's (arms, fingers, legs)（手足を切断する）	「身体の四肢や部分」と結びつく
☐ **artículàte** one's (vision, words, idea, view)（はっきり述べる［発音する］）	「言葉・考え」と結びつきやすい
☐ **báffle** (doctors, scientists, authorities)（困惑させる）	「専門家・権威」と結びつきやすい

☐ **belíttle** sb's (influence, importance, efforts, achievement)（軽視する・見下す）	「影響・功績」と結びつきやすい
☐ **bícker** over trivial (matters, issues, problems)（口論する）	「問題」と結びつく
☐ **bluff** one's way out of the (trouble, crisis, danger)（〜をはったりで切り抜ける）	「困難」と結びつく
☐ **bólster** one's (confidence, support, position, career)（強化する）	「信頼・地位」と結びつきやすい
☐ **bombárd** (a city, an enemy, someone with questions)（爆撃する・攻め立てる）	「場所・敵」と結びつきやすい
☐ be **coérced** into (retirement, resignation, confession)（強制して〜させる）	「嫌がること」と結びつきやすい
☐ **cìrcumvént** the (problem, danger, rule, regulation)（避ける）	「問題・危険・規則」と主に結びつく
☐ **commúne** with (nature, animals, god)（心を交わす）	「自然・動物」と主に結びつく
☐ **concóct** a (an) (story, excuse, plot, alibi)（作り上げる・でっち上げる）	「話・口実」と主に結びつく
☐ **condóne** the (violence, crime, offense)（〜を大目に見る・許す）	「犯罪・悪行」と結びつく

☐ **cónfiscàte** (assets, property, drugs, weapons)(押収する・没収する)	「資産・違法品」と主に結びつく
☐ **confóund** (critics, doctors, sb's expectation [prediction])(当惑させる)	「専門家・予想」と結びつきやすい
☐ **cónjure** up the (images, pictures, ideas)(思い浮かべる)	「イメージ・考え」と結びつく
☐ **cúlminàte** in one's (victory, death, resignation, arrest)(ついに〜となる)	「事件・出来事」と主に結びつく
☐ **curb** (one's power[influence], growth, air pollution)(抑制する・抑える)	「権力[影響]・成長・害」と結びつきやすい
☐ **dámpen** (sb's spirit [enthusiasm], growth, demand)(くじく・鈍らせる)	「精神・成長・需要」と結びつきやすい
☐ **decípher** the (codes, messages, technical jargon)(解読する)	「暗号・情報」と結びつく
☐ **decrý** (racism, violence, execution)((公然と)非難する)	「非道徳的行為」と結びつく
☐ **defléct** (attention, criticism, questions, pressure)(そらせる)	「注意・批判・質問」と結びつきやすい

英検1級重要頻出単語 その3

語彙は洋画やドラマなどで用いられたのを聞いて、「疑似体験」を通じて覚えるのが非常に効果的です。私の場合は、最初の「スタートレック」で語彙力がUPし、その時覚えた単語は忘れませんでした。

【過去3回以上使われた頻出語彙】
fetter, **fiasco**, fluctuate, formidable, **fraught**, **frisk**, **hoard**, impasse, impeccable, imperative, **incarcerate**, incessant, incur, ingenious, innate, intangible, intimidate, **inundate**, **languish**, liability, mediocre, misgiving, **mollify**

☐ **délve** into the (matter, crime, details) （徹底的に調査する）	「問題・詳細」と結びつきやすい
☐ **demóte** an (employee, executive, official)（降格させる）	「肩書」と結びつく
☐ **deríde** sb's (idea, attempt, ignorance) （あざ笑う・ばかにする）	「考え・試み」と結びつきやすい
☐ **dilúte** (alcohol, whisky, power, value) （薄める・弱める）	「液体・力」と主に結びつく
☐ **disbánd** a (an) (party, team, army, parliament)（解散する）	「団体・組織」と結びつく

☐ **dismántle** the (system, structure, engine, machine, army)(解体する)	「組織・機械」と主に結びつく
☐ **dissémináte** (information, messages, news, knowledge)(広める)	「情報」と結びつく
☐ **divérge** from the (common ancestor, point, course)(～からそれる)	「派生の元」と主に結びつく
☐ **divést** someone of one's (position, right, property)(人から～を剥奪する)	「地位・権利」と結びつきやすい
☐ **dóuble-cróss** the (partner, gang, mob boss)(裏切る)	「パートナー」と結びつきやすい
☐ **éarmàrk** the (budget, funds, money) for the project(割り当てる)	「お金」と結びつく
☐ **elícit** (information, responses, feelings)(引き出す)	「情報・反応」と主に結びつく
☐ **elúde** (responsibility, punishment, criticism)(逃れる)	「責任・罪・批判」と結びつきやすい
☐ **émanàte** (light, smell, sound)(発する・発散する・広がる)	「光・音」と主に結びつく
☐ **embéllish** a (story, tale, room, dress)(装飾する・飾り立てる)	「話・装飾されるもの」と主に結びつく

II 一般語彙力パワーUPコロケーション

☐ **émulàte** sb's (success, achievement, deeds)（まねる・見習う・競う）	「成功・業績」と主に結びつく
☐ **encróach** on sb's (privacy, right, territory)（侵入する）	「権利・領域」と結びつく

> 音素の力で
> ボキャブラリー
> UP〔9〕

fl

ふらふら、ひらひら、ぺらぺら軽いよ軽い！ひらひら **fly** と飛んで行く

flap　　（はためく）パタパタゆれる、バタバタ動かす
flutter　（羽ばたき）パタパタ
flicker　（明滅する）光がちらちら
flip　　（ピンとはじく）ぺらぺらとページをめくる
flimsy　ぺらぺらと（軽い薄い、薄弱な）
flirt　　（浮気する）ふらふらっと浮気する
flit　　（ひらひら飛ぶ）
flake　　（薄片）ひらひらはがれ落ちる
flee　　（逃げる）ひらひらっと逃げていく
flop　　（バタバタ動く）

☐ **encúmber** the (progress, process, success)(妨げる)	「進行」と結びつく
☐ **engénder** (anxiety, suspicion, problems, conflict)(引き起こす)	「感情・問題」と結びつきやすい
☐ **engráve** (names, words, designs) on a ring (彫り込む)	「言葉・デザイン」と結びつく
☐ be **engúlfed** in (flames, fight, violence) (〜に包まれる・〜に巻き込まれる)	「炎・争い」と主に結びつく
☐ **enlíst** sb's (support, help, aid, cooperation)(協力を求める)	「援助・協力」と主に結びつく
☐ **entáil** (loss, risk, cost) (〜を伴う・引き起こす)	「損失・リスク・支出」と主に結びつく
☐ **enúmeràte** several (issues, items, reasons)(列挙する)	「項目」と結びつく
☐ **enúnciàte** one's (words, idea, policy)(明確に述べる)	「言葉・考え」と結びつく
☐ **erádicàte** the (problem, disease, poverty) (撲滅させる)	「問題」と結びつく
☐ **evóke** sb's (memory, response, feeling, emotion)(呼び起こす)	「記憶・反応・感情」と結びつきやすい

II 一般語彙力パワーUPコロケーション

☐ **exhórt** the (employees, soldiers, students) to work hard（強く勧める・忠告する）	「大衆」と結びつきやすい
☐ **extól** the (virtues, benefits, advantages, merits) of capitalism（賞賛する）	「美点・長所」と主に結びつく
☐ **fétter** sb's (freedom, liberty, movement)（束縛する）	「自由・動き」と結びつきやすい
☐ **fóil** sb's (plan, scheme, attempt, plot)（くじく・失敗させる）	「計画・試み」と主に結びつく
☐ **forestáll** the (attack, trouble, conspiracy, plot)（〜を未然に防ぐ）	「攻撃・企み」と主に結びつく
☐ **gárner** (votes, attention, support, information, fact)（獲得する・集める）	「票・支持」と主に結びつく
☐ **grápple** with the (task, problem, issue)（〜に取り組む）	「問題」と結びつく
☐ **immérse** oneself in (work, study, water)（〜に没頭する）	「仕事・水」と主に結びつく
☐ **incúr** (charges, costs, penalties, losses, expenses)（被る・負う）	「費用・罰則」と主に結びつく
☐ be **infátuàted** with (women, love, gambling)（〜に夢中になった）	「恋愛・興味の対象」と結びつきやすい

☐ **ínstigàte** a (an) (riot, legal action, investigation)（扇動する・始めさせる）	「騒動・法律上の手続き」と主に結びつく
☐ **instíll** (discipline, ideas, confidence) into someone（教え込む）	「主義・考え・自信」と結びつきやすい
☐ **ìntercépt** a (call, message, missile)（傍受する・迎撃する）	「通信・ミサイル」と主に結びつく
☐ **invóke** the (law, rule, image, memory)（発動する・呼び起こす）	「法律・イメージ・記憶」と結びつきやすい
☐ **jéopardìze** sb's (future, prospect, position, career)（危うくする）	「将来性・職」と結びつきやすい
☐ **júggle** the (jobs, tasks, balls)（やりくりする）	「仕事」と結びつきやすい
☐ **levy** a (charge, fine, tax)（課す）	「料金・税金」と結びつく
☐ be **mired** in (poverty, controversy, scandal, crisis)（～にはまり込む）	「窮状・危機」と主に結びつく
☐ **meándering** (river, canyon, conversation, novel)（曲がりくねった・とりとめのない）	「川・話の筋」と主に結びつく

II 一般語彙力パワーUPコロケーション

☐ **mésmerìze** the (audience, crowds, TV viewers)(魅了する)	「聴衆」と結びつく
☐ **mítigàte** the (impact, effects, damage, problems)(軽くする・和らげる)	「影響・問題」と主に結びつく
☐ **mútilàted** (body, corpse, bank note)(破損した・ばらばらの)	「体・紙幣」と結びつきやすい
☐ **oblíteràte** the (sign, data, memories, the entire city)(消し去る・全滅させる)	「記録・記憶」と結びつきやすい

■ 復習テスト

Choose the best answer from the 10 words below for each blank.

1. (　) one's (confidence, support, position, career)
2. (　) (discipline, idea, confidence) into someone
3. (　) the (attack, trouble, conspiracy, plot)
4. (　) sb's (memory, response, feeling, emotion)
5. (　) the (problem, disease, poverty)
6. (　) (information, messages, news, knowledge)
7. (　) (poverty, suffering, fears, concerns)
8. (　) the (budget, funds, money) for the project
9. (　) (responsibility, punishment, criticism)
10. (　) the (violence, crime, offense)

> A. alleviate　B. bolster　C. condone　D. disseminate
> E. earmark　F. elude　G. eradicate　H. evoke　I. forestall
> J. instill

■解 答
1. B 2. J 3. I 4. H 5. G 6. D 7. A 8. E 9. F 10. C

皆さん、お疲れ様でした。以上で第9日の「動詞編 必須レベル Part1」は終了です。次回は「動詞編 必須レベル Part2」です。それでは、明日に向かってボキャブラリービルディング！
Let's enjoy the process!（陽は必ず昇る！）

アルファベットの意味を知る！その2

英単語を覚える時に、アルファベットの語感を持つことは非常に役立つことが多いので、ぜひ知っておきましょう！

- **N**：何もなくなるゼロと新生（**nothing, nature, naked, new, novice, null**）
- **O**：丸く全体的に統一する円の境地（**organize, orchestra, order, origin, oval**）
- **P**：ピューッと突き出て進む（**push, penetrate, plunge, puke, pierce, press**）
- **Q**：キューッと圧力を加えて縮小する（**quell, quench, squeeze, squash**）
- **R**：力強く回転して元に戻る（**around, rotate, range, return, receive**）
- **S**：進んで出てくる音・視界（**sound, sight, speak, sing, search, success**）
- **T**：まっすぐ高く立てる（**tower, institute, statistics, tomb, taut, tit, tilt**）
- **U**：欠けてなくなり補う（**but, cut, unhappy, support, supply, hurt, ugly**）

V：力強くブアーッと飛び出す（vital, violence, vivid, valor, virtue）

W：曲がりくねる（wrinkle, wrestle, wring, wind, wriggle, wiggle）

X：交わり固定する（fix, mix, sex, obnoxious, orthodox, taxonomy）

Y：ヨガのように広がってゆく（yell, yawn, yearn, yard, young, yield）

Z：激しく揺さぶるエネルギー！（zenith, zeal, zest, zip, zap, zephyr, zing）

2-10　第10日
一般語彙力パワーUP
動詞編　必須レベル Part2

第10日目は、「動詞編 必須レベルPart2（8千～1.2万語水準）」です。それでは、皆さんの語彙力をぐーんとパワーUPしていただきましょう!!

□ **óffsèt** the (loss, gains, cost, expense)（埋め合わせる・相殺する）	「損益・費用」と主に結びつく
□ **óstracìze** (criminals, political activists, religious extremists)（追放する・葬り去る）	「犯罪者・活動家」と主に結びつく
□ **óust** someone from (the post [party], power)（追い出す）	「地位・組織」と主に結びつく
□ **òutstríp** (sb's ability, supply, demand)（～を凌駕する）	「能力・需要供給」と結びつきやすい
□ **òverhául** the (system, industry, engine)（～を徹底的に点検する）	「制度・組織・機械」と結びつきやすい

☐ **òverríde** (sb's decision [vote, consideration], a veto)(覆す・無視する)	「決定・投票」と主に結びつく
☐ **òverrún** the (country, enemy forces, budget, schedule)(侵略する・超過する)	「敵国・予算・時間」と結びつきやすい
☐ **péddle** (goods, drugs, one's idea)(〜を小売する・売り込む)	「商品・アイデア」と主に結びつく
☐ **pérmeàte** the (air, room, society, soil)(浸透する・広がる)	「空間・社会」と結びつきやすい
☐ **pérpetràte** a (an)(crime, fraud, attack, assault)(悪事を犯す)	「犯罪・暴力」に主に結びつく
☐ **pínpòint** the (cause, problem, location)(特定する・突き止める)	「原因・問題・場所」と結びつきやすい
☐ **plácate** (sb's anger, protesters, critics, customers, investors)(なだめる・静める)	「怒り・抗議（批判）者」と主に結びつく
☐ **plúmmeting** (birth rate, stock prices, popularity)(急速に減少する)	「数字・価格」と主に結びつく
☐ **plúnder** (a village [vessel], art treasures)(略奪する)	「略奪の対象・物品」と結びつきやすい
☐ **preclúde** (the possibility, sb's attempt [misunderstanding])(妨げる)	「可能性・試み」と主に結びつく

☐ **própagàte** (information, ideas, the race [plants])(広める・繁殖させる)	「情報・種」と主に結びつく
☐ **protrúding** (stomach, teeth, eyes, lips)(突き出ている)	「身体」と主に結びつく
☐ **quash** (the decision [revolt, strike] conviction, rumors)(無効にする・鎮圧する)	「判決・反乱・噂」と結びつきやすい
☐ **quell** (the violence [disturbance, riot], fear, doubts)(鎮圧する・和らげる)	「暴動・不快な感情」と主に結びつく
☐ **quench** the (flames, one's thirst [appetite])(消す・癒す)	「炎・生理的欲求」と結びつく
☐ **quíbble** over (minor details, trivial issues, small matters)(あれこれ言う・口論する)	「ささいな物事」と結びつく
☐ **ráze** the (village, building, forest, jungle)(破壊する)	「地域・建物・自然」と主に結びつく
☐ **rebúff** sb's (offer, suggestion, request)(拒絶する)	「提案・要求」と結びつきやすい
☐ **recóunt** one's (experience, story, history)(詳しく話す)	「体験・話題」と結びつきやすい

☐ **réctifỳ** the (problem, mistake, situation)(是正する)	「問題・状況」と主に結びつく
☐ **recúperàte** from (illness, injury, losses)(～から回復する)	「病気・ケガ・損失」と結びつく
☐ **redóuble** one's (efforts, exertions, support)(強める)	「努力・支援」と主に結びつく

語呂合わせで覚える英検1級単語 その5

☐ shun（しゃんとしないと人は寄りつかない）
☐ singe（伸治くんが服を焦がした！）
☐ sly（こっそりと悪事すらーい！）
☐ smother（キス、マザーにしすぎて窒息させる）
☐ sultry（サル・鳥参る蒸し暑さ！）
☐ supplant（何さぷらっと来て地位を奪い取るとは！）
☐ surly（去ーれー！不機嫌な奴は）
☐ tenet（手に取るように分かる彼らの信条が）
☐ thwart（タバコ吸おーとするのを邪魔するな！）
☐ torrid（鳥どれも丸焼け！焦熱の）
☐ tumult（便秘で詰まると 大騒動！）
☐ turmoil（またーもいるゴキブリ大騒動）
☐ vacillate（ばしばし入れーと、優柔不断な奴に焼き入れる）
☐ villain（ビラーンと悪者スカートめくる）
☐ wobble（うお〜！ブルブル よろよろふらつく）
☐ zenith（絶頂期に銭にするのが一番！）

☐ **redréss** the (balance, imbalance, situation, injustice)（是正する）	「均衡［不均衡］・不正」と結びつきやすい
☐ **refúrbish** a (building, house, hotel)（改装する）	「建物」と結びつく
☐ **rèinstáte** a (member, law, penalty)（復職［復活］させる）	「構成員・法律」と主に結びつく
☐ **relínquish** (power, control, one's position [responsibility])（放棄する）	「権力・役職・責任」と主に結びつく
☐ **repéal** the (law, bill, tax)（無効にする・取り消す）	「法律・法案」と結びつく
☐ **retráct** one's (statement, remarks, criticism)（撤回する）	「発言」と主に結びつく
☐ **retrénch** the (staff, workers, expenses)（削減する）	「人員・経費」と主に結びつく
☐ **retríeve** (information, data, one's honor [freedom])（読み出す・回復する）	「情報・名誉・自由」と結びつきやすい
☐ **revámp** (the system, a house, one's image)（改める・刷新する）	「制度・家屋・イメージ」と結びつきやすい
☐ **revítalize** (communities, economy, industry, organization)（活性化する）	「地域・経済・組織」と結びつきやすい

Ⅱ 一般語彙力パワーUPコロケーション

☐ **revóke** a (license, law, contract)（取り消す・無効にする）	「免許・法律・契約」と主に結びつく
☐ **rout** the (enemy, rival, opponent)（負かす）	「敵・ライバル」と結びつく
☐ **rúmmage** through one's (pocket, desk, room)（くまなく探す）	「収納場所」と主に結びつく
☐ **sávor** (the food [wine], one's victory [freedom])（味わう）	「飲食物・喜ばしい経験」と主に結びつく
☐ **scoff** at sb's (idea, notion, fear)（あざ笑う）	「考え」と結びつきやすい
☐ **séver** (connections, ties, relations) with someone（断つ）	「関係」と結びつく
☐ **slay** (innocent people, enemies, animals)（虐殺する）	「人・動物」と結びつく
☐ **smóther** (a cry [yawn, scandal, crime], the fire [opposition])（抑える・もみ消す）	「感情・悪事・炎」と結びつきやすい
☐ **spawn** (eggs, a crisis, problems)（生む）	「卵・危機・問題」と主に結びつく
☐ **squánder** (money, opportunities, time)（浪費する）	「お金・時間」と主に結びつく

☐ **stréamlìne** the (management, operation, procedure, process)（合理化する）	「経営・事業」と主に結びつく
☐ **stýmie** (the growth [process], one's attempt)（妨害する）	「成長・過程・試み」と結びつきやすい
☐ **súblimàte** one's (desire, energy, drive)（昇華する）	「欲望・衝動」と結びつきやすい
☐ **succúmb** to the (temptation, desire, pressure)（〜に屈する）	「誘惑・欲望・圧力」と結びつきやすい
☐ **swérve** (from one's course, off the road, to the right [left])（それる）	「コース・道」と主に結びつく
☐ **thwart** sb's (attempt, efforts, conspiracy, plan, ambition, desire)（阻止する・妨げる）	「企み・計画・野望」と主に結びつく
☐ **tilt** (the balance [scale], a chair, one's head)（傾ける）	「均衡・バランス」と結びつきやすい
☐ **tínker** with (the system [law, engine], nature, genes)（いじくる）	「法律・機械・自然」と結びつきやすい

II 一般語彙力パワーUPコロケーション

> 音素の力でボキャブラリーUP〔10〕

sn

sn スヌッと鼻でクンクン **sniff**
ぱっと、取る **snap, snatch**

s<u>n</u>arl	（がみがみ言う、うなる）
s<u>n</u>eer	（せせら笑う、軽蔑する）
s<u>n</u>ore	鼻で（いびきをかく）
s<u>n</u>obbish	地位（知識）を（鼻にかけた、俗物根性の）
s<u>n</u>oop	（こそこそ詮索する、かぎ回る）
s<u>n</u>ide	鼻でけなして（いやみな、皮肉な）
s<u>n</u>ivel	（鼻をすすって泣く）
s<u>n</u>ot	（鼻汁）、snub（鼻であしらう）
s<u>n</u>uffle	（鼻をならす）
s<u>n</u>ip	（はさみでチョキンと切る［切り取る］）
s<u>n</u>itch	（ぱっとひったくり、告げ口する）

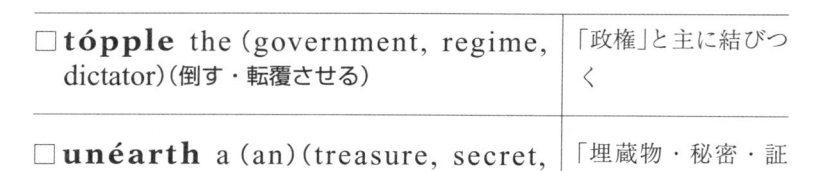

□ **tópple** the (government, regime, dictator) (倒す・転覆させる)	「政権」と主に結びつく
□ **unéarth** a (an) (treasure, secret, evidence) (掘り起こす)	「埋蔵物・秘密・証拠」と結びつきやすい

☐ The (event, drama, story, plot) **unfólded.**（展開する）	「出来事・話の筋」と主に結びつく
☐ **unrável** (threads, the mystery [plot, riddle])（ほぐす・解明する）	「糸・謎・企み」と主に結びつく
☐ **úpstáge** (the main character, one's rivals [opponents])（人気を奪う）	「主役・ライバル」と主に結びつく
☐ **usúrp** sb's (power, authority, position, role, right)（奪う）	「権力・地位・権利」と結びつきやすい
☐ **vácate** the (position, premises, seat)（明け渡す・立ち退く）	「地位・建物」と主に結びつく
☐ **veer** (away to the left, off course, from the road)（それる）	「進路・方向」と主に結びつく
☐ **vie** for (power, supremacy, support, the championship)（争う・張り合う）	「権力」と主に結びつく
☐ **víndicàte** one's (decision, claim, action, conduct)（正当性を立証する）	「主張・行動」と主に結びつく
☐ **vóuch** for the (quality, authenticity, validity)（保障する）	「品質・信頼性・有効性」と主に結びつく
☐ **wáge** a (war, battle, campaign)（（戦争・運動など）を行う）	「戦争・運動」と主に結びつく

☐ **wáver** between (hope and despair, consent and refusal)(揺れ動く・迷う)	「相反する感情」と主に結びつく
☐ **wéather** the (crisis, storm, recession)(乗り切る)	「難局・嵐」と主に結びつく
☐ **whet** one's (appetite, curiosity, imagination, taste)(刺激する)	「食欲・興味・創造」と結びつきやすい
☐ **wield** (power, influence, authority, a sword [weapon])(行使する・巧みに使う)	「権力・武器」と主に結びつく
☐ **woo** (women, consumers, voters)(言い寄る)	「女性・客・有権者」と結びつきやすい
☐ **wréstle** with a [an](problem, issue, question)(〜に取り組む)	「問題」と主に結びつく

■ 復習テスト

Choose the best answer from the 10 words below for each blank.
1. (　) a (license, law, contract)
2. (　) with a (an) (problem, issue, question)
3. (　) sb's (power, authority, position, role, right)
4. (　) the (management, operation, procedure, process)
5. (　) the (balance, imbalance, situation, injustice)
6. (　) the (loss, gains, cost, expense)
7. (　) (money, opportunities, time)
8. (　) (the violence [disturbance, riot], fear, doubts)
9. (　) sb's (attempt, efforts, conspiracy, plan, ambition, desire)
10. (　) a (an) (crime, fraud, attack, assault)

A. offset　B. perpetrate　C. quell　D. redress　E. revoke
F. squander　G. streamline　H. thwart　I. usurp　J. wrestle

■ 解　答
1. E　2. J　3. I　4. G　5. D　6. A　7. F　8. C　9. H　10. B

皆さん、お疲れ様でした。以上で第10日の「動詞編 必須レベル Part2」は終了です。次回は「動詞編 完成レベル」です。それでは、明日に向かってボキャブラリービルディング！

Let's enjoy the process!（陽は必ず昇る！）

2-11 第11日
一般語彙力パワーUP
動詞編 完成レベル

　第11日目は1万～1.5万語水準というハイレベルな語彙の「完成レベル」の動詞です。この水準が分かれば、洋書や英字紙はもちろんのこと、英検1級語彙を完全にマスターできるレベルで、国連英検・GRE（米国大学院入試試験）などの上級英語資格試験対策になります。それでは「動編 完成レベル」を気合を入れて頑張りましょう!!

□ **àcquiésce** to sb's (demands, decision, request)（同意する・黙認する）	「要求・決定」と結びつきやすい
□ **appráise** sb's (property, ability, work)（評価する）	「財産・能力」と主に結びつく
□ **belíe** (the fact, one's age [words])（偽る・裏切る）	「事実・年齢」と結びつきやすい
□ **bequéath** one's (fortune, legacy, assets) to someone（遺贈する）	「財産・遺産」と結びつく
□ **besíege** a (castle, fortress, garrison, town)（取り囲む）	「要塞・場所」と主に結びつく

☐ **brándish** a (gun, knife, sword, club)（振りかざす）	「武器」と結びつく
☐ **broach** a (matter, subject, topic)（持ち出す）	「話題」と結びつく
☐ **búngle** the (operation, response, attempt)（やり損なう）	「業務・対応・試み」と結びつきやすい
☐ **cápitalìze** on one's (idea, ability, experience, popularity)（利用する）	「考え・能力・経験・人気」と結びつきやすい
☐ **capítulàte** to (sb's demand [pressure], an enemy)（屈服する）	「要求・圧力」と結びつく
☐ **códdle** a (baby, child, cat)（大事に育てる・甘やかす）	「子供・動物」と主に結びつく
☐ **conníve** at (a shady deal, a criminal act, sb's fault)（大目に見る）	「悪行・犯罪・過失」と主に結びつく
☐ **consórt** with (the enemy, prostitutes, drug-dealers)（付き合う）	「敵・いかがわしい人物」と結びつきやすい
☐ **corróborate** the (statement, explanation, information)（実証する）	「発言・情報」と結びつく

☐ **cróuching** (position, posture, tiger, cat)(しゃがんだ)	「姿勢・動物」と主に結びつく
☐ **cull** (flowers, animals, data from multiple sources)((花を)摘む・間引く・集める)	「動植物・情報」と結びつきやすい
☐ **dábble** in (painting, music, literature)(かじる・軽く手を出す)	「趣味・学問」と主に結びつく
☐ **debáse** the (currency, quality, value, moral)(価値・品性を下げる)	「価値・品質」と主に結びつく
☐ **décimàte** (the population [army, industry], agricultural crops)(殺す・台無しにする)	「集団・産業・農作物」と結びつきやすい
☐ **defíle** the (holy place, image, body)(けがす・損なう)	「聖地・イメージ」と結びつきやすい
☐ **defráud** (investors, companies, government)(だます)	「投資家・会社・組織」と結びつきやすい
☐ **defráy** the (costs, expenses, charges)(費用を払う)	「費用」と結びつく
☐ **delíneàte** the (picture, role, character, boundary)(描写する・輪郭を描く)	「像・役割・境界線」と結びつきやすい

☐ **demárcate** the (border, areas, zones) （境界を定める）	「地域・境界線」と結びつく
☐ **désiccated** (fruit, milk, skin)（乾燥した）	「飲食物・肌」と結びつきやすい
☐ **dìsavów** (any responsibility [connection, involvement])（否定する）	「責任・関係」と主に結びつく
☐ **dìsengáge** the (brake, clutch, lock) （離す・切る）	「機器・鍵」と主に結びつく
☐ **dismémber** a [an] (body, company, organization)（ばらばらにする・解体する）	「体・組織」と主に結びつく

英検１級重要頻出単語 その４

CNN や BBC などのニュースを通じて、語彙力を UP させる場合は、覚えたい単語が使われた時に、繰り返し声に出して頭に叩き込む努力をすると効果的です。

【過去３回以上使われた頻出語彙】

niche, obsolete, **opulent**, **ostensible**, **ostracize**, **penitent**, perpetrate, plummet, polarization, prerequisite, **pristine**, procrastinate, **prodigy**, **prognosis**, proliferate, prolific, propagate, **propensity**, proposition, provision

☐ **disséct** the (body, specimens, problem) (解剖する・分析する)	「標本・問題」と主に結びつく
☐ **dissémble** one's (embarrassment, fear, intention, innocence) (隠す)	「感情」と結びつく
☐ **díssipàte** (money, fortune, energy, heat) (浪費する・散らす)	「お金・エネルギー」と主に結びつく
☐ **divúlge** the (secrets, information, details) (漏らす・暴露する)	「秘密・情報」と結びつく
☐ **elúcidate** the (problem, origin, mechanism, structure) (解明する・説明する)	「問題・仕組み」と主に結びつく
☐ **eschéw** (alcohol, meat, comment, violence) (避ける)	「望ましからざる行為」と主に結びつく
☐ **espóuse** a (doctrine, principle, belief, concept) (支持する)	「主義・方針」と結びつく
☐ **exóneràte** someone from (charges, responsibility, blame) (免除する・解放する)	「容疑・責任・非難」と結びつく
☐ **éxpedìte** the (process, construction, business, decision) (促進する・はかどらせる)	「プロセス・ビジネス」と主に結びつく
☐ **expóund** one's (theory, doctrine, views) (詳しく説明する)	「理論・主義」と結びつく

☐ **flaunt** one's (power, knowledge, wealth, skills)(誇示する・ひけらかす)	「権力・知識・富」と結びつきやすい
☐ **flóundering** (economy, company, business)(四苦八苦している)	「経済・会社」と主に結びつく
☐ **fomént** (trouble, disorder, revolution)(扇動する)	「問題・反乱」と主に結びつく
☐ **fúmble** (a ball, for words, in one's pocket)(しくじる・探す)	「物・言葉・場所」と結びつきやすい
☐ **gálvanìze** (action, the economy, public opinion)(活性化する)	「行動・経済・世論」と結びつきやすい
☐ **hággle** over the (price, fare, cost)(値切る・交渉する)	「値段・費用」と結びつく
☐ **hóne** (the edge, one's skills [abilities])(研ぐ・研ぎすます)	「刃・技能」と主に結びつく
☐ **imbúe** someone with (enthusiasm, compassion, the belief)(吹き込む)	「感情・信条」と結びつきやすい
☐ **impóverish** the (country, soil, mind)(貧困化させる・やせさせる)	「国・土地・精神」と結びつきやすい
☐ be **incapácitàted** by (illness, injury, accident)(再起不能になる)	「病気・事故」と結びつく

II 一般語彙力パワーUPコロケーション

☐ **incúlcàte** (the ideology [doctrine], virtue, discipline)（教え込む）	「道徳・教え」と結びつきやすい
☐ **infíltràte** the (territory, enemy, crime ring)（潜入する）	「領域・組織」と主に結びつく

音素の力でボキャブラリーUP〔11〕

gr-

ぐりぐりえぐって、苦しいよう！
ガリガリきしんで不満だよ！
groan とうめき、**grate** ときしる

<u>gr</u>imace　　（しかめ面をする）
<u>gr</u>avel　　　ガリガリ（砂利）の音
<u>gr</u>uelling　　ぐりぐりえぐって（へとへとに疲れさせる、苛酷な）
<u>gr</u>udge　　　ぐりぐり（ねたむ、憎む、恨み）
<u>gr</u>ate　　　　えぐる（すりおろす、きしませる）
<u>gr</u>ope　　　（手探りで捜す、捜し求める、まさぐる）
<u>gr</u>uesome　（心えぐる、恐ろしい、ぞっとする）
<u>gr</u>ipe　　　　（不平［ぐち］を言う、きりきり痛ませる）
<u>gr</u>ouch　　　（不平［ぐち］を言う）
<u>gr</u>ieve　　　心をえぐる（深く悲しませる）
<u>gr</u>oan　　　心をえぐる（うめく、きしむ）

☐ **infúse** (spirit, courage, passion) into someone（注ぎ込む）	「精神・感情」と結びつきやすい
☐ **móored** (ship, vessel, boat)（係留［停泊］している）	「船」と結びつく
☐ **mórtify** one's (body, flesh, mind)（苦行する）	「肉体・精神」と主に結びつく
☐ **múddle** one's (mind, brain, thought, life)（台無しにする・混乱させる）	「考え方」と主に結びつく
☐ **núllìfy** the (law, agreement, contract, decision)（無効にする）	「法律・取り決め」と主に結びつく
☐ **óozing** (blood, water, wound)（にじみ出る・ジクジクした）	「液体・傷口」と結びつく
☐ **pertúrb** (the system [order], one's mind)（かき乱す）	「制度・秩序・精神」と結びつきやすい
☐ **píque** sb's (interest, anger, vanity)（そそる・あおる）	「感情」と主に結びつく
☐ **ránsack** a (room, house, town)（あさり回る・荒らし回る）	「家屋・地域」と結びつく
☐ **recánt** one's (allegation, statement, view)（撤回する）	「主張・発言」と主に結びつく

II 一般語彙力パワーUPコロケーション

☐ **reek** of (alcohol, sweat, smoke)(〜のにおいがする)	「悪臭の元」と主に結びつく
☐ **repúdiàte** the (contract, treaty, payment)(拒否する)	「契約・支払い」と結びつきやすい
☐ **rescínd** the (law, contract, penalty)(撤回する)	「法律・契約」と主に結びつく
☐ **rúminàte** about the (past, issue, problem)(熟考する)	「過去・問題」と主に結びつく
☐ **scówling** (face, countenance, look)(しかめっ面の・渋った表情の)	「顔・表情」と結びつく
☐ **smóldering** (fire, combustion, anger, resentment)(くすぶっている)	「燃焼・悪い感情」と主に結びつく
☐ **squirm** in (discomfort, embarrassment, the spotlight, court)(落ち着きがない)	「不快・位置を表す語」と結びつきやすい
☐ **sùperséde** the old (system, method, law, rule)(取って代わる)	「制度・手法・法律」と結びつきやすい
☐ **trámple** on (rules, human rights, sb's feelings)(踏みにじる)	「法律・人権」と主に結びつく
☐ **transgréss** the (law, rule, boundary, territory)(違反する・超える)	「法律・境界線［領域］」と主に結びつく

☐ **vácillàte** between (love and hate, consent and refusal)(揺れ動く)	「相反するもの」と結びつく
☐ **vánquish** the (enemy, opponent, fear)(負かす・克服する)	「敵・不安」と主に結びつく
☐ **vílifỳ** sb's (character, image, opponents)(非難する)	「性格・敵」と結びつきやすい
☐ **wáde** through the (crowds, river, book)(〜を通り抜ける・〜を歩いて渡る・目を通して読む)	「群集・川・本」と結びつきやすい
☐ **wean** a (baby, child, toddler) from the mother(乳離れさせる)	「子供」と主に結びつく
☐ **wínce** in (pain, agony, shock)(ひるむ)	「痛み・ショック」と主に結びつく
☐ **wrench** one's (ankle, wrist, knee)(痛める)	「体の関節」と結びつきやすい

■ 復習テスト

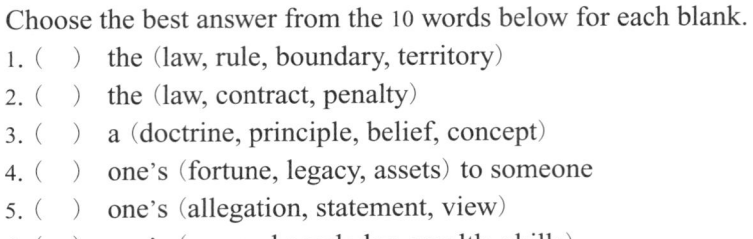

Choose the best answer from the 10 words below for each blank.

1. (　) the (law, rule, boundary, territory)
2. (　) the (law, contract, penalty)
3. (　) a (doctrine, principle, belief, concept)
4. (　) one's (fortune, legacy, assets) to someone
5. (　) one's (allegation, statement, view)
6. (　) one's (power, knowledge, wealth, skills)
7. (　) a (gun, knife, sword, club)
8. (　) (trouble, disorder, revolution)
9. (　) (money, fortune, energy, heat)
10. (　) the (ideology [doctrine], virtue, discipline)

A. bequeath　B. brandish　C. dissipate　D. espouse
E. flaunt　F. foment　G. inculcate　H. recant　I. rescind
J. transgress

■ 解　答
1. J　2. I　3. D　4. A　5. H　6. E　7. B　8. F　9. C　10. G

皆さんお疲れ様でした。以上で第11日の「動詞編 完成レベル」は終了です。次回は「名詞編」です。それでは、明日に向かってボキャブラリービルディング！

Let's enjoy the process!（陽は必ず昇る！）

2-12　第12日
一般語彙力パワーUP
名詞編　必須レベル

　第12日目は、基礎・必須・完成レベルの語彙水準の「名詞編」で、英語学習者の素養としてはどれも欠かせない重要な単語を収録しています。それでは、皆さんの語彙力をぐーんとパワーUPしていただきましょう!!

□ **ábstinence** from (food, meat, alcohol, sex)（節制）	「飲食物・快楽」と結びつく
□ (international, worldwide, public) **accláim**（賞賛）	「世界・民衆」と結びつく
□ (business, political, financial) **ácumen**（洞察力・見識）	「ビジネス・政治」と主に結びつく
□ the **ádvent** of (the Internet [computer], television)（到来）	「発明品」と主に結びつく
□ (political, voter, public, general) **ápathy**（無関心）	「政治・一般」と主に結びつく

☐ (hospital, political, grave) **blúnder**（大失敗・へま）	「組織・程度」と主に結びつく
☐ **boon** to (business, economy, industry)（恩恵・利益）	「経済・産業」と結びつく
☐ **cátalyst** for (change, development, prosperity)（触媒）	「変化・発展」と結びつきやすい
☐ **complícity** in a (crime, plot, conspiracy)（共謀）	「犯罪・企み」と結びつく
☐ the **crux** of the (matter, problem, issue)（要点）	「問題」と結びつく
☐ (cheerful, nervous, sunny, aggressive, amiable) **dìsposítion**（気質）	「性格を表す形容詞」と結びつく
☐ **déarth** of (resources, support, talent, information)（不足）	「資源・人材・情報」と結びつきやすい
☐ **déference** to the (authority, leader, elderly)（敬意）	「敬意の対象」と結びつく
☐ **déluge** of (letters, questions, claims)（殺到）	「手紙・質問・要求」と結びつきやすい
☐ **disìntegrátion** of the (country, society, empire)（崩壊・分裂）	「組織」と結びつく

☐ (economic, income, racial) **dispárity**（格差）	「経済・人種」と結びつきやすい
☐ (political, business, commercial) **éntity**（団体）	「政治・経済」と結びつく
☐ the **epítome** of (life, success, power)（典型・縮図）	「人生・成功・権力」と結びつきやすい
☐ **èquilíbrium** of (trade, industry, power)（均衡・釣り合い）	「経済・力」と結びつきやすい
☐ (complete, total, political, financial) **fiásco**（大失敗）	「完全・政治・経済」と結びつきやすい
☐ (media, buying, killing, festival) **frenzy**（熱狂）	「メディア・取引・催し」と結びつきやすい
☐ **gárment** (industry, factory, manufacturer)（衣類・服飾）	「産業・製造者」と主に結びつく

英検1級重要頻出単語 その5

　語彙をどんどん増やすには何よりも、英単語・表現がとても好きだと自己暗示にかける必要があります。決して苦手意識を持つのではなく、まずは言葉から自分を暗示にかけていきましょう。

> **【過去３回以上使われた頻出語彙】**
>
> prudence, redeem, reiterate, **repulse**, **respite**, retaliate, **reticent**, revoke, rustle, speculate, **squander**, stagger, stipulate, stringent, submerge, substantiate, swindle, tangible, **taunt**, tedious, ubiquitous, vie, **voracious**

☐ **gist** of a (statement, speech, story) （要点・骨子）	「発言・話」と結びつきやすい
☐ pay **hómage** to the (king, saint, war dead)（敬意）	「敬意の対象」と結びつく
☐ **hárbinger** of (doom, death, trouble) （前触れ・前兆）	「運命・死」と主に結びつく
☐ **héydày** of one's (time, life, power) （全盛期・絶頂）	「時代・人生・権力」と結びつきやすい
☐ give (new, fresh, initial, further, major) **ímpetus**（推進力・勢い・弾み）	「初期・新規・重要」と結びつきやすい
☐ **láyman's** (idea, view, guide)（素人）	「考え方・見方」と結びつく
☐ **lust** for (power, fame, money) （欲・強い欲望）	「権力・名声・お金」と主に結びつく

☐ **lúster** of (gold, pearl, furniture) (輝き)	「金属・装飾品」と主に結びつく
☐ (grave, serious, deep) **mìsgívings** (不安・心配)	「深刻さ」と結びつく
☐ (medical, nuclear, traffic, minor) **míshap**（不幸な出来事・事故）	「医療・原発・交通」と結びつきやすい
☐ a **mýriad** of (problems, factors, opportunities)（無数）	「問題・要素・機会」と結びつきやすい
☐ **nádir** of one's (career, life, existence)（底・最悪の状態）	「経歴・人生」と結びつきやすい
☐ **nóvice** (computer user, monk, teacher)（初心者・新米・見習い）	「ユーザー・職業」と主に結びつく
☐ (political, racial, emotional, romantic) **óvertòne**（含み・ニュアンス）	「政治・感情」と主に結びつく
☐ the **óutsèt** of (the administration [negotiation], one's career)（初期）	「政権・交渉・経歴」と結びつきやすい
☐ **ónslàught** of (the enemy, calls, information)（猛攻撃）	「敵・電話・情報」と結びつきやすい
☐ (basic, central, false, first, underlying) **prémise**（根拠・覆建物）	「基礎・中心・誤り」と結びつきやすい

II 一般語彙力パワーUPコロケーション

☐ (close, geographical, physical) **proxímity**（近さ）	「密接さ・地理的」と結びつきやすい
☐ (moral, basic, divine) **précept**（処世訓・戒め）	「道徳・基礎」と結びつく
☐ **páragòn** of (beauty, virtue, courage)（典型）	「美・美徳」と主に結びつく
☐ **páucity** of (information, evidence, resources)（不足・少量）	「情報・証拠・資源」と結びつきやすい
☐ **pínnacle** of one's (power, success, career)（絶頂）	「権力・成功・経歴」と結びつきやすい
☐ a **pléthora** of (information, choices, options)（大量）	「情報・選択」と結びつきやすい
☐ **plíght** of the (refugees, victims, homeless)（苦境）	「難民・被害者」と主に結びつく
☐ **pórtent** of (death, calamity, disaster, danger)（前兆）	「死・災難」と結びつきやすい
☐ **precúrsor** of the (Internet, earthquake, social movement)（前触れ・前兆）	「科学技術・災害・社会運動」と結びつきやすい
☐ (political, financial, economic) **predícament**（苦境）	「政治・経済」と結びつきやすい

☐ **prèdiléction** for (wine, books, clothes, songs, color)（特別の好み・偏愛）	「嗜好の対象」と結びつく
☐ **prèdisposítion** to (disease, cancer, violence)（傾向・質）	「病気・暴力」と主に結びつく
☐ **preséntiment** of (danger, disaster, earthquakes)（予感）	「危険・災害」と主に結びつく
☐ **prétext** for (war, crackdown, one's arrest)（口実・言い訳）	「戦争・取締り」と結びつきやすい
☐ **proclívity** for (crime, violence, unethical behavior)（傾向・性癖）	「犯罪・暴力」と結びつきすい
☐ **propénsity** for (drinking, gambling, overspending)（性癖）	「悪習慣」と結びつく
☐ **púrport** of one's (speech, letter, remark)（意図・目的）	「発言・言葉」と主に結びつく
☐ (military, political, economic) **qúagmìre**（泥沼・窮地）	「軍事・政治・経済」と結びつきやすい
☐ **quirk** of (fate, nature, timing)（気まぐれ・予測のつかない出来事）	「運命・自然」と主に結びつく

II 一般語彙力パワーUPコロケーション

> 音素の力でボキャブラリー UP〔12〕

| wr | タオルをねじってねじってしぼり出す、**wring** としぼる |

wring　（しぼる、ねじる）リング！とタオルをしぼる。
wriggle　（のたうち回る）リグル！と体をのたうち回る。
wrinkle　（しわ）リンクる！と服にしわが寄る。
wrest　（ねじる、ねじり取る）レスト！とものをねじり取る。
wrestle　（取っ組み合う）レスル！とレスリングで、取っ組み合う。
wry　（しかめる）ライ！と顔をしかめる。

☐ (shooting, killing, murderous) **rámpage**（凶暴な行動）	「殺人」と結びつく
☐ (legal, political, economic) **ràmificátion**（結果・悪影響）	「法律・政治・経済」と結びつきやすい
☐ **rémnant** of the (medieval times, Roman empire, feudal system)（名残・面影）	「昔を偲ばせるもの」と結びつく
☐ **rénegàde** (elements, terrorist, nation)（裏切り）	「メンバー・組織」と主に結びつく

☐ **réspite** from (work, competition, attack)(中断・小休止)	「仕事・競争・攻撃」と結びつきやすい
☐ **resúrgence** of (militarism, nationalism, racism)(復活)	「主義」と結びつく
☐ **revúlsion** against (war, crime, violence)(嫌悪)	「戦争・犯罪・暴力」と結びつきやすい
☐ **rift** between (the rich and poor, black and white)(対立・亀裂)	「相反するもの・異なる集団」と結びつく
☐ **rúbble** of (buildings, war, earthquakes)(がれき)	「建物・災害」と結びつきやすい
☐ **rúbric** of the (examination, rituals, constitution)(指示・説明書)	「試験・儀式・法律」と結びつきやすい
☐ **stígma** of (obesity, AIDS, suicide)(汚名・不名誉)	「悪印象の事象」と結びつく
☐ **scóurge** of (war, terrorism, drugs)(災難・惨劇)	「戦争・破壊行為」と結びつく
☐ **sémblance** of (confidence, dignity, peace, order)(見せかけ)	「内面[外面]を表す語・平和秩序」と結びつきやすい
☐ **sháckles** of (slavery, communism, convention)(束縛・足かせ)	「因習・組織」と主に結びつく

☐ a **smáttering** of (knowledge, intelligence, French)（少しばかり・少量）	「知識・外国語」と結びつきやすい
☐ **smear** (attack, campaign, tactics)（中傷）	「攻撃・戦術」と結びつきやすい
☐ **spasm** of (fear, laughter, muscle, stomach)（発作・けいれん）	「感情・身体」と主に結びつく
☐ **swarm** of (ants, bees, tourists, refugees)（群れ・群集）	「昆虫・人」と主に結びつく
☐ **synópsis** of the (speech, play, presentation, story)（概要）	「スピーチ・劇」と結びつきやすい
☐ **ténets** of (Buddhism, Islam, communism)（教義・原理）	「宗教・イデオロギー」と結びつく
☐ pay **tríbute** to (sb's courage [contribution], the war dead)（賛辞）	「偉業・人」と主に結びつく
☐ (political, economic, financial, social) **túrmoil**（混乱）	「政治・経済・社会」と結びつきやすい
☐ **témperance** in (one's conduct, eating, drinking)（節度・自制）	「行い」と主に結びつく
☐ **stink** of (alcohol, fish, garlic, burning rubber)（におい）	「飲食物・化学物質」と結びつく

☐ a **throng** of (shoppers, onlookers, spectators)(多数・大群)	「群集」と主に結びつく
☐ **tínge** of (irony, regret, sadness, pink)(かすかな様子・色合い)	「感情・色彩」と主に結びつく
☐ **tírade** against (illegal aliens, parasite singles, pay cuts)(厳しい批判・攻撃演説)	「社会問題」と主に結びつく
☐ **trávesty** of (justice, truth, the law)(曲解・こじつけ)	「正義・法律」と主に結びつく
☐ **trìbulátions** of (war, life, competition)(試練・苦難)	「戦争・競争」と主に結びつく
☐ **únderpìnning** of (democracy, market economy, the society)(基盤・土台)	「社会・経済」と結びつきやすい
☐ **úpròar** over (the scandal, tax increase, human cloning)(反対の声・わめき声)	「社会問題」と主に結びつく
☐ the **úpshòts** of the (investigation, event, experiment)(結果・結末)	「調査・出来事」と主に結びつく
☐ **véngeance** against the (enemy, criminal, murderer)(復讐・報復)	「敵・犯罪者」と主に結びつく
☐ **véstige** of (tradition, Western culture, colonialism)(名残・痕跡)	「伝統・文化」と結びつきやすい

II 一般語彙力パワーUPコロケーション

☐ in the **vicínity** of the (station, airport, $1 million)（付近・周辺）	「場所・数値」と結びつく
☐ **vicíssitùdes** of (one's life [career], the seasons)（浮き沈み・絶え間ない変化）	「人生・市場・気候」と主に結びつく
☐ (political, diplomatic, legal) **wrángle**（論争）	「政治・外交・法律」と結びつきやすい
☐ **wreath** of (flowers, smoke, laurel)（花輪・輪状のもの）	「花・煙」と主に結びつく

■ 復習テスト

Choose the best answer from the 10 words below for each blank.
1. (　) of one's (career, life, existence)
2. (international, worldwide, public) (　)
3. (　) of the (speech, play, presentation, story)
4. (complete, total, political, financial) (　)
5. (　) of (beauty, virtue, courage)
6. (　) of (doom, death, trouble)
7. (　) to (disease, cancer, violence)
8. (　) of (gold, pearl, furniture)
9. (　) of the (country, society, empire)
10. (　) of (war, terrorism, drugs)

> A. acclaim　B. disintegration　C. fiasco　D. harbinger
> E. luster　F. nadir　G. paragon　H. predisposition
> I. scourge　J. synopsis

■ 解 答
1. F 2. A 3. J 4. C 5. G 6. D 7. H 8. E 9. B 10. I

皆さん、お疲れ様でした。以上で第12日の「名詞編」は終了です。これで、一般語彙力パワーUP大特訓は終了です。それでは、明日に向かってボキャブラリービルディング！

Let's enjoy the process!（陽は必ず昇る！）

英単語の意味と英和辞典の訳はどれだけズレている！

　日本人が英語で発信する時に一番厄介な問題の1つが類語の使い分けですが、英和辞典や単語集で「翻訳型の学習法」で主にメインの意味を覚えることで語彙補強をしてきたほとんどの日本人は、文脈に合った適語の選びや類語の使い分けがうまくできません。よく使われる refer to は英和辞典によく記されているような「言及する」といった文語的な語ではないし、statement も「陳述」ほど堅くはありません。その他、approve と「是認する」、get と「得る」などもフォーマル度にズレがあります。また develop と「発展する［させる］」、contribute と「貢献する」などは、意味の幅にかなりのズレがあり、5段階で言えば3ぐらいでしょう。これに対して、ズレの少ないもの、つまり5段階で5のものは、progress と「進歩」、improve と「改善する」、supply と「供給する」、infer と「推論する」、estimate と「推定する」などで、success と「成功」、presume と「推定する」、assassinate と「暗殺する」なども、かなり近い（5段階で4.5）と言えます。これらをしっかりと認識していれば、文脈に合った適語の選びや類語の使い分けがしやすくなるでしょう。

第3章

分野別語彙力パワーUP
文系語彙

3-1　第13日
政治語彙に強くなる

　政治分野の語彙の知識は、英字新聞を始め、タイム、ニューズウィーク、エコノミストなどの英字誌を読んだり、CNNやBBC放送を聞き取れるようになるために重要であることは言うまでもありません。また、資格検定試験対策としては、英検1級・準1級の1次・2次試験、国連英検A級・特A級などに合格するためには、それらをある程度覚えておく必要があります。それでは皆さん、最後まで頑張ってこの分野の語彙力UPに励みましょう。

政治関係語彙に強くなる　　　CD 1-13

- [ ] checks and balances / separation of powers　三権分立
- [ ] legislative branch　立法府（executive branch は「行政府」、judiciary branch は「司法府」）
- [ ] parliamentary system　議会制
- [ ] plenary〔plí:nəri〕convention　総会（plenary session は「本会議」）
- [ ] Capitol Hill　国会議事堂（speaker は「議長」、the floor は「議員席、議員」）
- [ ] Diet dissolution　国会解散（Diet resolution は「国会決議」）
- [ ] the House of Councilors / the Upper House　参議院 ⇔ 衆議院

the House of Representatives / the Lower House
- [ ] cabinet reshuffle [shakeup]　内閣改造（coalition cabinetは「連立内閣」、the Cabinet Secretariatは「内閣官房」）
- [ ] casting vote　決裁票：議会で賛否同数の時、議長が持つ決定票
- [ ] steamrolling / railroading　強行採決
- [ ] constitutional amendment　憲法改正
- [ ] federal mandate〔mǽndeit〕連邦指令：上級裁判所から下級裁判所への職務執行令状、選挙民から議員への要求、委任
- [ ] fiscal expansionism　財政拡張政策（fiscal policyは「財政政策」）
- [ ] appropriation bill　歳出法案
- [ ] agrarian〔əgréəriən〕[agricultural] reform　農地改革
- [ ] State of the Union Message / State-of-the-Nation Address　一般教書：大統領が憲法上の義務に基づき連邦の状況について議会に報告する
- [ ] presidential veto〔víːtou〕大統領拒否権（line-item vetoは「個別条項拒否権」）
- [ ] presidential aide〔éid〕大統領補佐官
- [ ] the First Amendment　合衆国憲法修正第1条：表現や宗教の自由
- [ ] filibustering〔fíləbʌstəriŋ〕senate　議事妨害する上院議員
- [ ] Chancellor〔tʃǽnsələ〕ドイツの首相
- [ ] deputy Prime Minister　副総理（acting chairpersonは「議長代理」）
- [ ] incumbent〔inkʌ́mbənt〕mayor　現職の市長（outgoing mayorは「退職する市長」）
- [ ] inaugural〔inɔ́ːgjərəl〕address　就任演説（keynote addressは「基本方針演説」）
- [ ] vote of confidence　信任案（vote of nonconfidenceは「不信任案」）

- ☐ impeachment〔impíːtʃmənt〕vote　弾劾投票
- ☐ government dignitary〔dígnitèri〕　政府高官
- ☐ red-tape system　複雑な官僚制度
- ☐ government-ruled municipality〔mjuːnìsəpǽləti〕　政府直轄市
- ☐ governmental immunity〔imjúːnəti〕　政府免責［特権］：政府の許諾がない限り、政府を相手に訴訟を提起することができないこと

■ **政治の略語クイズにチャレンジ!!**

1. ERA	2. G.O.P.	3. KKK	4. NPO	5. NRA
6. OSCE	7. TMD	8. ACS	9. ANC	10. CIS
11. IAEA	12. NSC	13. MIRV	14. OECD	15. PSI
16. ICBM	17. IPCC	18. OAU	19. OAS	20. PKF

■ 解　答

1. Equal Rights Amendment　男女同権憲法修正法案
2. Grand Old Party　共和党
3. Ku Klux Klan　米国の秘密結社
4. Nonprofit Organization　民間非営利組織
5. National Rifle Association　全米ライフル協会
6. Organization for Security and Cooperation in Europe
　全欧安全保障協力機構（2008年現在で56カ国加盟）
7. Theater Missile Defense　戦域ミサイル防衛（NMD［National Missile Defense］は「米本土ミサイル防衛」）
8. Association of Caribbean States　カリブ諸国連合（1995年発足）

9. African National Congress　アフリカ民族会議（1912年発足）
10. Commonwealth of Independent States　独立国家共同体：旧ソビエト連邦の12カ国で形成
11. International Atomic Energy Agency　国際原子力機関
12. National Security Council　〈米〉国家安全保障理事会
13. Multiple Independently-targetable Reentry Vehicle　複数目標弾頭
14. Organization for Economic Cooperation and Development　経済協力開発機構
15. Proliferation Security Initiative　（大量破壊兵器の）拡散防止構想
16. Intercontinental Ballistic Missile　大陸間弾道ミサイル
17. Intergovernmental Panel for Climate Change　気候変動に関する政府間パネル
18. Organization of African Unity　アフリカ統一機構
19. Organization of American States　米州機構
20. U.N. Peacekeeping Force　国連平和維持軍

- [ ] ethnocentric〔èθnouséntrik〕mentality / chauvinism〔ʃóuvənìzm〕自民族中心主義（nation state は「民族国家」）
- [ ] Balkanization　小国分割主義政策
- [ ] absolute dictatorship　絶対的独裁制（totalitarian〔toutǽlətéəriən〕regime は「全体主義体制」）
- [ ] corrupt autocracy〔ɔːtákrəsi〕[authoritarianism]〔ɔːθɔ̀əritéəriənìzm〕腐敗した独裁主義
- [ ] veneered jingoism〔dʒíŋgouìzm〕うわべだけの好戦的愛国主義者

- ☐ appeasement〔əpíːzmənt〕policy　宥和政治
- ☐ middle-of-the-road party　中道政権
- ☐ left-wing extremist　極左翼 ⇔ 右翼 right-wing
- ☐ mainstream faction　主流派 ⇔ 反主流派 anti-mainstream faction
- ☐ Islamic fundamentalism　イスラム原理主義
- ☐ Israel enclave〔énkleiv〕　イスラエル人居住地
- ☐ political manifesto〔mæn∂féstou〕　政治綱領（communiqué〔kəmjúːnikèi〕は「公式声明」）
- ☐ political turmoil [upheaval〔ʌphíːvl〕]　政治的混乱［混迷］
- ☐ political clout　政治的影響力
- ☐ political assassination　政治的暗殺（political maneuvering〔mənúːvəriŋ〕[engineering]は「政治工作」）
- ☐ political backlash　政治反動
- ☐ political contribution　政治献金（slush fundは「不正政治資金」）
- ☐ pork-barrel politics　利益誘導型政治
- ☐ power breakfast　有力者との朝食会（power broker は「実力者、黒幕」）
- ☐ rainmaker　やり手の弁護士
- ☐ retail politics　小売政治：一般大衆に迎合した政治
- ☐ ruling party　与党 ⇔ 野党 opposition party
- ☐ secession〔siséʃən〕from the party　党からの脱退
- ☐ sectarian〔sektéəriən〕strife　分派抗争（splinter groupは「政党の分派」）
- ☐ Foggy Bottom / the Department of State　米国国務省
- ☐ defense expenditure [outlay]　防衛費
- ☐ anti-insurgency campaign　反乱弾圧作戦
- ☐ civil war　内戦（martial law は「戒厳令」）

- □ preliminary [prior] talks　事前協議
- □ census bureau〔bjúərou〕　国勢調査局
- □ local autonomy　地方自治（local chapter は「地方支部」）
- □ entitlement program　（失業手当などの）公的給付金プログラム
- □ provisional government　暫定政府
- □ provincial government　州政府：カナダは10州 province と２準州 territory からなる連邦国家である
- □ propaganda war　（主に政治目的の意味がある）宣伝戦争
- □ Boy Scout　ボーイスカウト：妥協せず自分の理想を追求する政治家
- □ Democratic pollster　民主党の調査専門家
- □ privacy act　プライバシー保護法
- □ Politburo〔pálətbjùərou〕　旧ソビエト共産党中央委員会政治局
- □ political dissident　政治的反体制者（political activist は「反対分子」）
- □ the Tokyo Metropolitan Police Department　警視庁
- □ online resident registry network　住基ネット

選挙関係語彙に強くなる　　CD 1-14

- □ bankrolled election　金権選挙
- □ cabinet approval rate　内閣支持率（resign en masse は「総辞職」）
- □ campaign platform　選挙公約（campaign trail は「選挙遊説」）
- □ caretaker Cabinet　選挙管理内閣
- □ closely-contested constituency〔kənstítʃuənsi〕　激戦区
- □ controversial gerrymandering〔dʒérimændəriŋ〕　問題ある勝手な選挙区改定
- □ Democratic caucus〔kɔ́:kəs〕　民主党幹部会（Democratic ticket は「民主党公認候補者」）

- ☐ Republican convention　共和党大会 ⇔ 民主党大会 Democratic convention
- ☐ electoral college　大統領選挙人団
- ☐ running mate　副大統領候補
- ☐ the Liberal Democratic Party's primaries〔práimèəriz〕　自民党総裁予備選挙（presidential election は「大統領選」）
- ☐ official party endorsement　党の公認
- ☐ major contender [contestant] / hopeful　有力候補（front-runner は「最有力候補」）
- ☐ also-ran　落選者
- ☐ lame duck　落選議員（president-elect は「次期大統領」）
- ☐ gubernatorial〔gùːbənətɔ́əriəl〕election　知事選挙（mayoral election は「市長選」）
- ☐ off-year election　中間選挙
- ☐ lopsided victory　一方的勝利
- ☐ election returns　開票結果（voter turnout は「投票率」）
- ☐ by-election results　補欠選挙の結果
- ☐ mudslinging barrage　（政治運動などの）中傷合戦
- ☐ smear campaign　組織的中傷
- ☐ proportional representation system　比例代表制（single-seat constituency system は「小選挙区制」）
- ☐ revolving door　政府高官が政権交代によって、政府と民間企業の間を行き来すること
- ☐ universal suffrage〔sʌ́fridʒ〕　普通参政権
- ☐ referendum legislation　国民投票に基づく法律制定
- ☐ eligible voter　有権者
- ☐ runoff voting　決選投票
- ☐ sympathy vote　同情票

- □ ballot box　投票箱（ballot initiative は「住民投票」）
- □ absentee〔ǽbsntíː〕vote　不在投票（abstention rate は「棄権率」）
- □ nonaffiliated voters / unaffiliated voters　無党派層
- □ sound bite　一口発言：テレビやラジオで引用される、政治家などの短い発言
- □ spin doctor　スピンドクター：政治家の広報アドバイザー

タイム・エコノミストエンジョイ必須句動詞マスター！①

お金を払う − shell out［cough up, fork out［over, up］］money
でっち上げる − cook［trump, make］up an alibi
防ぐ − fend［ward, stave, head］off the danger
上げる − jack［drive, send］up the price
高める − step［shore, beef, prop, rev］up the economy
乗り越える − ride out［tide over, pull through］the difficulty
奮い起こす − summon［muster, pluck, screw］up one's
　　　　　　　courage
打ち出す − hammer［thrash, hash］out a compromise
元気づける − perk［cheer, pep, buoy, buck］her up
抑える − hold back［choke back, bottle up］one's anger
獲得する − rack up［chalk up, carry off］victories
しくじる − screw［goof, mess, foul, fuck］up the business
ごまかす − gloss over［paper over, cover up］the failure
削減する − scale［whittle, pare, cut］down the salary
屈服する − cave in［knuckle under, bow to］the pressure
和らげる − tone［water］down one's criticism

■ 米国の政治機構

Legislative power 立法権	Constitution of the U.S.A. (米国憲法)	Judicial power 司法権
議会(上院・下院) Senate & House of Representatives		最高裁判所　Supreme Court 控訴裁判所　Appellate Court 地方裁判所　District Court

Executive Power（行政権）

EOP ［Executive Office of the President］（大統領府）

President（大統領）／ Vice President（副大統領）

国務省 Department of State	国防総省 Department of Defense	司法省 Department of Justice
商務省 Department of Commerce	内務省 Department of Interior	労働省 Department of Labor
運輸省 Department of Transportation	健康社会福祉省 Department of Health and Human Services	住宅都市開発省 Department of Housing and Urban Development
教育省 Department of Education	エネルギー省 Department of Energy	復員軍人省 Department of Veterans Affairs
財務省 Department of Treasury	農務省 Department of Agriculture	

■ 日本の政治機構

```
┌─────────────────────────┐  ┌──────────┐  ┌─────────────────────────┐
│ 国会(Diet)              │  │Constitution│  │ 裁判所(Court)           │
│ 議会(衆議院・参議院)    │──│of Japan   │──│ 最高裁判所(Supreme Court)│
│ House of Representatives &│  │(日本国憲法)│  │ 高等裁判所(Hight Court) │
│ House of Councilors     │  │          │  │ 地方裁判所(District Court)│
└─────────────────────────┘  └──────────┘  └─────────────────────────┘
                    │
          ┌─────────────────────┐
          │ Executive Power(行政権)│
          └─────────────────────┘
```

内閣(Cabinet)

内閣総理大臣(Prime Minister)

国務大臣(State Minister)

総務省 Ministry of Internal Affairs and Communications	農林水産省 Ministry of Agriculture, Forestry and Fisheries
法務省 Ministry of Justice	経済産業省 Ministry of Economy, Trade and Industry
外務省 Ministry of Foreign Affairs	国土交通省 Ministry of Land, Infrastructure and Transport
財務省 Ministry of Finance	環境省 Ministry of Environment
厚生労働省 Ministry of Health, Labor and Welfare	防衛省 Ministry of Defense
文部科学省 Ministry of Education, Culture, Sports, Science and Technology	

※ 補足語彙　Financial Services Agency　金融庁

　　　　　　Imperial Household Agency　宮内庁

分野別語彙力パワーUP文系語彙

外交関係語彙に強くなる　　　CD 1-15

- asylum 〔əsáiləm〕 migration　亡命移民（Jewish émigré 〔émigrèi〕は「ユダヤ人亡命者」）
- exodus 〔éksədəs〕 of refugees　難民の大量流出（refugee repatriation 〔ri:pèitriéiʃən〕は「難民送還」）
- deportee 〔dì:pɔətí:〕　国外追放者
- the Arab street　アラブ世界の世論
- axis of evil　悪の枢軸（rouge state は「ならず者国家」）
- bilateral 〔bailǽtərəl〕 [trilateral 〔tràilǽtərəl〕] discussion　二者［三者］会談
- bargaining power　交渉力（brinkmanship は「瀬戸際外交」）
- consulate 〔kánsələt〕 general　総領事館（consul は「領事」）
- embassy civilian　大使館の民間人（ambassador は「大使」）
- courtesy call [visit]　表敬訪問（goodwill visit は「親善訪問」）
- diplomatic immunity　外交官特権
- extraterritorial right　治外法権
- belligerent 〔bəlídʒərənt〕 countries　交戦国
- ultimatum 〔ʌ̀ltəméitəm〕　最後通告
- military action　軍事力行使（military intervention は「軍事的介入」）
- military reprisal 〔ripráizl〕 [retaliation 〔ritæ̀liéiʃən〕]　軍事的報復
- preemptive 〔priémptiv〕 attack　先制攻撃（opening gambit 〔gǽmbit〕は「先手」）
- legitimate self-defense　正当防衛
- proxy 〔práksi〕 war　代理戦争（war of attrition は「消耗戦」）
- blitz tactics [strategy]　電撃作戦（D-day は「作戦開始日」）
- border skirmish 〔skə́:miʃ〕　国境地帯での小競り合い
- torpedo 〔tɔəpí:dou〕 -boat destroyer　駆逐艦

- [ ] ground-controlled interception　管制迎撃
- [ ] missile deployment　ミサイル配備（nuclear warhead は「核弾頭」）
- [ ] reconnaissance〔rikánəzəns〕plane　偵察機（stealth bomber は「ステルス爆撃機」）
- [ ] salvo〔sǽlvou〕bombing　爆弾の一斉投下
- [ ] Agent Orange / defoliant〔di:fóuliənt〕　枯葉剤（tear gas は「催涙ガス」）
- [ ] hand grenade　手榴弾（grenade blast は「手榴弾攻撃」）
- [ ] time bomb　時限爆弾（booby trap は「しかけ爆弾」）
- [ ] logistic assistance [support]　後方支援
- [ ] supply depot〔dépou〕/ supply base　補給基地
- [ ] militia〔məlíʃə〕commander　民兵指揮官
- [ ] undercover agent　諜報部員
- [ ] intelligence infiltration〔ìnfiltréiʃən〕　秘密情報機関による潜入調査
- [ ] disinformation [blowback] alert　偽〔逆〕情報警戒
- [ ] suspicious vessel / unidentified boat [ship]　不審船
- [ ] wartime atrocity〔ətrásəti〕　戦争時の残虐行為
- [ ] wholesale slaughter〔slɔ́:tə〕　大量殺戮
- [ ] war dead　戦没者（war-displaced orphan は「戦争孤児」）
- [ ] withdrawal [pullout] deadline　撤退期限
- [ ] cease-fire / truce　停戦（conflict resolution は「紛争解決」）
- [ ] mediation clause　調停条項
- [ ] rapprochement〔ræ̀prouʃmá:ŋ〕talks　国交回復交渉
- [ ] war reparation〔rèpəréiʃən〕　戦争賠償金
- [ ] conscientious objector　良心的参戦拒否者
- [ ] disarmament talks　軍縮会議
- [ ] weapons inspector　武器査察官

タイム・エコノミストエンジョイ必須句動詞マスター！②

取り組む – grapple [wrestle, deal, cope] with the problem
熟考する – mull over [chew over, chew on, sleep on, kick around] the matter
頼る – count [bank, fall back] on her help
整頓する – spruce [tidy, straighten] up the room
根絶する – stamp [root, weed, wipe] out corruption
終える – wind [wrap, clean] up the job
調べる – pore over [sift through, check on] the document
応える – measure [live, come] up to their expectations
解決する – iron [straighten, work, smooth] out the problems
現れる – crop [spring, pop, turn, show] up
いじくる – fiddle [tinker, tamper, monkey, play, mess] with the machine
突きとめる – ferret out [track down, pin down] the truth
けなす – put [run, call] down the student
求める – fish for [jockey for, be gunning for] a position / be spoiling [itching] for a fight
味方する – stand by [stand up for, stick up for] the woman
尻込みする – shy [shrink, back] away from the challenge

- [ ] peaceful coexistence　平和共存
- [ ] state sponsor of terrorism　テロ支援国家
- [ ] homeland security　国土安全保障：米国をテロから守ること
- [ ] extradition of terrorists　テロリスト引き渡し（eco-terrorism は「環境テロリズム」：環境保護目的で行われるテロ行為）

- □ G8 communiqué　G8首脳による共同声明（summit talks は「首脳会談」、joint communiqué は「共同声明」）
- □ global hegemony〔hədʒéməni〕　世界覇権
- □ globocop　世界の警察
- □ military junta〔húntə〕　軍事政権
- □ most-favored-nation treatment　最恵国待遇
- □ non-aggression treaty [pact]　不可侵条約
- □ nonaligned neutrality　非同盟中立（permanent neutrality は「永世中立」）
- □ nuclear proliferation〔prəlìfəréiʃən〕　核拡散
- □ nuclear freeze agreement　核凍結合意
- □ nuclear holocaust〔hάləkɔ̀ːst〕　核の大惨事（radioactive fallout は「放射能の死の灰」）
- □ deterrent〔ditə́ːrənt〕capability　抑止能力（nuclear deterrence は「核による戦争抑止」）
- □ ODA [Official Development Assistance]　政府開発援助
- □ Ostpolitic〔άstpɑlitìːk〕　東欧政策、東方外交
- □ papal emissary〔péipl | éməsèəri〕　ローマ法王の使者（courier は〔kúriər〕「急使、特使」）
- □ peace envoy〔énvɔi〕　平和使節（peace pact は「平和条約」）
- □ ratification〔rætəfikéiʃən〕instrument　批准書
- □ stationing garrison〔gǽərisn〕　駐屯軍（troop deployment は「軍隊の派遣」）
- □ territorial issue　領土問題（Northern Territories は「北方領土」）
- □ the territorial waters　領海（the high seas は「公海」）
- □ the U.N. Charter　国連憲章（U.N. resolution は「国連決議」）
- □ the U.N. General Assembly　国連総会（the U.N. Secretary-General は「国連事務総長」）

III　分野別語彙力パワーUP文系語彙

- ☐ the United Nations Security Council　国連安全保障理事会
- ☐ ministerial [working] level talks　閣僚級［事務レベル］会議
- ☐ political asylum　政治亡命
- ☐ zero immigration　不法移民をゼロにする政策
- ☐ the Nolan Committee　ノーラン委員会：官僚・議員の粛正基準を定めるために設置された機関
- ☐ the Amsterdam [ǽmstədæm] Treaty　アムステルダム条約：EUを創設したマーストリッヒ条約の改正条約
- ☐ Brussels　ブリュッセル：EUの本部があることからEUの代名詞
- ☐ the Dayton Agreement　デイトン合意：ボスニア戦争を終結
- ☐ the Oslo [ázlou] Agreement　オスロ合意：イスラエルとPLOが紛争解決を目指して1993年に調印
- ☐ Whitewater Affair　ホワイトウォーター疑惑：クリントン前大統領が1980年代に関与したとされる土地開発・不正融資をめぐる疑惑

■ 政治語彙復習テストにチャレンジ！

1	内閣改造	11	亡命移民
2	三権分立	12	軍事政権
3	連邦指令	13	交戦国
4	弾劾投票	14	抑止能力
5	正当防衛	15	悪の枢軸
6	大統領拒否権	16	親善訪問
7	ドイツの首相	17	後方支援
8	不在投票	18	不可侵条約
9	民主党幹部会	19	核拡散
10	決選投票	20	戦争賠償金

■ 政治語彙復習テスト（解答）

1	cabinet reshuffle［shakeup］	11	asylum migration
2	Checks and balances	12	military junta
3	federal mandate	13	belligerent countries
4	impeachment vote	14	deterrent capability
5	legitimate self-defense	15	axis of evil
6	presidential veto	16	goodwill visit
7	Chancellor	17	logistic assistance［support］
8	absentee vote	18	non-aggression treaty［pact］
9	Democratic caucus	19	nuclear proliferation
10	runoff voting	20	war reparation

最難関国連英検特 A 突破攻略法

　あらゆる英語資格の中でも非常に難関とされる国連英検特 A を合格するには、まずエッセイ問題で高得点を取るために必要な国際情勢の知識（中東・北朝鮮・ＥＵなど地域別に、歴史的見地に基づいた現状分析）を Input したエッセイを書き、その添削指導トレーニングを受けることが重要です。次に、英検１級語彙問題ではカバーできない、タイム、ニューズウィークによく見られる時事問題を語る際の頻出フレーズ（たとえば、dig one's heels in「自分の意向に固執する」、pyrrhic victory「犠牲を払って得た勝利」、moral high ground「精神的な優位」）を覚えながら、最難関の文法・語法問題は、全文を読まずにコロケーションだけで解いてしまうトレーニングをする必要があります。それによって試験では、250語のエッセイを書くのに必要な時間 30 分を当てることができます。というのも読解問題の量が非常に多いため、大部分の人がエッセイライティング問題に十分な

時間が割けず、手抜きのエッセイを書いてしまい試験にパスできない状況がよく起こっているからです。国連英検特Aは、試験自体は難しいのですが、合格点は60点前後なので、時間内に問題処理ができ、エッセイをきちんと書ききれば合格の可能性が高くなります。

　2次試験対策としては、質問内容が大体分かっているので十分準備をすることができます。評価の項目はComprehension、Speaking、Communication、Knowledge（International Affairs）で、試験直前に面接シミュレーション＆トレーニングをすれば、各項目で満点を取ることは不可能ではありません。ただし平易なspoken Englishではなく、学識経験者の話す語彙豊富で正確なwritten Englishを話すように心がけましょう。そしてこれは面接試験に共通することですが、試験としてとらえるのではなく、試験官と国際情勢について意見を交わすことをエンジョイする姿勢が合格への近道です。

3-2 第14日

経済・ビジネスの語彙に強くなる Part1（経済・金融関係）

　経済・ビジネス分野の語彙の知識は、ビジネス会話をしたり、英字新聞やタイム、ニューズウィーク、エコノミストの他、ビジネスウィーク、フォーチュンなどの経済誌を読めるようになるために重要であることは言うまでもありません。また、資格検定試験対策としては、TOEICで高得点を取るためにも、英検1級1次・2次試験、英検準1級1次・2次試験、ビジネス英検、ビジネス通訳士［翻訳士］検定などを突破するためにも、最低必要なものを覚えておく必要があります。それでは皆さん、最後まで頑張ってこの分野の語彙力UPに励みましょう。

財政・景気語彙に強くなる　　　　CD 1-16

- □ subprime loan　サブプライムローン：信用度の低い人向けの住宅ローン
- □ trickle-down economics　トリクルダウン政策：大企業優先の経済政策（easy monetary policy は「金融緩和政策」）
- □ laissez-faire〔leséiféə〕自由放任主義
- □ pump-priming measures　呼び水政策
- □ tight-money policy / belt-tightening　金融引き締め政策

- [ ] economic-stimulus package　景気刺激策
- [ ] fiscal〔fískl〕policy　財政政策 ⇔ 金融政策 monetary policy
- [ ] national treasury / government coffers〔kɔ́:fəz〕　国庫
- [ ] revenue　歳入 ⇔ 歳出 expenditure
- [ ] supplementary budget　補正予算
- [ ] outstanding government bonds　国債発行残高
- [ ] local allocation〔æ̀ləkéiʃən〕tax　地方交付税
- [ ] value-added tax　付加価値税
- [ ] excise tax [duty]　（酒、タバコなどの）物品税
- [ ] gift tax　贈与税（inheritance tax は「相続税」）
- [ ] withholding tax / pay-as-you-go　源泉徴収課税（progressive tax は「累進課税」）
- [ ] tax deduction〔didʌ́kʃən〕for spouse [dependents]　配偶者［扶養家族］控除
- [ ] tax return　所得申告（blue return は「青色申告」）
- [ ] direct-indirect tax ratio　税の直間比率
- [ ] indexation〔ìndekséiʃən〕　物価スライド制
- [ ] utility charges　公共料金
- [ ] grant / bounty　助成金（spoon-fed は「助成金を与える」）
- [ ] housing subsidy　住宅助成金（food subsidy は「食料助成金」）
- [ ] official discount rate　公定歩合（prime rate は「貸付金利」）
- [ ] denomination〔dinɑ̀mənéiʃən〕　額面単位（revaluation は「平価切り上げ」）
- [ ] federal funds rate　FFレート：民間銀行同士で貸し借りする時の利率
- [ ] yen-denominated〔dinɑ́mənèitid〕bond　円建て債券［法］
- [ ] yen-based loan / yen credit　円借款
- [ ] quantitative monetary easing　金融の量的緩和

- ☐ reserve-requirement ratio　預金準備率
- ☐ rock-bottom interest rates　超低金利
- ☐ exchange gains from strong yen　円高差益
- ☐ per capita income　1人当たり所得
- ☐ excess liabilities / negative net worth　債務超過
- ☐ boom-and-bust〔bʌst〕　一時的活況（diffusion index は「景気動向指数」）
- ☐ economic fluctuation　景気の変動
- ☐ inflationary spiral　悪性インフレ
- ☐ double-digit inflation　2桁インフレ（taxflation は「増税によるインフレーション」）
- ☐ stagflation〔stæɡfléiʃən〕　スタグフレーション：景気停滞下のインフレ（hyperinflation は「物価の上昇と通貨価値の下落が急激に起こる極度のインフレ」）

■ ビジネスの略語クイズにチャレンジ!!

1. CLI	2. EMU	3. FRB	4. IBRD	5. IRS
6. ECB	7. FOMC	8. FTC	9. BIS	10. UNCTAD

■ 解　答

1. cost-of-living index　消費者物価指数
2. Economic and Monetary Union　EUの経済通貨同盟
3. Federal Reserve Board　連邦準備制度理事会
4. International Bank for Reconstruction and Development
　国際復興開発銀行

5. Internal Revenue Service 〈米〉内国税歳入局
6. European Central Bank 欧州中央銀行
7. Federal Open Market Committee 〈米〉連邦公開市場委員会
8. Federal Trade Commission 〈米〉連邦取引委員会
9. Bank for International Settlements 国際決済銀行
10. United Nations Conference on Trade and Development 国連貿易開発会議

- [ ] financial meltdown 金融破綻
- [ ] default〔difɔ́:lt〕債務不履行（insolvencyは「支払い不能」）
- [ ] microfinance マイクロファイナンス：貧困層・低所得者層のための金融サービス
- [ ] heavily-indebted poor countries [HIPCs] 重債務貧困国
- [ ] Corporate Rehabilitation Law 会社更生法（Chapter 11は「連邦破産法第11章（会社更生法）」）
- [ ] mint 造幣局
- [ ] the Social Insurance Agency 社会保険庁
- [ ] post-office businesses 郵政事業
- [ ] operation by the public and private sectors 第3セクター方式
- [ ] pension contributions [premiums] 年金掛け金（pension reserveは「年金積立金」）
- [ ] nursing care insurance 介護保険
- [ ] endowment〔endáumənt〕insurance 養老保険
- [ ] revenue stamp 収入印紙

貿易・国際経済語彙に強くなる

- balance of payment　国際収支
- key currency　基軸通貨
- convertible currency　兌換紙幣：金や世界各国の通貨と容易に交換することができる紙幣（hard currency は「交換可能通貨」）
- foreign exchange rate　外国為替レート　（floating exchange rate は「変動為替相場」）
- foreign reserve　外貨準備
- yen quotation　円相場（quotation in yen は「円建て」）
- appreciation [depreciation] of the yen　円高 [円安]
- dollar-buying intervention　ドル買い介入
- dollar-denominated bond　ドル建て債券
- foreign exchange gain　為替差益（foreign exchange loss は「為替差損」）
- trade friction [dispute]　貿易摩擦
- trade deficit　貿易赤字 ⇔ 貿易黒字 trade surplus
- protectionism　保護貿易主義（trade liberalization は「貿易自由化」）
- import quota　輸入割当（import surcharge は「輸入課徴金」）
- preferential tariff〔tǽrif〕　特恵関税（most favored nation clause は「最恵国待遇条約」、non-tariff barrier は「非関税障壁」）
- punitive〔pjúːnətiv〕[retaliatory〔ritǽliətɔ̀ːri〕] tariff　報復関税（across-the-board tariff reductions は「関税の一括引き下げ」）
- safeguard clause　緊急輸入制限条項
- economic blockade〔blɑkéid〕　経済封鎖（embargo は「通商禁止」）
- exclusive economic zone [EEZ]　排他的経済水域

■ **新語クイズにチャレンジ!! その1**

1. K-12
2. enrichment class
3. deadbeat dad
4. healthspan
5. intact family
6. energy drink
7. killer wave
8. eternity leave
9. biometric passport
10. baggage meltdown
11. BILF
12. deshop
13. fart gag
14. metrosexual
15. intellidating

■ **解　答**

1. 義務教育期間（Kはkindergartenのことで、12は高校3年のこと）
2. 補習授業や優秀な学生のための特別クラス
3. 養育費を払わない父親
4. 医者にかからず健康でいる期間
5. 両親がそろっている家庭
6. スタミナドリンク
7. 津波
8. 死に向かう肉親を看病するために取る末期介護休暇
9. 生態識別情報を含んだパスポート
10. 飛行機の荷物が行方不明になること
11. イケメン（boy I'd like to fuckのこと）
12. 品物を買って使用後に返品する
13. くだらないギャグ
14. メトロセクシャル（「美的センスのある都会の男性」、ubersexualは「男らしい男」）
15. 知的に興奮するデート

投資関係語彙に強くなる　　　CD 1-18

- assets and liabilities　資産と負債（liquid assets は「流動資産」）
- government bond　国債（deficit-covering bond は「赤字国債」）
- debenture　社債（derivative は「金融派生商品」）
- gilt-edged bond　優良債券
- bearish market　弱気市場 ⇔ 強気市場 bullish market
- bellwether　主要株、主要指標［数］（the Dow Jones average は「ダウ平均株価」）
- equities〔ékwətiz〕　普通株式（blue chip は「優良株」）
- listed stock　上場株 ⇔ 非上場株 unlisted stock
- selected stock［issue］　主要銘柄（specific issue［stock］は「指定銘柄」）
- outstanding share　発行済み株式、総発行株数
- over-the-counter stock market　店頭株式市場
- pre-listed shares / not-yet-offered stocks　未公開株
- gaining［advancing］issues　値上がり株（most active issue は「最も人気を集めた株」）
- speculative stock［issue］　仕手株
- price-earnings ratio　株価収益率
- derivative　デリバティブ：先物（futures）、スワップ（swap）、先渡し（forward）、オプション（option）の4種類がある
- futures market　先物市場（spot market は「現物市場」）
- hedge fund　ヘッジファンド：世界の金持ちや機関投資家から集めた資金を運用して高利回りを得ようとする国際投機マネー
- speculation　投機（speculator は「投機家」）
- institutional investor　機関投資家
- capital gain　（株式などの）資産売却所得
- arbitrage〔ɑ́ːrbətrɑ̀ːʒ〕　さや取り：相場などの利ざやで儲けること

- [ ] back [negative] spread　逆ざや（latent loss は「含み損」）
- [ ] corner the market　株の買い占め
- [ ] support buying　買い支え
- [ ] takeover bid [TOB] / tender offer　株式公開買い付け：株式の所有者に買い付け価格を公告して買い取りを提案する
- [ ] greenmail payment　グリーンメール・ペイメント：買収対象となった会社が、仕掛人の取得した株式を高額で譲り受けること
- [ ] stock option　株式購入権
- [ ] mutual fund　投資信託会社（trust fund は「信託資金」）
- [ ] margin trading　信用取引（stock exchange は「証券取引所」）
- [ ] real estate investment trust [REIT]　不動産投資信託
- [ ] title deed　不動産権利証書
- [ ] investment portfolio〔pɔːrtfóuliòu〕　有価証券明細書
- [ ] negotiable instrument　譲渡可能証券
- [ ] retail banking　小口金融取引
- [ ] disinvestment　投資の食いつぶし
- [ ] earnings per share [EPS]　1株当たり利益
- [ ] net income　純益
- [ ] net selling / net buying　売り越し［買い越し］
- [ ] return on investment [ROI]　投資利益率（ROE は「運用益」）
- [ ] speculative portfolio / return [performance]-oriented portfolio　利回り重視のポートフォリオ［有価証券］
- [ ] oligopoly〔àləgápəli〕market　寡占市場
- [ ] market equilibrium〔ìːkwəlíbriəm〕　市場均衡：需要曲線と供給曲線の交点
- [ ] dividend〔dívədènd〕　配当（volume は「出来高」、yield は「高利回り」）
- [ ] markup　値上げ ⇔ 値下げ markdown

- ☐ goods and chattels〔tʃætlz〕 家財道具一切
- ☐ treasury bond 米国の財務省長期証券 (treasury bill は「財務省証券」)
- ☐ Big Board ニューヨーク証券取引所の通称
- ☐ bourse〔búəs〕 ヨーロッパの株式市場
- ☐ certified financial analyst [CFA] 米国証券アナリスト
- ☐ the Tokyo Stock Exchange 東京証券取引所
- ☐ the Topix index / the Tokyo Stock Price Index 東証株価指数

企業活動・会計その他の語彙に強くなる　CD 1-19

- ☐ pretax profit / current profit 経常利益
- ☐ borrowed capital [capital] 他人資本［自己資本］
- ☐ solvency margin / claim-paying ability ソルベンシーマージン：保険会社の支払い能力の指標
- ☐ outstanding debt 未払いの負債
- ☐ appraisal [paper / unrealized] loss 含み損、評価損
- ☐ tax in arrears〔əríəz〕 延滞税 (separate taxation は「分離課税」)
- ☐ licensed tax accountant 税理士
- ☐ money laundering 不正資金浄化
- ☐ tax haven〔héivn〕 税逃れの場所 (tax break は「税優遇措置」)
- ☐ overheads 間接費：原材料費と労働費を除く
- ☐ depreciation 減価償却：土地・貨幣などの目減り
- ☐ insurance beneficiary 保険受取人
- ☐ surrender value 生命保険の解約払戻金
- ☐ inheritance waiver〔wéivə〕 相続放棄
- ☐ compulsory automobile liability insurance 自賠責保険
- ☐ consolidated statement 連結決算
- ☐ creditor account 貸方勘定 ⇔ 借方勘定 debtor account

- ☐ welfare pension / employees' pension plan　厚生年金
- ☐ local procurement　現地調達
- ☐ local [domestic] content legislation　ローカルコンテント法：輸入車に対し部品の現地調達を規定した法律
- ☐ penetration〔pènətréiʃən〕[ownership] rate　普及率
- ☐ collective bargaining　団体交渉
- ☐ interim report　中間報告
- ☐ voucher　取引証票、引換券
- ☐ early scouting of university students　青田買い
- ☐ catastrophe〔kətǽstrəfi〕reserve　災害損失積立金

■ 経済・ビジネス語彙復習テストにチャレンジ！ Part1

1	景気動向指数	11	税逃れの場所
2	財政政策	12	不正資金浄化
3	超低金利	13	相続放棄
4	弱気の市場	14	公共料金
5	普通株式	15	円借款
6	店頭株式市場	16	未払いの負債
7	源泉徴収課税	17	団体交渉
8	預金準備率	18	自由放任主義
9	さや取り	19	上場株
10	経済封鎖	20	国債

■ 経済・ビジネス語彙復習テスト Part1（解答）

1	diffusion index	11	tax haven
2	fiscal policy	12	money laundering
3	rock-bottom interest rates	13	inheritance waiver
4	bearish market	14	utility charges
5	equities	15	yen-based loan / yen credit

6	over-the-counter stock market	16	outstanding debt
7	withholding tax / pay-as-you-go	17	collective bargaining
8	reserve-requirement ratio	18	laissez-faire
9	arbitrage	19	listed stock
10	economic blockade	20	government bond

TOEIC 満点突破：意外な意味に要注意！①

produce one's passport（パスポートを提示する）
promptly at 10 a.m.（10時ちょうどに）
sanction the action（その措置を認可する）
report to work（出社する）
draft（隙間風、生ビール、徴兵召集）
fare（乗客、食べ物、出し物）
local **chapter**（地方支部、「連続」の意味もある）
commute the sentence（刑を減刑する）
lodge a **complaint**（告訴する、「病気」の意味もある）
engineering **concern**（土木会社）
contract AIDS（エイズにかかる、「収縮する」の意味もある）
return on the investment（投資に関する見返り）
tender a resignation（辞表を出す）
surrender value（保険の解約払戻金）
grace the **function**（行事に出席する）
champion the cause（主義を擁護する）

3-3 第15日

経済・ビジネスの語彙に強くなる Part2（ビジネス・オフィス関係）

会社・職場　最重要語彙表現をマスター！　　CD 2-1

- □ corporate headquarters [head office]　本社 (subsidiary は「子会社」)
- □ affiliated company　関連会社 (foreign affiliate は「外資系企業」)
- □ small-and-medium-sized business　中小企業
- □ deficit-ridden company　赤字会社
- □ divestiture〔daivéstitʃə〕　子会社または事業部の売却（downsizing は「企業縮小」）
- □ auditor〔ɔ́:ditə〕　会計検査官、監査役
- □ board meeting　役員会議
- □ rank and file / employees with no title　平社員
- □ bookkeeper　帳簿係 (liaison は「連絡係」)
- □ skeleton staff　最小限度のスタッフ
- □ career track　昇進コース
- □ glass ceiling　ガラスの天井：昇進を妨げる見えない壁
- □ job opening　就職口
- □ reference letter / recommendation　推薦状 (resume は「履歴書」)

- [ ] probation [proubéiʃən] period　見習い期間（probationer は「見習い」、hands-on training は「実地訓練」）
- [ ] temporary worker　臨時雇い（contingent worker は「臨時雇用の労働者」）
- [ ] moonlighting　アルバイト
- [ ] personnel [pə̀:snél] cost　人件費
- [ ] fringe benefit　付加給付（perquisite [pə́:kwəzit] は「役得」）
- [ ] paid vacation [holiday]　有給休暇
- [ ] maternity [paternity] leave　育児休業（sick leave は「病欠」）
- [ ] severance [sévərns] pay　解雇手当
- [ ] lifetime employment　終身雇用
- [ ] mandatory [mǽndətɔ̀əri] retirement　定年退職（voluntary retirement [resignation] は「希望退職」）
- [ ] seniority system　年功序列 ⇔ 能率給 performance-based wage system
- [ ] physical [commodity] distribution　物流
- [ ] absenteeism [ǽbsntí:ìzm]　無断欠勤（dress code は「服装規定」）
- [ ] briefing　簡単な報告（debriefing は「報告徴収」）
- [ ] extension number　内線番号
- [ ] invoice　送り状（ledger [lédʒə] は「元帳」）
- [ ] clerical error [mistake]　事務上の誤り
- [ ] labor union / trade union　労働組合
- [ ] walkout / strike　ストライキ

■ 新語クイズにチャレンジ!! その2

1. identity theft 2. senior moment 3. henna tattoo
4. nip and tuck 5. BBW 6. blitz 7. bod-mod
8. bottomless cup of coffee 9. cash-for-trash
10. cultural Chernobyl 11. go ballistic
12. level-playing field 13. nail-down
14. affluenza 15. sizist

■ 解　答

1. 個人情報を盗むこと
2. ど忘れ、うっかり行動
3. ヘナタトゥー、消えるタトゥー
4. 美容整形
5. 大柄な美人（big beautiful woman）
6. Eメール：瞬時に相手に届くことから
7. ピアス、タトゥーなどで体に装飾をすること
8. コーヒーのお変わり自由
9. お金目当てにスキャンダルを暴露すること
10. 文化や芸術が台無しにされる場所
11. キレる：go nuclearとも言う
12. 機会の均等
13. 客寄せのために広告に載せた安価な商品
14. アフルエンザ［金持ち病］：贅沢に慣れ、それが当たり前になること
15. 身長や体重で人を判断する体格差別的な人

- ☐ commission / percentage　手数料
- ☐ warranty〔wɔ́rənti〕　保証書
- ☐ CIF〔cost, insurance and freight〕　「運賃保険料込み値段」
- ☐ installment plan　分割払い（lumpsum payment は「一括払い」）
- ☐ dishonored bill　不渡り手形（bounced check は「不渡り小切手」）
- ☐ reminder / demand note　督促状
- ☐ credit sale　信用販売、掛け売り
- ☐ low-end product　低価格商品
- ☐ price busting　価格破壊
- ☐ quotation〔kwoutéiʃən〕　時価、費用の見積もり
- ☐ money back guarantee　返金保証
- ☐ return privilege〔prívlidʒ〕　返品特約
- ☐ opinion ad　意見広告
- ☐ testimonial〔tèstəmóuniəl〕advertising　テスティモニアル広告：専門家、著名人などに広告商品の優秀性を証言させる形の広告
- ☐ package deal　一括取引
- ☐ segmental breakdown　部門別内訳
- ☐ point of sale［POS］　販売時点情報管理
- ☐ sales channel　販売経路、販売ルート
- ☐ selling point　セールスポイント
- ☐ earnings estimate　企業の業績予想
- ☐ window-dressing statements　粉飾決算
- ☐ chain-reaction of bankruptcies　連鎖倒産
- ☐ collateral〔kəlǽtərəl〕/ security　担保（物件）

会社・職場　最重要語彙表現をマスター！　CD 2-2

- managing director　常務取締役（executive director は「専務取締役」）
- acting chairperson　会長代理
- administration office　総務局
- expense accounters　社用族（expense account は「交際費」）
- troubleshooter　修理係、問題解決者
- commuting allowance　通勤手当
- employer matching plans　会社側一部負担制度
- social security holdings　（社員の）社会保障積立高［金額］
- log　業務日誌、連絡簿（organ は「機関紙」）
- letterhead　便箋の頭書（cover letter は「添え状、添付説明書」）
- office supplies　事務用備品
- durable years　耐用年数
- partitioning 〔pɑːtíʃənin〕（オフィス空間などの）仕切り方
- three-martini 〔mɑətíːni〕 lunch　社用の昼食、豪華な昼食
- night shift　夜勤（work shift は「交代制勤務」）
- downtime　（機械の故障・修理などによる）操業停止時間
- featherbedding　（組合による）水増し雇用、生産制限行為
- mid-career recruiting　中途採用（percentage working は「就労率」）
- performance appraisal ［evaluation / review］　勤務評定
- minimum wage　最低賃金（overtime allowance は「残業手当」）
- promotion transfer　栄転（demotion transfer は「左遷」）
- arbitrary 〔ɑ́ːbitrəri〕 layoff　一方的解雇（exploitation ［èksplɔitéiʃən］ of workers は「労働者搾取」）
- maternalism　（デイケア・フレックスタイムなど）仕事と家庭を両立できるように女性従業員に配慮した雇用体制

- □ unemployment allowance　失業手当
- □ retirement allowance　退職手当（seniority allowance は「勤続手当」）
- □ annuity〔ən(j)úːəti〕/ pension　年金
- □ liquidated〔líkwidèitid〕company　清算会社
- □ subcontractor　下請会社
- □ job action　（労働組合の）抗議行動
- □ underemployed　不完全雇用の：学歴や職歴から考えると、能力を発揮できない、畑違いの仕事に従事していること
- □ just-in-time marketing　店頭で顧客が出した反応に即時に対応しようとするマーケティング（just-in-time employee は「契約社員」）
- □ walk-in　アポなしの客

■ 経済・ビジネス語彙復習テストにチャレンジ！Part2

1	赤字会社	11	隙間産業
2	外資系企業	12	水増し雇用
3	帳簿係	13	運送費
4	粉飾決算	14	商品損害賠償責任
5	年功序列	15	24時間営業
6	見習い期間	16	薄利多売
7	解雇手当	17	販売戦略
8	最小限度のスタッフ	18	組立工場
9	大量購入割引、一括購入割引	19	借入金をてこにした企業買収
10	受注残高	20	産業スパイ活動

■ 経済・ビジネス語彙復習テスト Part2（解答）

| 1 | deficit-ridden company | 11 | niche business |
| 2 | foreign affiliate | 12 | featherbedding |

3	bookkeeper	13	shipping cost
4	window-dressing statements	14	product liability
5	seniority system	15	around-the-clock operation
6	probation period	16	low-margin high-turnover
7	severance pay	17	sales-promotion gimmick
8	skeleton staff	18	assembly plant
9	bulk discount	19	leveraged buyout
10	order backlog	20	industrial espionage

商業・経営・ビジネス　最重要語彙表現をマスター！

☐ mail order business　通信販売　　　　　　　　　CD 2-3

☐ niche〔nítʃ〕business　隙間産業：隙間やニーズを発掘して、サービスを中心に行う新しいビジネス（niche product は「隙間商品」）

☐ garment industry　服飾業界

☐ no-frills flight　余分なサービスはしない航空便

☐ classified ad　求人広告（want ad は「募集広告」）

☐ leaflet / flier　チラシ（mailer は「郵便広告、メール広告」）

☐ word-of-mouth advertising　口コミによる宣伝

☐ around-the-clock operation　24時間営業

☐ clearance sale　処分セール（inventory は「在庫」）

☐ bulk〔bʌ́lk〕discount　大量購入割引、一括購入割引

☐ patron〔péitrən〕ひいき客、顧客（prospective customer は「見込み客」）

☐ creditor　債権者 ⇔ 債務者 debtor

☐ guarantor〔gæ̀rəntɔ́ː〕保証人

☐ product liability　商品損害賠償責任

☐ defective〔diféktiv〕[reject] product　不良品

☐ order processing　注文の処理［手続き］

- □ order backlog　受注残高（backorder は「未処理受注残」）
- □ proceeds　売上高
- □ track record　実績、業績
- □ sales quota〔kwóutə〕　販売ノルマ（sales-promotion gimmick〔gímik〕は「販売戦略」、sales pitch は「しつこい売り」）
- □ low-margin high-turnover　薄利多売
- □ outsourcing　外注
- □ royalty　印税、特許権
- □ retail outlet　小売店（outlet は「店舗」、retail price は「小売価格」、wholesale price は「卸売価格」）
- □ shipping cost　運送費（warehouse は「倉庫」）
- □ special public corporation　特殊法人
- □ independent corporation　独立法人
- □ industrial restructuring　業界再編
- □ the Labor Standards Law　労働基準法
- □ overdue wages　未払い賃金
- □ phony business trip　カラ出張
- □ turnover rate　離職率
- □ annual wage bargaining　春闘
- □ job transfer away from one's home　単身赴任
- □ absence without leave［AWOL］　無断欠勤
- □ personal information protection law　個人情報保護法
- □ applicant screening / candidate screening　応募者選考
- □ informal job offer　内定（mid-career recruiting は「中途採用」）
- □ incentive〔inséntiv〕system　報奨制度（staff incentives は「従業員報酬制」）
- □ upscale consumer　金持ち消費者

■ 組織図

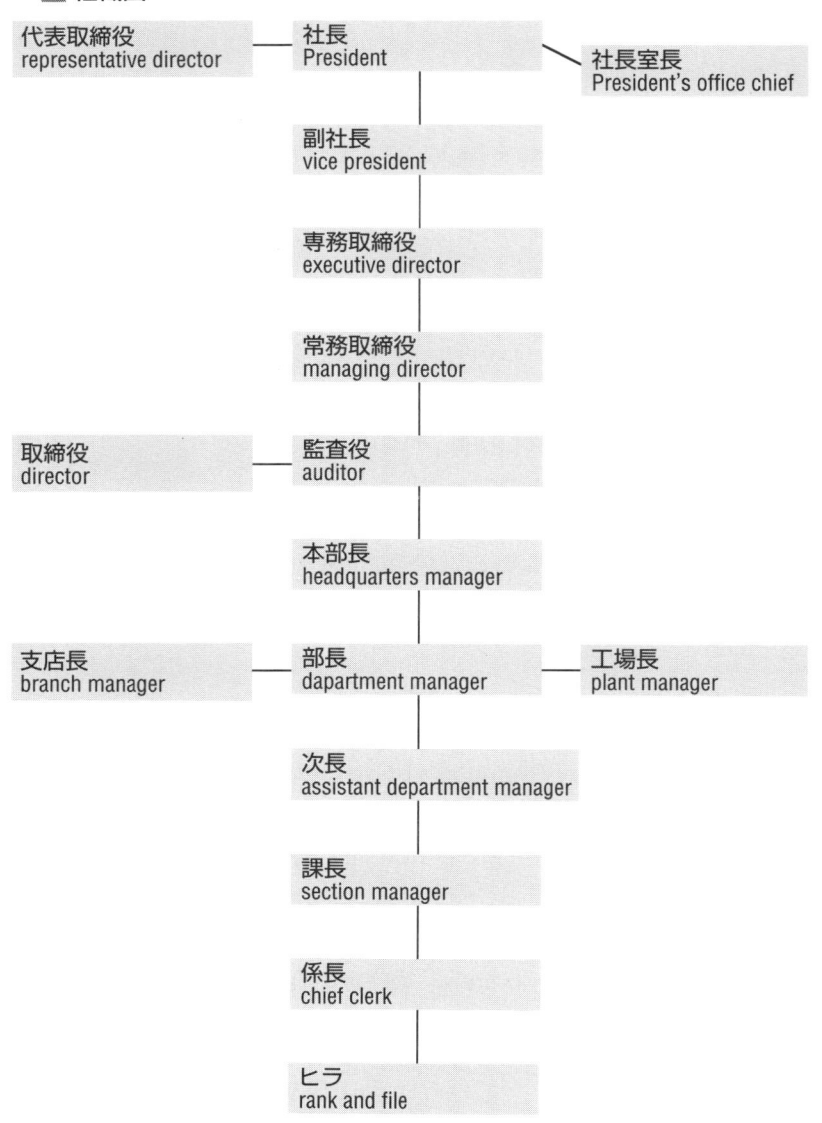

- 代表取締役 representative director — 社長 President — 社長室長 President's office chief
- 副社長 vice president
- 専務取締役 executive director
- 常務取締役 managing director
- 取締役 director — 監査役 auditor
- 本部長 headquarters manager
- 支店長 branch manager — 部長 dapartment manager — 工場長 plant manager
- 次長 assistant department manager
- 課長 section manager
- 係長 chief clerk
- ヒラ rank and file

商業・経営・ビジネス　重要語彙表現をマスター！

- advertorial〔ædvətɔ́ːriəl〕　記事広告（advocacy advertising は「意見広告」）
- comparative advertising　比較広告
- dealer spot　（小売業者による）スポット広告（point of purchase advertising は「小売店頭広告」）
- drive time　（朝夕の）マイカー出勤者向けコマーシャル
- repeat sales　リピート販売戦略
- consignment〔kənsáinmənt〕sale　委託販売（tie-in は「抱き合わせ販売」）
- fly-by-night operation　一発商売（peddler は「行商人」）
- home delivery　宅配（special delivery は「速達」）
- asking price　（売り手が買い手に示す）提示価格、言い値
- bargain-basement price　特売価格
- list price　定価
- trade-in price　下取り価格（unit price は「セット料金」）
- renewal charge　更新料（resale price は「再販価格」）
- money-back guarantee　返金保証
- flagship　主力商品（loss leader / come-on は「目玉商品」）
- high-ticket items　高額商品（low-end product は「低価格商品」）
- prototype / pre-production　試作品
- AIDMA's rule　アイドマの法則：人間の消費行動の特徴を表す attention、interest、desire、memory、action へと移行するプロセス
- wish list　購入予定の商品一覧表
- exclusive contract　独占契約
- reciprocal〔risíprəkl〕[bilateral] contract　双務契約
- feasibility〔fìːzəbíləti〕study　実行可能性調査
- fixtures and fittings　付帯設備

- [ ] IOU [I owe you]　借用証書
- [ ] voluntary closure　自主廃業
- [ ] safety recall　安全のための欠陥商品回収
- [ ] chamber [tʃéimbə] of commerce　商工会議所
- [ ] upmarket　高級品市場
- [ ] upholstery [ʌphóulstəri]　室内装飾業、家具製造販売業
- [ ] confectionery [kənfékʃənèəri]　菓子屋

■ 企業の最高責任者名

CEO [Chief Executive Officer]（最高経営責任者）
CFO [Chief Financial Officer]（最高財務責任者）
COO [Chief Operating Officer]（最高業務執行責任者）
CMO [Chief Marketing Officer]（最高営業責任者）
CAO [Chief Administrative Officer]（最高総務責任者）
CTO [Chief Technical Officer]（最高技術責任者）
CNO [Chief Network Officer]（最高ネットワーク責任者）
CPO [Chief Project Officer]（最高計画責任者）
CDO [Chief Development Officer]（最高開発責任者）
CCO [Chief Communication Officer]（最高コミュニケーション責任者）

産業　重要語彙表現をマスター！　CD 2-5

- [ ] primary industry　第1次産業（tertiary industryは「第3次産業」）
- [ ] subsistence [səbsístəns] agriculture　自給自足農業
- [ ] aquaculture [ǽkwəkʌ̀ltʃə] / aquafarming　養殖
- [ ] deep-sea fishing　遠洋漁業（coastal fishing は「沿岸漁業」）

- [ ] dairy〔déəri〕farming　酪農業
- [ ] sericulture〔séərəkʌ̀ltʃə〕養蚕（textile industry は「繊維産業」）
- [ ] farm belt　穀倉地帯、農業地帯（the Farm Belt は「米国中西部の大農業地帯」、farm produce は「農作物」）
- [ ] assembly plant　組立工場
- [ ] cottage industry　家内工業
- [ ] blast furnace〔blǽst | fə́ːnəs〕溶鉱炉
- [ ] industrial complex　コンビナート
- [ ] oil refinery　精油所（oil glut は「石油のだぶつき」）
- [ ] the petrochemical industry　石油化学産業
- [ ] oil concession　石油採掘権（oil rig は「油田掘削機」）
- [ ] the pharmaceutical〔fɑ̀ːməs(j)úːtikl〕industry　製薬産業
- [ ] the shipbuilding industry　造船業
- [ ] precision machinery　精密機械
- [ ] low-fare carrier　低料金運送業者（mover / forwarding agent は「運送業者」）
- [ ] knowledge-intensive industry　知識集約型産業（knowledge worker は「頭脳労働者」）
- [ ] deindustrialization / industrial hollowing-out　産業の空洞化：基幹産業としての製造業が衰弱化する現象
- [ ] proprietary〔prəpráiətèəri〕technology　独自技術
- [ ] amalgamation〔əmæ̀lgəméiʃən〕/ merger　合併
- [ ] realignment〔rìəláinmənt〕再編成、再整理
- [ ] streamline / rationalize〔rǽʃənəlàiz〕簡素化［合理化］する
- [ ] shakeout　業界再編成：競争が激化し、業界で１社か２社だけが生き残ること
- [ ] leveraged buyout［LBO］借入金をてこにした企業買収、レバレッジド・バイアウト（MBO［management buyout］は「経営

者による企業買収」)
- [ ] consortium〔kənsɔ́ːʃiəm〕 共同事業体、企業体
- [ ] business line 営業品目、事業分野
- [ ] brain drain 頭脳流出（brain gain は「頭脳流入」）
- [ ] COE (Center of Excellence) センターオブエクセレンス：優秀な頭脳と最先端の設備環境を備えた世界的評価の高い中核的研究拠点
- [ ] land [property] development 土地開発
- [ ] pilot plant 試験的工場（test-market は「試験的に販売する」）
- [ ] offshore procurement〔prəkjúəmənt〕 域外調達
- [ ] crash program 突貫計画（due date は「締め切り日、納入日」）
- [ ] breach〔bríːtʃ〕of contract 契約違反（contract terms は「契約条件」）
- [ ] competitive price 競争価格
- [ ] price cap 料金上限規制
- [ ] tax break 税制上の優遇措置
- [ ] industrial espionage 産業スパイ活動
- [ ] escrow〔éskrou〕 エスクロー [第三者預託]：物の受け渡しと代金の支払いを第三者を介して行う仕組み
- [ ] planned obsolescence〔àbslésns〕 計画的陳腐化：製品や部品が老朽化するように作る方法
- [ ] AFL-CIO 米国総同盟産別会議
- [ ] the Rust Belt ラストベルト地域：デトロイトのようなかつて産業などで栄えて倒産した企業や工場が集中する米国東部および北部中央工場地帯
- [ ] the Sunset Belt 米国南部地域：ノースカロライナ州からメキシコ湾岸諸州を経てカリフォルニア州に至る米国南部諸州

TOEIC 満点突破：意外な意味に要注意！②

honor the contract（契約を守る）
outstanding issue ［debt］（未解決の問題、未払いの借金）
executive **material**（重役の器である）
modest tax cuts（小規模減税）
immediate supervisor（直属の上司「すぐ隣の」の意味もある）
conservative estimate（控えめな見積もり）
handsome profits（かなりの利益）
matured insurance（満期保険）
principal and interest payment（元利払い）
projected deficit（見込まれる赤字）
title deed（土地の権利書）
sleeping **quarters**（寝泊りする部屋、「地区・4半期」の意味もある）
proceeds from a bazaar（バザーの収益）
the **minutes** of the meeting（議事録）
the last **leg** of the tour（最後の訪問地）

3-4　第16日
教育語彙に強くなる

　現代社会を語る時、ある意味で最も重要なのが教育と言語コミュニケーションです。特に英語圏留学を考えている人は、この分野の語彙・表現を絶対に覚えておく必要があります。

学問分野の語彙に強くなる　　　　　　CD 2-6
- [ ] aesthetics〔esθétiks〕　美学
- [ ] anthropology〔æ̀nθrəpálədʒi〕　人類学
- [ ] applied science　応用科学
- [ ] archaeology〔à:rkiálədʒi〕　考古学
- [ ] ethics　倫理学
- [ ] geology〔dʒiálədʒi〕　地質学
- [ ] etymology〔ètəmálədʒi〕　語源学
- [ ] health and physical education　保健体育
- [ ] meteorology〔mì:tiərálədʒi〕　気象学
- [ ] psycholinguistics　心理言語学
- [ ] seismology〔saizmálədʒi〕　地震学
- [ ] pedagogy〔pédəgòudʒi〕　教育学、教授法
- [ ] zoology　動物学

学校・クラス・試験の語彙に強くなる　　CD 2-7

- [ ] associate dean〔díːn〕 副学部長（registrar は「教務係」）
- [ ] emeritus〔iméritəs〕[honorary] professor　名誉教授
- [ ] substitute teacher　代用教員（teaching certificate は「教員免状」）
- [ ] board of education　教育委員会
- [ ] board of trustees〔trʌstíːz〕 理事会（colloquium [kəlóukwiəm] は「会議、セミナー」）
- [ ] multiple-choice exam　多肢選択方式試験（true-false question は「○×式問題」、placement test は「組み分けテスト」）
- [ ] school recommendation　内申書
- [ ] acceptance letter　合格通知（admission criterion は「入学基準」）
- [ ] documentary elimination　書類選考
- [ ] probationary〔proubéiʃənèəri〕 acceptance　仮入学許可
- [ ] teaching practicum　教育実習（trainee [cadet] teacher は「教育実習生」）
- [ ] valedictorian〔væ̀lədiktɔ́əriən〕 speech　卒業式総代のスピーチ（commencement adress は「卒業式の演説」、graduation ceremony は「卒業式」）
- [ ] alma mater〔ǽlməmɑ́ːtə〕 母校、出身校（accredited school は「認定校」）
- [ ] field study [work]　野外研究
- [ ] honors student　優等生（cum laude〔kum | láudi〕 は「優等で卒業した人」）
- [ ] alumnus〔əlʌ́mnəs〕 同窓生男性（alumna〔əlʌ́mnə〕 は「同窓生女性」）
- [ ] alumni〔əlʌ́mnai〕 association / class reunion　同窓会
- [ ] co-education　男女共学

- ☐ compulsory education　義務教育
- ☐ credit-system high school　単位制高校
- ☐ charter school　特別認可校：保護者や教師が自治体から特別認可を受けて開く学校
- ☐ voucher system　バウチャー制度：親が州政府に学校券を発行し、学費を負担する制度
- ☐ remedial〔rimíːdiəl〕education　補習教育（secondary education は「中等教育」）
- ☐ course syllabus　講義要綱
- ☐ undergraduate curriculum　学部カリキュラム（graduate student は「大学院生」）
- ☐ required course　必修科目（elective / course selective は「選択科目」）
- ☐ crash program　特訓コース（examination ordeal は「受験地獄」）
- ☐ extension courses [lectures]　大学公開講座
- ☐ term paper　学期末レポート
- ☐ final [exam]　（大学などの）期末試験
- ☐ GPA [grade point average]　学業成績平均点（academic transcript は「学業成績証明書」）
- ☐ deviation〔dìːviéiʃən〕value　偏差値
- ☐ prize fellowship　成績優秀者特別奨学金
- ☐ bachelor's〔bǽtʃləz〕degree　学士号
- ☐ master's degree　修士号（doctorate は「博士号、学位」）
- ☐ dissertation〔dìsərtéiʃən〕博士論文（master's thesis は「修士論文」）
- ☐ interdisciplinary〔ìntədísəplənèəri〕approach　超学際的アプローチ
- ☐ nursery school　保育園

- ☐ polytechnic school　工芸学校（preparatory school は「予備校」）
- ☐ theological seminary　神学校（vocational school は「職業学校」）
- ☐ prestigious〔prestí:dʒəs〕university　名門大学
- ☐ academic clique　学閥
- ☐ roll book　出席簿
- ☐ truancy〔trú:ənsi〕/ refusal to attend school　不登校
- ☐ carrel〔kǽrəl〕庫内読書席（checkout desk / circulation desk は「貸し出しデスク」）
- ☐ dormitory / dorm / residential hall　寄宿舎
- ☐ room and board　部屋と食事費
- ☐ forensic〔fərénsik〕club　スピーチクラブ
- ☐ gymnastics〔dʒimnǽstiks〕club　器械体操クラブ

■ 世界大学ランキング

① Harvard University（US）
② University of Cambridge（UK）
③ University of Oxford（UK）
④ Massachusetts Institute of Technology（US）
⑤ Yale University（US）
⑥ California Institute of Technology（US）
⑦ Princeton University（US）
⑧ Stanford University（US）
⑨ University of California, Berkeley（US）
⑩ Imperial College London（UK）
⑪ University of Chicago（US）
⑫ Columbia University（US）
⑬ Duke University（US）

⑭ University of Tokyo (Japan)
⑮ London School of Economics (UK)
⑯ Australia National University (Australia)
⑰ Cornell University (US)
⑱ University College London (UK)
⑲ McGill University (US)
⑳ Beijing University (China)

(2004〜2007年度のタイム誌より)

言語・コミュニケーションの語彙に強くなる　　CD 2-8

- [ ] lingua franca〔líŋgwə | frǽŋkə〕　共通語、通商語
- [ ] intercultural [cross-cultural] communication　異文化間コミュニケーション
- [ ] command of English / English proficiency　英語運用力
- [ ] Creole〔kríːoul〕混交言語：ピジン混交語が造語や借用語を加えて語数を増し母国語化したもの
- [ ] Ebonics〔ibániks〕　エボニックス：アメリカ黒人の言葉
- [ ] vernacular〔vənǽkjələ〕　自国語、お国言葉
- [ ] linguistic xenophobia〔zènəfóubiə〕　外国語嫌い
- [ ] Braille〔bréil〕edition　点字版（index glossary は「索引用語集」）
- [ ] linguistic semantics〔səmǽntiks〕　言語学的意味論
- [ ] connotation〔kànətéiʃən〕　内包的意味
- [ ] syntax〔síntæks〕analysis　構文解析
- [ ] stylistic rule　文体規則
- [ ] prescriptive〔priskríptiv〕grammar　規範文法
- [ ] grammatical competence〔kámpətns〕　文法的言語能力
- [ ] suffix〔sʌ́fiks〕form　接尾語形 ⇔ 接頭辞 prefix〔príːfiks〕
- [ ] honorific prefix　敬称

- □ adjective declension 〔diklénʃən〕 形容詞語形変化
- □ alliterated 〔əlítərèitid〕 poem 頭韻を踏んだ詩
- □ onomatopoeia 〔ὰnəmæ̀təpíːə〕 擬音、擬声語
- □ pictographic language 絵文字的言語（phonetic は「音声的」）
- □ hieroglyphic 〔hàiərəglífik〕 inscription 象形文字の碑文
- □ lexicographic 〔lèksikəgrǽfik〕 work 辞書編さん
- □ author bibliography 〔bìbliágrəfi〕 著作目録
- □ calligraphy 〔kəlígrəfi〕 master 書道の大家
- □ impromptu 〔imprámpt(j)uː〕 [extemporaneous 〔ikstèmpəréiniəs〕 / offhand] speech 即興のスピーチ
- □ the Shakespeare corpus 〔kɔ́ːpəs〕 シェークスピア全集

教育全般の語彙に強くなる　　　　　　　　　　CD 2-9

- □ corporal 〔kɔ́ː(r)pərəl〕 punishment 体罰
- □ mnemonic [nimánik] device 記憶術（rote memorization は「丸暗記」）
- □ lifelong [continuing] education 生涯教育
- □ correspondence course / distance learning 通信教育
- □ the Fields prize フィールズ賞：数学の分野でのノーベル賞に相当
- □ inner-city school 荒廃した都市中心部の学校
- □ literacy rate 識字率（illiteracy rate は「文盲率」）
- □ prom date （大学・高校の）学年末のダンスパーティーのパートナー
- □ qualified applicant 資質ある志願者
- □ sabbatical 〔səbǽtikl〕 term 研究休暇期間
- □ social integration 〔ìntigréiʃən〕（人種・障害者差別の廃止等の）社会的統合

■ 教育語彙復習テストにチャレンジ！

1	保健体育	11	組分けテスト
2	学閥	12	内申書
3	合格通知	13	庫内読書席
4	副学部長	14	教育実習
5	理事会	15	共通語、通商語
6	卒業式総代のスピーチ	16	外国語嫌い
7	単位制高校	17	体罰
8	偏差値	18	書類選考
9	名誉教授	19	記憶術
10	多肢選択方式試験	20	丸暗記

■ 教育語彙復習テスト（解答）

1	health and physical education	11	placement test
2	academic clique	12	school recommendation
3	acceptance letter	13	carrel
4	associate dean	14	teaching practicum
5	board of trustees	15	lingua franca
6	valedictorian speech	16	linguistic xenophobia
7	credit-system high school	17	corporal punishment
8	deviation value	18	documentary elimination
9	emeritus[honorary] professor	19	mnemonic device
10	multiple-choice exam	20	rote memorization

3-5 第17日
一般社会語彙に強くなる

　一般社会語彙の知識は、社会問題について英語でディスカッションをしたり、様々な英字新聞や英字誌や、CNN、BBCなどの英語放送や洋画などをエンジョイできるようになるためにも非常に重要です。また英検1級・準1級を始めとするすべての資格検定試験対策にも重要で、この分野は、できるだけ多くの語彙・表現を覚えておきましょう。それでは皆さん、最後まで頑張ってこの分野の語彙力UPに励みましょう。

結婚・家庭・ライフスタイルの語彙に強くなる　　CD 2-10

- □ rite of passage　（誕生・結婚・成人・死などの）**通過儀礼**
- □ ceremonial functions　冠婚葬祭（betrothal gift は「結納」）
- □ birth certificate　出生証明書
- □ life expectancy　余寿命（life span は「平均寿命」）
- □ monogamy〔mənάgəmi〕family　一夫一婦家族（polygamy は「一夫多妻性」）
- □ extended family　拡大家族（bereaved family は「遺族」）
- □ maternal [paternal] lineage〔líniidʒ〕　母方［父方］の家系
- □ kissing cousin　遠い親類

- ☐ Electra complex　ファザコン (Oedipus〔édəpəs〕complexは「マザコン」)
- ☐ latchkey〔lǽtʃkìː〕child　鍵っ子
- ☐ adoption agency　養子縁組斡旋業者 (foster parent は「里親」)
- ☐ surrogate〔sə́ːrəgèit〕mother　代理母
- ☐ the age of discretion〔diskréʃən〕　分別年齢：英米の法律は14歳
- ☐ bottle-fed baby　牛乳で育った赤ん坊 (breast-fed は「母乳」)
- ☐ eligible man　結婚相手にふさわしい男性
- ☐ teddy bear syndrome　テディベア症候群：孤独を癒すための軽はずみな結婚傾向
- ☐ heterosexual contact　異性との接触
- ☐ extramarital sex　婚外交渉 (premarital sexは「婚前交渉」)
- ☐ amicable〔ǽmikəbl〕[uncontested] divorce　協議離婚
- ☐ in-home separation　家庭内離婚
- ☐ joint custody〔kʌ́stədi〕(離婚した［別居中の］両親による) **共同親権**
- ☐ binuclear family　(子供を持つ夫婦が離婚することによって生じる片方の親と子供だけの) 2つの核家族
- ☐ battered [abused] wife　虐待を受ける妻
- ☐ marital rape　配偶者への暴力的セックス
- ☐ feudalistic〔fjùːdlístik〕family system　封建的な家制度
- ☐ sheltered upbringing〔ʌpbríŋiŋ〕温室育ち (emotional dependence は「甘え」)
- ☐ family squabble〔skwábl〕/ internecine strife　内輪もめ
- ☐ sibling〔síbliŋ〕rivalry　兄弟間の競争意識
- ☐ filial piety〔páiəti〕/ devotion to one's parents　親孝行
- ☐ boomerang kid　都会から故郷に戻り、親と一緒に生活する子供
- ☐ empty-nest syndrome　空っぽの巣症候群：子供が独立して夫婦がしばしば憂うつ症になること

- ☐ party line　親子電話（call-waiting telephone は「キャッチホン」）
- ☐ adolescent〔ǽdlésnt〕problems [crisis]　青年期の諸問題［情緒的混乱］
- ☐ moral vacuum　モラルの真空：青少年の道徳感の喪失
- ☐ crash diet　無謀なダイエット
- ☐ freeloader　居候(いそうろう)

専門職の語彙に強くなる　　　CD 2-11

- ☐ minister　牧師（clergy は「聖職者」）
- ☐ public servant　公務員（national public servant は「国家公務員」、local public servant は「地方公務員」）
- ☐ customs official　税関職員
- ☐ corporate warrior　企業戦士
- ☐ side-tracked employees / window-side workers　窓際族
- ☐ temporary employee　嘱託社員
- ☐ second-generation politician / hereditary Diet member　世襲議員（special-interest legislator は「族議員」）
- ☐ anchor　ニュースキャスター
- ☐ weather forecaster　気象予報士
- ☐ sign language interpreter　手話通訳者（simultaneous interpreter は「同時通訳者」）
- ☐ pharmacist〔fάəməsist〕　薬剤師
- ☐ veterinarian〔vètərənéəriən〕　獣医
- ☐ usher　（劇場などの）案内係、守衛、案内する
- ☐ concierge〔kɔ́nsjèəʒ〕　接客係
- ☐ caterer　仕出し業者
- ☐ wine connoisseur〔kὰnəsə́ː〕　ワインの目利き
- ☐ curator　館長

- □ import trade agency　輸入代行業者
- □ insurance canvasser　保険外交員
- □ migrant worker　出稼ぎ労働者
- □ moving company　引っ越し業者
- □ ombudsman〔ámbudzmən〕　苦情調査係
- □ dubbing artist　声優
- □ comic storyteller　落語家
- □ plumber〔plʌmə〕　配管工
- □ utility person　便利屋
- □ security guard　ガードマン
- □ private detective / private eye　私立探偵
- □ land shark　地上げ屋
- □ scalper〔skǽlpə〕　ダフ屋
- □ part-timer / jog-hopping part-timer　フリーター
- □ house sitter　家人に代わって留守番をする人

宗教・イデオロギーの語彙に強くなる　CD 2-12

- □ atheism〔éiθiìzm〕　無神論
- □ lax agnosticism〔ægnástisìzm〕　寛大な不可知論
- □ mystic animism〔ǽnəmìzm〕　神秘的な霊魂信仰
- □ God-given revelation〔rèveléiʃən〕　神の啓示
- □ ecumenicalism〔èkjəméniklìzm〕　世界教会主義：教派を超えて宣教活動にあたろうとするキリスト教徒の主張や運動
- □ evangelical〔ìːvændʒélikl〕doctrine　福音主義
- □ eschatology〔èskətálədʒi〕　終末論：眼前の現実を末世とみなし、この末世から解脱して千年王国や王道楽土を希求する考え
- □ apocalyptic〔əpàkəlíptik〕belief　黙示録的な信仰
- □ millennium celebration　千年紀の祝典

- □ Protestant denomination〔dinὰmənéiʃən〕 プロテスタント派 (Protestant Reformation は「宗教改革」)
- □ domestic prelate〔prélət〕 教皇付き名誉高位聖職者
- □ Sabbath〔sǽbəθ〕school 安息日学校
- □ Moslem〔mázləm〕 イスラム教徒
- □ Shiite〔ʃíːait〕Arab シーア派アラブ人
- □ Sunni〔súni〕Islam スンニー派イスラム教徒
- □ guru's adherents〔ədhíərənts〕[followers] 教祖の信者
- □ fanatic believer / religious fanatic 狂信的な信者
- □ esoteric Buddhism 密教
- □ Buddhist monastery〔mánəstèəri〕 仏教の僧院（Buddhist scripture / sutra は「経典」）
- □ Taoist hermit〔táuìst | həˊːrmit〕 道教の隠者
- □ Confucian〔kənfjúːʃən〕ethics 孔子の教え
- □ ancestor worship 先祖崇拝
- □ dialectic〔dàiəléktik〕materialism 弁証法的唯物論 ⇔ 唯心論 spiritualism
- □ utilitarian〔juː(ː)tìlitéəriən〕theory 功利主義理論
- □ religious eclecticism〔ikléktisìzm〕 宗教折衷主義
- □ existential approach 実存的方法
- □ extroverted〔èkstrəvəˊːtid〕nature 外交的な性格
- □ androphobic〔æ̀ndroufóubik〕attitude 男性恐怖症的態度
- □ obsessive personality disorder 強迫性人格障害
- □ personal magnetism 人間的魅力
- □ communicative competence 会話能力
- □ latent〔léitənt〕ability 潜在的能力（subconscious desire は「潜在的願望」）
- □ herd mentality 群集心理、大衆心理

- □ moral obligation　義理（duty and obligations は「義理人情」）
- □ physiognomy〔fiziágnəmi〕　人相判断
- □ extrasensory perception [ESP]　超能力（paranormal phenomenon は「超常現象」）
- □ scientology〔sàiəntálədʒi〕　サイエントロジー：宗教と心理学とを結びつけた精神療法と能力開発
- □ self-fulfilling prophecy　自己成就的予言：誤情報に基づく思い込みが、思い込みどおりの現実を生み出してしまう現象

格差社会の語彙に強くなる　　　CD 2-13

- □ egalitarian〔igælitéəriən〕society　平等社会（hierarchical society は「縦社会」）
- □ plural society　多元社会（androgynous〔ændrádʒənəs〕society は「中性化社会」）
- □ racial persecution　民族的迫害
- □ gender segregation　性的差別 ⇔ 性差別撤廃 gender integration
- □ hate crime　憎悪犯罪：人種・性差別への憎しみから起きる犯罪
- □ color bar　有色人種への社会的差別
- □ degreeocracy　学歴社会（plutocracy〔pluːtákrəsi〕は「金権社会」）
- □ reverse discrimination　（少数派優先策のために起こる）逆差別
- □ tokenism〔tóukənìzm〕　（学校・職場などでの名目ばかりの）少数派優遇策
- □ male chauvinist pig [MCP]　極端な男性優越主義者
- □ weightism　体重による差別：肥満者を不当に差別すること
- □ high [low] income bracket〔brǽkət〕　高［低］所得者層
- □ seniors [senior citizens]　65歳以上の老人
- □ barrier-free society [facilities]　バリアフリー社会［設備］
- □ sensibility gap　（民族や世代などの違いから生じる）感覚のズレ

- □ hyphenated〔háifəneitid〕American　外国系アメリカ人
- □ immigrant [population] influx　移民の [人口] 流入
- □ WASP [White Anglo-Saxon Protestant]　ワスプ：白人でアングロサクソン系でプロテスタントの人々
- □ Aussie〔ɔ́:si〕　オーストラリア人（Down Underは「オーストラリアやニュージーランド」）
- □ Caucasoid〔kɔ́:kəsɔ̀id〕　白色人種、コーカソイド人種
- □ Chicano〔tʃiká:nou〕　メキシコ系米国人
- □ career consumer　時間も財力もある専業主婦
- □ expatriate〔ekspéitrièit〕[returnee] children　帰国子女
- □ sexual [child] exploitation〔èksplɔitéiʃən〕　性的 [児童労働] 搾取
- □ social alienation　社会からの疎外
- □ social stigma〔stígmə〕　社会的不名誉

文化・歴史・風俗の語彙に強くなる　CD 2-14

- □ the National Medal of Honor　国民栄誉賞
- □ the Order of Culture / the Order of Cultural Merit　文化勲章
- □ the Paleolithic〔pèiliəlíθik〕Age　旧石器時代（medieval〔mì:dí:vl〕age は「中世」）
- □ indigenous〔indídʒənəs〕tribes　土着の部族（indigenous people は「先住民族」）
- □ mausoleum〔mɔ̀:səlí:əm〕　壮大な墓（morgue〔mɔ́:g〕, mortuary〔mɔ́:tʃuəri〕は「遺体安置所」）
- □ demise〔dimáiz〕of Emperor　天皇の崩御
- □ landmark [watershed] deal　歴史的取り決め
- □ glocalism　グローカリズム：地球的規模で発想し、地域ごとに活動しようとする考え方

- ☐ double standard （特に性差に基づき使い分ける道徳上の）二重基準
- ☐ pro-choice activist　人工中絶に賛成の活動家（pro-lifeは「中絶反対者」）
- ☐ pros and cons / supporters and detractors　賛否両論
- ☐ silent majority　物言わぬ大衆、声なき声
- ☐ epicurean〔èpikjuərí:ən〕tastes　食い道楽（vegetarianは「菜食主義者」）
- ☐ compulsive clotheshorse　流行の服を追わずにいられない人
- ☐ couch potato　カウチポテト族：自宅のソファーに寝そべりながら気ままに時間を過ごす都市型の生活様式
- ☐ teenage prostitution　10代の売春（prostituteは「売春婦」、brothel / whore houseは「売春宿」）
- ☐ massage brothel〔bráθl〕マッサージ・パーラー
- ☐ telephone dating club　テレクラ
- ☐ health spa　健康ランド
- ☐ homogeneous society　同質的社会 ⇔ 雑多な社会 heterogeneous society
- ☐ community chest　共同募金
- ☐ social implications　社会的影響
- ☐ geek / nerd　オタク
- ☐ Seeing-Eye dog　盲導犬
- ☐ disposable camera　使い捨てカメラ（disposable incomeは「可処分所得」）
- ☐ chocolate out of courtesy　義理チョコ
- ☐ graffiti〔grəfí:ti〕落書き
- ☐ alpha male　アルファメール：組織などの精悍(せいかん)で頼もしい男性指導者
- ☐ sex pervert〔pə́:və:t〕変態性欲者（closet transvestite

〔trænsvéstait〕は「隠れ服装倒錯者」）
- [ ] quitter / person who gives up easily　三日坊主
- [ ] road rage　車を運転中に逆上し、暴力行為に走ること
- [ ] keeping a useless person on the payroll for life　飼い殺し

■ 一般語彙復習テストにチャレンジ！

1	食道楽	11	社会的不名誉
2	帰国子女	12	代理母
3	盲導犬	13	温室育ち
4	オタク	14	里親
5	ダフ屋	15	無神論
6	文化勲章	16	壮大な墓
7	経典	17	親孝行
8	神の啓示	18	学歴社会
9	密教	19	極端な男性優越主義者
10	群集心理、大衆心理	20	兄弟間の競争意識

■ 一般語彙復習テスト（解答）

1	epicurean tastes	11	social stigma
2	expatriate[returnee] children	12	surrogate mother
3	Seeing-Eye dog	13	sheltered upbringing
4	geek / nerd	14	foster parent
5	scalper	15	atheism
6	the Order of Culture / the Order of Cultural Merit	16	mausoleum
7	Buddhist scripture / sutra	17	filial piety
8	God-given revelation	18	degreeocracy
9	esoteric Buddhism	19	male chauvinist pig
10	herd mentality	20	sibling rivalry

III 分野別語彙力パワーUP文系語彙

TOEIC 満点突破：意外な意味に要注意！③

prospecting for oil（石油探査）
take up one's station（持ち場につく）
brave the storm（嵐をものともしない）
commit more money for the project（その計画にもっとお金を投入する —— 幅広い意味のある重要多義語）
condemn a building（ビルを廃棄処分にする、「刑の宣告」もある）
account（得意先、会計、報告、口座と意味が多い）
acknowledge the letter（手紙を受け取ったことを伝える）
process the application（申し込みを処理する、「加工する・現像する」もある）
sample the food（食品を試食する、「経験する」の意味もある）
track the students（生徒を能力別に分ける）
screen the applicants（応募者を選別する、「守る」の意味もある）
stagger the commuting hours（通勤時間をずらす）
sweep the country（全国的に圧勝する、［広まる］）
quote the price（値段を見積もる）
posted prices of crude oil（原油の公示価格）

3-6　第18日
スポーツ・アート語彙に強くなる

　この分野の語彙表現は、スポーツなどの娯楽番組や記事をエンジョイするのに役立つので、ぜひ覚えておきましょう。

スポーツの語彙に強くなる　　CD 2-15

- [ ] affiliated team　所属球団
- [ ] ball park　野球場（backstop は「バックネット」）
- [ ] base hit　安打（batting average は「打率」）
- [ ] capacity crowd　超満員客
- [ ] grand slam / bases-loaded home run　満塁ホームラン
- [ ] grandstand play　スタンドプレー
- [ ] the Senior High School Baseball Championships　高校野球大会
- [ ] runs batted in　打点
- [ ] sandlot baseball　草野球
- [ ] broad jump / running long jump　走り幅跳び
- [ ] discus throw　円盤投げ（hammer throw は「ハンマー投げ」）
- [ ] high jump　走り高跳び（triple jump は「三段跳び」）
- [ ] javelin〔dʒǽvəlin〕throw　槍投げ（shot put は「砲丸投げ」）
- [ ] runup　助走（take-off は「踏み切り」）

- ☐ track and field　陸上競技（Ekiden road relay は「駅伝」）
- ☐ tug of war　綱引き
- ☐ rope skipping [jumping]　なわとび
- ☐ uneven parallel bars　段違い平行棒
- ☐ balance beam　平均台（floor exercise は「床運動」）
- ☐ gymnastic rings　吊輪（horizontal bar は「鉄棒」）
- ☐ long horse vault　跳馬（pommel〔pΛml〕horse は「鞍馬（あんば）」）
- ☐ vaulting wooden box　跳び箱
- ☐ rhythmic gymnastics　新体操
- ☐ push-up / press-up　腕立て伏せ（handstand は「逆立ち」）
- ☐ radio gymnastic exercises　ラジオ体操（shape-up exercise / calisthenics〔kæləsθéniks〕は「美容体操」）
- ☐ backstroke　背泳ぎ（breast stroke は「平泳ぎ」、dog paddle は「犬かき」）
- ☐ horsemanship　馬術
- ☐ preliminary competition / elimination　予選（first-round elimination は「第１次予選」）
- ☐ final game [match]　決勝
- ☐ winners' podium〔póudiəm〕　表彰台
- ☐ bronze medal　銅メダル
- ☐ certificate of merit / certificate of commendation　賞状
- ☐ bout sheet　取組表（national sport は「国技」）
- ☐ having more wins than losses　勝ち越し
- ☐ doping test　ドーピングテスト
- ☐ Paralympics　身障者オリンピック
- ☐ physical strength and fitness test　体力テスト
- ☐ player's number　ゼッケン
- ☐ punching bag　サンドバッグ

- ☐ bamboo sword　竹刀

アート・レジャーの語彙に強くなる　　CD 2-16

- ☐ figurative arts / plastic art　造形芸術
- ☐ retrospective exhibition　回顧展
- ☐ forthcoming book　近刊書（supplementary edition は「増刊号」）
- ☐ "I" novel / novel based on the author's own life　私小説
- ☐ pocketbooks　文庫本（serial novel は「連載小説」）
- ☐ literary coterie〔kóutəri〕　文学の同人
- ☐ revised edition　改訂版（abridged edition は「簡約版」）
- ☐ first run of a film　映画の封切り
- ☐ trilogy〔trílədʒi〕3部作（posthumous [pástʃəməs] work は「遺著」）
- ☐ subtitles　字幕スーパー
- ☐ animated movie　アニメ映画
- ☐ cloak-and-dagger story　スパイ物語
- ☐ slapstick comedy　ドタバタ喜劇（situation comedy は「ホームドラマ」）
- ☐ intermission　（映画・舞台などの）幕間、休憩時間
- ☐ leading role / starring role　主演
- ☐ life-size statue　実物大の銅像
- ☐ long-running program　長寿番組
- ☐ period adventure drama　時代劇
- ☐ nepotistic〔nèpətístik〕succession　世襲（accredited master は「名取り」）
- ☐ concerto〔kəntʃéətou〕協奏曲（musical score は「楽譜」）
- ☐ costume pageant〔pǽdʒənt〕コスチュームショー（musical

extravaganza は「音楽の催し」)
- ecclesiastical〔iklì:ziǽstikl〕music　教会音楽
- jazz improvisation〔imprὰvəzéiʃən〕ジャズの即興演奏
- sought-after singer　売れっ子の歌手
- golden oldie / old hit song　なつメロ
- percussion〔pəkʌ́ʃən〕instrument　打楽器（xylophone〔záiləfòun〕は「木琴」）
- ventriloquism〔ventríləkwìzm〕腹話術
- embroidery〔embrɔ́idəri〕刺繍
- handicraft　手芸

■ スポーツ・アート語彙復習テストにチャレンジ！

1	なつメロ	11	なわとび
2	映画の封切り	12	砲丸投げ
3	ジャズの即興演奏	13	満塁ホームラン
4	実物大の銅像	14	腕立て伏せ
5	回顧展	15	草野球
6	綱引き	16	馬術
7	背泳ぎ	17	文庫本
8	3部作	18	刺繍
9	字幕スーパー	19	打楽器
10	世襲	20	ドタバタ喜劇

■ スポーツ・アート語彙復習テスト（解答）

1	golden oldie / old hit song	11	rope jumping / rope skipping
2	a first run of a film	12	shot put
3	jazz improvisation	13	grand slam / bases-loaded home run
4	life-size statue	14	push-up / press-up

5	retrospective exhibition	15	sandlot baseball
6	tug of war	16	horsemanship
7	backstroke	17	pocketbooks
8	trilogy	18	embroidery
9	subtitles	19	percussion instrument
10	nepotistic succession	20	slapstick comedy

Gothic Cathedral(ゴシック建築教会)

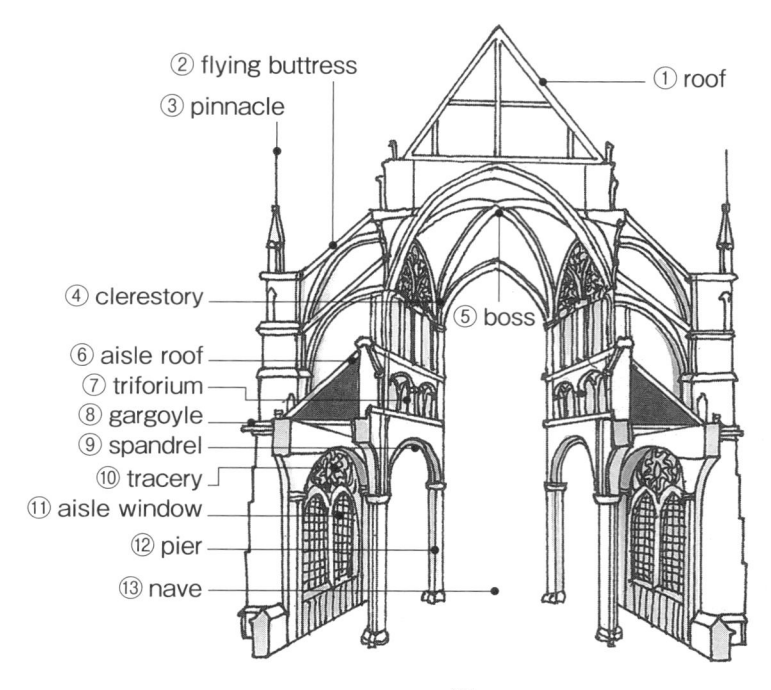

① roof
② flying buttress
③ pinnacle
④ clerestory
⑤ boss
⑥ aisle roof
⑦ triforium
⑧ gargoyle
⑨ spandrel
⑩ tracery
⑪ aisle window
⑫ pier
⑬ nave

① roof(屋根)　② flying buttress(飛び梁)　③ pinnacle(小尖塔)
④ clerestory(クリアストーリー[明かり層])
⑤ boss(浮き出し飾り)　⑥ aisle roof(側廊屋根)
⑦ triforium(トリフォリウム:側廊上部)
⑧ gargoyle(ガーゴイル:怪物の形の屋根の水落とし口)
⑨ spandrel(スパンドレル[三角小間])
⑩ tracery(トレーサリー[はざま飾り])　⑪ aisle window(側廊窓)
⑫ pier(ピア[窓間壁])　⑬ nave(身廊)

3-7　第19日
乗り物・交通・旅行語彙に強くなる

　この分野の語彙は、乗物に乗ったり、旅行する時に重要なものばかりなので完全にマスターしましょう。

乗り物の語彙に強くなる　　　　　CD 2-17
- [ ] four-wheeled car　4輪駆動車
- [ ] courtesy car　送迎サービス車
- [ ] convertible　オープンカー
- [ ] rent-a-car　レンタカー
- [ ] camper　キャンピングカー
- [ ] unlicensed taxi　白タク
- [ ] water truck [wagon / cart]　給水車
- [ ] sprinkler truck　散水車
- [ ] honey truck　バキュームカー
- [ ] hearse　霊柩車
- [ ] armored car　装甲車 (lightly armored vehicle は「軽装甲車両」)
- [ ] patrol wagon / prison van　護送車
- [ ] high-mileage car / fuel-efficient car / gas-sipper　低燃費車
- [ ] license plate　ナンバープレート (steering wheel は「ハンドル」)

- [ ] side-view mirror　サイドミラー（rearview mirror は「バックミラー」）
- [ ] commuter train　通勤電車
- [ ] out-of-service train　回送列車
- [ ] tube〈英〉/ underground〈英〉/ subway〈米〉　地下鉄
- [ ] trolley　市街電車（tramcar / streetcar は「路面電車」）
- [ ] up train　上り列車（banquet room train は「お座敷列車」）
- [ ] women-only car / women-only train coach　女性専用車両
- [ ] windowless train for sightseeing purposes　トロッコ列車
- [ ] stopover　途中下車
- [ ] aisle seat　通路側の席（coach は「客車」）
- [ ] priority seat / seat reserved for the elderly and disabled　優先座席
- [ ] hydrofoil〔hàidrəfɔ́il〕　水中翼船
- [ ] liner　定期船（tramp ship は「不定期船」）
- [ ] greenway　歩行者自転車専用道路

交通の語彙に強くなる　CD 2-18

- [ ] ticket wicket〔wíkit〕/ ticket window　改札口
- [ ] commuter pass / season ticket　定期券
- [ ] round-trip ticket　往復切符（platform ticket は「駅入場券」）
- [ ] student discount / special discount rate for students　学割
- [ ] flag drop / drop fee　初乗り料金（excess fare は「乗り越し運賃」）
- [ ] fare adjustment office　運賃精算所
- [ ] fare chart / fare table　運賃表
- [ ] holiday train schedule　休日ダイヤ
- [ ] junction　乗り換え駅
- [ ] railway crossing　踏切

- ☐ intersection　交差点（median strip は「中央分離帯」）
- ☐ No Stopping / No Standing　停車禁止
- ☐ No Thoroughfare　通行止め
- ☐ multi-storied parking lot〔garage〕　立体駐車場
- ☐ pedestrians'〔pədéstiənz〕overpass　歩道橋（underpass / underground は「地下道」）
- ☐ solid crossing　立体交差
- ☐ toll road　有料道路
- ☐ fuel replenishment〔ripléniʃmənt〕　燃料補給
- ☐ sobriety〔səbráiəti〕test / balloon test　飲酒テスト
- ☐ fork road / approach way　進入路、分岐路
- ☐ maiden〔méidn〕voyage　処女航海
- ☐ waterway　水路（wharf は「埠頭(ふとう)」）
- ☐ forced landing　不時着（runway は「滑走路」）
- ☐ multiple-car pileup / chain-reaction collision　玉突き衝突事故（「正面衝突」は head-on collision / frontal clash）

旅行の語彙に強くなる　　CD 2-19

- ☐ frequent flier　頻繁に飛行機を利用する人
- ☐ coach class　エコノミークラス
- ☐ baggage claim carousel　ベルトコンベヤ：空港の手荷物運搬用
- ☐ baggage claim tag　手荷物引換証（security screening は「手荷物検査」、excess baggage は「超過手荷物」）
- ☐ reserved seat　指定席（nonreserved seat は「自由席」）
- ☐ berth ticket　寝台券（excursion ticket は「周遊券」）
- ☐ no-show　（乗り物・宿泊などの）予約をして当日利用しなかった人
- ☐ reserved-ticket window　みどりの窓口
- ☐ commemorative photo　記念撮影（thirty-six exposure film

は「36枚撮りフィルム」)
- [ ] local specialty　地方の名産
- [ ] forest bath / walk in the woods for therapeutic purposes　森林浴

観光英検1級合格の秘訣

　観光英検1級は、通訳ガイドと英検1級を取得した人なら、世界の観光地(なかでも世界遺産)の知識をプラスするだけで優秀賞で合格できるかもしれません。世界の観光名所の記述を読んだり、リスニングして、地名を選択するような簡単な問題もありますが、語彙問題は建築など観光に関わる専門用語も出題され、決して易しくはありません。2次試験(native speaker 1名との面接)はあらかじめ、質問事項がある程度は分かっているため準備して臨むことが可能です。パッセージの音読、サマリー能力、短いQ&A、ディスカッションに対応できる能力なども試され、日本のみならず、世界の観光地についても詳しくなり、専門語彙習得のよい機会にもなる充実した内容の試験だと思いますので、ぜひチャレンジしていただきたいです。

3-8 第20日
日用品語彙に強くなる

　外国から来られた人に私たちの文化や生活習慣を説明するには背景知識に加え、表現するための語彙も重要です。的確な表現を知っていれば、相手に簡潔に伝えられます。高度な英語の根底となる基礎として、日常語彙を磨いていきましょう。それではまず、日常品から見てみましょう。

日用品・家庭用品の語彙に強くなる　　　CD 2-20

- [ ] fire extinguisher　消火器
- [ ] drainage〔dréinidʒ〕pipe　排水管（faucet〔fɔ́:sət〕は「蛇口」）
- [ ] household [home] appliance　家庭用電気器具
- [ ] durable goods　耐久消費財
- [ ] dehydrator〔di:háidreitə〕脱水機（water purifier〔pjúərəfàiə〕は「浄水器」）
- [ ] drier　乾燥機
- [ ] flash heater　瞬間湯沸し器（geyserは「湯沸し器」）
- [ ] dehumidifier〔dì:hju:mídəfàiə〕除湿器（humidifierは「加湿器」）
- [ ] microwave cooker　電磁調理器
- [ ] mosquito repellent〔ripélənt〕蚊取り線香

- ☐ gold-plated spoon　金メッキのスプーン
- ☐ duplicate〔d(j)úːplikət〕key　合鍵
- ☐ self-addressed envelope　返信用封筒
- ☐ binoculars　双眼鏡
- ☐ blowup　引き伸ばし写真
- ☐ insecticide / vermicide / bug spray　殺虫剤
- ☐ bunk bed　２段ベッド
- ☐ canteen / flask　水筒
- ☐ cardboard box　ダンボール箱（plywoodは「ベニヤ板」）
- ☐ clippers　バリカン
- ☐ miscellaneous / daily goods / everyday sundries / convenience goods　日用雑貨（sundry goods / groceriesは「雑貨品」）
- ☐ dental floss / dental tape　糸ようじ（toothpickは「爪ようじ」）
- ☐ disposable diaper [nappy]　使い捨て紙おむつ
- ☐ gimlet / drill / awl　錐（きり）
- ☐ dustpan　ちりとり（feather dusterは「はたき」）
- ☐ fluorescent〔fluərésnt〕lamp　蛍光灯（highlight penは「蛍光ペン」）
- ☐ folding chair　折りたたみ椅子（swivel chairは「回転椅子」）
- ☐ hair growth stimulant　発毛剤
- ☐ kerosene〔kéərəsìːn〕/ lamp oil / paraffin oil　灯油
- ☐ key chain / key ring　キーホルダー
- ☐ lever　てこ
- ☐ moist hot towel for cleaning hands before a meal　おしぼり
- ☐ nail clippers　爪切り（retractable knifeは「カッターナイフ」）
- ☐ earpick　耳掻き（tweezersは「毛抜き、ピンセット」）
- ☐ pacifier〔pǽsəfàiə〕/ dummy　おしゃぶり

- ☐ picture story book　絵本
- ☐ piggy bank　貯金箱
- ☐ prepaid cellular phone　プリペイド式携帯電話
- ☐ rake　熊手
- ☐ rubber band　輪ゴム（stapler は「ホッチキス」）
- ☐ special pen which looks like a writing brush　ふでペン
- ☐ Philips screwdriver　十字ドライバー
- ☐ pigment〔pígmənt〕/ coloring matter　絵の具
- ☐ plastic sheet　下敷き（wrapping cloth は「風呂敷」）
- ☐ ruler　ものさし（set square / triangle は「三角定規」）
- ☐ instant glue　瞬間接着剤（whiteout「白消し」）
- ☐ mechanical pencil　シャープペンシル
- ☐ adhesive tape　粘着テープ（packing tape は「ガムテープ」）
- ☐ Scotch tape / cellophane / adhesive tape　セロハンテープ
- ☐ scales　体重計
- ☐ scrub brush　たわし
- ☐ emery paper　紙やすり
- ☐ shoehorn　靴べら
- ☐ size AA battery　単3電池
- ☐ strainer　濾過器
- ☐ touch-tone phone / push-button phone　プッシュホン
- ☐ trash chute〔ʃúːt〕ダストシュート：ごみ棄て装置（vacuum cleaner は「掃除機」）
- ☐ tripod　三脚
- ☐ valuables　貴重品（vermillion〔vəmíljən〕inkpad used to ink signature seals は「朱肉」）
- ☐ ventilation〔vèntəléiʃən〕fan　換気扇
- ☐ washbowl　洗面器（washing machine は「洗濯機」）

- ☐ wash-toilet system　ウォッシュレット
- ☐ cistern / water tank　水槽
- ☐ wind-chime　風鈴

家・建物の語彙に強くなる　CD 2-21

- ☐ unit area (approx. 3.3m²)　坪
- ☐ aluminum window frame　アルミサッシ
- ☐ attic　屋根裏部屋（mezzanine〔mézənì:n〕は「中二階」）
- ☐ bay window　出窓
- ☐ canopy〔kǽnəpi〕　天蓋(てんがい)
- ☐ courtyard　中庭
- ☐ cross-beam　梁(はり)
- ☐ doorsill　敷居（lintel / head jamb は「鴨居(かもい)」）
- ☐ eaves　軒(のき)（gutter は「屋根のとい」）
- ☐ flower bed　花壇（gardening / horticulture は「園芸」）
- ☐ gatepost / heelpost / hinging post　門柱
- ☐ glossy finish　つや出し仕上げ（mat finish は「つや消し仕上げ」）
- ☐ ground-breaking ceremony / cornerstone-laying ceremony　起工式
- ☐ handrail　手すり（landing は「踊り場」）
- ☐ insulation　断熱材
- ☐ lattice work　格子
- ☐ lodging house　下宿（mountain hutは「ロッジ」）
- ☐ prefabricated house　プレハブ
- ☐ galvanized iron sheet　トタン板
- ☐ rain shutter　雨戸（screen door は「網戸」）
- ☐ drawing room　応接間（study は「書斎」）
- ☐ room layout / floor plan　間取り（skylight は「天窓」）

- louver〔lúːvə〕door / Venetian〔vəníːʃən〕shutter　鎧戸(よろいど)
- surveillance [monitoring] camera　監視カメラ
- flush toilet　水洗トイレ（waste water / sewage は「下水」)
- arbor　あずま屋：屋根つきのベンチつき休憩所
- castle renovation　城の改築
- lighthouse　灯台（clock tower は「時計台」)
- condominium　マンション（detached house は「一戸建て」)
- crematorium〔krìːmətɔ́ːriəm〕　火葬場
- ferroconcrete　鉄筋コンクリート
- high-rise　高層建築
- housing development　団地
- sewer〔súːə〕下水道
- sewage〔súːidʒ〕treatment facility　下水処理施設
- studio / apartment　ワンルームマンション
- suspension bridge　つり橋
- utility pole / telephone pole　電柱
- makeshift houses　仮設住宅
- fire hydrant　消火栓

■ 日用品語彙復習テスト

1	耐久消費財	11	カッターナイフ
2	合鍵	12	回転椅子
3	返信用封筒	13	掃除機
4	蚊取り線香	14	浄水器
5	殺虫剤	15	水洗トイレ
6	2段ベッド	16	プレハブ
7	バリカン	17	一戸建て
8	除湿器	18	起工式

| 9 | 蛍光ペン | 19 | 踊り場 |
| 10 | キーホルダー | 20 | ワンルームマンション |

■ 日用品語彙復習テスト（解答）

1	durable goods	11	retractable knife
2	duplicate key	12	swivel chair
3	self-addressed envelope	13	vacuum cleaner
4	mosquito repellent	14	water purifier
5	insecticide / vermicide / bug spray	15	flush toilet
6	bunk bed	16	prefabricated house
7	clippers	17	detached house
8	dehumidifier	18	ground-breaking ceremony /cornerstone-laying ceremony
9	highlight pen	19	landing
10	key chain / key ring	20	studio / apartment

第4章

日本のことは英語で何でも発信できる
日本事象語彙

4-1 第21日

日本のことは英語で何でも発信できる
通訳ガイド必須日本事象語彙（食生活編）

日本の食べ物に関する語彙に強くなる　　CD 2-22

　「発信型スーパーボキャブラリービルディング」の第4章、第21日から第23日は、日本のことは英語で何でも発信できるようになるための語彙・表現力UPトレーニングです。この章は外国人に日本のことを英語で説明する時に非常に役立つものが多いので、日本語から英語へという真の発信型アプローチを取りました。このセクションをマスターすれば、通訳案内士合格やボランティア通訳ガイドはもちろん、プロの通訳ガイドとしても通用する英語力が身につくことでしょう。それではまず最初は、日本の食べ物に関する語彙力UPトレーニングからです。張り切って参りましょう！

- □ ガリ　　　　　vinegared ginger
- □ ささみ　　　　chicken breast fillet 〔filéi〕
- □ だしの素　　　soup stock
- □ ぬか漬け　　　vegetables pickled in (salted) rice-bran paste
- □ ひき肉　　　　ground meat / minced meat
- □ メザシ　　　　dried sardines 〔sɑːrdíːnz〕(strung on a stick

		through the eyes)
☐	黄身（卵）	yolk〔jóuk〕/ yellow of an egg
☐	化学調味料	chemical seasoning
☐	人工甘味料	artificial sweetener
☐	食品添加剤	food additive
☐	食物繊維	dietary fiber
☐	真空パック	vacuum packaging〔vǽkjuəm｜pǽkidʒŋ〕
☐	生鮮食品	perishable food
☐	赤身肉	lean meat
☐	きな粉	(toasted) soybean flour
☐	醸造酒	brewage〔brúːidʒ〕(「蒸留酒」は spirits / distilled liquor)
☐	食前酒	aperitif〔əpèrətíːf〕
☐	サイダー	soda pop
☐	青汁	kale juice / green juice
☐	地ビール	local beer / microbrew
☐	発泡酒	low-malt beer (「梅酒」は plum wine)
☐	玉露(ぎょくろ)	refined green tea
☐	地酒	local sake / locally-brewed sake
☐	純米酒	sake made without added alcohol or sugar
☐	吟醸酒(ぎんじょうしゅ)	quality sake brewed from the finest rice (「大吟醸酒」は top-quality sake brewed from the finest rice)
☐	泡盛	strong liquor produced in Okinawa
☐	昆布茶	kelp tea / powdered tangle tea
☐	焼酎	(low-class) spirits distilled from sweet potatoes or grains
☐	酒粕(さけかす)	sake lees / sake sediment (「粕汁」は sake lees

IV　日本のことは英語で何でも発信できる日本事象語彙

		soup）
☐	酵母	yeast / leaven〔lévn〕
☐	もろみ	sake mash
☐	辛子明太子	cod roe〔róu〕seasoned with red pepper
☐	切り干し大根	dried radish strips
☐	千枚漬け	thin slices of turnip〔tə́:nəp〕pickled in vinegar
☐	地鶏(じどり)	free-range chicken / locally produced poultry
☐	豆腐	bean curd（「にがり」は bittern）
☐	氷砂糖	rock（sugar）candy
☐	米麹	rice malt / malted rice
☐	薬味	condiment / relish / spice
☐	油揚げ	fried bean curd
☐	麩(ふ)	breadlike pieces of dried wheat gluten〔glú:tn〕
☐	アク	scum / harsh taste
☐	味付け海苔	seasoned dried laver seaweed（「焼き海苔」は toasted laver、「青海苔」は green laver）
☐	あんかけ	thick starchy sauce made from arrowroot powder（arrowroot は「葛(くず)」）
☐	貝柱	shellfish ligament（「ホタテ貝柱」は scallop）
☐	数の子	herring roe（「イクラ」は salmon roe、「白子」は（globefish）milt / soft roe）

日本の食品を発信! 語彙クイズにチャレンジ!

■ 次の日本語を英語で説明してください。

1	冷奴	11	たくあん
2	玄米	12	昆布
3	味噌	13	小麦粉
4	梅干し	14	日本酒
5	和菓子	15	納豆
6	豆乳	16	ようかん
7	麦茶	17	団子
8	もち米	18	せんべい
9	かつおぶし	19	あんこ
10	かまぼこ	20	まんじゅう

■ 解 答

1	chilled soybean curd	11	pickled radish
2	brown (unpolished) rice	12	kelp / sea tangle
3	soybean paste	13	wheat flour
4	pickled plum	14	rice wine
5	Japanese confectionery	15	fermented soybeans
6	soybean milk /soymilk	16	sweet bean jelly
7	roasted barley tea	17	(rice) dumpling
8	sticky rice	18	rice cracker
9	dried bonito shavings (flakes)	19	sweet bean-paste
10	steamed fish-paste cake	20	bun with bean-jam filling

☐ かんぴょう　　dried gourd [gɔ́əd] shavings
☐ こんにゃく　　jelly made from devil's tongue starch
☐ 山菜　　　　　edible wild plants

☐	白身（卵）	(egg) white（「白身の魚」は white-meat fish）
☐	そば粉	buckwheat flour
☐	竹輪	tube-shaped, broiled fish-paste cake
☐	ちりめんじゃこ	boiled and dried baby sardines
☐	煮干「炒り子」	dried small sardines
☐	つくね	chicken meatball（「つみれ」は minced fish dumpling）
☐	とろろ昆布	kelp flakes / tangle flakes [shavings]
☐	奈良漬［粕漬］	vegetables pickled in sake lees
☐	ぬか	rice bran（「ぬか味噌」は salted rice-bran paste for pickling）
☐	パン粉	bread crumb [krʌm]（「片栗粉」は potato starch / dogtooth violet starch）
☐	みりん	sweet rice wine for cooking
☐	塩辛	salted fish entrails [éntreilz][guts]
☐	角砂糖	lump [cube] sugar
☐	銀杏	ginkgo [gingko][gíŋkou] nut
☐	春雨	bean-starch noodles（「糸こんにゃく」は devil's tongue-starch noodles）
☐	漬け物	pickles / pickled vegetable
☐	百合根	lily bulb
☐	冷凍食品	frozen food
☐	甘納豆	candied beans（「大学芋」は candied sweet potatoes）
☐	石焼いも	sweet potato baked in [roasted on] hot pebbles
☐	磯辺焼き	toasted rice cake wrapped in dried laver seaweed
☐	おこし	cake made of millet and rice
☐	かき氷	shaved ice with syrup on top

コンビニでも定番「おでん」のルーツとは!?

　冬の屋台（stall）につきもののおでんは、家庭料理（home cooking）としても手軽な軽食としても人気があり、コンビニの冬の定番商品（winter's regular item in convenience stores）となっている。魚のすり身（fish paste cakes）、大根（Japanese radish）、こんにゃく（jelly made from devil's tongue starch）、すじ肉（gristle）などを醤油ベースの出汁（soy-based stock soup）で煮込んだ煮物鍋の一種で、日本式ごった煮（Japanese hotchpotch）と言える。そのルーツは室町時代末期の、串に刺して味噌を塗って焼いた豆腐田楽（bean curd baked and coated with miso）で、形が田楽舞（ritual dancing performed at rice planting time）に似ているところからその名がついた。

□ かりんとう	fried dough〔dóu〕cake (coated with brown sugar)
□ ところてん	noodle-shaped gelatin made from seaweed
□ 寒天	agar-agar〔á:gɑɚ｜á:gɑɚ〕/ vegetable gelatin (「水飴」は starch syrup)
□ 甘酒	sweet drink made from fermented rice
□ 金平糖	sugar candy /Japanese candy originally made in Portugal
□ 綿菓子	cotton candy
□ あべかわ餅	rice cake covered with soybean powder

- □ あんころ餅　rice cake covered with sweet bean jam
- □ あんパン　bun filled with bean paste
- □ あんまん　steamed bean-jam bun
- □ 今川焼［回転焼］　gong-shaped pancake filled with bean jam
- □ おはぎ　rice dumpling covered with bean jam or soybean flour（「あんみつ」は syrup-covered bean jam, agar gelatin and fruit）
- □ こしあん　strained［pureed［pjuréid］］sweet bean jam
- □ 桜餅　rice cake with bean paste wrapped in a cherry leaf
- □ ぜんざい　sweet red-bean soup with rice cake
- □ たいやき　fish-shaped pancake filled with bean jam
- □ ちまき　rice dumpling wrapped in bamboo leaves
- □ どら焼き［三笠］　two small pancakes with bean jam in between
- □ もなか　wafer cake filled with bean jam（「カステラ」は sponge cake）
- □ 柏餅　rice cake wrapped in an oak leaf

語彙力UP　生き物の季語クイズにチャレンジ！（春編）

■次の俳句の春の季語を英語で言ってください。

①鶯（　　　　）②雉（　　　　）③雲雀（　　　　　）
④おたまじゃくし（　　　　）⑤虻（　　　　）⑥鱒（　　　　）
⑦若鮎（　　　　）⑧わかさぎ（　　　　）⑨鮑（　　　　）
⑩蛤（　　　　）⑪椿（　　　　）⑫菜の花（　　　　）
⑬藤の花（　　　　）⑭山吹（　　　　）⑮つつじ（　　　　）
⑯タンポポ（　　　　）⑰蓮華草（　　　　）⑱土筆（　　　　）
⑲ふきのとう（　　　　）⑳蓬（　　　　）

■ 解 答

① (Japanese bush warbler)　② (pheasant)　③ (skylark)
④ (tadpole)　⑤ (gadfly)　⑥ (trout)　⑦ (young sweetfish)
⑧ (pond smelt)　⑨ (abalone)　⑩ (clam)
⑪ (camellia)　⑫ (rape blossoms)　⑬ (wisteria blossoms)
⑭ (Japanese rose)　⑮ (azalea)　⑯ (dandelion)
⑰ (milk vetch)　⑱ (horsetail)　⑲ (butterbur sprout)
⑳ (mugwort)

日本の料理分野の語彙に強くなる　　CD 2-23

□ うどん　　　　Japanese wheat noodles (「手打ちうどん」は handmade noodles)
□ 鍋焼きうどん　noodles served hot in a pot
□ きつねうどん　wheat noodles in soup with thin pieces of fried bean curd
□ 鰻丼　　　　　a bowl of rice topped with broiled eel (「カツ丼」は～ topped with pork cutlet)
□ 親子丼　　　　a bowl of rice (topped) with chicken and eggs (「牛丼」は～ topped with seasoned beef、「天丼」は～ topped with deep-fried prawns)
□ おせち料理　　traditional New Year dishes
□ おつまみ　　　snacks eaten while drinking beer
□ おむすび　　　a triangular-shaped rice ball
□ かつおのたたき　lightly-roasted bonito〔bəníːtou〕
□ 栗きんとん　　mashed sweet potato with sweetened chestnuts
□ そば　　　　　buckwheat noodles (「そうめん」は thin wheat

		noodles served cold in summer）
☐	ざる蕎麦(そば)	buckwheat noodles served cold on a wickerwork tray
☐	冷やし素麺(そうめん)	chilled thin noodles / vermicelli〔vɚːmitʃéli〕served cold
☐	冷麺	Korean noodles served cold
☐	霜降り牛肉	marbled-beef（「赤身肉」は lean meat、「脂身肉」は fatty meat）
☐	しゃぶしゃぶ	thinly-sliced beef boiled with vegetables
☐	すき焼き	thin slices of beef cooked in a pan with various vegetables and tofu
☐	スルメ	dried squid〔skwíd〕
☐	てっさ［ふぐ刺し］	slices of raw globefish
☐	トロ	fatty tuna［meat］（「中トロ」は medium-grade fatty tuna meat）
☐	とろろ	grated yam
☐	山掛け	foods topped with grated yam
☐	豚汁	miso soup with pork and vegetables（「吸い物」は traditional Japanese clear soup seasoned with fish broth, salt, and soy sauce）
☐	なます	raw fish and vegetables［radish and carrot］marinated with sweet vinegar
☐	にぎりずし	small portion of vinegared rice with slices of raw fish on top
☐	ばら寿司［ちらし、五目］	vinegared rice topped with fish, vegetables and egg
☐	稲荷寿司	flavored boiled rice wrapped up with sweetly seasoned fried bean curd

お茶のルーツと心とは!?

　中国南部が原産の茶は、かつて薬用（for medicinal purpose）であったが、後に中国の禅僧（Zen Buddhist monks）の間で眠気覚まし（drinks to shake off sleep）として飲まれるようになった。茶道の基本精神は、一期一会（belief that each meeting should be cherished as a unique experience in life）の心と、四畳半の茶室（4.5-mat tatami tearoom）に象徴される、装飾を最小限に抑えた「わび」（elegant rusticity）の精神と、どんな貴人でも頭をかがめなければ茶室に入れない「にじり口」（main entrance used by the guests）に象徴される謙遜（humbleness）の心である。

□	巻き寿司	a roll of laver-covered vinegared rice (usually cut into mouthful pieces)
□	鉄火巻	raw tuna slices and vinegared rice rolled in laver seaweed
□	回転ずし	(revolving) conveyor-belt sushi bar / sushi-go-round restaurant
□	バイキング料理	smorgasbord〔smɔ́:gəsbɔ̀:d〕
□	ハヤシライス	hashed beef and rice
□	焼き魚	grilled [broiled] fish（「焼肉」はgrilled [broiled] meat）
□	レトルト食品	boil-in-the-bag food / retort pouch

IV 日本のことは英語で何でも発信できる日本事象語彙

☐	一品料理	à la carte 〔à: lɑ: kɑ́:ət〕
☐	駅弁	boxed station lunch / box lunches sold at railway stations
☐	加工食品	processed food
☐	会席料理	Japanese-style party dishes served on an individual tray
☐	懐石料理	tea-ceremony dishes
☐	本膳料理	formal Japanese full-course dinner
☐	釜めし	rice cooked with vegetables and chicken in a small individual pot
☐	五目飯	boiled rice mixed with fish [meat] and vegetables
☐	粥(かゆ)	rice porridge / gruel 〔grú:əl〕
☐	雑炊(ぞうすい)	rice and vegetable porridge
☐	干物	dried fish (「煮凝(にこご)り」は jellied fish or meat broth)
☐	甘露煮(かんろに)	sweetened boiled fish / candied chestnuts
☐	寄せ鍋	seafood and chicken pot
☐	郷土料理	local food
☐	持ち帰り用の袋	doggy bag
☐	七草粥(ななくさがゆ)	rice porridge with seven herbs

日本の料理を発信！　語彙クイズにチャレンジ！

■ 次の日本語を英語で説明してください。

1	天ぷら	11	和え物
2	湯葉	12	鍋物
3	おにぎり	13	茶碗蒸し
4	手打ちそば	14	鰻の蒲焼
5	丼物	15	厚揚げ

6	幕の内弁当	16	麦とろ
7	たこやき	17	佃煮
8	茶懐石	18	おから
9	照り焼き	19	おでん
10	お好み焼き	20	刺身盛り合わせ

■ 解 答

1	deep-fried food	11	dressed food / marinated food
2	boiled soymilk skim	12	hot-pot dishes/ one-pot cooking
3	rice ball wrapped with laver seaweed	13	cup-steamed egg custard
4	handmade buckwheat noodles	14	charcoal broiled eel / spitchcock
5	a bowl of rice with a topping	15	thick fried bean curd
6	variety box lunch	16	grated yam over barley rice
7	grilled octopus dumpling	17	food boiled down in soy sauce
8	light meal served before a formal tea ceremony	18	bean curd refuse / residue left after making tofu
9	glazed broiled fish or meat	19	Japanese hotchpotch
10	meat and vegetable pancake	20	assorted slices of raw fish

□ 焼き芋　　　roasted［baked］sweet potato
□ 焼き鳥　　　（skewered）grilled chicken
□ 新香　　　　pickled vegetables
□ 精進料理　　vegetarian diet［dish / meal / food］
□ 赤飯　　　　rice with red beans traditionally made to celebrate a happy occasion
□ 大根おろし　grated radish
□ 茶漬け　　　boiled rice with tea poured over it
□ 佃煮　　　　preserved food boiled down in soy

☐	定食	set [fixed] menu [meal] / combo
☐	湯豆腐	simmered tofu [bean curd]
☐	揚げだし豆腐	deep-fried tofu with amber sauce
☐	絹ごし豆腐	smooth fine-grained [silk-strained] tofu
☐	高野豆腐	freeze-dried bean curd (「長寿食」は macrobiotic food)
☐	豚角煮	braised pork
☐	肉じゃが	meat and potatoes stewed in sweetened soy sauce / braised meat and potatoes
☐	肉まん	steamed meat bun
☐	日替わりメニュー	today's special / menu of the day
☐	尾頭付き	fish served whole (with head and tail)
☐	付け合せ	garnish / relish
☐	弁当	box lunch
☐	目玉焼き	sunny-side up
☐	立ち飲み	stand-up bar serving alcoholic beverages
☐	赤だし	reddish brown miso soup
☐	活け作り	raw fish sliced while it is still alive
☐	おひたし	boiled leafy greens seasoned with soy sauce
☐	かき揚げ	a mixture of vegetable bits and shrimp deep-fried in batter
☐	餃子	Chinese dumplings stuffed with minced pork and vegetables
☐	雑煮	soup containing rice cakes and vegetables eaten on New Year's Day

語彙力UP　生き物の季語クイズにチャレンジ！（夏編）

■次の俳句の夏の季語を英語で言ってください。

①鮎（　　　　）　②くらげ（　　　　）　③メダカ（　　　　）
④雨蛙（　　　　）　⑤蛾（　　　　）　⑥天道虫（　　　　）
⑦不如帰（ほととぎす）（　　　　）　⑧蝉（せみ）（　　　　）　⑨黄金虫（こがねむし）（　　　　）
⑩あやめ（　　　　）　⑪蓮（はす）（　　　　）　⑫柿の花（　　　　）
⑬紫陽花（あじさい）（　　　　）　⑭牡丹（ぼたん）（　　　　）　⑮桐花（きりのはな）（　　　　）
⑯鈴蘭（すずらん）（　　　　）　⑰蘭（らん）（　　　　）　⑱枇杷（びわ）（　　　　）
⑲茄子（なす）（　　　　）

■解　答

①（sweetfish）　②（jellyfish）　③（Japanese killifish）　④（tree frog）　⑤（moth）　⑥（ladybug）　⑦（little cuckoo）　⑧（cicada）　⑨（scarab）　⑩（iris）　⑪（lotus）　⑫（persimmon blossoms）　⑬（hydrangea）　⑭（tree peony）　⑮（paulownia flowers）　⑯（lily of the valley）　⑰（orchid）　⑱（loquat）　⑲（eggplant）

食関連分野の語彙に強くなる　　CD 2-24

- □ おしぼり　　hot, moist hand towel / wet wipe
- □ おたま　　ladle / ladle spoon
- □ おろし金　　grater
- □ しゃもじ　　rice paddle / rice scoop
- □ つまようじ　　toothpick
- □ 銚子（ちょうし）［徳利（とっくり）］　　ceramic bottle for heating and pouring sake

		(「おちょこ」は small sake cup)
☐	ふきん	dishcloth / dish towel
☐	フライパン	frying pan / skillet
☐	ふるい	sieve 〔sív〕/ sifter
☐	焼き網	grill / grid / gridiron 〔grídàiən〕
☐	蒸籠(せいろ)	steaming basket
☐	水切りボール	colander (「洗いおけ」は dishpan)
☐	茶こし器	tea strainer
☐	箸	chopsticks (「割り箸」は disposable chopsticks)
☐	網杓子(あみじゃくし)	skimmer
☐	泡立て器	whisk
☐	まないた	chopping [cutting] board
☐	土鍋	earthenware pot
☐	1000円で食べ放題	all-you-can-eat for 1000 yen (「1000円で飲み放題」は all-you-can-drink for 1000 yen)
☐	居酒屋	Japanese-style pub / tavern
☐	立ち食い蕎麦屋	stand-up soba noodle shop
☐	持ち帰り料理	takeout food / food to go
☐	屋台	street [food] stall [stand] / food cart
☐	自炊	doing one's own cooking
☐	賞味期限	best before (date) / use-by [expiration] date / shelf life
☐	食べ残し	leftovers
☐	食べ放題のレストラン	all-you-can-eat restaurant
☐	食品宅配サービス	food catering service
☐	食糧貯蔵室	pantry
☐	料亭	traditional (high-class) Japanese-style restaurants

コラム　四字熟語でボキャブラリーパワー UP！

次の四字熟語は日本語でよく使われるので、ぜひ覚えて表現をUPしましょう！

単刀直入	(get right to the point)
電光石火	(with lightning speed)
一喜一憂	(swing from joy to sorrow)
軽挙妄動	(frivolous behavior)
五里霧中	(completely in the dark)
順風満帆	(smooth sailing)
付和雷同	(go along with the crowd)
馬耳東風	(take 〜 in stride)
天変地異	(extraordinary natural phenomenon)
暗中模索	(grope in the dark)
一触即発	(explosive situation)
外柔内剛	(gentle on the outside, tough on the inside)
千載一遇の機会	(one-in-a-million chance)
心機一転	(turn over a new leaf)
一刀両断	(take a drastic measure)
終始一貫	(through thick and thin)

動物に関する語彙に強くなる　　　CD 2-25

- □ アザラシ　　seal（「オットセイ」は fur seal）
- □ アシカ　　　sea lion（「セイウチ」は walrus）
- □ いもり　　　newt [n(j)úːt]（「やもり」は gecko / house lizard）

☐	カバ	hippopotamus 〔hìpəpátəməs〕/ hippo
☐	かめ	tortoise 〔tɔ́ːtəs〕（陸）/ turtle（海）
☐	かもしか	serow 〔sə́rou〕/ antelope 〔ǽntlòup〕
☐	かわうそ	otter 〔átə〕（「ラッコ」は sea otter）
☐	しまりす	chipmunk
☐	シャチ	killer whale（「シロナガスクジラ」は blue whale、「マッコウクジラ」は sperm whale、「ザトウクジラ」は humpback whale）
☐	たぬき	raccoon 〔rækúːn〕dog（「あらいぐま」は raccoon）
☐	はりねずみ	hedgehog（「ヤマアラシ」は porcupine /〈米〉hedgehog）
☐	ひきがえる	toad
☐	ひぐま	brown bear（「つきのわぐま」は white collar bear）
☐	ヒヒ	baboon 〔bæbúːn〕
☐	ひょう	leopard（「くろひょう」は panther）
☐	ムササビ	giant flying squirrel
☐	もぐら	mole
☐	両生類	amphibian
☐	原生動物	protozoan
☐	甲殻類	crustacean 〔krʌstéiʃən〕
☐	脊椎動物	vertebrate 〔və́ːtəbrət〕（「無脊椎動物」は invertebrate 〔invə́ːtəbrət〕）
☐	節足動物	arthropod 〔άːθrəpàd〕
☐	草食動物	herbivorous 〔həːbívərəs〕animal（「肉食動物」は carnivorous 〔kɑːnívərəs〕animal）
☐	軟体動物	mollusk 〔máləsk〕
☐	反すう動物	ruminant 〔rúːmənənt〕
☐	捕食動物	predator 〔prédətə〕

☐	猛禽類	birds of prey
☐	夜行動物	nocturnal 〔nɑktɚ́:nl〕 animal
☐	げっ歯動物	rodent
☐	霊長類	primate 〔práimeit〕
☐	哺乳類	mammal 〔mǽml〕
☐	爬虫類	reptile 〔réptail〕

コラム 「占い」の知識でボキャブラリーパワーUP！ Part1

親指や節も重要なファクターで、long thumb（親指の長い）の人は、leader material（リーダータイプ）、willpower tempered by sensibility（意志が強く判断力もすぐれ）、逆に短い人はsusceptible, indecisive（感受性が強く優柔不断）。knotty joints（節がごつごつした）人はdeep-thinking, dignified（思慮深く威厳があり）、large joints（節が大きい）人はmethodical, rational（几帳面で）、その反対にsmooth joints（節の少ない）人はquick-thinking, impulsive（頭の回転が速く衝動的）となっている。

鳥に関する語彙に強くなる

CD 2-26

☐	あほうどり	albatross 〔ǽlbətrɑ̀s〕
☐	うぐいす	nightingale 〔náitəngèil〕 / (Japanese) bush warbler 〔wɔ́:blə〕
☐	がちょう	goose（「雁」は wild goose）
☐	かっこう	cuckoo 〔kú:ku:〕（「ほととぎす」は little cuckoo）
☐	かも	wild duck / drake（「おしどり」は mandarin

		duck）
□	かもめ	sea gull
□	からす	crow
□	きじ	pheasant〔féznt〕
□	きつつき	woodpecker
□	くじゃく	peacock（雄）/ peahen（雌）/ peafowl（通称）
□	こうのとり	stork
□	こまどり	robin
□	さぎ	heron （「白さぎ」は white heron /egret）
□	すずめ	sparrow
□	とき	（Japanese crested）ibis
□	とんび	kite
□	はやぶさ	falcon
□	ひばり	skylark / lark
□	雷鳥	grouse / ptarmigan〔táːmign〕

魚介に関する語彙に強くなる　　CD 2-27

□	あさり	short-necked clam（「しじみ」はfreshwater clam）
□	あゆ	sweetfish / sweet smelt
□	あわび	abalone〔æbəlóuni〕（「さざえ」は turban（top）shell、「ほたて貝」はscallop）
□	あんこう	angler fish / angler
□	いか	squid（「コウイカ」は cuttlefish）
□	いかなご	sand eel
□	イソギンチャク	sea anemone〔ənéməni〕（「くらげ」は jellyfish）
□	うに	sea urchin〔ə́ːtʃən〕
□	なまこ	sea cucumber
□	エイ	ray（「アカエイ」は stingray）

□ えび	shrimp（「小えび」（「車えび」はprawn、「いせえび」は lobster）
□ かつお	bonito
□ かれい	（総称）flatfish（「ヒラメ」は flounder /（大）halibut）
□ キス	smelt-whiting / sand borer
□ さば	mackerel〔mǽkərəl〕（「あじ」は horse mackerel、「サワラ」は Spanish mackerel）
□ ザリガニ	crawfish / crayfish
□ いわし	sardine
□ さんま	saury〔sɔ́:ri〕/ mackerel pike（「トビウオ」は flying fish）
□ タツノオトシゴ	sea horse
□ たい	sea bream（「スズキ」は sea bass）
□ たにし	freshwater [pond / mud] snail
□ どじょう	loach（「なまず」は catfish）
□ とり貝	cockle clam（「赤貝」は ark shell / bloody clam）
□ にしん	herring（「たら」は cod、「たらこ」は cod roe）
□ ハゼ	goby
□ ふぐ	globefish / blowfish
□ フナ	crucian carp（「ボラ」は mullet）
□ ぶり	yellow tail（「ハマチ」は young yellow tail）
□ めだか	killifish / rice-fish（「出目金」は pop-eyed goldfish）
□ 穴子	conger〔kɑ́ŋɡə〕eel

生物を表現するための語彙クイズにチャレンジ！

■ 次の日本語を英語で説明してください。

1	いのしし	11	あやめ
2	おたまじゃくし	12	白樺
3	たぬき	13	こうのとり
4	すっぽん	14	きじ
5	いたち	15	とき
6	まむし	16	あめんぼ
7	いちょう	17	かまきり
8	びわ	18	まゆ
9	笹	19	あゆ
10	ひのき	20	かつお

■ 解　答

1	wild boar	11	iris
2	tadpole	12	white birch
3	raccoon dog	13	stork
4	soft-shell turtle	14	pheasant
5	weasel	15	ibis
6	viper / adder	16	water strider / pond skater
7	gingko / ginkgo	17	(praying) mantis
8	loquat	18	cocoon
9	bamboo grass	19	sweetfish / sweet smelt
10	Japanese cypress	20	bonito / skipjack tuna

昆虫に関する語彙に強くなる　　CD 2-28

☐ あげはちょう　　swallowtail（「もんしろちょう」は small white butterfly / cabbage butterfly）

☐ あめんぼ	water strider / pond skater
☐ いなご	locust（「かげろう」は dayfly / mayfly）
☐ うじ虫	maggot
☐ 蛾	moth
☐ かいこ	silkworm（「まゆ」は cocoon）
☐ かぶとむし	beetle（「くわがたむし」は stag beetle）
☐ かまきり	(praying) mantis
☐ ゲジゲジ [ヤスデ]	millipede 〔míləpìːd〕（「むかで」は centipede）
☐ けむし	(hairy) caterpillar（「イモ虫」は caterpillar）
☐ こおろぎ	cricket（「すずむし」は bell-ring cricket）
☐ こがねむし	goldbug / scarab
☐ さなぎ	pupa 〔pjúːpə〕/ chrysalis 〔krísəlis〕（「幼虫」は larva）
☐ しょうじょうばえ	fruit fly
☐ しらみ	louse
☐ しろあり	termite / white ant
☐ みつばち	honey bee（「くまばち」は carpenter bee）
☐ すずめばち	wasp / hornet（「あぶ」は horsefly / gadfly）
☐ せみ	cicada 〔sikéidə〕/〈米〉locust
☐ だに	tick / mite（「南京虫」は bedbug）
☐ てんとう虫	ladybug / ladybird
☐ とんぼ	dragonfly（「糸とんぼ」は damselfly）
☐ なめくじ	slug
☐ のみ	flea
☐ ひる	leech
☐ ぼうふら	wriggler / mosquito larva
☐ ほたる	firefly
☐ みのむし	bagworm

☐ みみず	earthworm

植物に関する語彙に強くなる　　　CD 2-29

☐ 梅	Japanese plum [apricot]（「あんず」は apricot、「スモモ」は plum）
☐ 瓜(うり)	gourd [gɔ́əd]
☐ 柿	persimmon（「びわ」は loquat）
☐ かぶ	turnip [tə́ːnəp]（「大根」は Japanese radish）
☐ きび	millet（「ひえ」は barnyard millet、「あわ」は foxtail millet）
☐ ごぼう	burdock [bə́ːdɑ̀k]（root）（「れんこん」は lotus root）
☐ ごま	sesame seeds（「夏みかん」は Chinese citron）
☐ ざくろ	pomegranate [pámə̀grænət]（「いちじく」は fig）
☐ 里芋	taro (potato)（「山芋」は yam）
☐ しそ	beefsteak plant（「山椒」は Japanese pepper）
☐ 春菊［菊菜］	edible [garland] chrysanthemum
☐ ぜんまい	royal fern / fiddlehead
☐ たけのこ	bamboo shoot（「ピーマン」は green pepper）
☐ ねぎ	green onion（「にら」は leek）
☐ ゆず	(small) aromatic citron [citrus fruit]
☐ らっきょう	scallion [skǽljən] / shallot bulb
☐ わさび	Japanese horseradish /（「みょうが」は Japanese ginger）
☐ わらび	bracken [brǽkn] /（「ふきのとう」は butterbur sprout）
☐ 三つ葉	trefoil [tríːfɔil] leaves
☐ 小豆(あずき)	red bean（「そら豆」は broad bean）

☐ いんげん豆	kidney bean	(「金時豆」は red kidney bean)
☐ 小麦	wheat 〔hwíːt〕(「大麦」は barley [báːli])	
☐ 大豆	soybean (「枝豆」は green soybean、「もやし」は bean sprout)	
☐ 唐辛子	red pepper	
☐ 白菜	Chinese cabbage (「菜の花」はrape blossoms)	
☐ 栗	chestnut (「くるみ」は walnut)	

4-2　第22日

日本のことは英語で何でも発信できる 通訳ガイド必須日本事象語彙 （伝統文化・風物編）

　第22日は日本の伝統文化・風物に関する発信力UPトレーニングです。日本独特の伝統文化事象はひと言の説明ですむものは少なく、それらを英語で説明するには背景知識が必要とされます。しかし、同時にそれを簡潔に表現することも重要です。そこでこのセクションでは、各分野にわたる日本の事象の語彙表現力UPにチャレンジしましょう。

伝統芸術分野の語彙に強くなる　　　　　CD 2-30

□ 家元	head (family) of a school (of traditional Japanese art)
□ 生け花［華道］	flower arrangement
□ 剣山(けんざん)	pinholder / needle point holder
□ 水墨画(すいぼくが)［墨絵(すみえ)］	India-ink painting
□ 硯(すずり)	ink stone [slab]
□ 墨(すみ)	India [Indian] ink stick
□ 錦絵	color woodblock print
□ 絵巻物	picture scroll
□ 掛け軸	hanging scroll

☐	屏風	folding screen
☐	錦	brocade〔broukéid〕(「金襴」は gold brocade)
☐	書道	calligraphy / penmanship
☐	草書	cursive style of writing
☐	抹茶	powdered tea
☐	初釜	the first tea ceremony of the New Year(「懐紙」は pocket paper used for tea ceremony or writing tanka, 31-syllable poem)
☐	野点(のだて)	outdoor tea ceremony
☐	茶屋	teahouse(「茶道具」は tea utensils〔ju(:)ténslz〕、「茶せん」は bamboo whisk)
☐	香道	incense burning / incense-smelling game
☐	雅楽	ancient Japanese court music (and dance)
☐	舞楽	court dance and music
☐	歌舞伎	traditional drama performed by male actors
☐	花道(歌舞伎)	elevated runway / passage through audience to stage
☐	隈取り(くまどり)(歌舞伎)	Kabuki stage makeup
☐	見得(歌舞伎)	actor's rigid pose at climax moment
☐	回り舞台(歌舞伎)	revolving stage
☐	セリ(歌舞伎)	trapdoor(せり出し舞台)
☐	屋号	stage name / trade [shop] name
☐	顔見せ	one's (first) appearance (on stage) / debuting
☐	花形	star (performer) / headliner
☐	長唄	long epic songs for Kabuki
☐	名取り	accredited master of Japanese dance
☐	講談	historical narrative
☐	大道芸	street performance

☐	落語	traditional comic storytelling / comic monologue
☐	小道具	props
☐	文楽 [人形浄瑠璃]	classical puppet show accompanied by joururi musical ballads and shamisen
☐	浄瑠璃	traditional ballad drama accompanying a Bunraku puppet show
☐	義太夫	a genre of reciting dramatic narratives for the puppet theater
☐	黒子	stage assistant dressed in black / stagehands in traditional Japanese theater
☐	人形遣い [文楽]	puppeteer〔pʌ̀pətíə〕(「足遣い」(文楽)はsecond assistant)
☐	田楽	ritual music and dancing originally performed at agricultural festivals
☐	能	Japanese classical stage art / Noh play
☐	薪能(たきぎのう)	(outdoor) torchlight Noh performances
☐	謡(うたい)	Noh chant / recitation in Noh
☐	囃子(はやし)(方)	musical accompaniment / musicians
☐	狂言	traditional short comical drama / farce〔fɑ́ːs〕performed between Noh plays
☐	シテ(能)	main actor / protagonist (「ワキ(能)」はbystander / secondary actor)
☐	般若(能)	(面) female demon's mask
☐	ひょっとこ	clown / clownish mask
☐	落語家	comic storyteller
☐	浪曲	musical recitation of admirable stories and tragedies
☐	詩吟	recitation〔chanting〕of a Chinese poem

☐	演歌	Japanese ballad full of sentimentality
☐	印籠(いんろう)	small case for a seal and medicine
☐	親方	master（職人）/ boss / supervisor / foreman（現場）/ stable master（相撲）
☐	こけし	limbless, cylindrical wooden doll with a round head
☐	盆栽	dwarf [miniature] potted tree
☐	わらじ	straw sandals
☐	起き上がり小法師	tumble doll / self-righting dharma doll
☐	だるま	hollow and round wish doll with no arms or legs / dharma [dάːmə] doll
☐	ちんどん屋	traditional Japanese street perfomers for sales promotion
☐	民謡	folk song
☐	こけらおとし	opening of a new theater
☐	琴	thirteen-stringed horizontal Japanese harp / long Japanese zither [zíθə] with thirteen strings
☐	琵琶	(four-stringed Japanese) lute (「ばち」は plectrum)
☐	大鼓	large hand drum
☐	鼓	hand drum
☐	尺八	five-holed bamboo flute [clarinet]
☐	陶芸	ceramic art / pottery
☐	磁器	porcelain [pɔ́ːsəlin]
☐	漆器	lacquerware [lǽkəwèə]
☐	青磁	celadon porcelain
☐	釉薬(ゆうやく)	glaze
☐	七宝焼き	cloisonné [klɔ̀izənéi] ware

IV 日本のことは英語で何でも発信できる日本事象語彙

語彙力UP　生き物の季語クイズにチャレンジ！（秋編）

■次の俳句の秋の季語を英語で言ってください。

① 懸巣（　　　　）　② 鵙（　　　　）　③ 渡り鳥（　　　　）
④ 啄木鳥（　　　　）　⑤ 雁（　　　　）　⑥ 蟋蟀（　　　　）
⑦ 赤蜻蛉（　　　　）　⑧ 蟷螂（　　　　）　⑨ 蓑虫（　　　　）
⑩ 団栗（　　　　）　⑪ 柿（　　　　）　⑫ 無花果（　　　　）
⑬ 石榴（　　　　）　⑭ 撫子（　　　　）　⑮ 朝顔（　　　　）
⑯ 菊（　　　　）　⑰ 鶏頭（　　　　）　⑱ 酸漿（　　　　）
⑲ 彼岸花［曼珠沙華］（　　　　）　⑳ 桔梗（　　　　）

■解　答

① (jay)　② (shrike)　③ (migratory bird)　④ (woodpecker)
⑤ (wild goose)　⑥ (cricket)　⑦ (red dragonfly)
⑧ (mantis)　⑨ (bagworm)　⑩ (acorn)　⑪ (persimmon)
⑫ (fig)　⑬ (pomegranate)　⑭ (pink)　⑮ (morning glory)
⑯ (chrysanthemum)　⑰ (cockscomb)　⑱ (ground cherry)
⑲ (cluster-amaryllis)　⑳ (Chinese bellflower)

宗教に関する語彙に強くなる

CD 2-31

□ 大仏　　　giant statue ［image］ of Buddha
□ 坊主　　　Buddhist priest ［monk］ / bonze〔bánz〕（「住職」は chief priest）
□ お水取り　sacred water-drawing ceremony at Nigatsu-do Hall of Nara's Todaiji Temple

☐ お布施	offering for Buddhist monks / Buddhist idea of giving offerings to others	
☐ お遍路さん	Buddhist pilgrim	
☐ お盆	Bon festival (「盆踊り」はBon dancing)	
☐ 観音菩薩	Goddess of Mercy / the Bodhisattva 〔bòudisʌ́tvə〕of Compassion	
☐ 四十九日	(memorial service held on) the forty-ninth day after a person's death	
☐ 三回忌	the second anniversary of one's death	
☐ 仁王	the guardian gods of Buddhism / the two deva 〔déivə〕kings	
☐ 鳳凰	mythical phoenix bird	
☐ 縁起	omen (「縁起物」は good luck talisman)	
☐ 縁日	temple or shrine fair / fairs / day of fair	
☐ 加持祈祷	Buddhist incantation 〔ìnkæntéiʃən〕(and prayer against misfortune)	
☐ 供養	memorial service	
☐ 駆け込み寺	shelter [temple] for battered women / refuge 〔réfju:dʒ〕temple for abused wives	
☐ 荒行	asceticism 〔əsétəsìzm〕/ austere discipline	
☐ 座禅	sitting in meditation / sitting in Zen meditation	
☐ 祭壇	altar 〔ɔ́:ltə〕(「位牌」は (Buddhist) memorial [ancestral] tablet)	
☐ 札所	temple which issues amulets to worshippers	
☐ 山伏	mountain ascetic 〔əsétik〕/ itinerant 〔aitínərənt〕priest	
☐ 氏寺	tutelary 〔t(j)ú:təlèəri〕Buddhist temple	

IV　日本のことは英語で何でも発信できる日本事象語彙

コラム 「占い」の知識でボキャブラリーパワー UP！Part2

占いには、astrology（星占い）、十二干支（oriental astrology）、手相占い（palmistry）、physiognomy（人相占い）、tarot（タロット占い）、numerology（姓名画数判断）、phrenology（骨相学）、blood type-based personality analysis（血液型性格分析）、crystal gazing[scrying]（水晶占い）、graphology（筆跡学）、divining sticks（筮竹）、oneiromancy（夢占い）、cartomancy（トランプ占い）、animal sign personality analysis（動物占い）、six-star astrology（六星占術）、molescopy（ほくろ占い）、voice-based personality analysis（声占い）、pyromancy（火占い）と、数多くのものがある。

□	舎利	remains of Buddha / remains
□	写経	transcription of a Buddhist sutra〔súːtrə〕（「宿坊」は temple lodging）
□	儒教	Confucianism〔kənfjúːʃənìzm〕
□	修験道	mountaineering asceticism
□	初七日	memorial service held on the sixth day after a person's death
□	除夜の鐘	temple bells speeding the old year
□	小乗仏教	Hinayana〔hìːnəjáːnə〕Buddhism（「大乗仏教」は Mahayana〔màːhəjáːnə〕Buddhism）
□	色即是空	All is vanity. Every form in reality is empty, and emptiness is the true form.
□	即身成仏	attaining Buddhahood while still in the flesh
□	他力本願	salvation by faith（「自力本願」は self-reliance）

☐ 托鉢	mendicancy〔méndikənsi〕(「托鉢僧」は mendicant / begging bonze)
☐ 地蔵	the Buddhist guardian deity of children and travelers / Jizo Bodhisattva〔bòudisʌ́tvə〕
☐ 弔辞(ちょうじ)	message [words] of condolence / memorial (funeral) address
☐ 読経(どきょう)	sutra-chanting (「念仏」は Buddhist invocation〔ìnvəkéiʃən〕/ prayer to Amitabha〔ʌ̀mitɑ́:bə〕)
☐ 尼寺	nunnery〔nʌ́nəri〕
☐ 煩悩(ぼんのう)	worldly desires
☐ 仏壇	Buddhist home altar (「仏像」は a Buddhist statue)
☐ 仏滅	very unlucky day of the Buddhist calendar
☐ 菩提寺(ぼだいじ)	family temple
☐ 法事	Buddhist memorial service
☐ 密教	esoteric Buddhism
☐ 木魚	fish-shaped wooden temple drum / wooden gong
☐ 輪廻(りんね)	transmigration / reincarnation
☐ 霊山	sacred mountain (「霊場」はholy place)
☐ 焼香	incense burning (「線香」はincense stick)
☐ 香典	condolence money
☐ 通夜	wake〔wéik〕
☐ 戒名	posthumous〔pɑ́stʃəməs〕Buddhist name
☐ 土葬	burial / interment of a dead body
☐ 命日	anniversary of a person's death
☐ 神輿(みこし)	portable shrine
☐ 神主(かんぬし)	Shinto priest (「宮司(ぐうじ)」は (Shinto) chief priest)

IV 日本のことは英語で何でも発信できる日本事象語彙

☐	巫女(みこ)	shrine maiden〔méidn〕(「絵馬」は votive picture tablet)
☐	鳥居	Shinto shrine gateway [archway]
☐	縁結び	matchmaking / marriage tie
☐	稲荷(いなり)	local guardian deity / the god of harvest
☐	氏子	Shinto shrine parishioner (「氏神」は tutelary deity)
☐	お供え	offering to the gods or ancestors
☐	鬼	demon / devil / fiend〔fíːnd〕/ ogre〔óugə〕
☐	おみくじ	fortune-telling paper / written oracle (「大吉」は excellent luck)
☐	お宮参り	newborn baby's first visit to a Shinto shrine
☐	お守り	good luck charm [talisman]〔tǽləsmən〕(「おふだ」は paper charm / amulet)
☐	御神酒(おみき)	rice wine offering for Shinto rites / sacred sake
☐	かしわ手	clapping one's hands in prayer (at a Shinto shrine)
☐	祝詞(のりと)	Shinto prayer
☐	ほこら	small shrine
☐	みそぎ	purification ceremony / ablutions〔əblúːʃənz〕
☐	宮大工	carpenter specializing in building shrines and temples

複数の宗教を同時に信仰する日本人

　日本の宗教は、神道（Shintoism）も仏教（Buddhisim）も信仰というより、生活に根をおろした伝統的慣習（ritualistic）であると言える。前者には明確な教義（doctrine）がなく、先祖崇拝（ancestor worship）、自然崇拝（nature worship）を基本とし、また「八百万の神（multitudinous gods）を崇めるために、釈迦（Buddha）もイエス・キリスト（Jesus Christ）も、日本では神々の一人と見なされている。後者はキリスト教（Christianity）のような絶対神（absolute God）がないので、他宗教に対して寛容になり、日本人は複数の宗教を同時に受け入れ（eclectic）てきた。日本では神仏習合［混交］（syncretization of Shinto with Buddhism）が長く続いたため、神棚（Shinto home altar）と仏壇（Buddhist altar）がある家も多く、両信者を合わせると日本の人口の２倍近くの数になる。

IV　日本のことは英語で何でも発信できる日本事象語彙

□ 玉ぐし料	offering for Shinto rites
□ 狛犬	stone (-carved) guardian dogs at Shinto shrine
□ 社殿	(main building of a) Shinto shrine /sanctuary
□ 神棚	Shinto home altar
□ 神道	Shintoism (which is the indigenous 〔indídʒənəs〕 Japanese religion)
□ 神仏混交	syncretism 〔síŋkrətìzm〕 of Buddhism and

		Shintoism
☐	注連縄(しめなわ)	sacred rice straw rope for warding off evils
☐	天照大神(あまてらすおおみかみ)	the Sun Goddess
☐	破魔矢(はまや)	sacred arrow bringing good luck
☐	厄除け	charm against bad luck（「厄払い」は exorcism〔éksɔːsìzm〕）
☐	賽銭箱(さいせんばこ)	offertory box / wooden box for receiving money offerings
☐	七福神	Seven Deities of Good Luck (Fortune)
☐	恵比須(えびす)	the god of commerce, fishing and shipping
☐	弁財天	the goddes of music, eloquence, wealth and wisdom
☐	大黒	the god of wealth
☐	道祖神	traveler's guardian deity
☐	仙人	mountain hermit
☐	陰陽道	ancient divination based on Yin and Yang
☐	五重塔	five-storied pagoda
☐	多神教	polytheism〔páliθìːzm〕

日本人の心を表す語彙に強くなる　　CD 2-32

☐	切腹	disemboweling〔dìsəmbáuəliŋ〕(oneself) / committing ritual suicide［harakiri］
☐	介錯	suicide assistant
☐	根回し	prior consultation / groundwork laying
☐	幽玄	the subtle and profound / quiet and elegant beauty
☐	わび	quiet refinement
☐	さび	refined rusticity

☐ 恩	moral obligation [indebtedness]
☐ 間	space / pause
☐ 辞世の句	poem composed on one's deathbed / farewell poem / tanka [haiku]
☐ 転生[輪廻]	transmigration of souls
☐ 判官びいき	sympathy or support for an underdog
☐ 武士道	the samurai code of chivalry〔ʃívəlri〕/ Japanese chivalry
☐ 腹芸	the art of conveying unspoken messages
☐ 無常	impermanence / transiency

文学に関する語彙に強くなる　CD 2-33

☐ 浮世草子	popular stories of everyday life in the Edo Period
☐ かぐや姫	The Moon Princess
☐ 季語	season word (in a haiku)
☐ 古今和歌集	Collection of Poems from Ancient and Modern Times
☐ 一寸法師	The Inch-High Samurai / Tom Thumb
☐ 歌集	anthology (「勅撰和歌集」は imperial-commissioned poem anthology)
☐ 戯曲	play / drama / theater
☐ 脚本	script (劇) / scenario (映画)
☐ 純文学	pure literature (「大衆文学」は popular literature、「文学賞」は literary prize)
☐ 随筆	essay (「散文」は prose、「紀行」は traveler's journal)
☐ 川柳	satirical〔sətírikl〕seventeen-syllable poem

IV　日本のことは英語で何でも発信できる日本事象語彙

☐	短歌	thirty-one syllable short poem written in a 5-7-5-7-7 line pattern
☐	伝記	biography (「自伝」は autobiography)
☐	童話	fairy tale (「民話」は folk tale / folklore、「説話」は narrative)
☐	枕草子	The Pillow Book

日本文化を発信するための語彙クイズにチャレンジ！ Part1

■ 次の日本語を英語で説明してください。

1	女形（歌舞伎）	11	神輿
2	寄席	12	先祖供養
3	茶道	13	本音と建前
4	神楽	14	義理
5	浮世絵	15	わび
6	三味線	16	玉虫色
7	悟り	17	檀家
8	数珠	18	俳句
9	お祓い	19	神話
10	ご利益	20	歌会

■ 解　答

1	female impersonator	11	portable shrine (carried in festivals)
2	vaudeville / variety show [theater / house]	12	Buddhist service for ancestors
3	tea ceremony	13	honest feelings and official stance
4	sacred Shinto music and dance	14	moral obligation

5	woodblock print (depicting everyday life in the Edo Period)	15	subtle [subdued] taste / quiet [austere] refinement
6	three-stringed guitar	16	ambiguous [equivocal/ weasel-worded] answer
7	enlightenment	17	Buddhist parishioner
8	Buddhist rosary	18	seventeen-syllable short poem written in a 5-7-5 line pattern
9	Shinto purification (ceremony)	19	mythology
10	divine favor	20	poetry party [competition]

コラム 「占い」の知識でボキャブラリーパワー UP！Part3

　「手相占い」をpalmistryと言うが、その1つである指占いでは、指の長い人はintelligent、短い人はimpulsive（衝動的）、そして指の大きい人はpainstaking（綿密で）and reflective（思慮深く）、またsquare（四角い形）をした人はcircumspect（用心深く）、spatulate（へら形）の人はvigorous（精力的）となっている。さらにtapered finger（先が細くなった指）の人はimpulsive（几帳面）、artistic（芸術的）、punctilious（規則にうるさい）、slender（細い）人はintroverted、aesthetic nature（内向的で審美眼がある）。これに対して、puffy（丸々した）人はhedonistic（快楽主義的）、thick and short（太短い）人はself-centered（利己主義）と言われている。

日本の行事に関する語彙に強くなる　　CD 2-34

- ☐ お年玉　　New Year's monetary gift
- ☐ 書き初め　　the first calligraphy of the New Year
- ☐ 門松　　New Year's pine and bamboo decoration
- ☐ 注連飾(しめかざ)り　　sacred Shinto rope with strips of white paper
- ☐ とそ　　spiced sake（served at New Year's）
- ☐ どんど焼き　　bonfire by which the New Year's decorations are burned
- ☐ 臼　　mortar / hand mill / millstone
- ☐ 鏡開き　　the custom of breaking and eating the New Year's rice cake
- ☐ 鏡餅　　large, round rice cake offered to the gods（at New Year's）
- ☐ 獅子舞　　ritual dance with a lion's mask
- ☐ 十二支　　the twelve signs of the Chinese zodiac[zóudiæ̀k]
- ☐ 出初式　　the New Year's fire brigade display
- ☐ 初詣　　New Year's visit to a shrine or a temple
- ☐ 初日の出　　the New year's first sunrise
- ☐ 初夢　　the first dream of the New Year
- ☐ 独楽(こま)　　(spinning) top（「独楽回し」はtop-spinning）
- ☐ お歳暮　　year-end gift
- ☐ 雪だるま　　snowman
- ☐ 大晦日(おおみそか)[除夜]　　New Year's Eve
- ☐ 年越しそば　　buckwheat noodles eaten on New Year's Eve
- ☐ 忘年会　　year-end party
- ☐ 内祝い　　family celebration / gifts for relatives or friends
- ☐ 見合い結婚　　arranged marriage（「見合い」は arranged marriage meeting）

□	水引き	ceremonial red-and-white paper cord for tying gifts
□	引き出物	gift given to those who attend a wedding reception
□	縁談	marriage proposal [offer] / engagement
□	嫁入り道具	trousseau [truːsóu] / bride's household effects
□	結納(ゆいのう)	betrothal [bitróuðəl] gift
□	三々九度	exchange of nuptial cups
□	祝儀袋	special envelope for monetary gifts
□	年中行事	annual events
□	百年祭	centennial [sonténiəl]（「二百年祭」は bicentennial (anniversary)）
□	屋台	stall（「夜店」は night stall (stand)）
□	厄年	unlucky year / critical [climacteric] year
□	冠婚葬祭	ceremonial functions
□	金婚式	golden wedding anniversary（「銀婚式」は silver wedding anniversary）
□	彼岸	equinoctial [ìːkwənákʃl] week (when Buddhist services are held)
□	花見	cherry blossom viewing
□	雛人形(ひな)	doll for Girls' Festival
□	鯉のぼり	carp streamer [banner]
□	七夕	the Star Festival (celebrated on July 7)
□	暑中見舞い	summer greeting card (inquiring after a person's health)
□	中元(ちゅうげん)	traditional mid-year gift
□	盆	the Buddhist festival of the dead / Bon festival
□	送り火	ceremonial bonfire to speed the spirits back to the other world

☐	精霊流し	floating lanterns or offerings for the spirits of the deceased
☐	月見	moon viewing
☐	針供養	memorial service for old needles
☐	成人の日	Coming-of-Age Day（2nd Monday. January）
☐	建国記念日	National Foundation Day（February 11）

年越しそばの由来とは⁉

　日本には昔から、大みそかの晩（New Year's Eve）には、新年に向けて人々の願いが込められた縁起物（good luck bringer）として、年越しそば（year-crossing buckwheat noodles）を食べる習わしがある。その由来は、「細長いそばから、長寿を願う（wish for long life）」がよく言われるが、他にも、開運（better luck）、邪気払い（drive away bad luck）などがある。そばは切れやすいところから、「旧年の災厄を断ち」（end last year's bad luck）が起こり、また、邪気を払う力を持つと信じられている三角形のそばの実から、金運（luck with money）をもたらすとされた。これは、金細工師（goldsmith）が金箔（gold leaf）を伸ばす時に、散った金粉（gold powder）を、そば粉（buckwheat dough）を練って集めたことから由来している。

☐ 節分　　　the eve of the first day of spring / bean

		throwing festival
☐	豆まき	bean-scattering [throwing] ceremony
☐	八十八夜	the eighty-eighth day from the setting-in of spring
☐	春分	vernal [spring] equinox〔íːkwənàks〕(「秋分」は autumnal equinox)
☐	雛祭り	Doll's Festival / Girls' Festival (March 3)
☐	昭和の日	Showa Day (April 29)
☐	憲法記念日	Constitution Day (May 3)
☐	みどりの日	Greenery Day (May 4)
☐	子供の日	Children's Day / Boys' Festival (May 5)
☐	海の日	Marine Day (3rd Monday. July)
☐	敬老の日	Respect-for-the-Aged Day (3rd Monday. September)
☐	体育の日	National Sports Day (2nd Monday. October)
☐	文化の日	Culture Day (November 3)
☐	勤労感謝の日	Labor Thanksgiving Day (November 23)
☐	天皇誕生日	Emperor's Birthday (December 23)
☐	七五三	festival [shrine visit] for children aged seven, five and three
☐	千歳飴(ちとせあめ)	red and white candy stick for children of three, five and seven
☐	夏至	summer solstice〔sálstəs〕(「冬至」は winter solstice)
☐	鬼	goblin / ogre
☐	綱引き	tug of war
☐	地鎮祭(じちんさい)	ground-breaking ceremony / Shinto ceremony for purifying a building site

IV 日本のことは英語で何でも発信できる日本事象語彙

4-3　第23日

日本のことは英語で何でも発信できる 通訳ガイド必須日本事象語彙（風物・娯楽編）

風物に関する語彙に強くなる（家の中編）　CD 3-1

- 油とり紙　　　absorbent paper
- 行灯（あんどん）　lamp with a paper shade
- ちょうちん　　lantern
- いろり　　　　sunken hearth〔hɑ́:θ〕
- 扇子　　　　　folding fan（「団扇（うちわ）」は round fan）
- 座敷　　　　　formal audience hall
- 床柱　　　　　alcove〔ǽlkouv〕post
- かまど　　　　cooking stove / kitchen range
- 家紋　　　　　family crest
- かんざし　　　ornamental hairpin
- 灸（きゅう）　moxibustion〔mɑ̀ksibʌ́stʃən〕/ moxa treatment
- こたつ　　　　low quilt-covered table with a heater underneath
- 火鉢　　　　　(charcoal) brazier〔bréiʒɚ〕/（「掘りごたつ」は charcoal brazier in a floor well）
- 実印　　　　　registered seal（「認め印」は personal〔unregistered〕seal）
- 朱肉　　　　　red ink pad / seal stamp pad

☐	そろばん	abacus
☐	畳	straw mat (used for floor covering)
☐	電気あんか	electric foot warmer
☐	湯たんぽ	hot-water bottle
☐	熨斗(のし)	special decoration put on the top of a gift box
☐	のれん	short split curtain (hung at home or a shop entrance)
☐	はちまき	headband
☐	福袋	lucky [grab] bag
☐	ふすま	sliding paper door with opaque paper on a wooden frame
☐	すだれ	bamboo blind
☐	障子(しょうじ)	sliding paper screen [door] with translucent paper on a wooden lattice frame
☐	孫(まご)の手	back scratcher
☐	鶯張(うぐいすば)り	squeaking security floor / nightingale floor
☐	下駄(げた)	wooden clogs
☐	鼻緒(はなお)	clog thong / sandal thong / straps of a geta
☐	草履(ぞうり)	Japanese straw sandals
☐	蚊帳(かや)	mosquito net
☐	桐ダンス	chest of drawers made of paulownia 〔pɔːlóuniə〕
☐	戸棚	cupboard
☐	呉服	cloth for traditional Japanese clothing
☐	根付け	miniature carving attached to the cord of a pouch
☐	招き猫	beckoning [welcoming] cat in shops
☐	喪服	mourning dress [attire]
☐	乳母車	baby buggy [carriage]

☐	洋服ダンス	wardrobe
☐	欄間(らんま)	decorative transom / [fan light]
☐	番傘	bamboo-and-paper umbrella

のれんのルーツとは!?

屋号（shop name）、商標（trademark）などを記し、商店の戸口（shop doorway）にかけたり、部屋の仕切り（divider）や装飾（ornament）として垂らすのれん（short split curtain）は、もとは禅寺で簾(すだれ)（bamboo screen）の隙間を覆う寒さよけ（ward off cold）に使われていたが、江戸時代に商屋（merchant houses）が営業権（goodwill）や信用（trustworthiness）を表す象徴として商業用（commercial purpose）に使われ始め、現在では、老舗の長年の歴史（the long-standing history of a shop）を示す役割を果たしている。

風物に関する語彙に強くなる（家の外編） CD 3-2

☐	縁側	veranda / porch
☐	鬼瓦	ridge-end tile with the figure of a devil / gargoyle 〔gá:gɔil〕
☐	かかし	scarecrow
☐	しっくい	plaster / mortar
☐	石庭	rock [stone] garden
☐	瓦	tile

☐	灯籠(とうろう)		Japanese (stone) lantern / garden lantern (「回り灯籠」は revolving lantern)
☐	堀		moat

日本文化を発信するための語彙クイズにチャレンジ！ **Part2**

■ 次の日本語を英語で説明してください。

1	振替休日	11	床の間
2	十五夜	12	相撲部屋
3	干支	13	駅伝
4	連休	14	決まり手
5	文金高島田	15	羽根つき
6	仲人	16	潮干狩り
7	土用	17	万華鏡
8	棟上式	18	観光地
9	いろり	19	無形文化財
10	長屋	20	露天風呂

■ 解　答

1	substitute holiday	11	alcove
2	the harvest moon / full moon night/	12	(sumo) stable
3	the twelve zodiac signs of Chinese astrology/ sexagenary cycle	13	long-distance relay road race
4	two or more holidays in succession	14	winning technique
5	upswept hairdo	15	battledore and shuttlecock / Japanese badminton
6	matchmaker / go-between	16	shellfish gathering
7	midsummer / dog days	17	kaleidoscope

8	topping-out (roof-raising) ceremony	18	tourist attraction / sightseeing spot
9	hearth made in the floor	19	intangible cultural asset
10	row house / terrace(d) house	20	open-air bath

風物に関する語彙に強くなる （服） CD 3-3

- 帯　　　　　broad sash for a kimono
- 袴（はかま）　long pleated skirt（worn over a kimono）
- 紋付き　　　crested kimono / garment bearing family crest
- 十二単（じゅうにひとえ）　layered ceremonial dress worn by court ladies
- 振り袖　　　long-sleeved kimono
- 足袋（たび）　Japanese split-toed socks
- 履物（はきもの）　footwear
- 浴衣　　　　informal cotton kimono for summer
- 留め袖　　　formal kimono for married women
- 礼服　　　　formal [ceremonial / full] dress
- ふんどし　　loincloth

風物に関する語彙に強くなる （その他） CD 3-4

- 女将（おかみ）　proprietress（hostess）of a Japanese inn
- 回覧板　　　circular notice（bulletin [búlətn]）
- 漢方薬　　　Chinese（herbal）medicine
- 熊手　　　　rake
- 宮内庁　　　the Imperial Household Agency
- 君が代　　　the Japanese national anthem
- 皇室　　　　the Imperial Household（Family）
- 皇太子　　　crown prince（「皇后」は empress）
- 銭湯（せんとう）　public bath

☐ 日本髪	Japanese-style hairdo / Japanese coiffure 〔kwɑːfjúə〕
☐ 忍者	secret agent in feudal times
☐ 手裏剣 (しゅりけん)	throwing-star / dirk / throwing-knife
☐ 風鈴 (ふうりん)	wind bell / wind chime
☐ 文鎮 (ぶんちん)	paperweight
☐ 鍼灸 (しんきゅう)	acupuncture and moxibustion
☐ 餞別 (せんべつ)	farewell [parting / going-away] gift [present]

伝統スポーツに関する語彙に強くなる　　CD 3-5

☐ 合気道	the art of self-defense that neutralizes attacks by minimum effort
☐ 空手	martial art characterized by sharp, quick punches, kicks, and knee or elbow strikes
☐ 剣道	Japanese swordsmanship
☐ なぎなた	halberd (「竹刀 (しない)」は bamboo sword)
☐ 弓道	Japanese archery / bowmanship
☐ 矢	arrow (「弓」は bow)
☐ 居合道	the art of drawing real swords
☐ 草野球	sandlot baseball
☐ 番付	ranking (list) (of sumo wrestlers, entertainers, etc.) (「取組表」は bout sheet)
☐ 行司 (ぎょうじ)	sumo (wrestling) referee
☐ 大相撲	grand sumo tournament
☐ まげ	topknot
☐ まわし	belt / sash (「化粧回し」は sumo-wrestler's ornamental apron)
☐ 寄り切り	forcing out

295

☐ 上手投げ	overarm throw / arm throw	
☐ 横綱	grand champion / highest rank wrestler	
☐ 大関	champion / second-highest rank wrestler	
☐ 関脇	junior champion / third-highest rank wrestler	
☐ 小結	junior champion second grade / sub-junior ［third］ champion /fourth-highest rank wrestler	
☐ 前頭	top-division wrestler	
☐ 十両	second-division wrestler / lower division	
☐ 敢闘賞	fighting spirit prize	
☐ 殊勲賞(しゅくん)	outstanding performance prize	
☐ 金星(きんぼし)	upset win over a yokozuna	
☐ 水入り	temporary halt	
☐ 千秋楽	the final day of a sumo tournament	
☐ 土俵入り	ring entering ceremony	
☐ 物言い	protest against the referee's decision	
☐ 立会い	initial charge	
☐ 勝越し	winning a majority of matches during the 15 days of the Grand Sumo Tournament	

語彙力ＵＰ　生き物の季語クイズにチャレンジ！（冬編）

■次の俳句の冬の季語を英語で言ってください。

①鴨（　　　　）　②水鳥（　　　　　）　③兎(うさぎ)（　　　　　）
④鶴（　　　　）　⑤梟(ふくろう)（　　　　）　⑥千鳥（　　　　　）
⑦河豚(ふぐ)（　　　　）　⑧牡蠣(かき)（　　　　）　⑨山茶花(さざんか)（　　　　）
⑩柊(ひいらぎ)（　　　　）　⑪水仙（　　　　）　⑫大根（　　　　　）
⑬枯れ尾花（　　　　　）

■ 解　答

① (duck)　② (water bird)　③ (rabbit)　④ (crane)　⑤ (owl)
⑥ (plover)　⑦ (blowfish)　⑧ (oyster)　⑨ (sasanqua)
⑩ (holly)　⑪ (narcissus)　⑫ (Japanese radish)
⑬ (withered Japanese pampas grass)

コンピューター囲碁は人間に勝てるか!?

　2人の対戦者が黒と白の石を交互に盤上に置き (alternately place black stones and white stones on a board)、相手の石と空間を取り合う囲碁 (Igo) は、奈良時代に、中国から朝鮮半島経由で日本に伝わり、現在では、囲碁人口約1000万人の人気のある室内ゲーム (indoor game) である。囲碁は、石を置く場所の制約が少なく、着手の選択肢に大きな幅を与える (give large latitude to placing stones)、戦略的に複雑なゲーム (strategically complicated game) であるため、コンピュータに世界チャンピオンが破られるチェスと違って、コンピュータ囲碁 (computer-programmed Igo player) はいまだにアマ中級程度である。

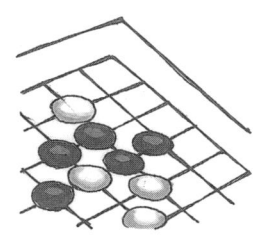

遊びに関する語彙に強くなる　CD 3-6

- ☐ あや取り　（play) cat's cradle / string game ［figures］
- ☐ 腕相撲　arm wrestling
- ☐ 鬼ごっこ　tag（「鬼ごっこの鬼」は it / tagger）
- ☐ おはじき［ビー玉］　marble
- ☐ おりがみ　the art of folding paper（into figures)（「千代紙」は paper with colored figures）
- ☐ 折り鶴　folded paper crane
- ☐ お手玉　beanbag
- ☐ かくれんぼ　hide-and-seek
- ☐ ゲームセンター　video game [amusement] arcade
- ☐ ジェットコースター　roller coaster
- ☐ じゃんけん　game of scissors-paper-stone to decide order
- ☐ 将棋　Japanese chess（「囲碁」は board game of capturing territory）
- ☐ しりとり　Japanese word-chain game
- ☐ チャンバラ　sword fight ［battle］ /（映画）samurai movie / sword-play film
- ☐ てるてる坊主　hanging doll made of white paper or cloth to wish for fine weather
- ☐ なぞなぞ　（play）riddle
- ☐ にらめっこ　staring ［stéəriŋ］ contest
- ☐ パチンコ　vertical pinball game / slingshot
- ☐ 羽子板　battledore
- ☐ ブランコ　swing（「空中ブランコ」は trapeze ［træpíːz］）
- ☐ ままごと　playing house
- ☐ 漫才　comic stage dialogue / comic backchat
- ☐ 滑り台　slide

☐	観覧車	Ferris wheel
☐	剣玉	cup-and-ball (game)
☐	砂場	sandbox / sand pit
☐	三輪車	tricycle
☐	紙芝居	picture-story show / traditional Japanese art of storytelling with pictures
☐	手品	magic trick
☐	雪合戦	snowball fight / snowballing
☐	双六(すごろく)	Japanese backgammon / child's dice game
☐	凧(たこ)揚げ	kite-flying
☐	竹とんぼ	bamboo dragonfly
☐	竹馬	(bamboo) stilts
☐	百人一首	the playing cards of 100 famous 31-syllable Japanese poems
☐	風車(かざぐるま)	pinwheel / windmill
☐	福笑い	game of comical face-making
☐	木馬	wooden horse /（小児用）rocking horse （「積み木」は building blocks）
☐	輪投げ	quoits 〔kwɔ́its〕

観光に関する語彙に強くなる　　　　　CD 3-7

☐	一見客(いちげんきゃく)	chance customer / first-time customer
☐	鵜飼(うかい)	cormorant 〔kɔ́ːmərənt〕 fishing
☐	温泉	hot spring / spa
☐	合掌造(がっしょうづく)り	wooden house with a steep rafter roof
☐	鐘楼(しょうろう)	bell tower / belfry 〔bélfriː〕
☐	枯山水	dry landscape garden (composed of rocks and sand)

IV　日本のことは英語で何でも発信できる日本事象語彙

299

☐	しゃちほこ	imaginary fish (with the head of a tiger and the body of a fish)
☐	ビジネスホテル	no-frills hotel
☐	モーニングサービス	breakfast special
☐	猿回し	monkey performance
☐	縁結び	marriage tie
☐	屋形船	(old-fashioned) houseboat/ roofed pleasure boat
☐	景勝地 [名勝]	scenic spot
☐	借景	borrowed landscape garden
☐	国立公園	national park
☐	国定公園	quasi [kwéizai] -national park
☐	史跡 [旧跡]	historic spots / places of historical interest
☐	周遊観光船	tour boat / sightseeing boat
☐	重要文化財	important cultural asset
☐	出国カード	embarkation [èmbɑːkéiʃən] card
☐	出入国管理局	Immigration (Control) Office
☐	植物園	botanical garden
☐	世界一周旅行	around-the-world trip
☐	世界文化遺産	World Cultural Heritage
☐	天然記念物	natural monument
☐	日本三景	the scenic trio of Japan
☐	舞妓	young apprentice geisha
☐	風致地区	nature preservation area
☐	保養地	health resort
☐	民芸品	folkcraft
☐	宿泊施設	accommodations
☐	国民宿舎	inexpensive hotel operated by a local government

| □ 民宿 | guest-house / private hotel（「旅館」は Japanese inn） |
| □ 旅程 | itinerary〔aitínərèəri〕|

通訳ガイド試験語彙問題対策

　通訳ガイド試験用語の出題傾向は、年度により、難易度や出題分野に変動があり、出題頻度が高い観光・文化用語以外に、時事用語、日常用語など、常識的な語彙から、通訳の現場で使うような、少々専門的なものまで幅広く身につけておく必要があります。また、決まった訳語が分からない場合でも、自分で考え出すことが大事です。ガイドの現場では即訳が求められることが多いので日頃から自分の言葉で、身の回りの事象を表現するように心がけましょう。

第5章

分野別語彙力パワーUP
理系語彙

5-1　第24日
物理語彙に強くなる

　科学が日進月歩に進歩する世の中で、グローバリゼーションが進み、世界がどんどんハイテク化するにつれて、サイエンスに関する英語での語彙表現力がますます重要性を帯びています。そこでここでは、サイエンティフィックアメリカンを始めとする科学の英字誌やサイエンスニュースがエンジョイできたり、英語で科学のプレゼンができたり、また英検1級はもちろん、工業英検やミシガン工業英検などの検定にも合格できるように、非常に効果的な科学の語彙表現力UPを行いたいと思います。それでは皆さん、最後まで頑張ってこの分野の語彙と知識力UPに励みましょう。

　物理はあらゆる工業の基本であり、機械製品・電気製品のほとんどは物理原理を基にして作られています。それゆえ、物理を機械・電気から明確に区別することは難しいのですが、ここでは原理的なものに絞りました。それでは皆さん、気合を入れて理系のボキャブラリービルディングに励みましょう！
Let's enjoy the process!（陽は必ず昇る！）

物理一般語彙に強くなる

CD 3-8

(1) 力

- □ universal gravitation　万有引力
- □ kinetic [kinétik] energy　運動エネルギー：速さで決まるエネルギー
- □ gravitational energy　重力エネルギー
- □ potential energy　位置エネルギー：高さで決まるエネルギー
- □ mechanical energy　力学的エネルギー
- □ the law of conservation of energy　エネルギー保存の法則：抵抗がない場合に成立
- □ gravitational force　重力（gravitational wave は「重力波」）
- □ momentum / moment　運動量（moment of inertia は「慣性モーメント」：回転運動における慣性の大きさを表す量）
- □ conservation of momentum　運動量保存
- □ the law of inertia [inə́ːʃə]　慣性の法則（inertial force は「慣性力」）
- □ principle of action and reaction　作用反作用の原理
- □ vertical motion　鉛直方向移動
- □ material point　質点：質量を持つ点
- □ point of action (application) / working point　作用点
- □ work function　仕事関数：1個の電子を外側に取り出すのに必要な最少エネルギー
- □ normal stress　垂直応力（allowable stress は「許容応力」：「応力」は荷重に応じて物体の内部に生ずる抵抗力）
- □ center of gravity　重心（concentrated load は「集中荷重」）
- □ centrifugal [sentrífjəgl] force　遠心力（centripetal [sentrípətl] force は「求心力」）

- [ ] critical mass [point]　臨界質量（点）（critical pressure は「臨界圧」）
- [ ] covariance〔kòuvéəriəns〕（物理法則の）**共変性**：時間・位置などが互いに物理学的関係を保ちながら変わること
- [ ] solid-state physics　固体物理
- [ ] lattice defect〔lǽtəs | díːfekt〕**格子欠陥**：結晶構造の欠陥
- [ ] crystal lattice　結晶格子（crystal axis は「結晶軸」）

(2) 振動、回転、速度　　CD 3-9

- [ ] standing wave　**定在波、定常波**：進行波と後退波が出合った時に生じる不動の波
- [ ] shock wave　**衝撃波**：空中で音速を超える速さの圧力変化の波
- [ ] wavelength　波長（wave front は「波面」）
- [ ] vibration [oscillation] frequency　振動数
- [ ] proper vibration　固有振動（natural frequency は「固有振動数」）
- [ ] damping oscillation〔àsəléiʃən〕減衰振動（deceleration は「減速」）
- [ ] tangential〔tændʒénʃl〕line　接線方向
- [ ] vibration analysis　振動解析
- [ ] angular velocity〔ǽŋgjələ | vəlásəti〕**角速度**：物体の回転速度（angular acceleration は「角加速度」）
- [ ] peripheral〔pərífərəl〕velocity　**周速度**：外周部表面の速度
- [ ] areal velocity　**面積速度**：惑星と太陽を結ぶ動経が描く面積

(3) 流体　　CD 3-10

- [ ] hydrodynamics　流体力学
- [ ] aerodynamics　空気力学
- [ ] hydraulics〔haidrɔ́ːliks〕水力学（hydraulic property は「水

硬性」、buoyancy〔bɔ́iənsi〕は「浮力」）
- [ ] convection〔kənvékʃən〕 対流（laminar flow は「層流」）
- [ ] surface tension　表面張力

■ 測定器のクイズにチャレンジ！

1. 熱量計　2. 高度計　3. 光度計　4. 圧力計　5. 震度計
6. 加速度計　7. 硬度計　8. 粘度計　9. 動力計　10. 比重計

■ 解　答

1. calorimeter　2. altimeter　3. photometer
4. pressure gauge　5. vibrometer
6. accelerometer　7. hardness meter
8. viscometer / viscosimeter　9. dynamometer
10. gravimeter / hydrometer

----

(4) 熱　　　　　　　　　　　　　　　　　　　　CD 3-11

- [ ] thermodynamics　熱力学
- [ ] thermal expansion coefficient　[TEC] 熱膨張係数
- [ ] thermal insulation　断熱（thermal conductivity は「熱伝導性」）
- [ ] thermal radiation　熱放射（thermocouple は「熱電対（ねつでんつい）」：温度差を測定するセンサー）
- [ ] thermal stress　熱応力（thermoelectric effect は「熱電効果」）
- [ ] radiation　輻射（ふくしゃ）、放射（radiation energy は「輻射エネルギー」）

(5) 光　　　　　　　　　　　　　　　　　　　　CD 3-12

- [ ] luminous〔lúːmənəs〕intensity　光度（luminanceは「輝度：ディスプレイ画面の明るさ」、chroma〔króumə〕は「彩度」、luminous objectは「発光体」）
- [ ] infrared〔ìnfrəréd〕rays　赤外線（ultraviolet raysは「紫外線」）
- [ ] interference fringe　干渉稿(じま)：空気層をはさんだ２枚の透明フィルムから反射される干渉縞（interferenceは「干渉、混信」）
- [ ] interferometry〔ìntəfəámətri〕干渉計測法（refractometer〔rìːfræktámətə〕は「屈折計」）
- [ ] light intensity　光強度、輝度（light waveは「光波」）
- [ ] magnification〔mæ̀gnəfikéiʃən〕拡大、倍率
- [ ] aberration〔æ̀bəréiʃən〕収差、（天文）光行差（chromatic aberrationは「色収差」）
- [ ] absorption spectrum　吸収スペクトル（absorptivityは「吸収率」）
- [ ] boundary surface　境界面
- [ ] coherence〔kouhíərəns〕コヒーレンス、可干渉性
- [ ] convergence〔kənvə́ːdʒəns〕収束（converging waveは「集中波」）
- [ ] condenser　凝縮器、集光装置（condensing lensは「集光レンズ」）
- [ ] convex〔kánveks〕lens　凸レンズ（concave〔kánkeiv〕lensは「凹レンズ」）
- [ ] eyepiece [ocular〔ákjələ〕] lens　接眼レンズ（field [objective] lensは「対物レンズ」、fisheye lensは「魚眼レンズ」、telephoto lensは「望遠レンズ」）
- [ ] false image　虚像（real imageは「実像」、focal lengthは「焦点距離」）
- [ ] entry [incidence / incident] angle　入射角

- □ reflection [specular] angle　反射角（solid angle は「立体角」）
- □ transmissivity　透過率：入射光に対する透過光の割合
- □ reflectivity / reflective index / index of reflection　反射率
- □ reflection　反射（reflection loss は「反射損」、irregular reflection は「乱反射」）
- □ spectroscopy〔spektráskəpi〕分光、分光学
- □ refraction〔rifrǽkʃən〕屈折（refraction angle は「屈折角」、refractive index は「屈折率」）
- □ gradient〔gréidiənt〕階調度、勾配（grating は「格付け」）
- □ diffraction〔difrǽkʃən〕grating　回折格子：光を回折させて、スペクトルを得るのに用いる装置（diffraction zone は「回折帯」）
- □ misalignment〔mìsəláinmənt〕（光軸などの）調整のズレ
- □ photogenic〔fòutədʒénik〕発光性の
- □ translucent〔trænslúːsnt〕半透明な

(6) 原子、量子　　　　　　　　　　　　　　　　CD 3-13

- □ half-life　半減期
- □ nanosecond　10億分の1秒
- □ neutron　中性子（elementary particle は「素粒子」）
- □ photon　光子、フォトン（photogenic は「発光性の」）
- □ physical quantity　物理量（physical constant は「物理定数」）
- □ quantum〔kwɑ́ntəm〕量子（quantum mechanics は「量子力学」）
- □ relativity theory　相対性理論（relaxation time は「緩和時間」）

Carbon Atom(炭素原子)

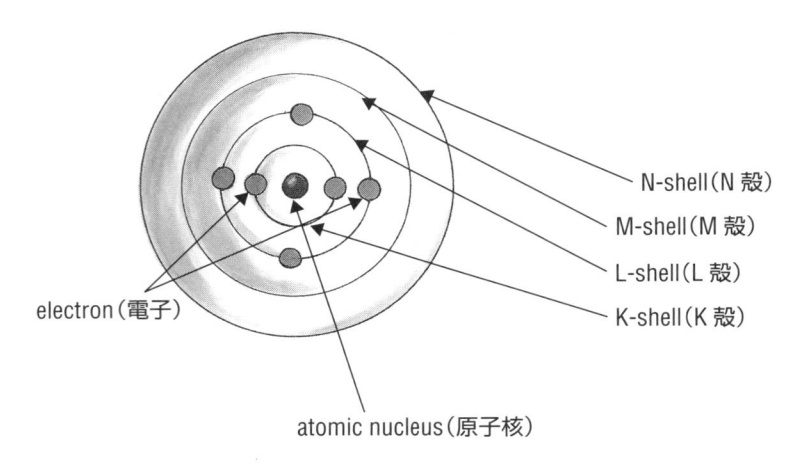

N-shell(N殻)
M-shell(M殻)
L-shell(L殻)
K-shell(K殻)
electron(電子)
atomic nucleus(原子核)

5-2　第25日
電気語彙に強くなる

　電気の技術革新では特にエレクトロニクス分野が目覚ましいです。ここではまず、その分野の語彙に重点を置いた語彙補強をしていただきましょう。目に見えない電気は回路を通して理解することが大切であり、実用面ではコンピュータ関連が重要です。

エレクトロニクス関連語彙表現に強くなる　　CD 3-14

(1) 電子物理
- atomic valence〔véiləns〕[value]　**原子価**：原子が他の原子と結合できる個数（valence band は「価電子帯」）
- free electron　**自由電子**：電気や熱伝導をする電子
- electric charge　**電荷**：物体が帯びている静電気の量、**充電**（electric discharge は「放電」）
- charged particles　**荷電粒子**：電子や陽子など
- positive charge　**正電荷**（positive pole は「陽極」、negative charge は「負電荷」）
- cathode〔kǽθoud〕　**陰極**（anode は「陽極」、static coupling は「静電結合：送電線や通信線間に静電容量が発生するなど」）

- ☐ conduction band　伝導帯（conductivity は「導電率、伝導率」）
- ☐ static charge [electricity]　静電気
- ☐ electric flux　電束：プラス極とマイナス極の間の電気力線の束
- ☐ electric potential　電位：2点間にある電気量を運ぶためのエネルギー（electric potential difference は「電位差、電圧」）
- ☐ electrostatic induction　静電誘導
- ☐ Coulomb〔kú:ləm〕force　クーロン力：正電荷と負電荷が引き合う力、または同種電荷の反発力
- ☐ capacitance〔kəpǽsətəns〕静電容量：コンデンサなどにどれだけの電気が蓄えられるかの大きさ
- ☐ polarization〔pòulərəzéiʃən〕分極：電界で電子分布が偏ること
- ☐ current density　電気密度（dielectric constant は「誘電率：2つの点電荷間に働く静電力、置かれる物質によって誘電率は異なる」）
- ☐ magnetic flux　磁束：N極とS極の間の磁力線の束（magnetic shield は「磁気遮蔽」）
- ☐ permeability〔pə́:(r)miəbíləti〕透磁率：磁気誘導の大きさと、磁界の強さとの比
- ☐ electromagnetic force　電磁力：電流と磁界の相互作用で生じる力
- ☐ electromagnetic induction　電磁誘導：電磁界の変化により、導体に起電力が生じること（magnetic susceptibility は「磁化率」：磁場によって物質に生じる磁化の度合い）
- ☐ thermoelectric effect　熱電効果
- ☐ heat & current conductivity　熱電流伝導性
- ☐ resistivity　抵抗率
- ☐ superconductivity　超伝導：極低温で電気抵抗がゼロになる現象
- ☐ piezoelectric〔pièizouiléktrik〕圧電性の
- ☐ electrolysis〔ilèktrálǝsis〕電気分解（electrode は「電極」、electrolyte は「電解液」）

- [ ] diffused reflection　乱反射

(2) 部品、材料

- [ ] insulation [insulator]　絶縁、絶縁体（insulating paper は「絶縁紙」、insulation resistance は「絶縁抵抗」）
- [ ] diode　ダイオード（junction diode は「接合ダイオード」）
- [ ] light emitting diode [LED]　発光ダイオード
- [ ] ferromagnetic 〔fèəroumægnétik〕 material　強磁性体：磁気が強く残る物質。例：鉄、ニッケル
- [ ] paramagnetic material　常磁性体：磁石の磁性と異なる極性が誘導される物質
- [ ] permanent magnet [PM]　永久磁石
- [ ] shadow mask　遮蔽板（shielding efficiency は「遮蔽効率」）
- [ ] battery plate　電池極板
- [ ] passive device　受動素子：抵抗、コイル、コンデンサなどエネルギーを消費するだけの素子
- [ ] active device　能動素子：トランジスタ、ダイオードなどエネルギー供給によって増幅、整流などの働きをする素子
- [ ] coaxial 〔kouǽksiəl〕 cable　同軸ケーブル（composite cable は「複合ケーブル」）
- [ ] photoelectric conversion　光電変換：デジカメのCCD（Charge Coupled Device）などの電荷結合素子がある
- [ ] variable capacitor　可変コンデンサ：容量を変化させることができる
- [ ] transducer　変換器、トランスデューサ：音を電気信号に変えたり、電気信号を機械運動に変えたりする変換器
- [ ] integrated circuit [IC]　集積回路：シリコン基板に抵抗、トランジスタなど多数の素子を集めた電子回路

□ cathode-ray tube [CRT]　ブラウン管
□ deflection〔diflékʃən〕偏向（deflecting circuit は「偏向回路：ブラウン管内の電子ビームを振らせる回路など」）

Direct current motor（直流モーター）

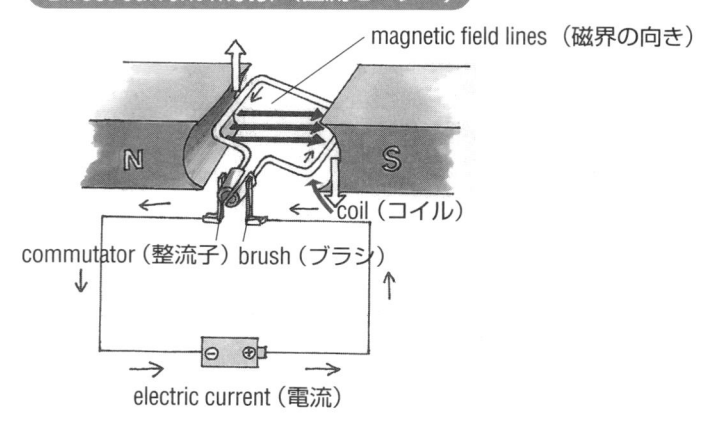

- magnetic field lines（磁界の向き）
- coil（コイル）
- commutator（整流子）　brush（ブラシ）
- electric current（電流）

(3) 回路　　　　　　　　　　　　　　　　　　　　CD 3-16

□ alternating current [AC]　交流電流（DC [direct current] は「直流電流」）
□ induced current　誘導電流
□ discharge current　放電電流
□ diffusion current　拡散電流（eddy current は「渦電流」）
□ holding current　保持電流（interrupted current は「断続電流」）
□ starting current　起動電流（steady flow は定常流）
□ working [operating] current　動作電流
□ saturation〔sætʃəréiʃən〕current　飽和電流
□ charging curve　充電曲線（continuous discharge は「連続放

電」)
- [ ] applied voltage　印加電圧（acceleration voltage は「加速電圧」）
- [ ] maximum output voltage　最大出力電圧
- [ ] output signal　出力信号（output unit は「出力装置」）
- [ ] overvoltage　過電圧（over current は「過電流」）
- [ ] threshold〔θréʃ(h)ould〕　敷居値（threshold voltage は「敷居電圧：電界効果トランジスタ等で反転層を形成するために必要な最少電圧」）
- [ ] sine wave　正弦波（rectangular wave は「矩形波」、saw-tooth wave は「のこぎり波」、oscillation [vibration] amplitude は「振幅」）
- [ ] resonance〔rézənəns〕　共振、共鳴（resonance frequency は「共振周波数」）
- [ ] resonating circuit　共振回路：周波数により回路が共振し最大電流が流れる（resonant cavity は「空洞共振器」）
- [ ] beat frequency　うなり周波数、うなり振動数
- [ ] bandwidth　周波数帯域
- [ ] harmonics　高調波：基本波の整数倍の波。音色、高調波ひずみなどを左右する（ordinary wave は「正常波」）
- [ ] connection diagram / wiring diagram　配線図
- [ ] series circuit　直列回路（series connection は「直列接続」）
- [ ] direct current circuit　直流回路：電流の向きが変わらない回路
- [ ] alternating current circuit　交流回路：時間とともに電流の向きと大きさが変化する回路
- [ ] rectifying circuit　整流回路：交流を直流に変える
- [ ] smoothing circuit　平滑回路：交流を直流に整流しても少し変動波が残っているのをさらに平滑にする回路
- [ ] oscillating circuit　振動回路、発振回路（oscillator は「発振器」）
- [ ] impedance〔impíːdns〕matching　インピーダンス整合：インピー

ダンスとは交流抵抗のことで、単位はオーム（Ω）
- [ ] amplification〔æmpləfikéiʃən〕circuit　増幅回路
- [ ] serial connection　直列接続（parallel connection は「並列接続」）
- [ ] cascade〔kæskéid〕connection　従属接続（cross connection は「交差接続」）
- [ ] amplifier　増幅器（attenuator は「減衰器」、coupler は「結合器」）
- [ ] gain　利得：増幅器の増幅度をデシベル（dB）に換算した値
- [ ] adjustable resistance　加減抵抗（variable resistance は「可変抵抗」、constant resistance は「不変抵抗」、parallel resistance は「並列抵抗」）
- [ ] in-phase　同相の：例えば２つの波形の時間的ズレを位相（phase）、ズレがないのを同相（同位相）という
- [ ] opposite phase　逆位相（phasing は「整相」）
- [ ] phase angle　位相角（phase deviation は「位相偏移」）
- [ ] retardation〔rìːtɑːdéiʃən〕遅延：波形の位相が時間的に遅れること

(4) 計測、試験　　　　　　　　　　　　　　　　CD 3-17

- [ ] downtime　休止時間、故障時間（rise time は「立ち上がり時間」）
- [ ] root-mean-square [rms] value　実効値
- [ ] feasibility〔fìːzəbíləti〕test　実現可能性試験
- [ ] maximum error　最大誤差
- [ ] measuring instrument　計測器（megger は「絶縁抵抗計」）
- [ ] galvanometer〔gælvənámətə〕検流計：微小電流検出計器
- [ ] shunt　分路：電流計等に並列に分流器（抵抗）を接続し多レンジメータとして使用
- [ ] distortion factor　ひずみ率：電流波形等のひずみ度合い
- [ ] delay distortion　遅延ひずみ

□ waveform distortion 波形ゆがみ

Motherboard（マザーボード）の構成

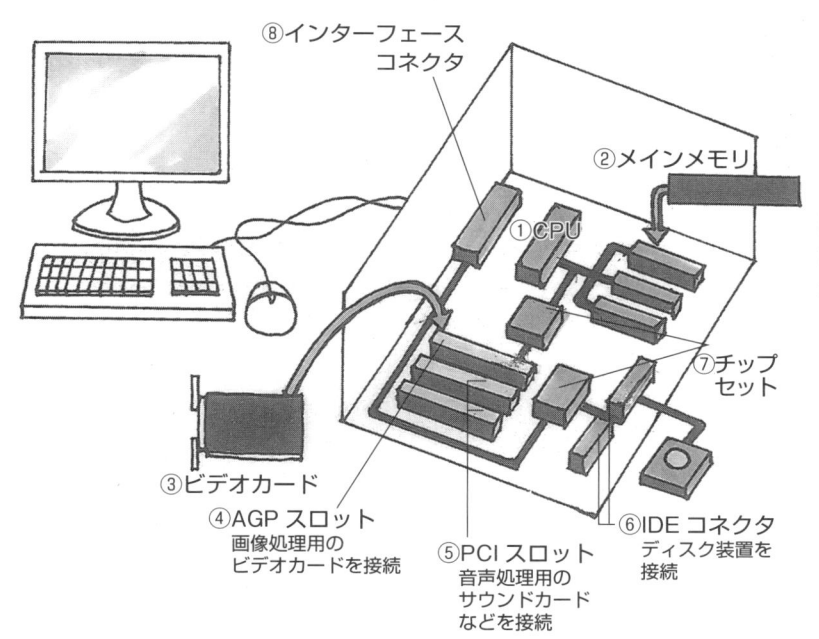

① CPU [Central Processing Unit]（中央演算処理装置）
② main memory（メインメモリ）
③ video card（ビデオカード）
④ AGP [Accelerated Graphics Port] slot（AGPスロット）
⑤ PCI [Peripheral Component Interconnect] slot（PCIスロット）
⑥ IDE [Integrated Drive Electronics] connector（IDEコネクタ）
⑦ chipset（チップセット）
⑧ interface connector（インターフェースコネクタ）

通信・コンピュータ関連語彙表現に強くなる

(1) 通信
CD 3-18

- [ ] audio frequency　可聴周波数（audio oscillatorは「可聴周波数発振器」）
- [ ] audible range　可聴範囲（audibility は「聴度」）
- [ ] hypersonic wave　極超音波（supersonic wave は「超音波」）
- [ ] high-frequency wave　高周波（low-frequency waveは「低周波」）
- [ ] microwave　極超短波：波長1m以下
- [ ] occupied band-width　占有周波数帯域幅
- [ ] cutoff frequency　遮断周波数
- [ ] acoustic efficiency　音響効率
- [ ] acoustic impedance　音響インピーダンス
- [ ] acoustics〔əkúːstiks〕音響学（acoustic wave は「音波」）
- [ ] woofer diaphragm〔dáiəfræm〕低音振動板：低音用スピーカ等の振動板
- [ ] directivity　指向性：マイクロホン等、音を拾う方向性等
- [ ] mouthpiece　送話口
- [ ] busy tone　話中の音（dial tone は「発信音」）
- [ ] switchboard　交換機、配電盤（switched line は「交換回線」）
- [ ] modulation〔màdʒəléiʃən〕変調：音声、映像など比較的低周波信号を搬送波（電波）に載せること（modulator は「変調器」）
- [ ] amplitude〔ǽmplət(j)ùːd〕modulation [AM]　振幅変調
- [ ] frequency modulation [FM]　周波数変調
- [ ] amplitude distortion　振幅ひずみ
- [ ] frequency response　周波数特性
- [ ] carrier current　搬送電流（carrier waveは「搬送波：電波等の高

周波数」)
- ☐ disturbing wave　妨害波
- ☐ longitudinal 〔làndʒətjúːdnl〕 wave　縦波 (transverse wave は「横波」)
- ☐ downlink　地上へのデータ通信
- ☐ electromagnetic wave　電磁波 (electromagnetic field は「電磁場」)
- ☐ radio wave　電波 (ultrashort wave / very high frequency は「超短波」)
- ☐ progressive wave　進行波 (plane wave は「平面波」)
- ☐ sideband wave　側帯波
- ☐ analog transmission　アナログ伝送
- ☐ multiple signal　多重信号
- ☐ aerial 〔éəriəl〕 cable　架空ケーブル
- ☐ optical fiber cable [fiber-optic cable]　光ファイバーケーブル
- ☐ fluctuation 〔flʌktʃuéiʃən〕 noise　揺らぎ雑音
- ☐ signal distortion　信号ゆがみ (static noise は「静電雑音」)
- ☐ ghost image　多重像、ゴーストイメージ
- ☐ high resolution　高レベル解像度
- ☐ high-definition television [HDTV]　高品位テレビ
- ☐ horizontal 〔hɔ̀ərəzántl〕 resolution　水平解像度 (vertical resolution は「垂直解像度」)
- ☐ scanning line　走査線
- ☐ video frequency　映像周波数
- ☐ voice recognition　音声認識
- ☐ wire broadcasting　有線放送
- ☐ cable network　有線テレビ網
- ☐ cable modem　ケーブルモデム：ケーブルテレビでインターネット

ができる装置

工業英検1級合格の秘訣

　工業英検で最も重要なのは、3C（clear、correct、concise）の原則に基づき、短時間に英文を書く能力です。「工業英検」というタイトルから連想される理系の知識は、それほど必要ではなく、それよりも優れた英文を書く能力を試す試験と言えます。工業英語では、spoken English ではなく、無生物主語を駆使した formal な written English が求められます。それらをすばやく発信するためには、百科事典の理系分野を最低10万語（「茅ヶ崎方式月刊英語教本」20冊分に相当。引き締まった英文を学ぶにはこれも有効）は音読し、体に染み込ませることが必須です。

(2) コンピュータ

CD 3-19

- [ ] general-purpose computer　汎用コンピュータ
- [ ] analog-to-digital [A/D] converter　アナログ-デジタル変換器
- [ ] boot　（コンピュータやソフトなどを）起動させる（reboot は「再起動する」）
- [ ] initialization　初期化（initialize は「初期化する」）
- [ ] forced termination　強制終了
- [ ] input and output devices　情報入出力装置
- [ ] readout　読み出し
- [ ] subroutine　サブルーチン：特定の小部分を処理するプログラム
- [ ] batch [bætʃ] processing　一括処理、バッチ処理
- [ ] processor / processing unit　処理装置
- [ ] remote processing　遠隔処理

- ☐ logical circuit　論理回路（logical operation は「論理演算」）
- ☐ transmission circuit　伝送回路（tuning circuit は「同調回路」）
- ☐ information retrieval　情報検索（data processing は「情報処理」）
- ☐ data compression　データ圧縮（decompression は「解凍」）
- ☐ extensibility　拡張性（file extension は「ファイル拡張子」）
- ☐ layered [hierarchical] structure　階層構造
- ☐ bug　バグ：プログラム中の不調
- ☐ parity〔pǽrəti〕bit　奇遇検査ビット、パリティビット：2進数字の集まりに付加する1個の2進数字
- ☐ debugging　デバッギング：誤りを探して修正すること
- ☐ diagnostic〔dàiəgnǽstik〕program　診断プログラム：ハードウェアとソフトウェアの故障を見つけるプログラム
- ☐ Computer Aided Design［CAD］　コンピュータ支援設計
- ☐ Computer-Assisted Instruction［CAI］　コンピュータ支援教育

■ ネットのクイズにチャレンジ!!

1. adware	2. BBS	3. emoticon
4. encryption	5. FAQ	6. FYI
7. flame	8. HTML	9. malware
10. key logger	11. lurk	12. meta-search engine
13. peer-to-peer	14. phishing	15. SNS
16. SMTP	17. thread	18. ticker
19. troll	20. twitter	

1. アドウェア：ソフトウェアを無料で使用できる代わりに画面に広告が表示されるソフトウェアのこと

2. **電子掲示板**：Bulletin Board Systemの略
3. **顔文字、絵文字**：メールなどで、人の顔を文字で描き、心情などを表したもの
4. **暗号、暗号化**：第三者への情報漏洩の防止のための暗号、暗号化
5. **よくある質問**：Frequently Asked Questionsの略
6. **参考までに**：For Your Informationの略
7. **フレーム、炎上**：相手を誹謗中傷することを目的にブログ、掲示板、メーリングリストに書き込む文書のこと
8. **HTML**：Hyper Text Markup Languageの略で、ウェブページを記述するために使われる言語
9. **マルウェア**：ウイルスや悪質なアドウェアなどの迷惑ソフトのこと
10. **キーロガー**：キーボード入力情報を、人に気づかれないように不正に監視、記憶し、パスワードを盗もうとするソフト
11. **ラーク、読み逃げ**：掲示板、チャットには直接参加しないで、ただ読んでいる人のこと
12. **メタ・サーチ・エンジン**：複数の検索エンジンを用いてキーワードを横断的に検索するシステム
13. **ピアツーピア**：複数のコンピュータが対等な関係でファイルを共有し合う技術
14. **フィッシング**：実在する企業を装い、偽のウェブページを使い、クレジットカードなどの暗証番号やパスワードを盗む詐欺のこと
15. **ソーシャルネットワーキングサービス**：Social Networking Serviceの略。インターネット上で構築された社会的ネットワークで、各人が自由に閲覧・書き込みができる
16. **SMTP**：Simple Mail Transfer Protocolの略。電子メールを配送するためのプロトコル
17. **スレッド**：電子掲示板やニュースグループ上の、同じ話題で連なった一連の記事

18. ティッカー：特定範囲内に文字列を流れるように表示させる表示方式
19. トロール、煽り：電子掲示板・ブログ荒らし。挑発的書き込みをし、返事を書かせようとすること
20. トゥイッター：コミュニティに登録されたユーザー同士が、「今、何をしているか」に対する回答のみ伝えるという非常にシンプルなコミュニケーションサービス

- [ ] Computer Aided Software Engineering [CASE]　コンピュータ支援ソフトウェア開発
- [ ] program optimization　プログラムの最適化
- [ ] termination　端末、終端
- [ ] logging　記録
- [ ] storage capacity　記憶容量（storage device は「記憶装置」）
- [ ] expansion memory　増設メモリ
- [ ] main memory　主記憶装置（memory capacity は「記憶容量」）
- [ ] auxiliary [ɔːgzíljəri] memory　補助記憶（auxiliary storage device は「補助記憶装置」）
- [ ] Magneto-Optical [MO]　光磁気：MO diskは繰り返し書き換えができる
- [ ] digital versatile [vˈəːsətl] disc [DVD]　光ディスク、デジタル多用途ディスク：ビデオ映像等を記録する大容量ディスク
- [ ] freeware　フリーウェア：無料で使用できるプログラム
- [ ] killer application　キラーアプリケーション：優れたソフトウェア
- [ ] vaporware　立ち切れソフトウェア：開発中のソフトや発売されずに消えてしまうソフト
- [ ] Matrix　マトリックス：コンピュータネットワークの総称

- [ ] image processing　画像処理（image analysis は「画像解析」）
- [ ] pixel〔píksl〕　画素：ディスプレイ上に画像を構成する最少単位
- [ ] split screen　画面分割
- [ ] liquid crystal display［LCD］　液晶ディスプレイ
- [ ] activation　ライセンス認証、起動
- [ ] address space　アドレス空間
- [ ] character recognition　文字認識
- [ ] digitization　数字化（digital divide は「情報格差」）
- [ ] discrete〔diskríːt〕units　別個の数
- [ ] encoder　符号器（encryption は「暗号」）
- [ ] error detection　誤り検出
- [ ] execution / run　実行
- [ ] code conversion　コード変換
- [ ] delimiter〔dilímitə〕　区切り文字
- [ ] breakpoint　区切り点：動作が途中で停止するようあらかじめ設定された区切り点
- [ ] serial number　通し番号
- [ ] ascending order　昇順（descending order は「降順」）
- [ ] latency〔léitnsi〕time　待ち時間（line speed は「伝送速度」）
- [ ] compatibility / interchangeability　互換性
- [ ] conformity　整合、適合
- [ ] scramble　暗号化、スクランブル
- [ ] sound clip　音声ファイル
- [ ] spam mail　迷惑メール
- [ ] courseware　教育用ソフトウェア
- [ ] cybernaut　インターネットをする人（cybernetics は「人工頭脳学」）
- [ ] stress test　ソフトウェア耐久度テスト（reload は「プログラムを入れ直す」）

- [ ] interactive computer shopping　双方向コンピュータ・ショッピング（interactivity は「双方向性」）
- [ ] Internaut　インターネット利用者（Internot は「ネット拒否者」）
- [ ] Internet-enabled people　インターネットに直結された人間
- [ ] intranet　企業内インターネット化
- [ ] payroll computation　給与計算
- [ ] spreadsheet application　表計算ソフト
- [ ] Structured Query Language［SQL］　構造化照会言語
- [ ] virtual image　仮想イメージ（virtual memory は「仮想記憶」）
- [ ] work station　ワークステーション：個人利用を原則とする高性能コンピュータ
- [ ] protocol〔próutəkàl〕　通信規約：異なるコンピュータ間データ通信に必要なルール

■ エレクトロニクスの略語クイズにチャレンジ！

1. ALGOL	2. ASCII	3. bps	4. COBOL
5. CAM	6. DNS	7. dpi	8. DSL
9. DTP	10. FDDI	11. FLOPS	12. FTP
13. HTTP	14. MIDI	15. MPEG	16. MSS
17. PCM	18. TCP/IP	19. URL	20. XML

■ 解　答

1. Algorithmic Language　アルゴル：科学計算向きの高水準言語
2. American Standard Code for Information Interchange　情報交換用米国標準コード：略称はASCII（アスキー）。符号、アル

ファベット、数字などを計算機へ入れるため16進数2桁（7ビット）で表したコード

3. bit per second　1秒当たりのビット数：データ転送速度の単位
4. Common Business-Oriented Language　コボル：事務処理用に開発されたプログラム
5. Computer-Aided Manufacturing　キャム：コンピュータ支援製造
6. Domain Name System　ドメイン名システム：インターネットで用いられるネーム・サービスシステム
7. dot per inch　1インチ当りのドット数：プリンタやディスプレイの解像度を表す
8. Digital Subscriber Line　デジタル加入者回線
9. Desk Top Publishing　デスクトップ・パブリッシング：コンピュータ上で出版物作成に必要な作業をすべて行うこと
10. Fiber Distributed Data Interface　光ファイバー分散データインターフェース：光ファイバーによるネットワーク
11. Floating-point Operation per Second　フロップス：コンピュータの演算速度の単位
12. File Transfer Protocol　ファイル転送プロトコル：ネットワーク上でファイルを転送するための通信規約
13. HyperText Transfer Protocol　HTTPプロトコル：HTML文書を送受信するための通信規約
14. Music Instrumental Digital Interface　ミディ：コンピュータで電子楽器を制御するための規格
15. Moving Pictures Experts Group　エムペグ：動画信号の国際標準符号化方式
16. Mass Storage System　大容量記憶システム
17. Pulse Code Modulation　パルス符号変調

18. Transmission Control Protocol / Internet Protocol：データで転送を低レベルでパケットにより処理するプロトコル
19. Uniform Resource Locator　ユーアルエル：インターネット上のファイルデータの場所表記法
20. Extensible Markup Language　拡張マークアップ言語：拡張可能なマーク付け情報表現言語

電力関連語彙表現に強くなる　　CD 3-20

- □ thermal power generation　火力発電（hydroelectric power generationは「水力発電」、nuclear power generationは「原子力発電」、wind power generationは「風力発電」、solar energy generation は「太陽光発電」、geothermal〔dʒìːouθə́ːml〕power generation は「地熱発電」）
- □ three-phase alternating current　三相交流：発電所では三相交流が発電され3本線で送電されるが、家庭には普通単相（2本線）で引き込まれる（revolving magnetic field は「回転磁界」）
- □ mean power　平均電力
- □ effective power　実効電力：実際に仕事をする電力で、単に電力と呼ばれるのはこの実効電力のこと
- □ reactive power　無効電力：回路中にコイルやコンデンサがあると仕事をしない電力が生じる
- □ stray capacity　浮遊容量：回路図にはないが実際には目に見えない静電容量が発生する
- □ dynamo / electric generator　発電機
- □ synchronizing circuit　同期回路（synchronizing signal は「同期信号」）
- □ commutator　整流子：直流モータ回転のための電流方向変換金属部

- ☐ stator　固定子：電動機等回転子に対する固定子部分
- ☐ changeover switch　切替スイッチ（cutout switch は「安全器」）
- ☐ contact breaker　断続器、電流遮断器
- ☐ control unit　制御装置（controlling circuit は「制御回路」）
- ☐ sequential〔sikwénʃəl〕control　シーケンス制御
- ☐ distributor　配電器（distribution cable は「配線ケーブル」）
- ☐ patch board　配線盤
- ☐ high-tension wire　高圧線（power voltage は「電圧」）
- ☐ high voltage　高電圧
- ☐ power transmission　送電（power distribution は「配電」）
- ☐ propagation〔pràpəgéiʃən〕loss　伝播損失
- ☐ load current　負荷電流（load factor は「負荷率」、dynamometer は「動力計」）
- ☐ transformer　変圧器（isolator は「絶縁装置、アイソレータ」）
- ☐ breaking current　遮断電流（leak breaker は「漏洩遮断器」）
- ☐ outlet / wall socket　コンセント
- ☐ blackout / power failure　停電
- ☐ screw-in type fluorescent〔fluərésnt〕lamp　電球型蛍光灯：白熱電球に似た光を出す省エネタイプの蛍光灯
- ☐ incandescent〔ìnkəndésnt〕lamp　白熱電球
- ☐ indirect lighting　間接照明
- ☐ life test　寿命試験（mean failure rate は「平均故障率」）
- ☐ rated value　定格値
- ☐ automatic voltage regulator　自動電圧調整器：出力電圧を常に一定に保つ装置（regulated power supply は「安定化電源」）
- ☐ regulation　整流、調整（regulator は「調節器、制御装置」）
- ☐ actuating〔ǽktʃuèitiŋ〕signal　動作信号
- ☐ release current　復旧電流（release equipment は「復旧装置」）

- [ ] actuator　作動装置：機械的動作を起こさせるための起動装置
- [ ] lightning rod　避雷針（earthing terminal は「接地端子」）
- [ ] internal safety valve　内部安全弁

■ 電気復習テスト（問題）

1	印加電圧	11	浮遊容量
2	実現可能性試験	12	増幅器
3	強磁性体	13	周波数帯域
4	検流計	14	集積回路
5	間接照明	15	最大出力電圧
6	計測器	16	アナログ伝送
7	コンセント	17	補助記憶装置
8	定格値	18	周波数変調
9	ブラウン管	19	水平解像度
10	実効値	20	静電雑音

■ 電気復習テスト（解答）

1	applied voltage	11	stray capacity
2	feasibility test	12	amplifier
3	ferromagnetic material	13	bandwidth
4	galvanometer	14	integrated circuit
5	indirect lighting	15	maximum output voltage
6	measuring instrument	16	analog transmission
7	outlet	17	auxiliary storage device
8	rated value	18	frequency modulation
9	cathode-ray tube	19	horizontal resolution
10	root-mean-square value	20	static noise

V　分野別語彙カパワーUP理系語彙

5-3 第26日
機械語彙に強くなる

　機械は物理原理を応用して作られているので、まずそれらを5項目に分けた機械一般用語を覚え、それから具体的な機械装置・部品に関する語彙補強を行います。ここでは工業英検合格に必須の工業製品語彙を中心にまとめましたので、しっかりボキャブラリーパワーUPに励みましょう。

機械一般用語関連語彙表現に強くなる　　CD 3-21

(1) 寸法、形状、力
- [ ] metrology〔mitrálədʒi〕 度量衡（学）
- [ ] minimum clearance　最小隙間（miniaturization は「小型化」）
- [ ] caliper〔kǽləpə〕 測径器：キャリパーやノギスなど
- [ ] thickness gauge〔géidʒ〕 厚み測定器
- [ ] tilt angle　傾斜角
- [ ] full scale　原寸、最大目盛（graduation は「等級、目盛り」）
- [ ] dimensional change　寸法変化（displacement は「変位」）
- [ ] effective area　実効面積（effective value は「実効値」）
- [ ] force per unit area　単位面積当たりの力

- □ cross section　断面（curvature は「曲率」）
- □ finished surface　仕上げ面（finishing temperature は「仕上げ温度」）
- □ supporting surface　支持面
- □ gravimetric analysis　重量分析（gravimeter〔grəvímitə〕は「重量計、重力計、比重計」）
- □ gross weight　総重量（net weight は「正味重量」）
- □ geometric distortion　形状ひずみ
- □ skewness〔skjúːnəs〕　ひずみ、ゆがみ、ひずみ度
- □ overshoot　行きすぎ量、オーバーシュート
- □ torsion〔tɔ́ːʃən〕　ねじり（torsional strength は「ねじれ強さ」）
- □ strain　ひずみ（strain gauge〔gage〈米〉〕は「ひずみ計」）
- □ inflection〔inflékʃən〕　屈曲
- □ breakdown test　破壊試験（endurance test は「耐久試験」）
- □ yield point load　降伏点荷重：物体に力を加えた時に元に戻れる限界点
- □ fatigue〔fətíːg〕failure　疲労破壊（fatigue life は「疲労寿命」）
- □ fracture　破断（shearing stress は「せん断応力」、fragmentation は「断片化」）
- □ cleavage〔klíːvidʒ〕　裂け目、開裂（化）（clogging は「詰まり、閉塞」）
- □ sliding contact　すべり接触
- □ slippage〔slípidʒ〕　滑り、ズレの量：理論と実際出力の差
- □ abrasion〔əbréiʒən〕　摩滅
- □ wear　磨耗、摩滅
- □ friction coefficient　摩擦係数：摩擦力とその物体に作用する重力との比
- □ static friction　静摩擦：物体が滑り出す直前の摩擦力（dynamic

friction は「動摩擦」)
- [ ] section line 断面線
- [ ] maximum torque〔tɔ́:k〕 最大トルク:物体を回転させる力の最大値
- [ ] manometer〔mənámətə〕/ pressure gauge 圧力計
- [ ] rigid body 剛体 (rigidity は「剛性」)
- [ ] hardness meter 硬度計 (hardness test は「硬さ試験」)
- [ ] plastic deformation〔dì:fɔ:méiʃən〕 塑性変形、永久変形
- [ ] elastic deformation 弾性変形 (elastic body は「弾性体」)
- [ ] elasticity 弾性 (elasto-plastic body は「弾塑性体」)
- [ ] ductility〔dʌktíləti〕 延性:弾性限界を超えて破壊されずに引き伸ばされる性質 (malleability〔mæliəbíləti〕は「可鍛性」、viscosity は「粘性、粘度」)
- [ ] duration 持続期間
- [ ] interrupted control 割り込み制御
- [ ] propulsion〔prəpʌ́lʃən〕 推進
- [ ] regeneration 再生 (reinforcement は「強化」)
- [ ] register 記録器 (registration は「書き留め、登録」)
- [ ] degeneration 縮退、退化
- [ ] schedule drawing 工程図 (schematic diagram は「概略図」)
- [ ] drawing 図面 (front view は「正面図」、side view は「側面図」、top view は「上面図、平面図」)
- [ ] constitutional diagram 状態図
- [ ] unit operation 単位操作
- [ ] consecutive operation (間を置かずに一定順序の) 連続動作
- [ ] omnidirectional 全方向性の (directional は「指向性の」)
- [ ] metastable〔mètəstéibl〕 準安定の
- [ ] accelerometer〔æksèlərámətə〕 加速度計

- [ ] creep　クリープ：一定の圧力や熱が物体を変形させること

(2) 振動、回転、速度
CD 3-22

- [ ] vibrometer〔vaibrəmətə〕　振動計
- [ ] waveguide　導波管、導波路
- [ ] reverse direction　反対方向（reversal は「反転」）
- [ ] clockwise rotation　時計方向回転（counterclockwiseは「反時計方向」）
- [ ] revolutions per minute [r.p.m.]　毎分回転数
- [ ] rotation　自転（revolution は「回転」、rotator は「回転体」）
- [ ] swing　旋回、振り
- [ ] speedometer　速度計
- [ ] accelerating curve　加速度曲線（accelerating deviceは「加速装置」）

(3) 流体
CD 3-23

- [ ] degassing　ガス抜き、化成
- [ ] vaporization〔vèipərəzéiʃən〕　気化、蒸発（vapor pressure は「蒸気圧」）
- [ ] stimulated emission　誘導放出（emission standards は「排出基準、排ガス」）
- [ ] circulated water cooling　循環水冷式
- [ ] dehydration　脱水（desorption は「脱着、脱離」）
- [ ] gasket　詰め物、ガスケット、パッキング：流体の漏れを防ぐための詰め物
- [ ] erosion〔iróuʒən〕　侵食
- [ ] degree of dispersion　分離度（degree of dissociation は「解離度」）

(4) 熱

- calorific capacity　熱容量
- defrosting cycle　霜取りサイクル
- emissivity　放射率（irradiation は「照射」）
- manual welding　手溶接（welding sequence は「溶接順序」）
- combustible〔kəmbʌ́stəbl〕可燃性の（incomplete combustion は「不完全燃焼」）

(5) 光

- exposure〔ikspóuʒɚ〕露光：写真での露出（opaque body は「不透明体」）
- photometer　光度計（photometric field は「測光視野」）
- radiograph　レントゲン写真（radiography は「X線写真法」）
- xerography〔ziərɑ́grəfi〕乾式複写、ゼログラフィー：静電写真法
- kaleidoscope〔kəláidəskòup〕万華鏡（periscope は「潜望鏡」）
- laser beam printer　レーザープリンタ
- laser scanning　レーザースキャン：バーコード読み取り

■ 力を表す力学用語にチャレンジ！

---

1. 浮力　　2. 回転力　　3. 遠心力　　4. 合力
5. 応力　　6. 張力　　　7. 反発力　　8. 耐久力
9. 起動力　10. 求心［向心］力

■ 解　答

1. buoyancy　「浮力」は、流体内にある物体の表面に働く流体の圧

力差によって、物体が重力に反して鉛直上方に押し上げられる力
2. torque 「回転力、トルク」は、物体を回転させる能力の大きさ
3. centrifugal force 「遠心力」は、回転運動をしている座標系において観測される慣性力
4. resultant force 「合力」は、同時に働く2つ以上の力を合成した力
5. stress 「応力」は、物体が荷重を受けた時、荷重に応じて物体の内部に生ずる抵抗力
6. tension 「張力」は、断面に垂直に働き、互いに引き合うような応力。ちなみに、tensile strength [force] は「引張力」
7. repulsive force 「反発力」は、加わった力に反発する力
8. durability 「耐久力」は、長く持ちこたえる力
9. impetus 「起動力」は、抵抗に逆らって動く物体の運動力
10. centripetal force 「求心[向心]力」は、円運動する物体が円の中心に向かって物体に働く力

機械装置関連語彙表現に強くなる

(1) 動力伝達装置

CD 3-26

□ axle〔ǽksl〕車軸 (ball-and-roller bearing は「転がり軸受け」)
□ shaft 軸 (shaft horsepower は「軸馬力」、feed shaft は「送り軸」)
□ bearing 軸受け (bearing stand は「軸受け台」)
□ bevel gear かさ歯車 (beveling は「面取り」)
□ cam gear カム歯車 (pinion は「小歯車」、worm gear は「ウォームギア」)
□ connecting rod 連結棒 (crankshaft は「クランク軸」)
□ pulley〔púli〕滑車
□ damper 緩衝器、制動子、調整弁 (damper unit は「緩衝装置」)

- [ ] front-wheel-drive　前輪駆動
- [ ] starting cam　始動カム（swivel bearing は「自在軸受け」）
- [ ] transmission　変速機（transmission gear は「伝動装置：gear は単独で「歯車」、複合語で「装置」）
- [ ] two-speed gear　2段変速装置
- [ ] automatic transmission　自動変速装置
- [ ] reduction gear　減速装置
- [ ] universal coupling [joint]　自在継手

Worm Gear（ウォームギア）

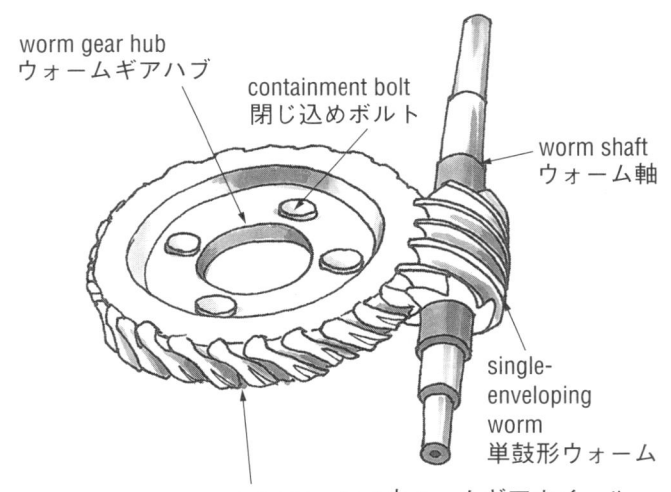

worm gear hub　ウォームギアハブ
containment bolt　閉じ込めボルト
worm shaft　ウォーム軸
single-enveloping worm　単鼓形ウォーム
worm gear wheel　ウォームギアホイール

(2) 振動、回転、速度　　　　　　　　　CD 3-27
- ultrasonic welding　超音波溶接
- current meter　流速計
- tachometer〔tækámətə〕　回転速度計、タコメータ

(3) 流体装置　　　　　　　　　　　　　CD 3-28
- suction〔sʌ́kʃən〕　吸引（suction pipe は「吸込管」）
- airflow meter　風量計（anemometer は「風速計」、barometer は「気圧計」）
- altimeter〔æltímətə〕　高度計
- carburetor〔kà:bjəréta〕　気化器（check valve は「逆止め弁」）
- pneumatic〔n(j)u(:)mǽtik〕tire　空気タイヤ
- hydraulic〔haidrɔ́:lik〕　水圧［油圧］式の
- oil diffusion〔difjú:ʒən〕pump　油拡散ポンプ
- throttle nozzle　絞りノズル
- reciprocating〔risíprəkèitiŋ〕pump　往復ポンプ
- compressor　圧縮機（instantaneous compressor は「瞬時圧縮機」）
- bellows〔bélouz〕　じゃばら、ふいご、ベロー
- air duct　通風ダクト
- ventilator〔véntəlèitə〕　換気装置
- feed pipe　給水管
- discharge regulator　流量調整装置
- centrifugal〔sentrífjəgl〕separator　遠心分離機（centrifugal dehydrator〔di:háidreitə〕は「遠心脱水機」）

> **ミシガン検定1級合格の秘訣**
>
> 　ミシガン工業英検で最も重要なのは、情報を文書全体、およびパラグラフ内でgeneral to specificに述べていくことです。これはtechnical writing の基本中の基本で、絶対にこの原則にのっとって英文を書かなければなりません。ゆえに、ミシガン英検1級の3つの構成要素、すなわち、英文和訳summary、英文editing、compositionは、その能力を厳密にテストしており、どの分野も最低6割以上を取らないと合格しません。また、audienceが混乱するような余計な情報は書かずに、最も重要な情報だけを選択して書くという、ビジネスの世界では必須の能力が必要です。これらの能力に欠けていると思う人は、添削指導を受けて、集中トレーニングをしておきましょう。

(4) 熱器具、装置　　　　　　　　　　　　CD 3-29

- tempering furnace〔fə́:nəs〕 焼き戻し炉：焼き戻しとは、焼き入れの温度より低い温度に熱し、冷却し粘り強くさせること
- thermostatic chamber〔tʃéimbə〕 恒温室
- cryogenic〔kràiədʒénik〕system　極低温装置 (detonator は「起爆装置」)
- soldering〔sádəiŋ〕iron　はんだごて（soldered joint は「はんだ接続」)
- ignition〔igníʃən〕coil　点火コイル　(incendiary deviceは「発火装置」)
- internal combustion〔kəmbʌ́stʃən〕engine　内燃機関
- extinguisher〔ikstíŋwiʃə〕 消火器 (incinerator は「焼却炉」)

(5) 工具、加工、工作、製造、建設機械　　CD 3-30

- [ ] wedge　くさび
- [ ] chisel 〔tʃízl〕　のみ（circular saw は「丸のこ」）
- [ ] emery 〔éməri〕 paper　紙やすり（square file は「角やすり」）
- [ ] tool angle　刃先（double armed lever は「二重てこ」）
- [ ] planing　平削り（pliers は「ペンチ」）
- [ ] tightening　締め付け（unscrew は「ネジを外す」）
- [ ] fitting　取り付け（flange は「つば、縁、フランジ」）
- [ ] sintering　焼結（smelting は「製錬」：鉱石などから金属を抽出精製すること）
- [ ] anneal 〔əníːl〕　焼きなます（hardening は「硬化、焼き入れ」）
- [ ] quenching 〔kwéntʃiŋ〕 / hardening　焼き入れ
- [ ] unglazed 〔ʌngléizd〕　素焼の
- [ ] rubbing　磨くこと、こすること（grinder は「研磨機」）
- [ ] lapping　研磨（luster は「光沢」）
- [ ] metal stamping　金属加工（metallurgy 〔métəlèːrdʒi〕は「冶金(やきん)」）
- [ ] working property　加工性
- [ ] press working / pressing　プレス加工（reaming は「リーマ加工」）
- [ ] rolling　圧延加工(あつえん)：ローラーで引き伸ばし材質を均質化すること
- [ ] vertical 〔vɚ́ːtəkl〕 press　縦プレス（viceは「万力(まんりき)、バイス」）
- [ ] shaping machine　形削り盤
- [ ] milling　フライス加工（milling machine は「フライス盤」）
- [ ] spine milling machine　溝切りフライス盤
- [ ] lathe 〔léið〕　旋盤（latch locking は「ラッチ旋錠」、automatic lathe は「自動旋盤」）
- [ ] numerical control [NC] machine　数値制御工作機械
- [ ] drilling machine　ボール盤

- [ ] ditching machine　掘削機（backhoe〔bǽkhòu〕も「掘削機」）
- [ ] grader　地ならし機（grooved rail は「みぞ型レール」）
- [ ] precision instrument　精密機械（precision lathe は「精密旋盤」）
- [ ] molding [machine]　成型（機）(mold は「金型」)
- [ ] gyrate〔dʒáiərèit〕　旋回する、らせん状の
- [ ] gyroscope〔dʒáiərəskòup〕　回転儀、ジャイロスコープ
- [ ] safeguard　安全装置（safety valve は「安全弁」）
- [ ] ratch　歯止め装置（ratchet〔rǽtʃit〕は「つめ車、ラチェット」）
- [ ] scaffold〔skǽfld〕　足場（selector は「選別機」）
- [ ] glitch　機械の不調［故障］
- [ ] idle time　遊休時間、遊び時間（idling は「無負荷運転」）
- [ ] maintenance engineer　整備エンジニア（maintainability は「保全度」）

(6) 部品、材料

CD 3-31

- [ ] laminated〔lǽmənèitid〕spring　重ね板ばね（laminated core は「成層鉄心」）
- [ ] spiral spring　うず巻きばね
- [ ] split bearing　割り軸受け（spur gear は「平歯車」）
- [ ] triangular thread　三角ねじ
- [ ] foundation bolt　基礎ボルト（front bearing は「前軸受け」）
- [ ] alloy〔ǽlɔi〕　合金（amorphous〔əmɔ́ːfəs〕substance は「非結晶性物質」）
- [ ] cast iron　鋳鉄（ちゅうてつ）：2％以上炭素を含む鉄合金（casting は「鋳造」）
- [ ] forged steel　鍛鋼（たんこう）（forging press は「鍛造プレス」）
- [ ] nonferrous〔nànférəs〕metal　非鉄金属
- [ ] iridium〔irídiəm〕　イリジウム（titanium〔taitéiniəm〕は「チタン」）
- [ ] precious metals　貴金属

- [ ] quartz〔kwɔ́:ts〕 石英（mica〔máikə〕は「雲母」、feldspar〔féldspɑ̀ə〕は「長石」）
- [ ] baking enamel　焼き付けエナメル
- [ ] protective coating　保護被膜
- [ ] rust prevention　さび止め
- [ ] explosives　火薬（heat insulator は「断熱材」）
- [ ] fuse wire　導火線
- [ ] plasticine〔plǽstəsì:n〕 工作用粘土（plasticity は「塑性」）
- [ ] refrigerant〔rifrídʒərənt〕 冷却材（refrigeration は「冷却、冷蔵」）
- [ ] lagging material　保温材
- [ ] substrate〔sʌ́bstreit〕 基材、基板（substratum〔sʌ́bstrèitəm〕は「基層」）
- [ ] mortar〔mɔ́:tə〕 モルタル、臼（ferroconcrete〔fèroukánkri:t〕は「鉄筋コンクリート」）
- [ ] receptacle〔riséptəkl〕 容器、（電気の）コンセント
- [ ] separator　隔離板、隔離符号

■ 機械語彙復習テストにチャレンジ！

1	測径器	11	弾性変形
2	疲労破壊	12	はんだごて
3	鍛鋼	13	回転儀
4	摩擦係数	14	内燃機関
5	毎分回転数	15	基礎ボルト
6	総重量	16	保護被膜
7	延性	17	旋盤
8	滑車	18	非鉄金属
9	自転	19	気化器
10	曲率	20	冷却材

■ 機械語彙復習テスト（解答）

1	caliper	11	elastic deformation
2	fatigue failure	12	soldering iron
3	forged steel	13	gyroscope
4	friction coefficient	14	internal combustion engine
5	revolutions per minute	15	foundation bolt
6	gross weight	16	protective coating
7	ductility	17	lathe
8	pulley	18	nonferrous metal
9	rotation	19	carburetor
10	curvature	20	refrigerant

5-4　第27日
化学語彙に強くなる

　世の中のすべての物質は100余りの異なる元素から成り立っており、化学元素は我々の生活に密接につながっています。自然環境・日常生活に用いられる食品や家電製品、スポーツを含む人体の働き、エネルギー資源等のあらゆる多岐の項目に及ぶ、非常に重要な分野です。

　当セクションでは、3つの分野、「化学一般」、「化合物」、「その他」に分けたものを覚えていただきましょう。

化学一般語彙に強くなる　　　　　　　　　　　CD 3-32

☐ adhesive〔ədhíːsiv〕 接着剤（adhesive agent は「粘着剤」）
☐ anticorrosive〔æntikəróusiv〕 さび止め剤（antifreezeは「不凍液」）
☐ antiseptic〔æntiséptik〕 防腐剤（deodorant は「脱臭剤」）
☐ aromatics〔ærəumǽtiks〕 芳香族物質：ベンゼン環を含む有機化合物
☐ carbohydrate 炭水化物（hydrocarbon は「炭化水素」）
☐ carbon compound 炭素化合物（carbonization は「炭化」）
☐ catalyst〔kǽtəlist〕action 触媒作用：化学反応速度を速める
☐ chemical fertilizer 化学肥料（chemical herbicide は「化学除

草剤」)
- [ ] chloride　塩化物（fluorideは「フッ化物」）
- [ ] coolant　冷却剤（antifreezeは「不凍液」）
- [ ] desiccant〔désikənt〕乾燥剤（detergentは「中性洗剤」）
- [ ] emulsion〔imʌ́lʃən〕乳剤（fusing agentは「融剤」）
- [ ] halogen〔hǽlədʒən〕ハロゲン（halide〔hǽlaid〕/ halogenated〔hǽlədʒenèitid〕compoundは「ハロゲン化合物」）
- [ ] high molecular compound　高分子化合物
- [ ] impurity　不純物（inert gasは「不活性ガス」）
- [ ] isotope〔áisətòup〕同位元素、アイソトープ（radioisotopeは「放射性同位元素」）
- [ ] nitric〔náitrik〕acid　硝酸（nitrateは「硝酸塩」、nitrideは「窒化物」）
- [ ] nitrogen oxide　窒素酸化物（peroxideは「過酸化物」）
- [ ] noble gas　希ガス（elemental gasは「元素ガス」）
- [ ] noncarbohydrate　非炭水化物
- [ ] nutrient　栄養物（nutrimentは「養分」）
- [ ] pesticide [agricultural chemical]　農薬（germicide〔dʒéːməsàid〕は「殺菌剤」）
- [ ] petrochemical　石油化学製品
- [ ] phosphate〔fásfeit〕リン酸塩（phosphate oilは「リン酸エステル油」）
- [ ] powdered material　粉末剤（preservativeは「防腐剤」）
- [ ] propellant〔prəpélənt〕促進剤（reducing agentは「還元剤」）
- [ ] reagent〔ri(ː)éidʒənt〕試薬
- [ ] solvent〔sálvənt〕溶剤：水やアルコールなど物質を溶かすのに用いる液体（solvabilityは「可溶性」）

化合物に関する語彙に強くなる

1. 無機化合物
CD 3-33

- calcium carbonate　炭酸カルシウム
- acid corrosion　酸腐食（acid phosphateは「酸性リン酸エステル」）
- active carbon / activated carbon　活性炭
- agate〔ǽgət〕めのう（garnetは「ざくろ石」、turquoise〔tə́ːkɔiz〕は「トルコ石」）
- heavy water　重水
- hydrogen sulfide〔sʌ́lfaid〕硫化水素（hydrogen chlorideは「塩化水素」）
- potassium〔pətǽsiəm〕カリウム（potassium nitrateは「硝酸カリウム」）
- siliceous〔səlíʃəs〕珪土質の：珪土は土状の無水珪酸でガラス成分（silica gel〔sílikə | dʒél〕は「シリカゲル」）
- slaked lime　消石灰
- sodium chloride〔sóudiəm | klɔ́ːraid〕塩化ナトリウム（sodium nitrateは「硝酸ナトリウム」）
- sulfuric〔sʌlfjúərik〕acid　硫酸（sulfurous〔sʌ́lfərəs〕acid gasは「亜硫酸ガス」）

2. 有機化合物
CD 3-34

- acetic〔əsíːtik〕acid　酢酸（lactic acidは「乳酸」）
- acetylene〔əsétlìːn〕gas　アセチレンガス：酸素と混ぜて鉄の切断や溶接に利用
- acrylic resin〔əkríːlək | rézin〕アクリル樹脂
- benzene〔bénziːn〕ベンゼン：無色の揮発性液体

- □ chitin〔káitin〕 **キチン質**：エビ・カニなどの殻の成分
- □ ether〔íːθɚ〕 **エーテル**：一般に中性で芳香のある液体（ether alcohol は「エーテル・アルコール」）
- □ ethyl〔éθl〕 alcohol **エチルアルコール**
- □ methanol〔méθənɔ̀(ː)l〕[methyl〔méθl〕] alcohol **メチルアルコール**
- □ ethylene〔éθəlìːn〕 **エチレン**：無色可燃性の気体（ethylene chloride は「塩化エチレン」）
- □ glycerin〔glísərin〕 **グリセリン**：代表的な３価のアルコール
- □ methane〔méθein〕gas **メタンガス**（propane gas は「プロパンガス」）
- □ methane hydrate **メタンハイドレイト**：深海の高圧環境で水と結合してシャーベット状になったメタン
- □ naphthalene〔næfθəliːn〕 **ナフタリン**：合成化学工業上の重要な原料（nylon resin は「ナイロン樹脂」）
- □ paraffin **パラフィン**：ロウソクや軟膏の原料
- □ polyethylene〔pàliéθəlìːn〕 **ポリエチレン**（polystyrene は「ポリスチレン」）
- □ synthetic fibers **合成繊維**（synthetic resin は「合成樹脂」）
- □ urea resin〔juəríːə | rézin〕 **尿素樹脂**：合成樹脂の１つ
- □ vinyl chloride **塩化ビニール**（vinyl resinは「ビニール樹脂」）
- □ xylene〔záiliːn〕 **キシレン**：芳香族炭化水素の１つ

Amino acid – Chemical Structural Formula
アミノ酸－化学構造式

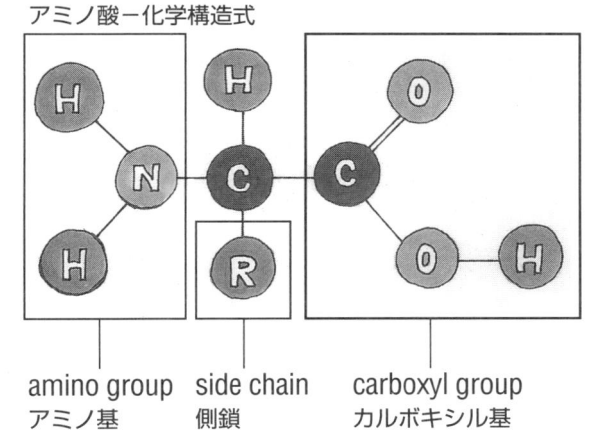

- amino group　アミノ基
- side chain　側鎖
- carboxyl group　カルボキシル基

その他の語彙に強くなる　　　CD 3-35

- ☐ aerification〔èərəfikéiʃən〕気化（carburetion、vaporization、volatilization は「液体から気体への変化」）
- ☐ alkaline〔ǽlkəlàin〕battery　アルカリ電池
- ☐ antistatic agent　帯電防止剤
- ☐ aqueous〔éikwiəs〕phase　水相（arsenic は「ヒ素」）
- ☐ bleach　漂白する
- ☐ bonding agent　接着剤、結合剤
- ☐ brine〔bráin〕食塩水（diluted acid は「希塩酸」）
- ☐ bromine〔bróumi:n〕臭素（iodine は「ヨウ素」）
- ☐ carbon nanotube　カーボンナノチューブ：ナノテクの新材料として注目されている
- ☐ cation〔kǽtàiən〕陽イオン（anion〔ǽnàiən〕は「陰イオン」）
- ☐ chemical bonding　化学結合（chemical compound は「化合物」）

- ☐ chemical formula 化学式 (chemical equation は「化学反応式」)
- ☐ coagulation〔kouǽgjəléiʃən〕[congealing / freezing] point 凝固点 (coagulant は「凝固剤」)
- ☐ cohesion〔kouhíːʒən〕 粘着、結合、凝集
- ☐ colloidal〔kalɔ́idl〕solution コロイド溶液：コロイド粒子が液体中に分散したもの
- ☐ covalent〔kouvéilənt〕bond 共有結合 (electrovalentは「イオン結合性」)
- ☐ ionic〔aiánik〕bond イオン結合 (ionic compoundは「イオン化合物」)
- ☐ Mixed oxide fuel [MOX] MOX燃料：酸化プルトニウムと酸化ウランの混合燃料で、プルサーマル燃料に使われる
- ☐ peptide〔péptaid〕bond ペプチド結合：アミノ酸間の結合
- ☐ crude oil 原油 (light oil は「軽油」、coal tar は「コールタール」)
- ☐ activation 活性化：触媒や酵素などを加えて機能を増大させるエネルギー
- ☐ decomposition 分解 (chemical combination は「化合」)
- ☐ density 濃度、密度 (densitometer〔dènsitámətə〕は「濃度計」)
- ☐ reduction / deoxidation〔diːɑksidéiʃən〕 還元
- ☐ deposition〔dèpəzítʃən〕 析出(せきしゅつ)：溶液から固体が現れること / 沈着
- ☐ disinfection 殺菌
- ☐ dissolution 溶解 (solution は「溶液」)
- ☐ distillation〔dìstəléiʃən〕 蒸留
- ☐ dry battery [cell] 乾電池 (floating battery は「浮動蓄電池」)
- ☐ electrochemistry 電気化学 (electrophoresis〔ilèktroufəríːsəs〕は「電気泳動」)
- ☐ epoxy〔epáksi〕resin エポキシ樹脂

- □ equilibrium〔ìːkwəlíbriəm〕 平衡（equilibrium composition は「平衡組成」）
- □ evaporation 蒸発（boiling point は「沸点」、endothermic〔èndou θə́ːmik〕は「吸熱反応の」、exothermicは「発熱反応」）
- □ extract〔ekstrǽkt〕 抽出物（extraction は「抽出」）
- □ fermentation〔fə̀ːmentéiʃən〕 発酵（fermentation time は「発酵時間」）
- □ filtration 濾過（filter paper は「濾紙」）
- □ flash [ignition] point 引火点（freezing point は「凝固点、凍結点」）
- □ fuel cell 燃料電池（fuel gauge は「燃料計」）
- □ fusibility〔fjùːzbíləti〕 可溶性
- □ gold plating 金めっき
- □ hydrolysis〔haidrásis〕 加水分解：水が作用して起こる分解反応
- □ hydrophilic 親水性の（hydrophobic は「疎水性の」）
- □ immersion 液浸：光学系で液体を使用する高性能化手段
- □ impermeable〔impə́ːmiəbl〕 不浸透性の（impervious は「通さない」）
- □ inorganic chemistry 無機化学（inorganic matter は「無機物」）
- □ issuing gas 発生ガス
- □ liquefied natural gas 液化天然ガス
- □ lithium〔líθiəm〕 リチウム（manganese は「マンガン」）
- □ lubricant〔lúːbrikənt〕 潤滑油 [剤]（lubricating property は「潤滑性」）
- □ mass spectrograph 質量分析器
- □ melting [fusing] point 融点
- □ mercury column 水銀柱
- □ microbiological [chemical] assays〔ǽseiz〕 微生物学的 [化学

的〕分析方法
- [ ] molecule　分子（molecular weight は「分子量」）
- [ ] monomer〔mάnəmə〕　単量体
- [ ] neutralization〔n(j)ù:trəlɘzéiʃən〕　中和
- [ ] normal solution　規定液（water solution / aqueous solution は「水溶液」）
- [ ] octane〔άktein〕number / octane rating　オクタン価：ガソリンのアンチノック性を表す指数
- [ ] organic chemistry　有機化学（organic matter は「有機物」）
- [ ] osmosis〔ɑzmóusəs〕　浸透（osmotic pressure は「浸透圧」）
- [ ] oxide　酸化物（oxidation は「酸化」）
- [ ] passivation layer　不活性化層
- [ ] periodic law　周期律（periodic table は「周期律表」）
- [ ] petroleum refinery　製油所（petroleum は「石油」、kerosene は「灯油」）
- [ ] polymer chemistry　高分子化学（polymerization は「重合」）
- [ ] precipitant　沈殿剤（precipitation は「沈殿」）
- [ ] pure matter　純粋物質（mixture は「混合物」）
- [ ] quantitative analysis　定量分析 ⇔ 定性分析 qualitative analysis
- [ ] reaction mixture　反応混合物（reaction accelerator は「反応促進剤」）
- [ ] recrystallization　再結晶
- [ ] refining　精製：方法には filtration / percolation〔pəˋ:kəléiʃən〕（ろ過）がある
- [ ] reforming reaction　改質反応（reversible reaction は「可逆反応」）
- [ ] saccharine〔sǽkərin〕　糖質の
- [ ] saturation point　飽和点（saturation curve は「飽和曲線」）

- [ ] softening temperature　軟化温度
- [ ] solidification　凝固（solidifying point は「凝固点」）
- [ ] solubility　溶解度
- [ ] suspended solid　浮遊固形物
- [ ] tap water　水道水（water vapor は「水蒸気」）
- [ ] thermal [heat] decomposition〔dìːkɑmpəzíʃən〕/ pyrolysis〔pairάləsis〕　熱分解
- [ ] thermoplastic material　熱可塑性樹脂
- [ ] thermosetting property　熱硬化性
- [ ] turbidity〔təːbídəti〕　濁度：水の濁りの程度を示す
- [ ] product　生成物質（reactant / reacting substance は「反応物質」）

■ 化学語彙復習テストにチャレンジ！

1	アルカリ電池	11	親水性の
2	触媒作用	12	リチウム
3	漂白する	13	メタンハイドレイト
4	炭水化物	14	単量体
5	キチン質	15	硝酸
6	コロイド溶液	16	加水分解
7	脱臭剤	17	糖質の
8	電気泳動	18	さび止め剤
9	乳剤	19	浮遊固形物
10	燃料電池	20	抽出物

■ 化学語彙復習テスト（解答）

1	alkaline battery	11	hydrophilic
2	catalyst action	12	lithium
3	bleach	13	methane hydrate
4	carbohydrate	14	monomer
5	chitin	15	nitric acid
6	colloidal solution	16	hydrolysis
7	deodorant	17	saccharine
8	electrophoresis	18	anticorrosive
9	emulsion	19	suspended solid
10	fuel cell	20	extract

5-5　第28日
数学語彙に強くなる

　数学の知識は自然科学だけでなく、経済学・社会学などの社会科学の研究においても重要で、特に米国では大学・大学院入試で不可欠です。そこでこのセクションも真剣に勉強しましょう。

CD 3-36

- [ ] algebraic〔ældʒəbréiik〕equation　代数方程式
- [ ] approximate value　近似値（characteristic value は「固有値」）
- [ ] arithmetic〔əríθmətìk〕operation　算術演算
- [ ] axis of coordinates　座標軸（axis of ordinates は「縦座標軸」）
- [ ] bar chart　棒グラフ（block diagram は「構成図」、histogram は「ヒストグラム」：度数分布図）
- [ ] binary〔báinəri〕system　2進法（binary code は「2進符号」）
- [ ] binominal〔bainάumənl〕distribution　二項分布：例えばコインを5回投げた時に表が出る確率の分布（bisection は「2等分」）
- [ ] cardinal〔kάːdinl〕number　基数
- [ ] circumference〔səkʌ́mfərəns〕円周
- [ ] complex number　複素数：実数＋虚数で表される数（imaginary number は「虚数」）
- [ ] composed function　合成関数

- ☐ correlation analysis　相関分析
- ☐ cubic centimeter　立方センチメートル
- ☐ decimal〔désml〕point　小数点（decimal fractionは「小数」、decimal systemは「10進法」）
- ☐ determinant　行列式（differential equationは「微分方程式」、matrixは「行列」：ベクトルに作用して別のベクトルに変換する作用素）
- ☐ diagonal〔daiǽgənl〕line　対角線（dotted lineは「点線」）
- ☐ variance〔véəriəns〕　分散、ばらつき（error varianceは「誤差分散」）
- ☐ divisor　除数（fractionは「分数、小部分」）
- ☐ inequality　不等式
- ☐ even number　偶数（odd numberは「奇数」）
- ☐ exponential〔èkspounénʃəl〕function　指数関数
- ☐ factorial　階乗（least squareは「最小二乗」）
- ☐ fundamental unit　基本単位
- ☐ horizontal axis　水平軸（perpendicularは「垂直の」）
- ☐ hyperbola〔haipə́:bələ〕/ hyperbolic curve　双曲線（parabola〔pərǽbələ〕は「放物線」）
- ☐ inclination　傾斜、傾角、伏角（inclined planeは「斜面」、hypotenuse〔haipátən(j)ù:s〕は「弦、斜辺」）
- ☐ integer〔íntidʒə〕　整数（irrational numberは「無理数」）

図形表現

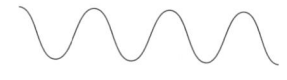

corrugate（波形）

jagged 〔dʒǽgid〕（尖った、突出した）

serrated / zigzag（ギザギザ）

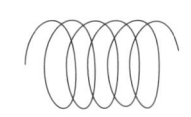

spiral（コイル、らせん）

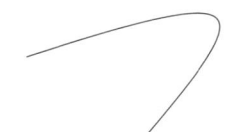

streamline（流線形）

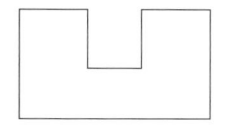

concave（凹形）

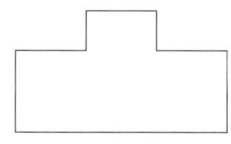

convex（凸形）

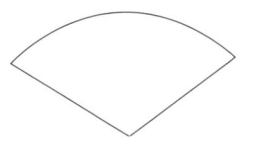

sector / fan-shaped（扇形）

平面図形

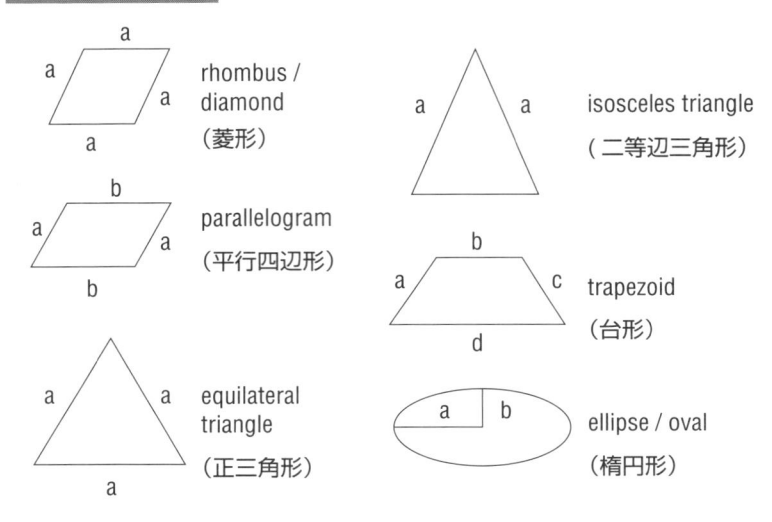

- rhombus / diamond（菱形）
- parallelogram（平行四辺形）
- equilateral triangle（正三角形）
- isosceles triangle（二等辺三角形）
- trapezoid（台形）
- ellipse / oval（楕円形）

- □ integrate　積分する（integral は「積分」）
- □ invariable　定数、不変の（multivariable は「多変数の」）
- □ inverse matrix〔méitriks〕　逆行列（inverse proportion は「反比例」）
- □ locus〔lóukəs〕　軌跡
- □ logarithm〔lɔ́:gəriðm〕　対数（common logarithm は「常用対数」）
- □ mean value　平均値（median〔mí:diən〕は「中央値 / 中線」）
- □ most probable value　最確値
- □ multiplying factor　倍率（multiplicity は「多重度」）
- □ nonlinear〔nɑnlíniə〕　非線形の：数学で一次式で表されない関係
- □ normal line　法線：曲線上の1点において、その点での接線に垂直な直線
- □ notation　記数法、表記

- □ numerator〔n(j)ú:mərèitə〕 分子（denominator は「分母」）
- □ numerical〔n(j)u:mérikl〕analysis 数値解析
- □ parameter〔pəræmətə〕 変数、パラメータ
- □ derivative 導関数：関数 f(x) の変化率
- □ permissible error 許容誤差（rounding error は「丸め誤差」）
- □ permutation〔pə̀:mjutéiʃən〕 順列
- □ polynomial〔pɑ̀lɔnóumiəl〕 多項式
- □ principal value 主値
- □ probability 確率
- □ product 積
- □ scalar product スカラー積：内積
- □ protractor〔prətræktə〕 分度器（radianは「弧度／ラジアン」）
- □ quadrant〔kwɑ́drənt〕 象限（quadrature〔kwɑ́drətʃə〕axisは「横軸」）
- □ quadratic〔kwɑdrǽtik〕equation 二次方程式（linear equationは「一次方程式」）
- □ radius of curvature〔réidiəs | əv | kə́:vətʃə〕 曲率半径：曲率円の半径

図表の種類

Line graph　線グラフ

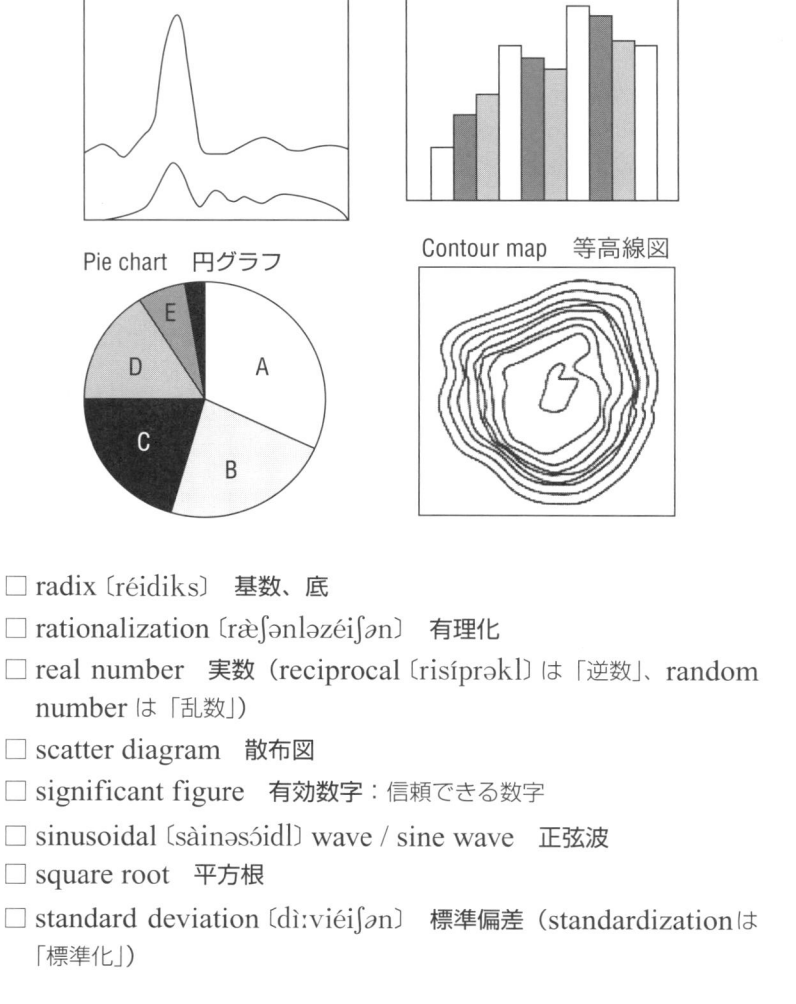

Bar graph　棒グラフ

Pie chart　円グラフ

Contour map　等高線図

- [ ] radix〔réidiks〕　基数、底
- [ ] rationalization〔ræ̀ʃənləzéiʃən〕　有理化
- [ ] real number　実数（reciprocal〔risíprəkl〕は「逆数」、random number は「乱数」）
- [ ] scatter diagram　散布図
- [ ] significant figure　有効数字：信頼できる数字
- [ ] sinusoidal〔sàinəsɔ́idl〕wave / sine wave　正弦波
- [ ] square root　平方根
- [ ] standard deviation〔dì:viéiʃne〕　標準偏差（standardizationは「標準化」）

- ☐ greatest common denominator　最大公約数（the least common multiple は「最小公倍数」）
- ☐ theorem　定理
- ☐ transfer function　伝達関数
- ☐ trigonometry　三角法（trigonometric function は「三角関数」）

■ 数学語彙復習テストにチャレンジ！

1	複素数	11	分子
2	座標軸	12	変数、パラメータ
3	小数点	13	順列
4	微分方程式	14	二次方程式
5	分散、ばらつき	15	有理化
6	指数関数	16	有効数字
7	虚数	17	標準偏差
8	不等式	18	最大公約数
9	整数	19	象限
10	軌跡	20	三角法

■ 数学語彙復習テスト（解答）

1	complex number	11	numerator
2	axis of coordinates	12	parameter
3	decimal point	13	permutation
4	differential equation	14	quadratic equation
5	variance	15	rationalization
6	exponential function	16	significant figure
7	imaginary number	17	standard deviation
8	inequality	18	greatest common denominator
9	integer	19	quadrant
10	locus	20	trigonometry

5-6 第29日
スペースサイエンス語彙に強くなる

　このスペースサイエンスでは、工業英検および英字新聞や雑誌のサイエンス記事に頻出する語彙の中で特に重要なものだけを集めました。

天文学語彙に強くなる　　　　　　　　　CD 3-37
- □ galaxy　銀河（the Milky Way は「銀河、天の川」）
- □ celestial〔səléstʃəl〕body　天体（constellation は「星座」、the zodiac は「十二宮図」）
- □ asteroid〔ǽstərɔ̀id〕　小惑星（nebula は「星雲」）
- □ meteor〔míːtiə〕/ meteorite　隕石、流星（comet は「彗星」）
- □ sunspot　黒点：太陽の光球面に見られる黒い小さな斑点（white dwarf〔dwɔ́ːf〕は「白色惑星」）
- □ prominence〔prámənəns〕　太陽の紅炎
- □ Neptune　海王星（Saturn は「土星」、Uranus は「天王星」）
- □ crescent〔krésnt〕moon　三日月（supernova は「超新星」）
- □ elliptical〔ilíptikl〕orbit　楕円軌道（geostationary orbit は「静止軌道」、orbiting は「軌道を回ること」）
- □ stratosphere〔strǽtəsfìə〕　成層圏（troposphere〔tróupəsfìə〕は「対流圏」）

- □ cosmic ray　宇宙線 (ionized layer / ionosphere [aiánəsfìə] は「電離層」)
- □ Polaris [pəlǽris] [the polestar]　北極星 (the Big Dipper は「北斗七星」)
- □ meridian [mərídiən]　子午線
- □ extraterrestrial [èkstrətəréstriəl]　地球外生物
- □ Search for Extraterrestrial Intelligence [SETI]　地球外知性探査
- □ lift-off　ロケットの打ち上げ (crash landing は「不時着」、splashdown は「着水」)
- □ interplanetary travel　惑星間旅行
- □ lunar module　月着陸船 (terraforming は「テラフォーミング：惑星を地球のように変化させて人が住めるようにすること」)
- □ spacewalk　宇宙遊泳 (weightlessness は「無重力」)
- □ debriefing　宇宙飛行士からの報告聴取
- □ stationary satellite　静止衛星 (the Solar System は「太陽系」、communication satellite [CS] は「通信衛星」)
- □ apogee [ǽpədʒiː]　遠地点 (perigee [pérɪdʒìː] は「近似点」)
- □ rocket trajectory [trədʒéktəri]　ロケットの軌跡
- □ Hubble Space Telescope [HST]　ハッブル宇宙望遠鏡
- □ National Aeronautics and Space Administration [NASA]　航空宇宙局 (Federal Aviation Administration [FAA] は「連邦宇宙局」)
- □ neutrino [n(j)uːtríːnou] astronomy　ニュートリノ天文学
- □ space debris [dəbríː]　宇宙ごみ (terrestrial magnetism は「地磁気」、cosmic ray は「宇宙線」、cosmic dust は「宇宙塵」)

Solar System（太陽系）

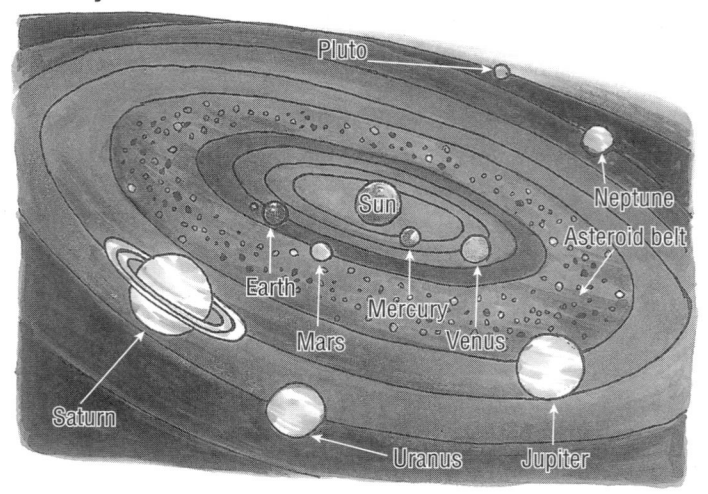

Pluto（冥王星：近年、太陽系惑星から格下げされた）、Neptune（海王星）、Uranus（天王星）、Saturn（土星）、Jupiter（木星）、Asteroid belt（小惑星帯）、Mars（火星）、Earth（地球）、Venus（金星）、Mercury（水星）、Sun（太陽）

5-7　第30日
環境語彙に強くなる

　地球の温暖化への危機感から、環境問題はますます重要性を帯びています。そこで、このセクションでは、エコロジー、気象、地形に関する語彙に分類して、一気に表現力をUPしていただきましょう。

　特にこの分野は重要なので、英語で発信できるようにCDを聞きながら、フレーズで日英の発信ができるようにトレーニングに励みましょう！

エコロジーの語彙に強くなる　　　　　　　　　CD 3-38

- □ biodiversity / biological diversity　種の多様性
- □ food chain　食物連鎖（natural habitat〔hǽbitæt〕は「生息地」）
- □ carnivorous〔kɑ:nívərəs〕animal　肉食動物（「草食動物」は herbivorous〔hə:bívərəs〕animal）
- □ nocturnal〔nɑktə́:rnl〕animal　夜行動物
- □ aquatic plants and animals　水生動植物（淡水は「fresh water」）
- □ coniferous〔kouníf ərəs〕trees　針葉樹林 ⇔ 落葉樹林 deciduous〔disídʒuəs〕trees（perennial〔pəréniəl〕plant は「多年生植物」）
- □ virgin forest　原生林（windbreak は「防風林」）

- □ deforestation〔di:fɔ̀ərəstéiʃən〕 森林破壊 ⇔ 植林 afforestation〔əfɔ̀ərəstéiʃən〕(desertification〔dizə̀:təfikéiʃən〕は「砂漠化」)
- □ ocean dumping 海洋投棄 (oil slick [spill]は「流出油」)
- □ radioactive contamination 放射能汚染
- □ car exhaust / exhaust gas / auto emission 廃棄ガス (acid rainは「酸性雨」)
- □ toxic substance 有毒物質
- □ incineration〔insínərèiʃən〕site 焼却場所 (incineratorは「焼却炉」、sootは「すす」)
- □ garbage [refuse] dump / waste-treatment site 廃棄物処理場 (garbage disposalは「ごみ処理」、dumping groundは「ごみ捨て場」、domestic drainage〔dréinidʒ〕は「生活排水」、drainageは「排水設備」)
- □ land reclamation〔rèkləméiʃən〕/ landfill 埋め立て
- □ liquefaction〔lìkwəfǽkʃən〕 液状化現象
- □ ozone depletion〔diplí:ʃən〕 オゾン枯渇 (ozone layerは「オゾン層」)
- □ photochemical smog 光化学スモッグ (「汚染物質」はpollutant)
- □ excess [excessive] packaging 過剰包装
- □ herbicide〔hə́:bəsàid〕 除草剤
- □ persistent〔pəsístnt〕organic pollutant 残留性有機汚染物質：DDTなど、分解しにくく土壌を汚染する人工化学物質
- □ evolutionism / evolutionary theory 進化論
- □ nature preservation 自然保護 (preserveは「保護地区」)
- □ deep ecology ディープエコロジー：すべての生命体が地球上で平等に生存する価値を持つという考え方
- □ ecofeminism エコフェミニズム：自然支配・破壊は男性の女性支配と同じであるという見方

- □ bird sanctuary〔sǽŋktʃuèəri〕 鳥保護地区（wildlife sanctuary は「鳥獣保護区」）
- □ endangered〔endéindʒəd〕species　絶滅寸前の種
- □ energy conservation　省エネ（fire hazard は「火の元」）
- □ emission control　排ガス規制（emission standard は「排ガス基準」）
- □ eco-friendly car / low-emission vehicle　低公害車
- □ biomass energy　バイオマスエネルギー
- □ cogeneration　廃熱発電：1つのエネルギーから2種類のエネルギーを取り出すこと
- □ biodegradable materials　生分解性物質（recyclable materials は「再利用可能物質」）
- □ nonrenewable energy　再生不能エネルギー
- □ sustainable development　持続可能な開発
- □ irrigation〔ìrigéiʃən〕灌漑（irrigated land は「灌漑地」）
- □ hydroponics〔hàidroupániks〕水耕栽培：養分を水溶液にして植物を栽培する方法
- □ tissue culture　組織培養
- □ photosynthesis〔fòutousínθəsis〕光合成
- □ the Kyoto Protocol　京都議定書
- □ emission trading　排出権取引：環境問題を市場メカニズムで解決しようとするもの

Food Chain（食物連鎖）

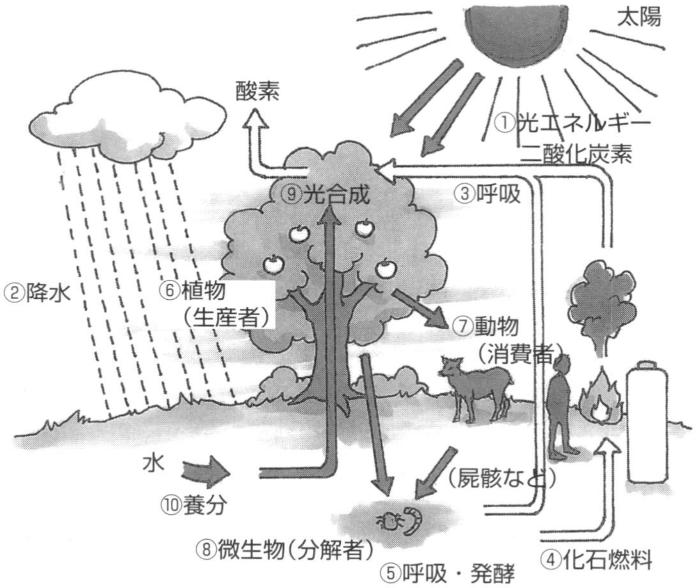

太陽
酸素
①光エネルギー
二酸化炭素
⑨光合成
③呼吸
②降水
⑥植物
（生産者）
⑦動物
（消費者）
水
（屍骸など）
⑩養分
⑧微生物（分解者）
⑤呼吸・発酵
④化石燃料

① light energy（光エネルギー）

② precipitation（降水）

③ respiration（呼吸）

④ fossil fuel（化石燃料）

⑤ respiration & fermentation（呼吸・発酵）

⑥ plant（植物）: producer（生産者）

⑦ animal（動物）: consumer（消費者）

⑧ microorganism（微生物）: decomposer（分解者）

⑨ photosynthesis（光合成）

⑩ nutrient（養分）

気象に関する語彙に強くなる

CD 3-39

□ climatology〔klàimətálədʒi〕 気候学、気象学

□ temperate〔témpərət〕climate 温帯気候（「亜寒帯気候」は

subarctic〔sʌbáːktik〕climate)
- [ ] the Frigid Zone　寒帯（the Temperate Zoneは「温帯」、the Torrid Zoneは「熱帯」）
- [ ] Meteorological Agency [Observatory]　気象庁［気象台］
- [ ] Automated Meteorological Data Acquisition System [AMEDAS]　アメダス
- [ ] atmospheric pressure　大気圧（depression は「低気圧」、cold air mass は「寒気団」）
- [ ] pressure trough〔trɔ́(ː)f〕気圧の谷（pressure pattern は「気圧配置」）
- [ ] cherry blossom front　桜前線
- [ ] seasonal rain front　梅雨前線
- [ ] cold front　寒冷前線（cold wave は「寒波」）
- [ ] tropical cyclone　熱帯低気圧（whirlwind〔hwə́ːlwìnd〕は「つむじ風」）
- [ ] precipitation〔prisìpitéiʃən〕降水量
- [ ] tempest〔témpəst〕暴風雨（tornado / whirlwind / twister は「竜巻」）
- [ ] torrential〔tɔrénʃəl〕rain / downpour / cloudburst　どしゃ降り（drizzle は「霧雨」）
- [ ] blizzard〔blízəd〕大吹雪
- [ ] hail　雹（ひょう）（sleet は「みぞれ」）
- [ ] dry spell / drought　干ばつ（flood damage / flooding は「水害」）
- [ ] air turbulence〔tə́ːbjələns〕乱気流（air current は「気流」）
- [ ] atmospheric discharge　空中放電
- [ ] westerlies / westerly gale　西風（gale は「疾風」）
- [ ] humidity / moisture　湿度
- [ ] dew point　露点：大気中の水蒸気が冷却して露を結び始める時の温

度
- □ mirage　蜃気楼（mist は「薄い霧」、haze は「かすみ、もや」）
- □ discomfort index　不快指数
- □ the International Date Line　日付変更線
- □ regression〔rigréʃən〕line / tropic　回帰線（Northern Tropic / the Tropic of Cancer は「北回帰線」）
- □ vernal [spring] equinox〔í:kwənàks〕春分（「冬至」は winter solstice〔sálstis〕、「夏至」は summer solstice）
- □ solar eclipse〔iklíps〕日食 ⇔ 月食 lunar eclipse
- □ evacuation drill　避難訓練
- □ tremor　微震（aftershock は「余震」）
- □ epicenter〔épəsèntə〕震央
- □ seismic〔sáizmik〕center　震源地（seismic intensity は「震度」）
- □ earthquake-proof construction [structure] 耐震構造
- □ ebb and flow　潮の干満（red tide は「赤潮」）
- □ tidal wave / tsunami　津波（storm surge は「高潮」）
- □ inundation〔ìnʌndéiʃən〕/ submersion under water　浸水
- □ flooding above the floor　床上浸水（flooding up to the floor は「床下浸水」）
- □ avalanche / snow slide　なだれ
- □ pyroclastic〔pàirəklǽstik〕flow　火砕流（molten lava は「噴き出た溶岩」）
- □ floating ice / drift ice　流氷
- □ trees covered with ice / trees with ice-covered foliage〔fóuliidʒ〕樹氷
- □ contour〔kántuə〕line　等高線（hazard map は「災害予測地図」）
- □ sludge〔slʌ́dʒ〕析出物、堆積物

Landform（地形）

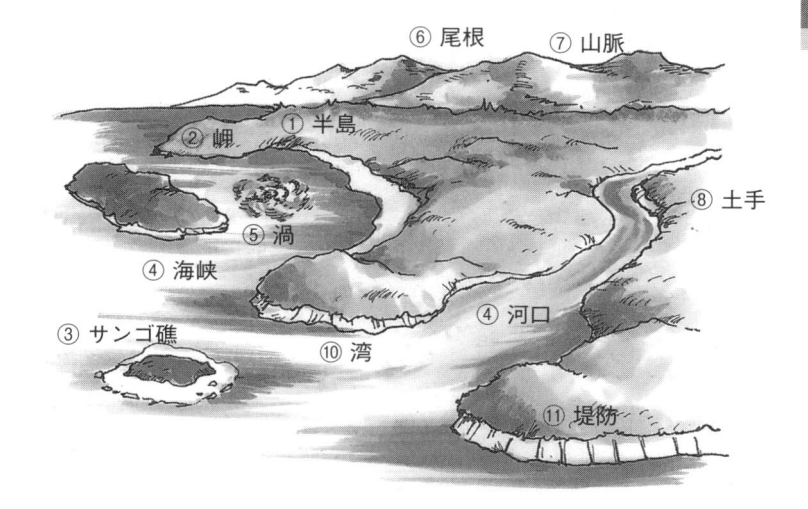

⑥ 尾根　⑦ 山脈
① 半島
② 岬
⑤ 渦
④ 海峡
⑧ 土手
③ サンゴ礁
⑨ 河口
⑩ 湾
⑪ 堤防

① peninsula（半島）　② cape（岬）　③ coral reef（サンゴ礁）
④ strait（海峡）　⑤ whirlpool（渦）　⑥ ridge（尾根）
⑦ mountain range（山脈）　⑧ bank（土手）　⑨ mouth（河口）
⑩ bay（湾）　⑪ levee（堤防）

地形に関する語彙に強くなる

CD 3-40

- [ ] the Northern hemisphere〔hémisfìə〕　北半球
- [ ] the Pacific rim　環太平洋
- [ ] the Japanese Archipelago〔à:kipéləgòu〕　日本列島（peninsula〔pənínsələ〕は「半島」）
- [ ] Antarctic　南極 ⇔ 北極 Arctic（「北極熊」は polar bear）
- [ ] latitude〔lǽtət(j)ù:d〕　緯度 ⇔ 経度 longitude〔lánʒet(j)ù:d〕
- [ ] mountain range　山脈（mountain pass は「峠」、ridge は「尾根」）
- [ ] dormant〔dɔ́:mənt〕volcano　休火山 ⇔ 活火山 active volcano

(extinct〔ikstínkt〕volcano は「死火山」)
- [ ] ocean [sea] trench / deep　海溝（the Mariana Trench は「マリアナ海溝」）
- [ ] plateau〔plætóu〕　高原（tableland は「台地、高原」）
- [ ] level ground　平地
- [ ] sand dune　砂丘（sand bar は「砂州」）
- [ ] ravine〔rəvíːn〕/ gorge〔gɔ́ːdʒ〕　峡谷：切り立つ狭い谷（大きいものは canyon、小さいのは gully〔gʌ́li〕）
- [ ] meadow / pasture　牧草地（ranch は「牧畜場、放牧場」）
- [ ] arable [farm] land　耕作地（cultivator は「耕運機」）
- [ ] reservoir　貯水池
- [ ] promontory〔prámentɔ̀ːri〕/ cape　岬
- [ ] river basin〔béisn〕　河川流域、重水域、(river>stream>brook [creek] は「川：順に小さくなる」)
- [ ] rapids　急流、早瀬（ford は「浅瀬」）（cascade〔kæskéid〕は「小滝」）
- [ ] first-grade river　一級河川（upper reaches は「上流」）
- [ ] sluice〔slúːs〕　水門
- [ ] estuary〔éstʃuèəri〕　河口　（inlet は「入り江」）
- [ ] mud land / tidal flat / tidal land　干潟
- [ ] strait / channel　海峡
- [ ] eddying current　渦潮
- [ ] embankment / dike / levee〔lévi〕　堤防
- [ ] atoll〔ǽtɔ(ː)l〕　環状珊瑚島 / 環礁（coral reef は「珊瑚礁」）
- [ ] iceberg　氷山
- [ ] desert island / uninhabited island　無人島
- [ ] stalagmite〔stəlǽgmait〕cave / limestone cave / stalactite〔stǽləktàit〕cave　鍾乳洞

- [ ] ice column　霜柱（icicle〔áisikl〕は「つらら」）
- [ ] intermittent〔ìntəmítənt〕spring / geyser　間欠泉
- [ ] pier〔píə〕/ wharf〔hwɔ́:f〕　岸壁（breakwater は「防波堤」）
- [ ] elevation above sea level　海抜
- [ ] crust〔krʌ́st〕　地殻（「地表」は surface、「マントル」は mantle）
- [ ] land shelf / continental shelf　大陸棚
- [ ] lava〔lá:və〕stream　溶岩流
- [ ] igneous〔ígniəs〕rock　火成岩（metamorphic〔mètəmɔ́:fik〕rock は「変成岩」）
- [ ] granite〔grǽnit〕　花崗岩（pumice〔pʌ́məs〕は「軽石」）
- [ ] limestone　石灰岩（sedimentary〔sèdəméntri〕rock は「堆積岩」）
- [ ] graphite〔grǽfait〕　黒鉛、グラファイト（gravel〔grǽvl〕は「砂利」）
- [ ] slate　粘板岩
- [ ] iron ore〔ɔ́:r〕　鉄鉱石（ore は「鉱石」）
- [ ] stratum〔stréitəm〕/ strata〔strǽtə〕　地層
- [ ] earthquake swarm　群発地震
- [ ] tectonic activity　地殻活動（tectonics は「構造地質学、地質構造」）
- [ ] volcanic eruption　火山の噴火、火山爆発
- [ ] active fault　活断層
- [ ] land [ground] subsidence　地盤沈下
- [ ] topography〔təpágrəfi〕/ topographical features　地勢（図）
- [ ] nautical〔nɔ́:tikl〕mile　海里（1 nautical mile は 1852m）
- [ ] oceanography〔òuʃənágrəfi〕　海洋学

■ 環境語彙復習テストにチャレンジ！

1	再生不能エネルギー	11	災害予測地図
2	原生林	12	活断層
3	等高線	13	避難訓練
4	峡谷	14	雹
5	鍾乳洞	15	気圧の谷
6	環状珊瑚島	16	みぞれ
7	岬	17	焼却場所
8	地殻	18	析出物
9	液状化現象	19	花崗岩
10	露点	20	海洋学

■ 環境語彙復習テスト（解答）

1	nonrenewable energy	11	hazard map
2	virgin forest	12	active fault
3	contour line	13	evacuation drill
4	ravine / gorge	14	hail
5	stalagmite ［limestone / stalactite］ cave	15	pressure trough
6	atoll	16	sleet
7	promontory / cape	17	incineration site
8	crust	18	sludge
9	liquefaction	19	granite
10	dew point	20	oceanography

5-8 第31日
医学語彙に強くなる

　2008年度から、英語診療スタッフおよび医療通訳者育成のため「医学英検」が始まりました。各級のレベルは4級（医科大学卒業程度）、3級（医療従事者、通訳・翻訳者レベル）、2級英語論文執筆・学会発表ができるレベル）、1級（英語研究論文の指導、国際学会で座長ができるレベル）となっています。そこでここでは、英語で医療について発信したり、通訳したりするだけでなく、医療翻訳者レベルの3級を目指すのに必要な語彙を集め、さらに医学用語の一般用語での言い換えも掲載しました。それでは皆さん、このハードな医学分野の語彙表現力UPにチャレンジしましょう！

医療に関する語彙に強くなる　　　　　　　　　　CD 3-41

□ endoscopic〔èndəskápik〕treatment [surgery]　内視鏡的治療[手術]

□ intravenous〔ìntrəvíːnəs〕drip　点滴（hypodermic〔hàipədə́ːmik〕injection は「皮下注射」）

□ orthopedic〔ɔ̀ːθəupíːdik〕[plastic] surgeon　整形外科医

□ osteopathy〔ɑ̀stiɑ́pəθi〕/ osteopathic treatment　整骨療法（chiropractic treatment は「背骨矯正」）

- [ ] regeneration medicine　再生医療
- [ ] stethoscope〔stéθəskòup〕　聴診器　(hearing aid は「補聴器」)
- [ ] suspended animation　仮死状態
- [ ] universal care　国民皆保険
- [ ] vital capacity　肺活量
- [ ] vital statistics / measurments　女性のスリーサイズ
- [ ] acupuncture anesthesia〔ǽkjəpʌ̀ŋktʃə | æ̀nəsθíːʒə〕　針麻酔 (acupuncturist は「針灸師」)
- [ ] moxibustion〔màksibʌ́stʃən〕/ cautery〔kɔ́ːtəri〕　灸
- [ ] American Medical Association [AMA]　米国医師会 (Health Maintenance Organization [HMO] は「健康管理機関」)
- [ ] antibiotic　抗生物質 (anti-cancer drug は「抗ガン剤」)
- [ ] anticonvulsant sedative〔æ̀ntikənvʌ́lsənt | sédətiv〕　抗痙攣鎮静剤
- [ ] antidote〔ǽntidòut〕　解毒剤
- [ ] antiseptic〔æ̀ntiséptik〕[disinfectant〔dìsinféktənt〕] capability　殺菌能力
- [ ] appendix〔əpéndiks〕operation　盲腸の手術
- [ ] abortion　中絶 (miscarriage は「流産」)
- [ ] artificial insemination〔insèmənéiʃən〕　人工受精
- [ ] bilateral mastectomy〔mæstéktəmi〕　両側乳房切除（術）
- [ ] blood donation　献血 (blood transfusion は「輸血」)
- [ ] blood product　血液製剤 (blood stanching〔stɔ́ːntʃiŋ〕は「止血」)
- [ ] blood-pressure gauge　血圧計
- [ ] body fat percentage　体脂肪率 (liposuction〔lípousʌ̀kʃən〕は「脂肪吸引」)

- Bone Marrow [mǽrou] Bank　骨髄バンク（bone marrow transplant は「骨髄移植」）
- cardiopulmonary resuscitation [kɑ̀:dioupʌ́lməneri | risʌ̀sitéiʃən] [CPR]　心肺蘇生法
- complete medical check-up　人間ドック
- compress [kámpres]　湿布
- cryosurgery [krɑ̀iəsə́:dʒəri]　冷凍外科手術
- euthanasia [jù:θənéiʒə] / mercy killing　安楽死
- death with dignity　尊厳死
- life-support system / life-prolonging device　延命装置
- dietary fiber　食物繊維
- dominant genes　優性遺伝子 ⇔ 劣性遺伝子 recessive genes
- dosage [dóusidʒ] adjustment　投薬量の調節
- E. coli [í: | kóulài] 157　大腸菌 O157
- electric scalpel [skǽlpl]　電気メス
- electrocardiogram [ilèktrouká:diəgrӕm]　心電図
- excretion [ikskrí:ʃən] amount　排泄量（urine は「小便」、stool は「大便」）
- first-aid kit　救急箱
- forensic psychiatrist [fərénsik | saikáiətrist]　法精神科医
- gastro [gǽstrou] - camera　胃カメラ
- generic [dʒənéərik] drug　商標未登録の薬
- hallucinogenic [həlù:sənədʒénik] drug　幻覚剤
- hypnotic [hipnátik] therapy　催眠治療（chemotherapy [kì:mouθéərəpi] は「化学治療」）
- immune [imjú:n] therapy / immunotherapy　免疫療法
- incubation [ìnkjəbéiʃən] period / latency [léitnsi] period　潜伏期

- □ informed consent　インフォームド・コンセント：手術の際の患者の同意
- □ kidney dialysis〔kídni | daiǽləsis〕　腎臓透析
- □ laxative〔lǽksətiv〕property　下剤作用
- □ living liver transplantation　生体部分肝移植
- □ local anesthesia〔æ̀nəsθíːʒə〕　局部麻酔（general anesthesia は「全体麻酔」）
- □ Medicaid eligibility　〈米〉メディケイド受益資格：低所得者と身障者を対象とする医療扶助制度受益資格

一般語と医学用語の違いとは !?

日本語訳	一般語	医学用語
腕	arm	brachium, brachial
背	back	dorsal
膀胱	bladder	cystic
骨	bone	osseous
臀部	buttocks	gluteal
胸	chest	thorax, thoracic
耳	ear	aural
眼	eye	ocular
頭	head	cranial
心臓	heart	cardiac
唇	lip	labial
肝臓	liver	hepatic
肺	lung	pulmonary, pulmonic
首	neck	cervical
皮膚	skin	dermal
大腿	thigh	femur, femoral
腰	waist	lumbar
気管	windpipe	trachea, tracheal

Human Body (人体)

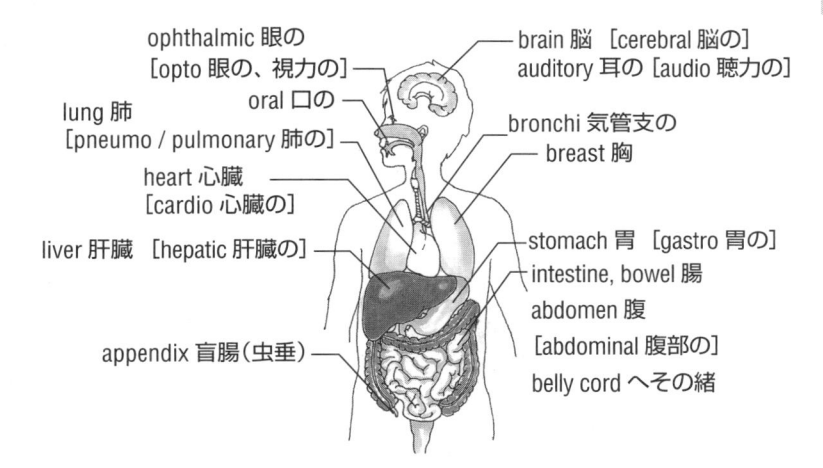

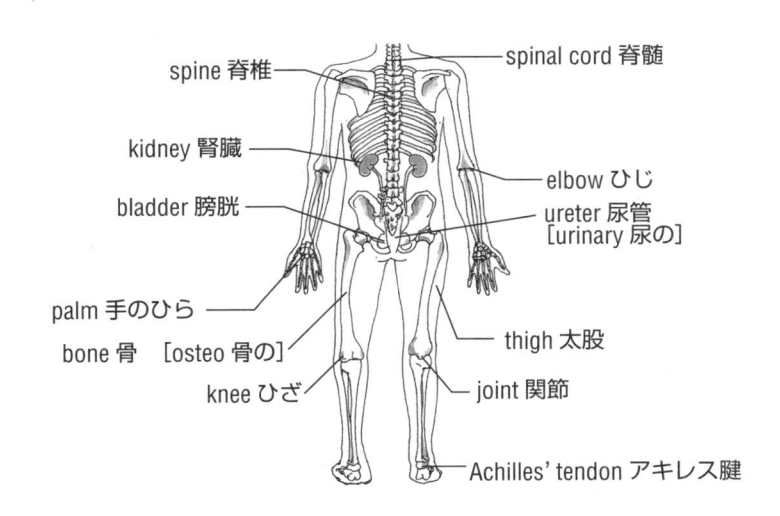

- ophthalmic 眼の [opto 眼の、視力の]
- oral 口の
- lung 肺 [pneumo / pulmonary 肺の]
- heart 心臓 [cardio 心臓の]
- liver 肝臓 [hepatic 肝臓の]
- appendix 盲腸（虫垂）
- brain 脳 [cerebral 脳の]
- auditory 耳の [audio 聴力の]
- bronchi 気管支の
- breast 胸
- stomach 胃 [gastro 胃の]
- intestine, bowel 腸
- abdomen 腹 [abdominal 腹部の]
- belly cord へその緒

- spine 脊椎
- kidney 腎臓
- bladder 膀胱
- palm 手のひら
- bone 骨 [osteo 骨の]
- knee ひざ
- spinal cord 脊髄
- elbow ひじ
- ureter 尿管 [urinary 尿の]
- thigh 太股
- joint 関節
- Achilles' tendon アキレス腱

- [ ] malpractice liability　医療過誤責任（misdiagnosis は「誤診」）
- [ ] medical diagnosis　医学的診断（prognosis は「予後診断」）
- [ ] morning calisthenics〔kælisθéniks〕　朝の体操
- [ ] normal delivery　通常分娩（painless delivery は「無痛分娩」）
- [ ] malnutrition〔mæln(j)u:tríʃən〕　栄養失調
- [ ] obesity〔oubí:səti〕remedy　やせ薬
- [ ] obstetrician〔àbstətríʃən〕　産婦人科医
- [ ] oncogene〔áŋkətdʒì:n〕expression　ガン遺伝子発現
- [ ] ophthalmologist〔àfθælmálədʒist〕/ oculist〔ákjəlist〕/ eye doctor　眼科医
- [ ] oral contraceptive〔kàntrəséptiv〕　経口避妊薬
- [ ] organ transplant　臓器移植（corneal〔kɔ́:niəl〕transplant は「角膜移植」）
- [ ] otorhinolaryngologist〔òutouràinəlæriŋgálədʒist〕/ ear, nose and throat [ENT] doctor　耳鼻咽喉科医
- [ ] outpatient department　外来診療部門 ⇔ 院内診療部門 inpatient department
- [ ] paramedic〔pæ̀rəmédik〕　救急救命士
- [ ] pediatrician〔pì:diətríʃən〕　小児科医
- [ ] placebo〔pləsí:bou〕effect　疑似薬効果（panacea [pæ̀nəsí:ə] / cure-all は「万能薬」）
- [ ] polio〔póuliòu〕vaccination　小児麻痺の予防接種
- [ ] practitioner / practicing doctor　開業医
- [ ] prescription medicine　処方薬（suppository は「座薬」）
- [ ] psychiatric center　精神療養所（mental hospital は「精神病院」）
- [ ] remission〔rimíʃən〕status　寛解状態：痛み、病状が和らぐこと
- [ ] serum〔síərəm〕antibody　血清抗体（stimulant は「覚せい剤」）
- [ ] sterilizer〔stéərəlàizə〕　消毒器

- □ sticking [adhesive] plaster for an injury　バンソウコウ
- □ stretcher〔strétʃə〕　担架
- □ cancer notification　ガン告知
- □ terminal care　末期医療（terminal patient は「末期患者」）
- □ therapeutic effect　治療効果
- □ twenty-twenty vision　正常な視力
- □ wheelchair-accessible station　車椅子で乗り入れ可能な駅

病気に関する語彙に強くなる　　CD 3-42

- □ acute appendicitis〔əpèndəsáitis〕　急性虫垂炎
- □ arthritis〔ɑːθráitis〕　関節炎（rheumatoid arthritis は「リウマチ性関節炎」）
- □ complication　合併症
- □ epilepsy seizure〔épəlèpsi | síːʒə〕　てんかん発作
- □ comatose〔kóumətòus〕patient　植物人間
- □ gonorrhea〔gànəríːə〕　淋病 （syphilis〔sífəlis〕は「梅毒」）
- □ hemophiliac〔hìːməfíliæk〕　血友病患者
- □ hives〔háivz〕/ nettle rash　じんましん
- □ osteoporosis〔àstioupəróusəs〕　骨粗鬆症
- □ phlegm〔flém〕　痰
- □ rabies inoculation〔réibiːz | inàkjəléiʃən〕　狂犬病予防接種
- □ schizophrenia〔skìtsoufríːniə〕　統合失調症
- □ sinusitis〔sàinəsáitəs〕/ sinus〔sáinəs〕problem / empyema〔èmpaiíːmə〕　蓄膿症
- □ sunstroke　日射病
- □ tetanus〔tétənəs〕vaccination　破傷風ワクチン接種
- □ tuberculosis〔t(j)ubə́ːkjəlóusis〕　結核
- □ venereal〔vəníəriəl〕disease　性病

- □ whiplash symptom　むち打ち症
- □ withdrawal symptom　禁断症状
- □ dental cavity〔kǽvəti〕/ decayed tooth　虫歯
- □ airborne infection / aerial〔éəriəl〕infection　空中感染
- □ AIDS epidemic〔èpidémik〕　エイズの流行
- □ alcohol dependence　アルコール依存症
- □ anemia〔əníːmiə〕　貧血
- □ anorexia nervosa〔æ̀nəréksiə | nəːvóusə〕　拒食症（bulimia〔bjuːlímiə〕は「過食症」）
- □ anthrax〔ǽnθræks〕　炭疽病
- □ arsenic〔ɑːsónik〕poisoning　砒素中毒（food poisoning は「食中毒」）

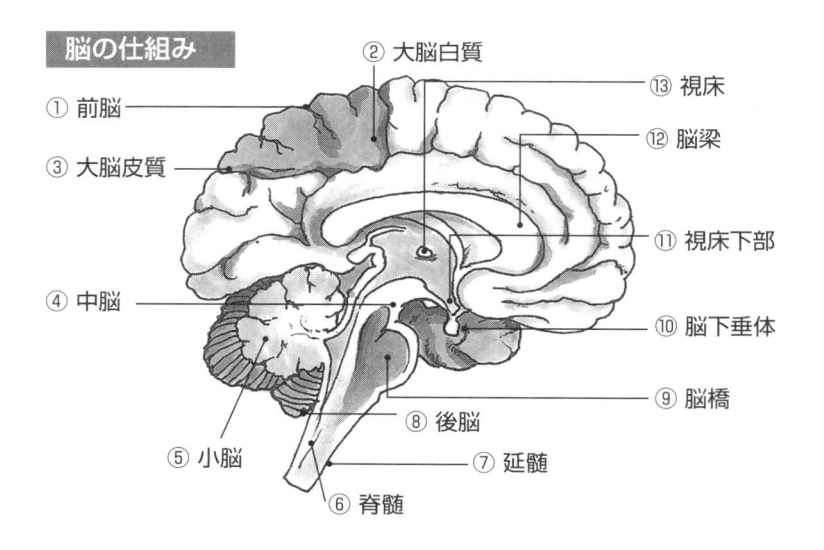

脳の仕組み

① 前脳
② 大脳白質
③ 大脳皮質
④ 中脳
⑤ 小脳
⑥ 脊髄
⑦ 延髄
⑧ 後脳
⑨ 脳橋
⑩ 脳下垂体
⑪ 視床下部
⑫ 脳梁
⑬ 視床

① forebrain（前脳）　② white matter（大脳白質）　③ cerebral cortex（大脳皮質）
④ midbrain（中脳）　⑤ cerebellum（小脳）

⑥ spinal cord（脊髄）　⑦ medulla oblongata（延髄）　⑧ hindbrain（後脳）
⑨ pons（脳橋）　⑩ pituitary gland（脳下垂体）　⑪ hypothalamus（視床下部）
⑫ corpus callosum（脳梁）　⑬ thalamus（視床）

....

- [ ] asthma〔ǽzmə〕care　喘息(ぜんそく)治療
- [ ] athlete's foot / water eczema〔éksəmə〕　水虫
- [ ] autonomic imbalance　自律神経失調症
- [ ] avian〔éiviən〕flu　鳥インフルエンザ
- [ ] bioinfomatics　生命情報学：遺伝子の構造を解析する分野
- [ ] mad cow disease [BSE]　狂牛病
- [ ] belch〔béltʃ〕/ burp〔bə́:p〕　ゲップ
- [ ] Caesarean〔sizéəriən〕section operation　帝王切開
- [ ] cardiac [heart] disease　心臓病（cardiac arrest は「心臓の停止」、angina pectoris〔ændʒáinə | péktərəs〕は「狭心症」、heart attack は「心臓発作」）
- [ ] cataract induction〔kǽtərækt | indʌ́kʃən〕　白内障誘発
- [ ] cerebral hemorrhage〔sérəbrəl | héməridʒ〕　脳出血（stroke は「脳溢血」、cerebral infarction は「脳梗塞」）
- [ ] chicken pox　水疱瘡(みずぼうそう)
- [ ] claustrophobia〔klɔ̀:strəfóubiə〕　閉所恐怖症（acrophobia〔ækrəfóubiə〕は「高所恐怖症」）
- [ ] color blindness　色盲
- [ ] complex fracture〔frǽktʃə〕　複雑骨折
- [ ] congenital〔kəndʒénitl〕disease　先天性の病気（hereditary disease は「遺伝病」）
- [ ] coronary aneurysm〔kɔ́:rənèri | ǽnjərìzm〕　冠動脈瘤(かんどうみゃくりゅう)（arteriosclerosis〔ɑ:tìəriouskləróusis〕は「動脈硬化」）

■ 重要病名クイズにチャレンジ！　中級 何割いえるか？

1. 便秘　2. 偏頭痛　3. 自閉症　4. 気管支炎　5. アトピー性皮膚炎
6. 下痢　7. 花粉症　8. 不眠症　9. 白血病　10. ものもらい

■ 解　答

1. constipation〔kànstəpéiʃən〕
2. migraine〔máigrein〕
3. autism〔ɔ́:tìzm〕
4. bronchitis〔brɑŋkáitis〕
5. atopic dermatitis〔eitápik | də̀:mətáitis〕(dermatologist〔də̀:mətálədʒist〕は「皮膚科医」)
6. diarrhea〔dàiərí:ə〕
7. hay fever
8. insomnia〔insámniə〕
9. leukemia〔lu(:)kí:miə〕(scurvy〔skə́:vi〕は「壊血病」)
10. sty〔stái〕

....

□ decayed tooth / dental cavity〔kǽvəti〕　虫歯 (denture〔déntʃə〕/ false tooth は「入れ歯」)
□ detached retina〔rétənə〕　網膜はく離 (「瞳孔」は pupil〔pjú:pl〕、「虹彩」は iris)
□ diabetes mellitus [DM]〔dàiəbí:ti:z meláitəs〕　真性糖尿病
□ disk herniation〔hə́:rnièiʃən〕/ slipped disk　椎間板ヘルニア
□ dislocation〔dìsloukéiʃən〕　脱臼

- □ vertigo / dizziness〔vɚ́ːtigòu〕 めまい
- □ drug-induced depression 薬物によるうつ病（manic depressive psychosis〔saikóusəs〕は「躁鬱症（そううつしょう）」）
- □ eye strain 眼精疲労 （farsightedness は「遠視」）
- □ food poisoning 食中毒（dysentery〔dísntèəri〕は「赤痢」）
- □ foot-and-mouth disease 口蹄疫
- □ forcible vomiting 強制嘔吐（nausea〔nɔ́ːziə〕は「吐き気」）
- □ gallstone〔gɔ́ːlstoun〕 胆石
- □ gastric〔gǽstrik〕hyperacidity 胃酸過多（gastroptosis〔gæstràptóusis〕は「胃下垂」）
- □ gastric ulcer〔ʌ́lsə〕 胃潰瘍（duodenal〔d(j)ùːədíːnl〕ulcer は「十二指腸潰瘍」）
- □ gastrointestinal〔gæstrouintéstənl〕disease 胃腸科系の病気
- □ geriatric〔dʒèəriǽtrik〕disease 老人病（geriatrics は「老人医学」）
- □ gout〔gáut〕attack 痛風発作
- □ hangover 二日酔い
- □ heartburn 胸焼け
- □ hepatitis〔hèpətáitəs〕C C型肝炎
- □ housekeeping gene ハウスキーピング遺伝子：老廃物の除去と細胞の生命維持活動全般に関わる遺伝子
- □ hypertension 高血圧 （internal bleeding は「内出血」）
- □ inflammation〔ìnfləméiʃən〕of the middle ear / otitis〔outáitəs〕media 中耳炎
- □ in-hospital infection 院内感染
- □ menstruation〔mènstruéiʃən〕/ period 生理
- □ kink in one's neck / sprained neck 寝違え
- □ lifestyle-related disease 生活習慣病

- □ lumbago〔lʌmbéigou〕/ lower back pain　腰痛（sprained lower back は「ぎっくり腰」）
- □ malignant tumor〔məlígnənt | t(j)úmə〕　悪性腫瘍（benign〔bənáin〕tumor は「良性腫瘍」）
- □ menopausal〔ménəpɔ́:zl〕discomfort [disorder]　更年期障害（menopause [change of life] は「更年期」、hot flash は「閉経期の一過性熱感」）
- □ mental retardation〔rì:tɑ:déiʃən〕[deficiency]　精神遅帯
- □ metabolic rate　新陳代謝率（metabolic syndrome は「メタボリックシンドローム」）
- □ middle-age bulge [spread]　中年太り
- □ morning sickness　つわり
- □ pathogen〔pǽθədʒən〕　病原体

■ 重要病名クイズにチャレンジ！　上級 何割言えるか？

1. 乱視	2. 肝硬変	3. 膀胱炎	4. 口内炎	5. 脳震盪
6. 痔	7. 神経痛	8. 坐骨神経痛	9. くも膜下出血	10. 子宮ガン

■ 解　答

1. astigmatism〔əstígmətìzm〕/ distorted vision（bifocals は「遠近両用メガネ」）
2. cirrhosis〔səróusis〕
3. cystitis〔sistáitəs〕（bladder〔blǽdə〕は「膀胱」）
4. canker sore〔kǽŋkər | sɔ́:r〕/ mouth inflammation ulcer〔ìnfləméiʃən | ʌ́lsə〕

5. brain concussion 〔kənkʌ́ʃən〕
6. hemorrhoids 〔hémərɔ̀idz〕 / piles
7. neuralgia 〔n(j)uərǽldʒə〕 (nervous breakdown は「神経衰弱」、rheumatism 〔rúmətìzm〕 は「リウマチ」)
8. sciatic neuralgia 〔saiǽtik | n(j)uərǽldʒə〕
9. subarachnoidal hemorrhage 〔sʌ̀bəræknɔ́idl | héməridʒ〕
10. uterine 〔júːtəràin〕 cancer (womb / uterus は「子宮」)

....

- □ gum disease / periodontitis 〔pèərioudəntáitis〕 歯周病
- □ pimple / acne 〔ǽkni〕 / boil 吹き出物
- □ pneumonia 〔n(j)umóuniə〕 肺炎 (respiratory disease は「呼吸器系の病気」)
- □ posttraumatic stress disorder [PTSD] 心的外傷後ストレス障害
- □ psychosomatic 〔sàikousoumǽtik〕 disease 心因性の病気
- □ rectum polyp 〔réktəm | pálip〕 直腸ポリープ
- □ scurvy 〔skə́ːvi〕 壊血病
- □ senile dementia 〔síːnail | diménʃə〕 老人性認知症 (Alzheimer disease は「アルツハイマー病」)
- □ severe acute respiratory syndrome [SARS] 重症急性呼吸器症候群
- □ sudden infant death syndrome [SIDS] 乳幼児突然死症候群
- □ rash / skin eruptions 発疹
- □ smallpox 天然痘
- □ convulsion 〔kənvʌ́lʃən〕 / spasm 〔spǽzm〕 痙攣(けいれん)
- □ speech disorder [impediment 〔impédəmənt〕] 言語障害
- □ sprained [strained] ankle 足関節捻挫 (sprained finger /

Ⅴ 分野別語彙力パワーUP理系語彙

dislocated finger は「突き指」)
- [ ] stomach cramp / gastralgia〔gæstrǽldʒiə〕 胃痙攣
- [ ] suppurative tonsillitis〔sʌ́pjurèitiv | tɑ̀nsláitəs〕 化膿性扁桃腺炎(tonsil は「扁桃腺」)

■ 医学語彙復習テストにチャレンジ！ その1

1	角膜移植	11	心肺蘇生法
2	内視鏡的治療	12	てんかん発作
3	整骨療法	13	点滴
4	解毒剤	14	聴診器
5	関節炎	15	灸
6	湿布	16	胃カメラ
7	合併症	17	肺活量
8	急性虫垂炎	18	再生医療
9	電気メス	19	整形外科医
10	骨髄バンク	20	国民皆保険

■ 医学語彙復習テスト（解答） その1

1	corneal transplant	11	cardiopulmonary resuscitation
2	endoscopic treatment	12	epilesy seizure
3	osteopathy / osteopathic treatment	13	intravenous drip
4	antidote	14	stethoscope
5	arthritis	15	cautery / moxibustion
6	compress	16	gastro-camera
7	complication	17	vital capacity
8	acute appendicitis	18	regeneration medicine
9	electric scalpel	19	orthopedic〔plastic〕surgeon
10	Bone Marrow Bank	20	universal care

人体に関する語彙に強くなる　　CD 3-43

- Achilles' tendon〔əkíli:z | téndən〕　アキレス腱
- armpit hair　わき毛
- artery〔á:tri〕　動脈（vein は「静脈」）
- bodily secretion〔sikrí:ʃən〕　分泌液（internal secretion は「内分泌」）
- bump / lump　こぶ（blister は「まめ」、callus は「たこ」）
- capillary〔kǽpəlèəri〕vessel　毛細血管
- cerebral cortex〔sérəbrl | kɔ́:rteks〕　大脳皮質（limbic system は「大脳辺縁系」、hypothalamus〔hàipouθǽləməs〕は「視床下部」、pituitary〔pit(j)ú:ətèəri〕gland は「脳下垂体」）
- dandruff〔dǽndrəf〕　フケ
- diaphragm〔dáiəfræm〕contraction　横隔膜収縮
- dimple　えくぼ　（mole [mole on the skin] は「ほくろ」）
- eardrum　鼓膜（lobe は「耳たぶ、肺葉や肝葉などの葉」）
- endocrine pancreas〔éndəkràin | pǽŋkriəs〕　すい臓内分泌部
- genitals〔dʒénətlz〕/ genital organs　性器（sperm は「精子」、semen〔sí:mən〕は「精液」、vagina〔vədʒáinə〕は「膣」、testicles〔téstəklz〕/ balls は「睾丸」）
- goose pimple　鳥肌（freckles〔fréklz〕は「そばかす」）
- groin〔grɔ́in〕　股
- involuntary muscle　不随意筋 ⇔ 随意筋 voluntary muscle
- large intestines〔intéstinz〕　大腸（small intestines は「小腸」）
- lymphatic〔limfǽtik〕gland　リンパ腺
- nostril〔nástrəl〕　鼻の穴
- pelvis〔pélvis〕　骨盤　（rib は「肋骨」、skull は「頭蓋骨」）
- plaque〔plǽk〕buildup　歯石の蓄積（full denture〔déntʃə〕は「総入れ歯」）

- □ recessive genes　劣性遺伝子 ⇔ 優性遺伝子 dominant genes
- □ red blood cell　赤血球（white blood cell は「白血球」）
- □ shin〔ʃín〕　すね（calf〔kǽf〕は「ふくらはぎ」）
- □ shoulder blade　肩甲骨（clavicle〔klǽvikl〕/ collarbone は「鎖骨」）
- □ spinal cord　脊髄　（spine / spinal column は「脊椎」）
- □ spleen〔splíːn〕　脾臓
- □ squeezed acne〔ǽkni〕[pimples]　つぶしたニキビ
- □ umbilical〔ʌmbílǝkl〕cord blood　臍帯血
- □ wisdom tooth　親知らず（「犬歯」は canine〔kéinain〕tooth）
- □ esophagus〔isáfǝgǝs〕/ gullet〔gʌ́lǝt〕　食道

■ 医学語彙復習テストにチャレンジ！　その2

1	淋病	11	蓄膿症
2	血友病患者	12	日射病
3	性病	13	仮死状態
4	動脈硬化	14	針麻酔
5	骨盤	15	親しらず
6	大脳皮質	16	植物人間
7	脳下垂体	17	めまい
8	経口避妊薬	18	口蹄疫
9	帝王切開	19	狂犬病予防接種
10	痰	20	破傷風ワクチン接種

■ 医学語彙復習テスト（解答）その2

1	gonorrhea	11	sinusitis / sinus problems / empyema
2	hemophiliac	12	sunstroke
3	venereal disease	13	suspended animation

4	arteriosclerosis	14	acupuncture anesthesia
5	pelvis	15	wisdom tooth
6	cerebral cortex	16	comatose patient
7	pituitary gland	17	vertigo
8	oral contraceptive	18	foot-and-mouth disease
9	Caesarean section operation	19	rabies inoculation
10	phlegm	20	tetanus vaccination

分野別語彙力パワーUP 理系語彙

英語索引 □チェックシートとしてもお使いください。

A

- [ ] abate 121
- [ ] abbreviated 54
- [ ] aberration 308
- [ ] abortion 374
- [ ] abrasion 331
- [ ] absence without leave 207
- [ ] absenteeism 201
- [ ] absentee vote 179
- [ ] absolute dictatorship 175
- [ ] absorption spectrum 308
- [ ] abstinence 157
- [ ] academic clique 217
- [ ] accelerating curve 333
- [ ] accelerometer 332
- [ ] acceptance letter 215
- [ ] accessible 33
- [ ] acclaim 157
- [ ] acetic acid 345
- [ ] acetylene gas 345
- [ ] Achilles' tendon 387
- [ ] acid corrosion 345
- [ ] acoustics 318
- [ ] acoustic efficiency 318
- [ ] acoustic impedance 318
- [ ] acquiesce 146
- [ ] acrimonious 54
- [ ] acrylic resin 345
- [ ] acting chairperson 204
- [ ] activation 324, 348
- [ ] active carbon 345
- [ ] active device 313
- [ ] active fault 371
- [ ] actuating signal 328
- [ ] actuator 329
- [ ] acumen 157
- [ ] acupuncture anesthesia 374
- [ ] acute appendicitis 379
- [ ] adamant 54
- [ ] address space 324
- [ ] adhesive 343
- [ ] adhesive tape 243
- [ ] adjective declension 219
- [ ] adjustable resistance 316
- [ ] administration office 204
- [ ] adolescent problems 223
- [ ] adoption agency 222
- [ ] adroit 54
- [ ] advent 157
- [ ] advertorial 209
- [ ] aerial cable 319
- [ ] aerification 347
- [ ] aerodynamics 306
- [ ] aesthetics 214
- [ ] affable 55
- [ ] affected 33
- [ ] affiliated company 200
- [ ] affiliated team 231
- [ ] AFL-CIO 212
- [ ] agate 345
- [ ] Agent Orange 183
- [ ] age of discretion 222
- [ ] aggravate 110
- [ ] agile 33
- [ ] agrarian reform 173
- [ ] AIDMA's rule 209
- [ ] AIDS epidemic 380
- [ ] airborne infection 380
- [ ] airflow meter 337
- [ ] air duct 337
- [ ] air turbulence 367
- [ ] aisle seat 238
- [ ] alarming 33
- [ ] alcohol dependence 380
- [ ] algebraic equation 353
- [ ] alkaline battery 347
- [ ] allay 123
- [ ] alleviate 123
- [ ] alliterated poem 218
- [ ] allocate 110
- [ ] allot 110
- [ ] alloy 340
- [ ] allude 110
- [ ] alma mater 215
- [ ] alpha male 228
- [ ] also-ran 178
- [ ] alternating current 314
- [ ] alternating current circuit 315
- [ ] altimeter 337
- [ ] altruistic 55
- [ ] aluminum window frame 244
- [ ] alumni 215
- [ ] alumni association 215
- [ ] alumnus 215

☐ amalgamation	211	☐ antibiotic	374	☐ ardent	33
☐ amass	111	☐ anticonvulsant sedative		☐ arduous	88
☐ ambiguous	33		374	☐ areal velocity	306
☐ amenable	88	☐ anticorrosive	343	☐ arid	88
☐ American Medical Association	374	☐ antidote	374	☐ arithmetic operation	353
☐ amiable	33	☐ antiquated	55	☐ armored car	237
☐ amicable	55	☐ antiseptic	343, 374	☐ armpit hair	387
☐ amicable divorce	222	☐ antistatic agent	347	☐ aromatics	343
☐ amplification circuit	316	☐ apathetic	55	☐ around-the-clock operation	206
☐ amplifier	316	☐ apathy	157	☐ arsenic poisoning	380
☐ amplitude distortion	318	☐ apocalyptic belief	224	☐ artery	387
☐ amplitude modulation	318	☐ apogee	361	☐ arthritis	379
☐ amputate	123	☐ appalling	55	☐ articulate	123
☐ Amsterdam Treaty	186	☐ appeasement policy	176	☐ artificial insemination	374
☐ analog-to-digital	320	☐ appendix operation	374	☐ ascending order	324
☐ analog transmission	319	☐ applicant screening	207	☐ ascetic	55
☐ ancestor worship	225	☐ applied science	214	☐ asking price	209
☐ anchor	223	☐ applied voltage	315	☐ assembly plant	211
☐ androphobic attitude	225	☐ appraisal loss	197	☐ assets and liabilities	195
☐ anemia	380	☐ appraise	146	☐ assiduous	88
☐ angular velocity	306	☐ appreciation of the yen	193	☐ assimilate	111
☐ animated movie	233	☐ appropriation bill	173	☐ associate dean	215
☐ anneal	339	☐ approximate value	353	☐ asteroid	360
☐ annual wage bargaining	207	☐ aquaculture	210	☐ asthma care	381
☐ annuity	205	☐ aquatic plants and animals	363	☐ astute	55
☐ anorexia nervosa	380	☐ aqueous phase	347	☐ asylum migration	182
☐ Antarctic	369	☐ arable land	370	☐ atheism	224
☐ anthrax	380	☐ Arab street	182	☐ athlete's foot	381
☐ anthropology	214	☐ arbitrage	195	☐ atmospheric discharge	367
☐ anti-insurgency campaign	176	☐ arbitrary layoff	204	☐ atmospheric pressure	367
		☐ arbor	245	☐ atoll	370
		☐ arcane	88	☐ atomic valence	311
		☐ archaeology	214		
		☐ archaic	55		

☐ atrocious	55	
☐ attentive	33	
☐ attic	244	
☐ audacious	56	
☐ audible range	318	
☐ audio frequency	318	
☐ auditor	200	
☐ augment	111	
☐ auspicious	33	
☐ Aussie	227	
☐ austere	33	
☐ authentic	34	
☐ authoritative	56	
☐ author bibliography		219
☐ autocratic	56	
☐ Automated Meteorological Data Acquisition System		367
☐ automatic transmission		336
☐ automatic voltage regulator		328
☐ autonomic imbalance		381
☐ auxiliary memory	323	
☐ avalanche	368	
☐ avaricious	56	
☐ avert	111	
☐ avian flu	381	
☐ axis of coordinates	353	
☐ axis of evil	182	
☐ axle	335	

B

☐ bachelor's degree	216	
☐ backstroke	232	
☐ backward	34
☐ back spread	196
☐ baffle	123
☐ baggage claim carousel	239
☐ baggage claim tag	239
☐ baking enamel	341
☐ balance beam	232
☐ balance of payment	193
☐ Balkanization	175
☐ ballot box	179
☐ ball park	231
☐ balmy	56
☐ bamboo sword	233
☐ banal	56
☐ bandwidth	315
☐ bankrolled election	177
☐ bargain-basement price	209
☐ bargaining power	182
☐ barrier-free society	226
☐ bar chart	353
☐ base hit	231
☐ batch processing	320
☐ battered wife	222
☐ battery plate	313
☐ bay window	244
☐ bearing	335
☐ bearish market	195
☐ beat frequency	315
☐ belch	381
☐ beleaguered	89
☐ belie	146
☐ belittle	124
☐ belligerent countries	182

☐ bellows	337
☐ bellwether	195
☐ benzene	345
☐ bequeath	146
☐ berth ticket	239
☐ besiege	146
☐ bevel gear	335
☐ bicker	124
☐ bigoted	89
☐ Big Board	197
☐ bilateral discussion	182
☐ bilateral mastectomy	374
☐ binary system	353
☐ binoculars	242
☐ binominal distribution	353
☐ binuclear family	222
☐ biodegradable materials	365
☐ biodiversity	363
☐ bioformatics	381
☐ biomass energy	365
☐ bird sanctuary	365
☐ birth certificate	221
☐ bizarre	56
☐ blackout	328
☐ bland	34
☐ blast furnace	211
☐ blatant	89
☐ bleach	347
☐ bleak	34
☐ blitz tactics	182
☐ blizzard	367
☐ blood-pressure gauge	374
☐ blood donation	374
☐ blood product	374

☐ blowup	242	☐ brittle	56	☐ canny	89		
☐ bluff	124	☐ broach	147	☐ canopy	244		
☐ blunder	158	☐ broad jump	231	☐ canteen	242		
☐ board meeting	200	☐ bromine	347	☐ capacitance	312		
☐ board of education	215	☐ bronze medal	232	☐ capacity crowd	231		
☐ board of trustees	215	☐ brusque	89	☐ capillary vessel	387		
☐ bodily secretion	387	☐ Brussels	186	☐ capitalize	147		
☐ body fat percentage	374	☐ Buddhist monastery	225	☐ capital gain	195		
☐ boisterous	89	☐ bug	321	☐ Capitol Hill	172		
☐ bolster	124	☐ bulk discount	206	☐ capitulate	147		
☐ bombard	124	☐ bump	387	☐ captivating	34		
☐ bonding agent	347	☐ bungle	147	☐ carbohydrate	343		
☐ Bone Marrow	375	☐ bunk bed	242	☐ carbon compound	343		
☐ bookkeeper	200	☐ buoyant	56	☐ carbon nanotube	347		
☐ boom-and-bust	191	☐ burgeoning	56	☐ carburetor	337		
☐ boomerang kid	222	☐ business line	212	☐ cardboard box	242		
☐ boon	158	☐ busy tone	318	☐ cardiac disease	381		
☐ boorish	89	☐ by-election results	178	☐ cardinal	34		
☐ boot	320			☐ cardinal number	353		
☐ border skirmish	182	**C**		☐ cardiopulmonary	375		
☐ borrowed capital	197	☐ cabinet approval rate	177	☐ career consumer	227		
☐ bottle-fed baby	222	☐ cabinet reshuffle	173	☐ career track	200		
☐ boundary surface	308	☐ cable modem	319	☐ caretaker Cabinet	177		
☐ bourse	197	☐ cable network	319	☐ carnivorous animal	363		
☐ bout sheet	232	☐ Caesarean section operation	381	☐ carrel	217		
☐ Boy Scout	177	☐ calcium carbonate	345	☐ carrier current	318		
☐ Braille edition	218	☐ caliper	330	☐ car exhaust	364		
☐ brain drain	212	☐ calligraphy master	219	☐ cascade connection	316		
☐ brandish	147	☐ callous	57	☐ castle renovation	245		
☐ brazen	89	☐ calorific capacity	334	☐ casting vote	173		
☐ breach of contract	212	☐ campaign platform	177	☐ cast iron	340		
☐ breakdown test	331	☐ camper	237	☐ catalyst	158		
☐ breaking current	328	☐ cam gear	335	☐ catalyst action	343		
☐ breakpoint	324	☐ cancer notification	379	☐ cataract induction	381		
☐ briefing	201	☐ candid	34	☐ catastrophe reserve	198		
☐ brine	347						
☐ brisk	34						

索引

393

☐ catchy	34		172	☐ coddle	147
☐ categorical	57	☐ chemical bonding	347	☐ code conversion	324
☐ cater	111	☐ chemical fertilizer	343	☐ COE	212
☐ caterer	223	☐ chemical formula	348	☐ coerce	124
☐ cathode	311	☐ cherish	111	☐ cogeneration	365
☐ cathode-ray tube	314	☐ cherry blossom front		☐ cogent	89
☐ cation	347		367	☐ coherence	308
☐ Caucasoid	227	☐ Chicano	227	☐ coherent	35
☐ cease-fire	183	☐ chicken pox	381	☐ cohesion	348
☐ celestial body	360	☐ chisel	339	☐ cold front	367
☐ censure	111	☐ chitin	346	☐ collaborate	111
☐ census bureau	177	☐ chloride	344	☐ collateral	203
☐ center of gravity	305	☐ chocolate out of		☐ collective bargaining	
☐ centrifugal force	305	courtesy	228		198
☐ centrifugal separator		☐ CIF	203	☐ colloidal solution	348
	337	☐ circulated water cooling		☐ color bar	226
☐ cerebral cortex	387		333	☐ color blindness	381
☐ cerebral hemorrhage		☐ circumference	353	☐ colossal	57
	381	☐ circumvent	124	☐ comatose patient	379
☐ ceremonial functions		☐ cistern	244	☐ combustible	334
	221	☐ civil war	176	☐ comic storyteller	224
☐ certificate of merit		☐ clandestine	57	☐ command of English	
	232	☐ classified ad	206		218
☐ certified financial		☐ claustrophobia	381	☐ commemorative photo	
analyst	197	☐ clearance sale	206		239
☐ chain-reaction of		☐ cleavage	331	☐ commensurate	89
bankruptcies	203	☐ clerical error	201	☐ commission	03
☐ chamber of commerce		☐ climatology	366	☐ communal	58
	210	☐ clippers	242	☐ commune	124
☐ Chancellor	173	☐ cloak-and-dagger story		☐ communicative	
☐ changeover switch			233	competence	225
	328	☐ clockwise rotation	333	☐ community chest	228
☐ character recognition		☐ closely-contested		☐ commutator	327
	324	constituency	177	☐ commuter pass	238
☐ charged particles	311	☐ co-education	215	☐ commuter train	238
☐ charging curve	314	☐ coach class	239	☐ commuting allowance	
☐ charter school	216	☐ coagulation point	348		204
☐ checks and balances		☐ coaxial cable	13	☐ comparable	35

- ☐ comparative advertising 209
- ☐ compatibility 324
- ☐ compelling 58
- ☐ competitive price 212
- ☐ compile 111
- ☐ complacent 35
- ☐ complete medical check-up 375
- ☐ complex fracture 381
- ☐ complex number 353
- ☐ complication 379
- ☐ complicity 158
- ☐ composed function 353
- ☐ compound 111
- ☐ compress 375
- ☐ compressor 337
- ☐ compulsive 36
- ☐ compulsive clotheshorse 228
- ☐ compulsory automobile liability insurance 197
- ☐ compulsory education 216
- ☐ Computer-Assisted Instruction 321
- ☐ Computer Aided Design 321
- ☐ Computer Aided Software Engineering 323
- ☐ concede 112
- ☐ conceivable 36
- ☐ concerto 233
- ☐ concierge 223
- ☐ concoct 124
- ☐ condenser 308
- ☐ condescending 58
- ☐ condominium 245
- ☐ condone 124
- ☐ conducive 58
- ☐ conduction band 312
- ☐ confectionery 210
- ☐ confiscate 125
- ☐ conform 112
- ☐ conformity 324
- ☐ confound 125
- ☐ Confucian 225
- ☐ congenital disease 381
- ☐ coniferous trees 363
- ☐ conjure 125
- ☐ connecting rod 335
- ☐ connection diagram 315
- ☐ connive 147
- ☐ connotation 218
- ☐ conscientious objector 183
- ☐ consecutive operation 332
- ☐ conservation of momentum 305
- ☐ consignment sale 209
- ☐ consolidated statement 197
- ☐ consort 147
- ☐ consortium 212
- ☐ constitutional amendment 173
- ☐ constitutional diagram 332
- ☐ consulate general 182
- ☐ consummate 90
- ☐ contact breaker 328
- ☐ contentious 58
- ☐ contour line 368
- ☐ contrive 112
- ☐ control unit 328
- ☐ controversial gerrymandering 177
- ☐ convection 307
- ☐ convergence 308
- ☐ convertible 237
- ☐ convertible currency 193
- ☐ convex lens 308
- ☐ convulsion 385
- ☐ coolant 344
- ☐ copious 90
- ☐ cordial 36
- ☐ corner the market 196
- ☐ coronary aneurysm 381
- ☐ corporal punishment 219
- ☐ corporate headquarters 200
- ☐ Corporate Rehabilitation Law 192
- ☐ corporate warrior 223
- ☐ corpulent 90
- ☐ correlation analysis 354
- ☐ correspondence course 219
- ☐ corroborate 147
- ☐ corrupt autocracy 175
- ☐ cosmic ray 361
- ☐ costume pageant 233
- ☐ cottage industry 211
- ☐ couch potato 228
- ☐ Coulomb force 312
- ☐ courseware 324
- ☐ course syllabus 216

☐ courtesy call	182	
☐ courtesy car	237	
☐ courtyard	244	
☐ covalent bond	348	
☐ covariance	306	
☐ coy	90	
☐ crafty	90	
☐ crash diet	223	
☐ crash program	212, 216	
☐ crass	58	
☐ credit-system high school	216	
☐ creditor	206	
☐ creditor account	197	
☐ credit sale	203	
☐ creep	332	
☐ crematorium	245	
☐ Creole	218	
☐ crescent moon	360	
☐ cripple	112	
☐ crisp	36	
☐ critical mass	306	
☐ crooked	36	
☐ cross-beam	244	
☐ cross section	331	
☐ crouch	148	
☐ crude oil	348	
☐ crumble	112	
☐ crumpled	58	
☐ crust	371	
☐ crux	158	
☐ cryogenic system	338	
☐ cryosurgery	375	
☐ cryptic	90	
☐ crystal lattice	306	
☐ cubic centimeter	354	
☐ cull	148	

☐ culminate	125	
☐ curator	224	
☐ curb	125	
☐ current density	312	
☐ current meter	337	
☐ cursory	90	
☐ curt	58	
☐ curtail	112	
☐ customs official	223	
☐ cutoff frequency	318	
☐ cybernaut	324	

D

☐ dabble	148	
☐ dainty	58	
☐ dairy farming	211	
☐ dampen	125	
☐ damper	335	
☐ damping oscillation	306	
☐ dandruff	387	
☐ daring	36	
☐ data compression	321	
☐ daunting	58	
☐ Dayton Agreement	186	
☐ deadly	36	
☐ dealer spot	209	
☐ dearth	158	
☐ death with dignity	375	
☐ debase	148	
☐ debenture	195	
☐ debriefing	361	
☐ debugging	321	
☐ decayed tooth	382	
☐ deceased	36	
☐ decimal point	354	
☐ decimate	148	
☐ decipher	125	
☐ decisive	36	

☐ decomposition	348	
☐ decrepit	90	
☐ decry	125	
☐ deep-sea fishing	210	
☐ deep ecology	364	
☐ default	192	
☐ defective product	206	
☐ defense expenditure	176	
☐ deference	158	
☐ deficit-ridden company	200	
☐ defile	148	
☐ deflect	125	
☐ deflection	314	
☐ deforestation	364	
☐ deformed	59	
☐ defraud	148	
☐ defray	148	
☐ defrosting cycle	334	
☐ deft	59	
☐ defunct	59	
☐ degassing	333	
☐ degenerate	112	
☐ degeneration	332	
☐ degreeocracy	226	
☐ degree of dispersion	333	
☐ dehumidifier	241	
☐ dehydration	333	
☐ dehydrator	241	
☐ deindustrialization	211	
☐ dejected	59	
☐ delay distortion	316	
☐ delimiter	324	
☐ delineate	148	
☐ deluge	158	
☐ delve	126	

☐ demanding 36	☐ dew point 367	☐ disarmament talks 183
☐ demarcate 149	☐ dexterous 59	☐ disavow 149
☐ demise of Emperor 227	☐ diabetes mellitus 382	☐ disband 126
☐ Democratic caucus 177	☐ diabolical 91	☐ discharge current 314
☐ Democratic pollster 177	☐ diagnostic program 321	☐ discharge regulator 337
☐ demote 126	☐ diagonal line 354	☐ discomfort index 368
☐ demure 90	☐ dialectic materialism 225	☐ discrete units 324
☐ denomination 190	☐ diaphragm contraction 387	☐ discus throw 231
☐ denounce 112	☐ didactic 91	☐ disengage 149
☐ density 348	☐ dietary fiber 375	☐ disgruntled 92
☐ dental cavity 380	☐ Diet dissolution 172	☐ dishonored bill 203
☐ dental floss 242	☐ diffident 91	☐ disinfection 348
☐ depict 112	☐ diffraction grating 309	☐ disinformation alert 183
☐ deportee 182	☐ diffuse 113	☐ disintegration 158
☐ deposition 348	☐ diffused reflection 313	☐ disinvestment 196
☐ depreciation 197	☐ diffusion current 314	☐ disk herniation 382
☐ deputy Prime Minister 173	☐ digital versatile disc 323	☐ dislocation 382
☐ deranged 90	☐ digitization 324	☐ dismal 37
☐ derelict 91	☐ dilapidated 91	☐ dismantle 127
☐ deride 126	☐ dilated 59	☐ dismember 149
☐ derivative 195, 357	☐ dilute 126	☐ disparaging 59
☐ derogatory 59	☐ dimensional change 330	☐ disparity 159
☐ desert island 370	☐ diminutive 92	☐ dispassionate 60
☐ desiccant 344	☐ dimple 387	☐ dispel 113
☐ desiccate 149	☐ diode 313	☐ disperse 114
☐ despicable 37	☐ diplomatic immunity 182	☐ displaced 37
☐ detached 37	☐ dire 59	☐ disposable camera 228
☐ detached retina 382	☐ direct-indirect tax ratio 190	☐ disposable diaper 242
☐ determinant 354	☐ directivity 318	☐ disposition 158
☐ deterrent capability 185	☐ direct current circuit 315	☐ disrupt 114
☐ deviate 112		☐ dissect 150
☐ deviation value 216		☐ dissemble 150
☐ devious 91		☐ disseminate 127
☐ devout 59		☐ dissertation 216
		☐ dissipate 150
		☐ dissolution 348

索引

- ☐ dissolve 114
- ☐ distillation 348
- ☐ distort 114
- ☐ distortion factor 316
- ☐ distract 114
- ☐ distributor 328
- ☐ disturbing wave 319
- ☐ ditching machine 340
- ☐ diverge 127
- ☐ divert 114
- ☐ divest 127
- ☐ divestiture 200
- ☐ dividend 196
- ☐ divisor 354
- ☐ divulge 150
- ☐ documentary elimination 215
- ☐ dollar-buying intervention 193
- ☐ dollar-denominated bond 193
- ☐ domestic prelate 225
- ☐ dominant genes 375
- ☐ doorsill 244
- ☐ doping test 232
- ☐ dormant volcano 369
- ☐ dormitory 217
- ☐ dosage adjustment 375
- ☐ double-cross 127
- ☐ double-digit inflation 191
- ☐ double standard 228
- ☐ downlink 319
- ☐ downtime 204, 316
- ☐ draconian 92
- ☐ drainage pipe 241
- ☐ drawing 332
- ☐ drawing room 244

- ☐ dreary 37
- ☐ drier 241
- ☐ drilling machine 339
- ☐ drive time 209
- ☐ drowsy 37, 61
- ☐ drug-induced depression 383
- ☐ dry battery 348
- ☐ dry spell 367
- ☐ dubbing artist 224
- ☐ dubious 37
- ☐ ductility 332
- ☐ duplicate 242
- ☐ duplicate 37
- ☐ durable goods 241
- ☐ durable years 204
- ☐ duration 332
- ☐ dustpan 242
- ☐ dwindle 114
- ☐ dynamo 327

E

- ☐ E. coli 375
- ☐ eardrum 387
- ☐ early scouting of university students 198
- ☐ earmark 127
- ☐ earnings estimate 203
- ☐ earnings per share 196
- ☐ earpick 242
- ☐ earthquake-proof construction 368
- ☐ earthquake swarm 371
- ☐ eaves 244
- ☐ ebb and flow 368
- ☐ Ebonics 218
- ☐ ebullient 92
- ☐ ecclesiastical music 234
- ☐ eco-friendly car 365
- ☐ ecofeminism 364
- ☐ economic-stimulus package 190
- ☐ economic blockade 193
- ☐ economic fluctuation 191
- ☐ ecumenicalism 224
- ☐ eddying current 370
- ☐ edifying 92
- ☐ eerie 92
- ☐ effective area 330
- ☐ effective power 327
- ☐ egalitarian society 226
- ☐ egregious 93
- ☐ elasticity 332
- ☐ elastic deformation 332
- ☐ elated 61
- ☐ election returns 178
- ☐ electoral college 178
- ☐ Electra complex 222
- ☐ electric charge 311
- ☐ electric flux 312
- ☐ electric potential 312
- ☐ electric scalpel 375
- ☐ electrocardiogram 375
- ☐ electrochemistry 348
- ☐ electrolysis 312
- ☐ electromagnetic force 312
- ☐ electromagnetic induction 312
- ☐ electromagnetic wave 319
- ☐ electrostatic induction 312
- ☐ elevation above sea

level	371	☐ endoscopic treatment		☐ eschatology	224
☐ elicit	127		373	☐ eschew	150
☐ eligible man	222	☐ endowment insurance		☐ escrow	212
☐ eligible voter	178		192	☐ esophagus	388
☐ elliptical orbit	360	☐ energy conservation		☐ esoteric	62
☐ elucidate	150		365	☐ esoteric Buddhism	225
☐ elude	127	☐ engaging	93	☐ espouse	150
☐ emaciated	61	☐ engender	129	☐ estranged	62
☐ emanate	127	☐ engrave	129	☐ estuary	370
☐ embankment	370	☐ engulf	129	☐ ether	346
☐ embassy civilian	182	☐ enigmatic	37	☐ ethics	214
☐ embedded	61	☐ enlist	129	☐ ethnocentric mentality	
☐ embellish	127	☐ ensuing	61		175
☐ embrace	114	☐ entail	129	☐ ethylene	346
☐ embroidery	234	☐ enterprising	38	☐ ethyl alcohol	346
☐ embryonic	61	☐ enticing	61	☐ etymology	214
☐ emeritus professor	215	☐ entitlement program		☐ euthanasia	375
☐ emery paper	243, 339		177	☐ evacuation drill	368
☐ emission control	365	☐ entity	159	☐ evade	115
☐ emission trading	365	☐ entry angle	308	☐ evangelical doctrine	
☐ emissivity	334	☐ enumerate	129		224
☐ empathic	61	☐ enunciate	129	☐ evaporation	349
☐ employer matching		☐ ephemeral	93	☐ evasive	38
plans	204	☐ epicenter	368	☐ even number	354
☐ empty-nest syndrome		☐ epicurean tastes	228	☐ evoke	129
	222	☐ epilepsy seizure	379	☐ evolutionism	364
☐ emulate	128	☐ epitome	159	☐ exacting	93
☐ emulsion	344	☐ epoxy resin	348	☐ exalted	62
☐ enchanting	37	☐ equilibrium	349	☐ exasperated	62
☐ encoder	324	☐ equilibrium	159	☐ excess liabilities	191
☐ encroach	128	☐ equitable	61	☐ excess packaging	364
☐ encumber	129	☐ equities	195	☐ exchange gains from	
☐ endangered species		☐ eradicate	129	strong yen	191
	365	☐ erode	114	☐ excise tax	190
☐ endearing	61	☐ erosion	333	☐ exclusive	38
☐ endocrine pancreas		☐ erratic	38	☐ exclusive contract	209
	387	☐ error detection	324	☐ exclusive economic	
☐ endorse	114	☐ erudite	62	zone	193

索引

- ☐ excretion amount 375
- ☐ excruciating 62
- ☐ execution 324
- ☐ exhilarating 93
- ☐ exhort 130
- ☐ existential approach 225
- ☐ exodus of refugees 182
- ☐ exonerate 150
- ☐ exorbitant 62
- ☐ expansion memory 323
- ☐ expatriate children 227
- ☐ expedite 150
- ☐ expense accounters 204
- ☐ explicit 38
- ☐ exploit 115
- ☐ explosives 341
- ☐ exponential function 354
- ☐ exposure 334
- ☐ expound 150
- ☐ exquisite 38
- ☐ extant 93
- ☐ extended family 221
- ☐ extensibility 321
- ☐ extension courses 216
- ☐ extension number 201
- ☐ extinguisher 338
- ☐ extol 130
- ☐ extract 349
- ☐ extradition of terrorists 184
- ☐ extramarital sex 222
- ☐ extrasensory perception 226
- ☐ extraterrestrial 361
- ☐ extraterritorial right 182
- ☐ extroverted nature 225
- ☐ exuberant 93
- ☐ eyepiece lens 308
- ☐ eye strain 383

F

- ☐ fabricate 115
- ☐ factorial 354
- ☐ false image 308
- ☐ faltering 62
- ☐ fanatic 38
- ☐ fanatic believer 225
- ☐ far-fetched 62
- ☐ far-reaching 62
- ☐ fare adjustment office 238
- ☐ fare chart 238
- ☐ farm belt 211
- ☐ fastidious 63
- ☐ fatigue failure 331
- ☐ feasibility study 209
- ☐ feasibility test 316
- ☐ feasible 38
- ☐ featherbedding 204
- ☐ federal funds rate 190
- ☐ federal mandate 173
- ☐ feed pipe 337
- ☐ fermentation 349
- ☐ ferocious 63
- ☐ ferroconcrete 245
- ☐ ferromagnetic material 313
- ☐ fervent 63
- ☐ fetter 130
- ☐ feudalistic family system 222
- ☐ fiasco 159
- ☐ fickle 63
- ☐ Fields prize 219
- ☐ field study 215
- ☐ figurative arts 233
- ☐ filial piety 222
- ☐ filibustering senate 173
- ☐ filtration 349
- ☐ final 216
- ☐ final game 232
- ☐ financial meltdown 192
- ☐ finished surface 331
- ☐ fire extinguisher 241
- ☐ fire hydrant 245
- ☐ first-aid kit 375
- ☐ first-grade river 370
- ☐ First Amendment 173
- ☐ first run of a film 233
- ☐ fiscal expansionism 173
- ☐ fiscal policy 190
- ☐ fitting 339
- ☐ fixtures and fittings 209
- ☐ flagrant 63
- ☐ flagship 209
- ☐ flag drop 238
- ☐ flamboyant 63
- ☐ flashy 66
- ☐ flash heater 241
- ☐ flash point 349
- ☐ flaunt 151
- ☐ fledgling 93
- ☐ flimsy 66
- ☐ flippant 93
- ☐ floating ice 368
- ☐ flooding above the floor 368
- ☐ flounder 151
- ☐ flower bed 244

☐ fluctuation noise	319	
☐ fluorescent lamp	242	
☐ flush toilet	245	
☐ fly-by-night operation	209	
☐ Foggy Bottom	176	
☐ foil	130	
☐ folding chair	242	
☐ foment	151	
☐ food chain	363	
☐ food poisoning	383	
☐ foot-and-mouth disease	383	
☐ forced landing	239	
☐ forced termination	320	
☐ force per unit area	330	
☐ forcible vomiting	383	
☐ foreign exchange gain	193	
☐ foreign exchange rate	193	
☐ foreign reserve	193	
☐ forensic club	217	
☐ forensic psychiatrist	375	
☐ forestall	130	
☐ forest bath	240	
☐ forge	115	
☐ forged steel	340	
☐ fork road	239	
☐ formidable	38	
☐ forthcoming book	233	
☐ fortuitous	66	
☐ foundation bolt	340	
☐ four-wheeled car	237	
☐ fractious	66	
☐ fracture	331	
☐ frantic	66	
☐ fraught	67	
☐ freeloader	223	
☐ freeware	323	
☐ free electron	311	
☐ frenzy	159	
☐ frequency modulation	318	
☐ frequency response	318	
☐ frequent flier	239	
☐ fret	115	
☐ friction coefficient	331	
☐ Frigid Zone	367	
☐ fringe benefit	201	
☐ frivolous	38	
☐ front-wheel-drive	336	
☐ fuel cell	349	
☐ fuel replenishment	239	
☐ full-fledged	67	
☐ full scale	330	
☐ fumble	151	
☐ fundamental unit	354	
☐ furtive	93	
☐ fuse wire	341	
☐ fusibility	349	
☐ futures market	195	

G

☐ G8 communique	185	
☐ gain	316	
☐ gaining issues	195	
☐ galaxy	360	
☐ gallstone	383	
☐ galvanize	151	
☐ galvanized iron sheet	244	
☐ galvanometer	316	
☐ garbage dump	364	
☐ garbled	94	
☐ garish	94	
☐ garment	159	
☐ garment industry	206	
☐ garner	130	
☐ garrulous	94	
☐ gasket	333	
☐ gastric hyperacidity	383	
☐ gastric ulcer	383	
☐ gastrointestinal disease	383	
☐ gastro - camera	375	
☐ gatepost	244	
☐ gaunt	67	
☐ geek	228	
☐ gender segregation	226	
☐ general-purpose computer	320	
☐ generic drug	375	
☐ genitals	387	
☐ geology	214	
☐ geometric distortion	331	
☐ geriatric disease	383	
☐ ghost image	319	
☐ giddy	67	
☐ gift tax	190	
☐ gigantic	39	
☐ gilt-edged bond	195	
☐ gimlet	242	
☐ gist	160	
☐ glamorous	39	
☐ glass ceiling	200	
☐ glib	67	
☐ glitch	340	
☐ global hegemony	185	

索引

- ☐ globocop 185
- ☐ glocalism 227
- ☐ glossy 40
- ☐ glossy finish 244
- ☐ glycerin 346
- ☐ gobble 115
- ☐ God-given revelation 224
- ☐ gold-plated spoon 242
- ☐ golden oldie 234
- ☐ gold plating 349
- ☐ gonorrhea 379
- ☐ goods and chattels 197
- ☐ goose pimple 387
- ☐ gout attack 383
- ☐ government-ruled municipality 174
- ☐ governmental immunity 174
- ☐ government bond 195
- ☐ government dignitary 174
- ☐ GPA 216
- ☐ grader 340
- ☐ gradient 309
- ☐ graffiti 228
- ☐ grammatical competence 218
- ☐ grandiose 94
- ☐ grandstand play 231
- ☐ grand slam 231
- ☐ granite 371
- ☐ grant bounty 190
- ☐ graphic 67
- ☐ graphite 371
- ☐ grapple 130
- ☐ gratuitous 94
- ☐ gravimetric analysis 331
- ☐ gravitational energy 305
- ☐ gravitational force 305
- ☐ greatest common denominator 359
- ☐ greenmail payment 196
- ☐ greenway 238
- ☐ gregarious 40
- ☐ groin 387
- ☐ grope 115
- ☐ gross weight 331
- ☐ grouchy 94
- ☐ ground-breaking ceremony 244
- ☐ ground-controlled interception 183
- ☐ groundless 40
- ☐ grudge 115
- ☐ grueling 67
- ☐ gruesome 94
- ☐ grumble 115
- ☐ guarantor 206
- ☐ gubernatorial election 178
- ☐ gullible 40
- ☐ gum disease 385
- ☐ guru's adherents 225
- ☐ gymnastics club 217
- ☐ gymnastic rings 232
- ☐ gyrate 340
- ☐ gyroscope 340

H

- ☐ haggard 67
- ☐ haggle 151
- ☐ hail 367
- ☐ hair growth stimulant 242
- ☐ halcyon 94
- ☐ half-life 309
- ☐ hallowed 94
- ☐ hallucinogenic drug 375
- ☐ halogen 344
- ☐ hamper 115
- ☐ handicraft 234
- ☐ handrail 244
- ☐ hand grenade 183
- ☐ hangover 383
- ☐ haphazard 67
- ☐ harbinger 160
- ☐ hardness meter 332
- ☐ harmonics 315
- ☐ harrowing 96
- ☐ hate crime 226
- ☐ haunting 40
- ☐ having more wins than losses 232
- ☐ hazardous 40
- ☐ hazy 67
- ☐ health and physical education 214
- ☐ health spa 228
- ☐ hearse 237
- ☐ heartburn 383
- ☐ heat & current conductivity 312
- ☐ heavily-indebted poor countries 192
- ☐ heavy water 345
- ☐ hectic 68
- ☐ hefty 68
- ☐ heinous 96
- ☐ hemophiliac 379

☐ hepatitis C	383	
☐ herald	116	
☐ herbicide	364	
☐ herd mentality	225	
☐ heretic	40	
☐ heterosexual contact	222	
☐ heyday	160	
☐ hieroglyphic inscription	219	
☐ high-definition television	319	
☐ high-frequency wave	318	
☐ high-mileage car	237	
☐ high-rise	245	
☐ high-tension wire	328	
☐ high-ticket items	209	
☐ high income bracket	226	
☐ high jump	231	
☐ high molecular compound	344	
☐ high resolution	319	
☐ high voltage	328	
☐ hilarious	68	
☐ hives	379	
☐ holding current	314	
☐ holiday train schedule	238	
☐ homage	160	
☐ homeland security	184	
☐ home delivery	209	
☐ homogeneous society	228	
☐ hone	151	
☐ honey truck	237	
☐ honorific prefix	218	
☐ honors student	215	
☐ horizontal axis	354	
☐ horizontal resolution	319	
☐ horrendous	68	
☐ horsemanship	232	
☐ household appliance	241	
☐ housekeeping gene	383	
☐ House of Councilors	172	
☐ house sitter	224	
☐ housing development	245	
☐ housing subsidy	190	
☐ Hubble Space Telescope	361	
☐ humdrum	68	
☐ humidity	367	
☐ hydraulic	337	
☐ hydraulics	306	
☐ hydrodynamics	306	
☐ hydrofoil	238	
☐ hydrogen sulfide	345	
☐ hydrolysis	349	
☐ hydrophilic	349	
☐ hydroponics	365	
☐ hyperbola	354	
☐ hypersonic wave	318	
☐ hypertension	383	
☐ hyphenated American	227	
☐ hypnotic therapy	375	

I

☐ "I" novel	233
☐ iceberg	370
☐ ice column	371
☐ idiosyncratic	96
☐ idle time	340
☐ idyllic	96
☐ igneous rock	371
☐ ignition coil	338
☐ ignoble	96
☐ illegible	40
☐ illustrious	96
☐ image processing	324
☐ imbue	151
☐ immaculate	68
☐ immerse	130
☐ immersion	349
☐ immigrant influx	227
☐ imminent	68
☐ immune	40
☐ immune therapy	375
☐ impassioned	96
☐ impeachment vote	174
☐ impeccable	68
☐ impedance matching	315
☐ impede	116
☐ impending	68
☐ imperative	40
☐ imperious	96
☐ impermeable	349
☐ impervious	68
☐ impetus	160
☐ import quota	193
☐ import trade agency	224
☐ impoverish	151
☐ impregnable	96
☐ impromptu	219
☐ improvise	116
☐ impudent	41
☐ impurity	344

☐ in-home separation 222	207	☐ insidious 70
☐ in-hospital infection 383	☐ inept 69	☐ insinuating 70
☐ in-phase 316	☐ inequality 354	☐ insipid 70
☐ inadvertent 96	☐ inexorable 97	☐ installment plan 203
☐ inaugural address 173	☐ infatuate 130	☐ instantaneous 41
☐ incandescent lamp 328	☐ infest 117	☐ instant glue 243
☐ incapacitate 97, 151	☐ infiltrate 152	☐ instigate 131
☐ incentive system 207	☐ infinitesimal 97	☐ instill 131
☐ incessant 41	☐ inflammation of the middle ear 383	☐ institutional investor 195
☐ incineration site 364	☐ inflationary spiral 191	☐ insulation 244, 313
☐ incipient 69	☐ inflection 331	☐ insurance beneficiary 197
☐ incisive 97	☐ inflict 117	☐ insurance canvasser 224
☐ inclination 354	☐ informal job offer 207	☐ insurmountable 71
☐ incorporate 117	☐ information retrieval 321	☐ integer 354
☐ incorrigible 97	☐ informed consent 376	☐ integral 41
☐ incubation period 375	☐ infrared rays 308	☐ integrate 356
☐ inculcate 152	☐ infuse 153	☐ integrate 117
☐ incumbent mayor 173	☐ ingenious 41	☐ integrated circuit 313
☐ incur 130	☐ ingenuous 69	☐ intelligence infiltration 183
☐ indebted 41	☐ ingrained 69	☐ intelligible 41
☐ indelible 69	☐ ingratiating 97	☐ interactive computer shopping 325
☐ independent corporation 207	☐ inheritance waiver 197	☐ intercept 131
☐ indexation 190	☐ inhibit 117	☐ intercultural communication 218
☐ indigenous tribes 227	☐ inimical 97	☐ interdisciplinary approach 216
☐ indigent 69	☐ iniquitous 97	☐ interferometry 308
☐ indignant 41	☐ initialization 320	☐ interim report 198
☐ indirect lighting 328	☐ inner-city school 219	☐ intermission 233
☐ indisposed 97	☐ inordinate 97	☐ intermittent 371
☐ indolent 41	☐ inorganic chemistry 349	☐ internal combustion engine 338
☐ induce 117	☐ input and output devices 320	☐ internal safety valve
☐ induced current 314	☐ inquisitive 70	
☐ indulgent 41	☐ insatiable 70	
☐ industrial complex 211	☐ inscrutable 70	
☐ industrial espionage 212	☐ insecticide 242	
☐ industrial restructuring		

☐		329
☐ International Date Line		
		368
☐ Internaut		325
☐ Internet-enabled people		
		325
☐ interplanetary travel		
		361
☐ interrupted control		332
☐ intersection		239
☐ intimidate		117
☐ intoxicated		43
☐ intractable		71
☐ intranet		325
☐ intravenous drip		373
☐ intrepid		98
☐ intricate		43
☐ intrinsic		43
☐ introspective		100
☐ intrude		117
☐ inundation		368
☐ invariable		356
☐ inverse matrix		356
☐ investment portfolio		
		196
☐ invincible		71
☐ invoice		201
☐ invoke		131
☐ involuntary muscle		387
☐ ionic bond		348
☐ IOU		210
☐ irate		100
☐ iridium		340
☐ iron ore		371
☐ irrefutable		71
☐ irrelevant		43
☐ irrevocable		71
☐ irrigation		365
☐ Islamic fundamentalism		
		176
☐ isotope		344
☐ Israel enclave		176
☐ issuing gas		349

J

☐ jaded		100
☐ Japanese Archipelago		
		369
☐ javelin throw		231
☐ jazz improvisation		234
☐ jeopardize		131
☐ job action		205
☐ job opening		200
☐ job transfer away from		
one's home		207
☐ joint custody		222
☐ jovial		71
☐ jubilant		71
☐ juggle		131
☐ junction		238
☐ just-in-time marketing		
		205

K

☐ kaleidoscope		334
☐ keeping a useless		
person on the payroll		
for life		229
☐ kerosene		242
☐ key chain		242
☐ key currency		193
☐ kidney dialysis		376
☐ killer application		323
☐ kinetic energy		305
☐ kink in one's neck		383
☐ kissing cousin		221
☐ knotty		100
☐ knowledge-intensive		
industry		211
☐ Kyoto Protocol		365

L

☐ Labor Standards Law		
		207
☐ labor union		201
☐ lackluster		71
☐ laconic		100
☐ lagging material		341
☐ laissez-faire		189
☐ lame duck		178
☐ laminated spring		340
☐ landmark deal		227
☐ land development		212
☐ land reclamation		364
☐ land shark		224
☐ land shelf		371
☐ land subsidence		371
☐ lapping		339
☐ large intestines		387
☐ laser beam printer		334
☐ laser scanning		334
☐ latchkey child		222
☐ latency time		324
☐ latent ability		225
☐ lathe		339
☐ latitude		369
☐ lattice defect		306
☐ lattice work		244
☐ laudable		71
☐ lava		371
☐ lavish		43
☐ law of conservation of		
energy		305
☐ law of inertia		305

- ☐ laxative property 376
- ☐ lax agnosticism 224
- ☐ layered structure 321
- ☐ layman 160
- ☐ leading role 233
- ☐ leaflet 206
- ☐ left-wing extremist 176
- ☐ legislative branch 172
- ☐ legitimate self-defense 182
- ☐ lenient 71
- ☐ letterhead 204
- ☐ level ground 370
- ☐ lever 242
- ☐ leveraged buyout 211
- ☐ levy 131
- ☐ lewd 72
- ☐ lexicographic work 219
- ☐ Liberal Democratic Party's primaries 178
- ☐ licensed tax accountant 197
- ☐ license plate 237
- ☐ life-size statue 233
- ☐ life-support system 375
- ☐ lifelong education 219
- ☐ lifestyle-related disease 383
- ☐ lifetime employment 201
- ☐ life expectancy 221
- ☐ life test 328
- ☐ lift-off 361
- ☐ lighthouse 245
- ☐ lightning rod 329
- ☐ light emitting diode 313
- ☐ light intensity 308
- ☐ limestone 371
- ☐ liner 238
- ☐ lingering 44
- ☐ lingua franca 218
- ☐ linguistic semantics 218
- ☐ linguistic xenophobia 218
- ☐ liquefaction 364
- ☐ liquefied natural gas 349
- ☐ liquidated company 205
- ☐ liquid crystal display 324
- ☐ listed stock 195
- ☐ listless 72
- ☐ list price 209
- ☐ literacy rate 219
- ☐ literary coterie 233
- ☐ lithium 349
- ☐ living liver transplantation 376
- ☐ load current 328
- ☐ local allocation tax 190
- ☐ local anesthesia 376
- ☐ local autonomy 177
- ☐ local content legislation 198
- ☐ local procurement 198
- ☐ local specialty 240
- ☐ locus 356
- ☐ lodging house 244
- ☐ log 204
- ☐ logarithm 356
- ☐ logging 323
- ☐ logical circuit 321
- ☐ logistic assistance 183
- ☐ long-running program 233
- ☐ longitudinal 319
- ☐ long horse vault 232
- ☐ looming 44
- ☐ lopsided victory 178
- ☐ loquacious 101
- ☐ louver door 245
- ☐ low-end product 203
- ☐ low-fare carrier 211
- ☐ low-margin high-turnover 207
- ☐ lubricant 349
- ☐ lucid 72
- ☐ lucrative 72
- ☐ ludicrous 72
- ☐ lukewarm 72
- ☐ lumbago 384
- ☐ luminous intensity 308
- ☐ lunar module 361
- ☐ lurid 101
- ☐ lurk 117
- ☐ lush 101
- ☐ lust 160
- ☐ luster 161
- ☐ luxuriant 72
- ☐ lymphatic gland 387

M

- ☐ macabre 101
- ☐ mad cow disease 381
- ☐ magnanimous 44
- ☐ magnetic flux 312
- ☐ Magneto-Optical 323
- ☐ magnification 308
- ☐ maiden voyage 239
- ☐ mail order business 206

☐ mainstream faction 176	☐ maximum torque 332	☐ microbiological assays 349
☐ maintenance engineer 340	☐ meadow 370	☐ microfinance 192
☐ main memory 323	☐ meager 44	☐ microwave 318
☐ major contender 178	☐ meander 131	☐ microwave cooker 241
☐ makeshift houses 245	☐ mean power 327	☐ mid-career recruiting 204
☐ malevolent 72	☐ mean value 356	☐ middle-age bulge 384
☐ male chauvinist pig 226	☐ measuring instrument 316	☐ middle-of-the-road party 176
☐ malignant tumor 384	☐ mechanical energy 305	☐ migrant worker 224
☐ malnutrition 378	☐ mechanical pencil 243	☐ military action 182
☐ malpractice liability 378	☐ meddle 118	☐ military junta 185
☐ managing director 204	☐ mediation clause 183	☐ military reprisal 182
☐ mandatory retirement 201	☐ Medicaid eligibility 376	☐ militia commander 183
☐ manipulate 118	☐ medical diagnosis 378	☐ millennium celebration 225
☐ manometer 332	☐ mediocre 73	☐ milling 339
☐ manual welding 334	☐ melting point 349	☐ mingle 118
☐ margin trading 196	☐ menial 73	☐ minimum clearance 330
☐ marital 44	☐ menopausal discomfort 384	☐ minimum wage 204
☐ marital rape 222	☐ menstruation 383	☐ minister 223
☐ market equilibrium 196	☐ mental retardation 384	☐ ministerial level talks 186
☐ markup 196	☐ mercenary 74	☐ mint 192
☐ massage brothel 228	☐ mercury column 349	☐ mirage 368
☐ mass spectrograph 349	☐ meridian 361	☐ mire 131
☐ master's degree 216	☐ mesmerize 132	☐ misalignment 309
☐ material point 305	☐ metabolic rate 384	☐ miscellaneous daily goods 242
☐ maternalism 204	☐ metal stamping 339	☐ miserly 44
☐ maternal lineage 221	☐ metastable 332	☐ misgiving 161
☐ maternity leave 201	☐ meteor 360	☐ mishap 161
☐ Matrix 323	☐ Meteorological Agency 367	☐ misleading 44
☐ mausoleum 227	☐ meteorology 214	☐ misplace 118
☐ maximum error 316	☐ methane gas 346	☐ missile deployment 183
☐ maximum output voltage 315	☐ methane hydrate 346	☐ mitigate 132
	☐ methanol alcohol 346	
	☐ methodical 44	
	☐ meticulous 44	
	☐ metrology 330	

- ☐ Mixed oxide fuel 348
- ☐ mnemonic device 219
- ☐ modulation 318
- ☐ moist hot towel for cleaning hands before a meal 242
- ☐ molding 340
- ☐ molecule 350
- ☐ momentum 305
- ☐ money-back guarantee 203, 209
- ☐ money laundering 197
- ☐ monogamy family 221
- ☐ monomer 350
- ☐ monumental 44
- ☐ moonlighting 201
- ☐ moor 153
- ☐ moot 101
- ☐ moral obligation 226
- ☐ moral vacuum 223
- ☐ morbid 74
- ☐ morning calisthenics 378
- ☐ morning sickness 384
- ☐ mortar 341
- ☐ mortify 153
- ☐ Moslem 225
- ☐ mosquito repellent 241
- ☐ most-favored-nation treatment 185
- ☐ most probable value 356
- ☐ mountain range 369
- ☐ mouthpiece 318
- ☐ moving company 224
- ☐ moxibustion 374
- ☐ muddle 153
- ☐ mudslinging barrage 178
- ☐ mud land 370
- ☐ muggy 45
- ☐ multi-storied parking lot 239
- ☐ multiple-car pileup 239
- ☐ multiple-choice exam 215
- ☐ multiple signal 319
- ☐ multiplying factor 356
- ☐ mundane 74
- ☐ murky 101
- ☐ mutilate 132
- ☐ mutual fund 196
- ☐ myriad 161
- ☐ mystic 74
- ☐ mystic animism 224

N

- ☐ nadir 161
- ☐ nail clippers 242
- ☐ nanosecond 309
- ☐ naphthalene 346
- ☐ National Aeronautics and Space Administration 361
- ☐ National Medal of Honor 227
- ☐ national treasury 190
- ☐ nature preservation 364
- ☐ nautical mile 371
- ☐ nebulous 101
- ☐ nefarious 101
- ☐ negligible 45
- ☐ negotiable instrument 196
- ☐ nepotistic succession 233
- ☐ Neptune 360
- ☐ net income 196
- ☐ net selling 196
- ☐ neutralization 350
- ☐ neutralize 118
- ☐ neutrino astronomy 361
- ☐ neutron 309
- ☐ niche business 206
- ☐ night shift 204
- ☐ nimble 45
- ☐ nitric acid 344
- ☐ nitrogen oxide 344
- ☐ no-frills flight 206
- ☐ no-show 239
- ☐ noble gas 344
- ☐ nocturnal animal 363
- ☐ Nolan Committee 186
- ☐ non-aggression treaty 185
- ☐ nonaffiliated voters 179
- ☐ nonaligned neutrality 185
- ☐ noncarbohydrate 344
- ☐ nonchalant 101
- ☐ nonferrous metal 340
- ☐ nonlinear 356
- ☐ nonrenewable energy 365
- ☐ normal delivery 378
- ☐ normal line 356
- ☐ normal solution 350
- ☐ normal stress 305
- ☐ Northern hemisphere 369
- ☐ nostril 387
- ☐ nosy 45

- ☐ notation 356
- ☐ novice 161
- ☐ noxious 101
- ☐ No Stopping 239
- ☐ No Thoroughfare 239
- ☐ nuclear freeze agreement 185
- ☐ nuclear holocaust 185
- ☐ nuclear proliferation 185
- ☐ nullify 153
- ☐ numerator 357
- ☐ numerical 357
- ☐ numerical control machine 339
- ☐ nursery school 216
- ☐ nursing care insurance 192
- ☐ nurture 118
- ☐ nutrient 344

O

- ☐ obesity remedy 378
- ☐ obliterate 132
- ☐ obnoxious 74
- ☐ obscene 45
- ☐ obscure 45
- ☐ obsess 118
- ☐ obsessive personality disorder 225
- ☐ obsolete 45
- ☐ obstetrician 378
- ☐ obtrusive 102
- ☐ occupied band-width 318
- ☐ oceanography 371
- ☐ ocean dumping 364
- ☐ ocean trench 370
- ☐ octane number 350
- ☐ ODA 185
- ☐ off-year election 178
- ☐ office supplies 204
- ☐ official discount rate 190
- ☐ official party endorsement 178
- ☐ officious 102
- ☐ offset 135
- ☐ offshore procurement 212
- ☐ oil concession 211
- ☐ oil diffusion pump 337
- ☐ oil refinery 211
- ☐ oligopoly market 196
- ☐ ombudsman 224
- ☐ ominous 45
- ☐ omnidirectional 332
- ☐ oncogene expression 378
- ☐ onerous 102
- ☐ online resident registry network 177
- ☐ onomatopoeia 219
- ☐ onslaught 161
- ☐ ooze 153
- ☐ operation by the public and private sectors 192
- ☐ ophthalmologist 378
- ☐ opinionated 74
- ☐ opinion ad 203
- ☐ opportune 74
- ☐ opposite phase 316
- ☐ optical fiber cable 319
- ☐ oral contraceptive 378
- ☐ order backlog 207
- ☐ Order of Culture 227
- ☐ order processing 206
- ☐ organic chemistry 350
- ☐ organ transplant 378
- ☐ ornate 102
- ☐ orthopedic surgeon 373
- ☐ oscillating circuit 315
- ☐ Oslo Agreement 186
- ☐ osmosis 350
- ☐ ostensible 74
- ☐ ostentatious 74
- ☐ osteopathy 373
- ☐ osteoporosis 379
- ☐ Ostpolitic 185
- ☐ ostracize 135
- ☐ otorhinolaryngologist 378
- ☐ oust 135
- ☐ out-of-service train 238
- ☐ outgrow 118
- ☐ outlet 328
- ☐ outpatient department 378
- ☐ output signal 315
- ☐ outrageous 45
- ☐ outset 161
- ☐ outsourcing 207
- ☐ outstanding debt 197
- ☐ outstanding government bonds 190
- ☐ outstanding share 195
- ☐ outstrip 135
- ☐ outweigh 118
- ☐ over-the-counter stock market 195
- ☐ overcast 74
- ☐ overdue 45

- ☐ overdue wages 207
- ☐ overhaul 135
- ☐ overheads 197
- ☐ override 136
- ☐ overrun 136
- ☐ overshoot 331
- ☐ overthrow 119
- ☐ overtone 161
- ☐ overvoltage 315
- ☐ oxide 350
- ☐ ozone depletion 364

P

- ☐ Pacific rim 369
- ☐ pacifier 242
- ☐ package deal 203
- ☐ pagan 75
- ☐ paid vacation 201
- ☐ Paleolithic Age 227
- ☐ paltry 75
- ☐ papal emissary 185
- ☐ paraffin 346
- ☐ paragon 162
- ☐ Paralympics 232
- ☐ paramagnetic material 313
- ☐ paramedic 378
- ☐ parameter 357
- ☐ paramount 75
- ☐ parity bit 321
- ☐ parliamentary system 172
- ☐ parochial 75
- ☐ part-timer 224
- ☐ partitioning 204
- ☐ party line 223
- ☐ passivation layer 350
- ☐ passive device 313
- ☐ patch board 328
- ☐ pathogen 384
- ☐ patrol wagon 237
- ☐ patron 206
- ☐ patronizing 75
- ☐ paucity 162
- ☐ payroll computations 325
- ☐ peaceful coexistence 184
- ☐ peace envoy 185
- ☐ pedagogy 214
- ☐ pedantic 75
- ☐ peddle 136
- ☐ pedestrians' overpass 239
- ☐ pediatrician 378
- ☐ pejorative 102
- ☐ pelvis 387
- ☐ penetration rate 198
- ☐ penitent 75
- ☐ pension 205
- ☐ pension contributions 192
- ☐ pent-up 75
- ☐ peptide bond 348
- ☐ perceptive 46
- ☐ percussion instrument 234
- ☐ peremptory 75
- ☐ performance appraisal 204
- ☐ perfunctory 77
- ☐ periodic law 350
- ☐ period adventure drama 233
- ☐ peripheral velocity 306
- ☐ permanent magnet 313
- ☐ permeability 312
- ☐ permeate 136
- ☐ permissible error 357
- ☐ permissive 46
- ☐ permutation 357
- ☐ pernicious 102
- ☐ perpetrate 136
- ☐ perpetual 47
- ☐ persistent organic pollutant 364
- ☐ personal information protection law 207
- ☐ personal magnetism 225
- ☐ personnel cost 201
- ☐ pertinent 47
- ☐ perturb 153
- ☐ pervasive 47
- ☐ per capita income 191
- ☐ pesticide 344
- ☐ petrochemical 344
- ☐ petrochemical industry 211
- ☐ petroleum refinery 350
- ☐ pharmaceutical industry 211
- ☐ pharmacist 223
- ☐ phase angle 316
- ☐ Philips screwdriver 243
- ☐ phlegm 379
- ☐ phony business trip 207
- ☐ phosphate 344
- ☐ photochemical smog 364
- ☐ photoelectric conversion 313

☐ photogenic	309	
☐ photometer	334	
☐ photon	309	
☐ photosynthesis	365	
☐ physical distribution		201
☐ physical quantity	309	
☐ physical strength and fitness test		232
☐ physiognomy	226	
☐ pictographic language		219
☐ picture story book	243	
☐ pier	371	
☐ piezoelectric	312	
☐ piggy bank	243	
☐ pigment	243	
☐ pilot plant	212	
☐ pimple	385	
☐ pinnacle	162	
☐ pinpoint	136	
☐ pique	153	
☐ pithy	77	
☐ pivotal	77	
☐ pixel	324	
☐ placate	136	
☐ placebo effect	378	
☐ placid	77	
☐ plaintive	102	
☐ planing	339	
☐ planned obsolescence		212
☐ plaque buildup	387	
☐ plasticine	341	
☐ plastic deformation	332	
☐ plastic sheet	243	
☐ plateau	370	
☐ plausible	47	

☐ player's number	232
☐ plenary convention	172
☐ plethora	162
☐ plight	162
☐ plumber	224
☐ plummet	136
☐ plunder	136
☐ plural society	226
☐ pneumatic tire	337
☐ pneumonia	385
☐ pocketbooks	233
☐ poignant	77
☐ point of action	305
☐ point of sale	203
☐ Polaris	361
☐ polarization	312
☐ polemic	102
☐ polio vaccination	378
☐ Politburo	177
☐ political assassination	176
☐ political asylum	186
☐ political backlash	176
☐ political clout	176
☐ political contribution	176
☐ political dissident	177
☐ political manifesto	176
☐ political turmoil	176
☐ polyethylene	346
☐ polymer chemistry	350
☐ polynomial	357
☐ polytechnic school	216
☐ pork-barrel politics	176
☐ portent	162
☐ positive charge	311
☐ post-office businesses	192

☐ posttraumatic stress disorder	385
☐ potassium	345
☐ potential energy	305
☐ powdered material	344
☐ power breakfast	176
☐ power transmission	328
☐ practitioner	378
☐ pre-listed shares	195
☐ precarious	78
☐ precept	162
☐ precious metals	340
☐ precipitant	350
☐ precipitation	367
☐ precipitous	102
☐ precision instrument	340
☐ precision machinery	211
☐ preclude	136
☐ precocious	78
☐ precursor	162
☐ predicament	162
☐ predilection	163
☐ predisposition	163
☐ predominant	47
☐ preemptive attack	182
☐ prefabricated house	244
☐ preferential tariff	193
☐ preliminary competition	232
☐ preliminary talks	177
☐ premise	161
☐ prepaid cellular phone	243
☐ preposterous	78

索引

☐ prescription medicine 378	☐ proclivity 163	☐ prototype 209
☐ prescriptive grammar 218	☐ procure 119	☐ protracted 47
	☐ prodigal 78	☐ protractor 357
	☐ prodigious 78	☐ protrude 137
☐ presentiment 163	☐ product 351, 357	☐ provincial government 177
☐ presidential aide 173	☐ product liability 206	
	☐ profane 78	☐ provisional government 177
☐ presidential veto 173	☐ profuse 78	
☐ pressure trough 367	☐ program optimization 323	☐ proximity 162
☐ press working 339		☐ proxy war 182
☐ prestigious 47	☐ progressive wave 319	☐ prudent 48
☐ prestigious university 217	☐ prolific 78	☐ psychiatric center 378
	☐ prominence 360	☐ psycholinguistics 214
☐ presumptuous 47	☐ promontory 370	☐ psychosomatic disease 385
☐ pretax profit 197	☐ promotion transfer 204	
☐ pretentious 47	☐ prom date 219	☐ publicize 119
☐ pretext 163	☐ propaganda war 177	☐ public servant 223
☐ price-earnings ratio 195	☐ propagate 137	☐ pugnacious 103
	☐ propagation loss 328	☐ pulley 335
☐ price busting 203	☐ propellant 344	☐ pump-priming measures 189
☐ price cap 212	☐ propensity 163	
☐ primary industry 210	☐ proper vibration 306	☐ punching bag 232
☐ principal value 357	☐ prophetic 78	☐ pungent 103
☐ principle of action and reaction 305	☐ propitious 102	☐ punitive tariff 193
	☐ proportional representation system 178	☐ pure matter 350
☐ priority seat 238		☐ purport 163
☐ pristine 78		☐ push-up 232
☐ privacy act 177	☐ proprietary technology 211	☐ pyroclastic flow 368
☐ private detective 224		
☐ prize fellowship 216	☐ propulsion 332	**Q**
☐ pro-choice activist 228	☐ prosaic 103	☐ quadrant 357
☐ probability 357	☐ prospective 47	☐ quadratic equation 357
☐ probationary acceptance 215	☐ pros and cons 228	☐ quagmire 163
	☐ protectionism 193	☐ quaint 48
☐ probation period 201	☐ protective coating 341	☐ qualified applicant 219
☐ proceeds 207	☐ Protestant denomination 225	☐ quantitative analysis 350
☐ processor 320		
☐ proclaim 119	☐ protocol 325	☐ quantitative monetary

easing	190	
☐ quantum	309	
☐ quartz	341	
☐ quash	137	
☐ quell	137	
☐ quench	137	
☐ quenching	339	
☐ quibble	137	
☐ quirk	163	
☐ quitter	229	
☐ quixotic	104	
☐ quotation	203	

R

☐ rabies inoculation	379
☐ racial persecution	226
☐ radiant	79
☐ radiation	307
☐ radioactive contamination	364
☐ radiograph	334
☐ radio gymnastic exercises	232
☐ radio wave	319
☐ radius of curvature	357
☐ radix	358
☐ railway crossing	238
☐ rainmaker	176
☐ rain shutter	244
☐ rake	243
☐ ramification	164
☐ rampage	164
☐ rank and file	200
☐ ransack	153
☐ rapids	370
☐ rapprochement talks	183

☐ rash	48, 385
☐ ratch	340
☐ rated value	328
☐ ratification instrument	185
☐ rationalization	358
☐ ravine	370
☐ ravishing	79
☐ raze	137
☐ reaction mixture	350
☐ reactive power	327
☐ readout	320
☐ reagent	344
☐ realignment	211
☐ real estate investment trust	196
☐ real number	358
☐ reassuring	48
☐ rebuff	137
☐ recant	153
☐ recede	119
☐ receptacle	341
☐ receptive	79
☐ recessive genes	388
☐ reciprocal contract	209
☐ reciprocating pump	337
☐ reclusive	79
☐ reconnaissance plane	183
☐ recount	137
☐ recrystallization	350
☐ rectify	138
☐ rectifying circuit	315
☐ rectum polyp	385
☐ recuperate	138
☐ red-tape system	174
☐ redolent	104

☐ redouble	138
☐ redress	139
☐ reduction	348
☐ reduction gear	336
☐ red blood cell	388
☐ reek	154
☐ reference letter	200
☐ referendum legislation	178
☐ refining	350
☐ reflection	309
☐ reflection angle	309
☐ reflectivity	309
☐ reforming reaction	350
☐ refraction	309
☐ refractory	104
☐ refrigerant	341
☐ refurbish	139
☐ regeneration	332
☐ regeneration medicine	374
☐ register	332
☐ regression line	368
☐ regulation	328
☐ reinstate	139
☐ reiterate	119
☐ relativity theory	309
☐ release current	328
☐ relentless	79
☐ religious eclecticism	225
☐ relinquish	139
☐ relish	119
☐ remedial education	216
☐ reminder	203
☐ remission status	378
☐ remnant	164
☐ remorseful	79

索引

413

☐	remote processing	320	☐	retirement allowance	205	☐	roll book	217
☐	remunerative	80	☐	retract	139	☐	room and board	217
☐	render	119	☐	retrench	139	☐	room layout	244
☐	renegade	164	☐	retrieve	139	☐	root-mean-square value	316
☐	renewal charge	209	☐	retrospective exhibition	233	☐	rope skipping	232
☐	rent-a-car	237	☐	return on investment	196	☐	rotation	333
☐	repeal	139	☐	return privilege	203	☐	round-trip ticket	238
☐	repeat sales	209	☐	revamp	139	☐	rout	140
☐	repent	119	☐	revenue	190	☐	royalty	207
☐	replete	104	☐	revenue stamp	192	☐	rubber band	243
☐	repress	120	☐	reverse direction	333	☐	rubbing	339
☐	Republican convention	178	☐	reverse discrimination	226	☐	rubble	165
☐	repudiate	154	☐	revised edition	233	☐	rubric	165
☐	repugnant	80	☐	revitalize	139	☐	ruler	243
☐	repulsive	104	☐	revoke	140	☐	ruling party	176
☐	required course	216	☐	revolutions per minute	333	☐	ruminate	154
☐	rescind	154	☐	revolving door	178	☐	rummage	140
☐	reserve-requirement ratio	191	☐	revulsion	165	☐	running mate	178
☐	reserved-ticket window	239	☐	rhythmic gymnastics	232	☐	runoff voting	178
☐	reserved seat	239	☐	rife	80	☐	runs batted in	231
☐	reservoir	370	☐	rift	165	☐	runup	231
☐	resilient	80	☐	rigid body	332	☐	rustic	80
☐	resistivity	312	☐	rigorous	48	☐	Rust Belt	212
☐	resonance	315	☐	rite of passage	221	☐	rust prevention	341
☐	resonating circuit	315	☐	river basin	370	☐	ruthless	48
☐	resourceful	48	☐	road rage	229			
☐	respite	165	☐	roam	120		**S**	
☐	resplendent	104	☐	robust	48	☐	Sabbath school	225
☐	resurgence	165	☐	rock-bottom interest rates	191	☐	sabbatical term	219
☐	retail banking	196	☐	rocket trajectory	361	☐	saccharine	350
☐	retail outlet	207	☐	rolling	339	☐	safeguard	340
☐	retail politics	176				☐	safeguard clause	193
☐	retard	120				☐	safety recall	210
☐	retardation	316				☐	salacious	104
☐	reticent	80				☐	sales channel	203
						☐	sales quota	207
						☐	salient	80

☐ salutary	104
☐ salvo bombing	183
☐ sandlot baseball	231
☐ sand dune	370
☐ sanguine	81
☐ sardonic	81
☐ saturation current	314
☐ saturation point	350
☐ savor	140
☐ scaffold	340
☐ scalar product	357
☐ scales	243
☐ scalper	224
☐ scanning line	319
☐ scatter diagram	358
☐ schedule drawing	332
☐ schizophrenia	379
☐ school recommendation	215
☐ scientology	226
☐ scoff	140
☐ scorching	81
☐ scornful	48
☐ Scotch tape	243
☐ scourge	165
☐ scowl	154
☐ scramble	324
☐ screw-in type fluorescent lamp	328
☐ scrub	120
☐ scrub brush	243
☐ scrupulous	81
☐ scrutinize	120
☐ scurvy	385
☐ Search for Extraterrestrial Intelligence	361
☐ seasonal rain front	367
☐ secession from the party	176
☐ second-generation politician	223
☐ sectarian strife	176
☐ section line	332
☐ secular	48
☐ security guard	224
☐ sedentary	81
☐ seduce	120
☐ Seeing-Eye dog	228
☐ segmental breakdown	203
☐ seismic center	368
☐ seismology	214
☐ selected stock	195
☐ self-addressed envelope	242
☐ self-fulfilling prophecy	226
☐ selling point	203
☐ semblance	165
☐ senile dementia	385
☐ Senior High School Baseball Championship	231
☐ seniority system	201
☐ seniors	226
☐ sensibility gap	226
☐ sensual	81
☐ separator	341
☐ sequential control	328
☐ serial connection	316
☐ serial number	324
☐ sericulture	211
☐ series circuit	315
☐ serum antibody	378
☐ sever	140
☐ severance pay	201
☐ severe acute respiratory syndrome	385
☐ sewage treatment facility	245
☐ sewer	245
☐ sexual exploitation	227
☐ sex pervert	228
☐ shabby	49
☐ shackle	165
☐ shadow mask	313
☐ shaft	335
☐ shaggy	104
☐ shakeout	211
☐ Shakespeare corpus	219
☐ sham	104
☐ shaping machine	339
☐ sheltered upbringing	222
☐ Shiite Arab	225
☐ shin	388
☐ shipbuilding industry	211
☐ shipping cost	207
☐ shock wave	306
☐ shoehorn	243
☐ shoulder blade	388
☐ shun	120
☐ shunt	316
☐ sibling rivalry	222
☐ side-tracked employees	223
☐ side-view mirror	238
☐ sideband wave	319
☐ signal distortion	319
☐ significant figure	358

索引

☐ sign language interpreter	223
☐ silent majority	228
☐ siliceous	345
☐ sine wave	315
☐ sinister	49
☐ sintering	339
☐ sinusitis	379
☐ sinusoidal wave	358
☐ size AA battery	243
☐ sizzling	81
☐ skeleton staff	200
☐ skewness	331
☐ slaked lime	345
☐ slapstick comedy	233
☐ slate	371
☐ slay	140
☐ sleek	105
☐ sliding contact	331
☐ slippage	331
☐ sloppy	49
☐ slovenly	81
☐ sludge	368
☐ sluice	370
☐ sly	49
☐ small-and-medium-sized business	200
☐ smallpox	385
☐ smattering	166
☐ smear	166
☐ smear campaign	178
☐ smolder	154
☐ smoothing circuit	315
☐ smother	140
☐ snug	105
☐ sobriety test	239
☐ social alienation	227
☐ social implications	228

☐ Social Insurance Agency	192
☐ social integration	219
☐ social security holdings	204
☐ social stigma	227
☐ sodium chloride	345
☐ softening temperature	351
☐ solar eclipse	368
☐ soldering iron	338
☐ solid-state physics	306
☐ solidification	351
☐ solid crossing	239
☐ solubility	351
☐ solvency margin	197
☐ solvent	344
☐ somber	49
☐ soothe	120
☐ sordid	81
☐ sought-after singer	234
☐ sound bite	179
☐ sound clip	324
☐ spacewalk	361
☐ space debris	361
☐ spam mail	324
☐ sparse	81
☐ spasm	166
☐ spawn	140
☐ special pen which looks like a writing brush	243
☐ special public corporation	207
☐ specious	105
☐ spectroscopy	309
☐ speculation	195
☐ speculative portfolio	196

☐ speculative stock	195
☐ speech	219
☐ speech disorder	385
☐ speedometer	333
☐ spinal cord	388
☐ spine milling machine	339
☐ spin doctor	179
☐ spiral spring	340
☐ spleen	388
☐ split bearing	340
☐ split screen	324
☐ sporadic	82
☐ sprained ankle	385
☐ spreadsheet application	325
☐ sprinkler truck	237
☐ squalid	82
☐ squander	140
☐ square root	358
☐ squeamish	105
☐ squeezed acne	388
☐ squirm	154
☐ stagflation	191
☐ staggering	49
☐ stalagmite cave	370
☐ stale	49
☐ standard deviation	358
☐ standing wave	306
☐ standoffish	105
☐ starting cam	336
☐ starting current	314
☐ State of the Union Message	173
☐ state sponsor of terrorism	184
☐ static charge	312

- [ ] static friction 31
- [ ] stationary satellite 361
- [ ] stationing garrison 185
- [ ] stator 328
- [ ] staunch 82
- [ ] steamrolling 173
- [ ] sterilizer 378
- [ ] stethoscope 374
- [ ] sticking plaster for an injury 379
- [ ] stifle 120
- [ ] stigma 165
- [ ] stimulated emission 333
- [ ] stink 166
- [ ] stock option 196
- [ ] stomach cramp 386
- [ ] stopover 238
- [ ] storage capacity 323
- [ ] strain 331
- [ ] strainer 243
- [ ] strait 370
- [ ] stratosphere 360
- [ ] stratum 371
- [ ] stray capacity 327
- [ ] streamline 141, 211
- [ ] strenuous 49
- [ ] stress test 324
- [ ] stretcher 379
- [ ] strident 105
- [ ] stringent 82
- [ ] Structured Query Language 325
- [ ] student discount 238
- [ ] studio 245
- [ ] stuffy 50
- [ ] stunning 50
- [ ] stupendous 105

- [ ] stylistic rule 218
- [ ] stymie 141
- [ ] subcontractor 205
- [ ] subdue 120
- [ ] sublimate 141
- [ ] submissive 105
- [ ] subprime loan 189
- [ ] subroutine 320
- [ ] subsistence 210
- [ ] subsistence agriculture 210
- [ ] substitute teacher 215
- [ ] substrate 341
- [ ] subtitles 233
- [ ] succinct 105
- [ ] succumb 141
- [ ] suction 337
- [ ] sudden infant death syndrome 385
- [ ] suffix form 218
- [ ] sulfuric acid 345
- [ ] sumptuous 82
- [ ] Sunni Islam 225
- [ ] Sunset Belt 212
- [ ] sunspot 360
- [ ] sunstroke 379
- [ ] superconductivity 312
- [ ] supersede 154
- [ ] supple 106
- [ ] supplementary budget 190
- [ ] supply depot 183
- [ ] supporting surface 331
- [ ] support buying 196
- [ ] suppurative tonsillitis 386
- [ ] surface tension 307
- [ ] surrender value 197

- [ ] surreptitious 106
- [ ] surrogate mother 222
- [ ] surveillance camera 245
- [ ] susceptible 50
- [ ] suspended animation 374
- [ ] suspended solid 351
- [ ] suspension bridge 245
- [ ] suspicious vessel 183
- [ ] sustainable development 365
- [ ] swarm 166
- [ ] sweltering 106
- [ ] swerve 141
- [ ] swing 333
- [ ] switchboard 318
- [ ] sympathy vote 178
- [ ] synchronizing circuit 327
- [ ] synopsis 166
- [ ] syntax analysis 218
- [ ] synthetic fibers 346

T

- [ ] tachometer 337
- [ ] tacit 51
- [ ] tainted 82
- [ ] takeover bid 196
- [ ] tangential line 306
- [ ] tantalizing 82
- [ ] tantamount 82
- [ ] Taoist hermit 225
- [ ] tap water 351
- [ ] tattered 107
- [ ] tax break 212
- [ ] tax deduction for spouse 190

索引

☐ tax haven	197	
☐ tax in arrears	197	
☐ tax return	190	
☐ teaching practicum	215	
☐ tectonic activity	371	
☐ teddy bear syndrome	222	
☐ tedious	51	
☐ teenage prostitution	228	
☐ telephone dating club	228	
☐ telling	82	
☐ telltale	107	
☐ temperamental	51	
☐ temperance	166	
☐ temperate climate	366	
☐ tempering furnace	338	
☐ tempest	367	
☐ temporary employee	223	
☐ temporary worker	201	
☐ tenacious	51	
☐ tenet	166	
☐ tenuous	82	
☐ tepid	107	
☐ terminal care	379	
☐ termination	323	
☐ term paper	216	
☐ territorial issue	185	
☐ territorial waters	185	
☐ terse	83	
☐ testimonial advertising	203	
☐ tetanus	379	
☐ theological seminary	216	

☐ theorem	359	
☐ therapeutic effect	379	
☐ thermal decomposition	351	
☐ thermal expansion coefficient	307	
☐ thermal insulation	307	
☐ thermal power generation	327	
☐ thermal radiation	307	
☐ thermal stress	307	
☐ thermodynamics	307	
☐ thermoelectric effect	312	
☐ thermoplastic material	351	
☐ thermosetting property	351	
☐ thermostatic chamber	338	
☐ thickness gauge	330	
☐ thorny	83	
☐ three-martini lunch	204	
☐ three-phase alternating current	327	
☐ threshold	315	
☐ throng	167	
☐ throttle nozzle	337	
☐ thwart	141	
☐ ticket wicket	238	
☐ ticklish	83	
☐ tidal wave	368	
☐ tight-money policy	189	
☐ tightening	339	
☐ tilt	141	
☐ tilt angle	330	
☐ time bomb	183	

☐ tinge	167	
☐ tinker	141	
☐ tirade	167	
☐ tissue culture	365	
☐ titillating	107	
☐ title deed	196	
☐ titular	107	
☐ tokenism	226	
☐ Tokyo Metropolitan Police Department	177	
☐ Tokyo Stock Exchange	197	
☐ toll road	239	
☐ tool angle	339	
☐ Topix index	197	
☐ topography	371	
☐ topple	142	
☐ torpedo-boat destroyer	182	
☐ torrential rain	367	
☐ torrid	83	
☐ torsion	331	
☐ touch-tone phone	243	
☐ toxic substance	364	
☐ track and field	232	
☐ track record	207	
☐ trade-in price	209	
☐ trade deficit	193	
☐ trade friction	193	
☐ trample	154	
☐ transducer	313	
☐ transfer function	359	
☐ transformer	328	
☐ transgress	154	
☐ transient	51	
☐ translucent	309	
☐ translucent	83	
☐ transmission	336	

- ☐ transmission circuit 321
- ☐ transmissivity 309
- ☐ trash chute 243
- ☐ travesty 167
- ☐ treasury bond 197
- ☐ trees covered with ice 368
- ☐ tremor 368
- ☐ triangular thread 340
- ☐ tribulation 167
- ☐ tribute 166
- ☐ trickle-down economics 189
- ☐ trifling 51
- ☐ trigonometry 359
- ☐ trilogy 233
- ☐ tripod 243
- ☐ trite 107
- ☐ trolley 238
- ☐ tropical cyclone 367
- ☐ troubleshooter 204
- ☐ truancy 217
- ☐ tube 238
- ☐ tuberculosis 379
- ☐ tug of war 232
- ☐ turbidity 351
- ☐ turmoil 166
- ☐ turnover rate 207
- ☐ twenty-twenty vision 379
- ☐ two-speed gear 336

U

- ☐ U.N. Charter 185
- ☐ U.N. General Assembly 185
- ☐ ulterior 83
- ☐ ultimatum 182
- ☐ ultrasonic welding 337
- ☐ umbilical cord blood 388
- ☐ unabashed 107
- ☐ unassuming 83
- ☐ uncanny 107
- ☐ uncouth 107
- ☐ undaunted 83
- ☐ undercover agent 183
- ☐ underemployed 205
- ☐ undergraduate curriculum 216
- ☐ undermine 121
- ☐ underpinning 167
- ☐ undulating 107
- ☐ unearth 142
- ☐ unemployment allowance 205
- ☐ uneven parallel bars 232
- ☐ unfold 143
- ☐ unglazed 339
- ☐ United Nations Security Council 186
- ☐ unit area 244
- ☐ unit operation 332
- ☐ universal care 374
- ☐ universal coupling 336
- ☐ universal gravitation 305
- ☐ universal suffrage 178
- ☐ unlicensed taxi 237
- ☐ unparalleled 51
- ☐ unprecedented 51
- ☐ unravel 143
- ☐ untenable 108
- ☐ upholstery 210
- ☐ upmarket 210
- ☐ uproar 167
- ☐ upscale consumer 207
- ☐ upshot 167
- ☐ upstage 143
- ☐ up train 238
- ☐ urea resin 346
- ☐ usher 223
- ☐ usurp 143
- ☐ utilitarian theory 225
- ☐ utility charges 190
- ☐ utility person 224
- ☐ utility pole 245

V

- ☐ vacate 143
- ☐ vacillate 155
- ☐ valedictorian speech 215
- ☐ valuables 243
- ☐ value-added tax 190
- ☐ vanquish 155
- ☐ vaporization 333
- ☐ vaporware 323
- ☐ variable capacitor 313
- ☐ variance 354
- ☐ vaulting wooden box 232
- ☐ veer 143
- ☐ vehement 51
- ☐ venal 108
- ☐ veneered jingoism 175
- ☐ venerable 51
- ☐ venereal 379
- ☐ vengeance 167
- ☐ vengeful 83
- ☐ venomous 84
- ☐ ventilation 243

索引

☐ ventilator	337	
☐ ventriloquism	234	
☐ verbatim	108	
☐ verbose	84	
☐ veritable	108	
☐ vernacular	218	
☐ vernal equinox	368	
☐ vertical motion	305	
☐ vertical press	339	
☐ vertigo	383	
☐ vestige	167	
☐ veterinarian	223	
☐ vexing	85	
☐ vibrant	85	
☐ vibration analysis	306	
☐ vibration frequency	306	
☐ vibrometer	333	
☐ vicinity	168	
☐ vicissitudes	168	
☐ video frequency	319	
☐ vie	143	
☐ vigilant	85	
☐ vile	52	
☐ vilify	155	
☐ vindicate	143	
☐ vindictive	108	
☐ vinyl chloride	346	
☐ virgin forest	363	
☐ virile	108	
☐ virtual image	325	
☐ virulent	108	
☐ visionary	85	
☐ vital capacity	374	
☐ vital statistics	374	
☐ vivacious	85	
☐ vociferous	108	
☐ voice recognition	319	

☐ volcanic eruption	371	
☐ voluntary closure	210	
☐ voluptuous	85	
☐ voracious	85	
☐ vote of confidence	173	
☐ vouch	143	
☐ voucher	198	
☐ voucher system	216	
☐ vulgar	52	

W

☐ wade	155	
☐ wage	143	
☐ walk-in	205	
☐ walkout	201	
☐ waning	85	
☐ wanton	108	
☐ warranty	203	
☐ wartime atrocity	183	
☐ wary	85	
☐ war dead	183	
☐ war reparation	183	
☐ wash-toilet system	244	
☐ washbowl	243	
☐ WASP	227	
☐ waterway	239	
☐ water truck	237	
☐ waveform distortion	317	
☐ waveguide	333	
☐ wavelength	306	
☐ waver	144	
☐ wayward	85	
☐ wean	155	
☐ weapons inspector	183	
☐ wear	331	
☐ weather	144	
☐ weather forecaster	223	

☐ wedge	339	
☐ weightism	226	
☐ welfare pension	198	
☐ westerlies	367	
☐ wheelchair-accessible station	379	
☐ whet	144	
☐ whimsical	86	
☐ whine	121	
☐ whiplashsymptom	380	
☐ Whitewater Affair	186	
☐ wholesale slaughter	183	
☐ wicked	52	
☐ wield	144	
☐ wince	155	
☐ wind-chime	244	
☐ window-dressing statements	203	
☐ windowless train for sightseeing purposes	238	
☐ wine connoisseur	223	
☐ winners' podium	232	
☐ wire broadcasting	319	
☐ wisdom tooth	388	
☐ wish list	209	
☐ wistful	108	
☐ withdrawal deadline	183	
☐ withdrawal symptom	380	
☐ withering	86	
☐ withhold	121	
☐ withholding tax	190	
☐ withstand	121	
☐ woeful	86	
☐ women-only car	238	

- ☐ woo 144
- ☐ woofer diaphragm 318
- ☐ word-of-mouth advertising 206
- ☐ working current 314
- ☐ working property 339
- ☐ work function 305
- ☐ work station 325
- ☐ wrangle 168
- ☐ wreath 168
- ☐ wrench 155
- ☐ wrestle 144
- ☐ wry 109

X

- ☐ xerography 334
- ☐ xylene 346

Y

- ☐ yen-based loan 190
- ☐ yen-denominated bond 190
- ☐ yen quotation 193
- ☐ yield point load 331

Z

- ☐ zero immigration 186
- ☐ zoology 214

日本事象語彙の日本語索引

あ

合気道	295
青汁	249
赤だし	260
赤身肉	249
アク	250
揚げだし豆腐	260
あげはちょう	268
アザラシ	263
あさり	266
アシカ	263
味付け海苔	250
小豆	270
穴子	267
油揚げ	250
油とり紙	290
あべかわ餅	253
あほうどり	265
甘酒	253
尼寺	279
天照大神	282
甘納豆	252
網杓子	262
あめんぼ	269
あや取り	298
あゆ	266
荒行	277
泡立て器	262
あわび	266
泡盛	249
あんかけ	250
あんこう	266
あんころ餅	254
行灯	290
あんパン	254
あんまん	254

い

居合道	295
家元	272
いか	266
いかなご	266
活け作り	260
生け花	272
居酒屋	262
石焼いも	252
イソギンチャク	266
磯辺焼き	252
一見客	299
一寸法師	283
一品料理	258
いなご	269
稲荷	280
稲荷寿司	256
今川焼	254
いもり	263
炒り子	252
いろり	290
いわし	267
いんげん豆	271
印籠	275

う

鵜飼	299
浮世草子	283
うぐいす	265
鶯張り	291
氏子	280
氏寺	277
うじ虫	269
臼	286
謡	274
内祝い	286
腕相撲	298
うどん	255
鰻丼	255
うに	266
乳母車	291
海の日	289
梅	270
瓜	270
上手投げ	296

え

エイ	266
駅弁	258
えび	267
恵比須	282
絵巻物	272
演歌	275
縁側	292
縁起	277
縁談	287
縁日	277
縁結び	280, 300

お

大相撲	295
大関	296
大晦日	286
尾頭付き	260
女将	294
起き上がり小法師	275
送り火	287
おこし	252

おしぼり	261	懐石料理	258	かぶ	270
お歳暮	286	回転ずし	257	歌舞伎	273
おせち料理	255	回転焼	254	かぶとむし	269
お供え	280	貝柱	250	かまきり	269
おたま	261	戒名	279	かまど	290
おつまみ	255	回覧板	294	釜めし	258
お手玉	298	顔見せ	273	紙芝居	299
お年玉	286	雅楽	273	神棚	281
鬼	280, 289	化学調味料	249	かめ	264
鬼瓦	292	かかし	292	かも	265
鬼ごっこ	298	鏡開き	286	かもしか	264
おはぎ	254	鏡餅	286	かもめ	266
おはじき	298	柿	270	家紋	290
帯	294	かき揚げ	260	蚊帳	291
おひたし	260	かき氷	252	粥	258
お布施	277	書き初め	286	辛子明太子	250
お遍路さん	277	角砂糖	252	からす	266
お盆	277	かぐや姫	283	空手	295
お守り	280	かくれんぼ	298	ガリ	248
御神酒	280	駆け込み寺	277	かりんとう	253
おみくじ	280	掛け軸	272	かれい	267
お水取り	276	加工食品	258	枯山水	299
お宮参り	280	風車	299	かわうそ	264
おむすび	255	加持祈祷	277	瓦	292
親方	275	歌集	283	冠婚葬祭	287
親子丼	255	かしわ手	280	かんざし	290
おりがみ	298	柏餅	254	寒天	253
折り鶴	298	粕漬	252	敢闘賞	296
おろし金	261	数の子	250	神主	279
恩	283	勝越し	296	観音菩薩	277
温泉	299	がちょう	265	かんぴょう	251
陰陽道	282	かつお	267	漢方薬	294
		かつおのたたき	255	観覧車	299
か		かっこう	265	甘露煮	258
蛾	269	合掌造り	299		
かいこ	269	華道	272	**き**	
介錯	282	門松	286	戯曲	283
会席料理	258	カバ	264	菊菜	270

季語	283
きじ	266
キス	267
義太夫	274
きつつき	266
きつねうどん	255
きな粉	249
絹ごし豆腐	260
きび	270
黄身	249
君が代	294
脚本	283
灸	290
旧跡	300
弓道	295
狂言	274
餃子	260
行司	295
郷土料理	258
玉露	249
桐ダンス	291
切り干し大根	250
金婚式	287
吟醸酒	249
銀杏	252
金星	296
勤労感謝の日	289

く

草野球	295
くじゃく	266
宮内庁	294
熊手	294
隈取り（歌舞伎）	273
供養	277
栗	271
栗きんとん	255
黒子	274

け

景勝地	300
敬老の日	289
ゲームセンター	298
夏至	289
ゲジゲジ	269
下駄	291
げっ歯動物	265
けむし	269
建国記念日	288
剣山	272
原生動物	264
剣玉	299
剣道	295
憲法記念日	289

こ

鯉のぼり	287
甲殻類	264
皇室	294
皇太子	294
講談	273
香典	279
香道	273
こうのとり	266
酵母	250
高野豆腐	260
氷砂糖	250
こおろぎ	269
こがねむし	269
古今和歌集	283
国定公園	300
国民宿舎	300
国立公園	300
こけし	275
こけらおとし	275
こしあん	254

五重塔	282
こたつ	290
琴	275
小道具	274
子供の日	289
呉服	291
ごぼう	270
独楽	286
ごま	270
狛犬	281
こまどり	266
小麦	271
小結	296
米麹	250
五目飯	258
こんにゃく	251
昆布茶	249
金平糖	253

さ

賽銭箱	282
サイダー	249
祭壇	277
さぎ	266
桜餅	254
ざくろ	270
酒粕	249
ささみ	248
座敷	290
座禅	277
里芋	270
さなぎ	269
さば	267
さび	282
ザリガニ	267
ざる蕎麦	256
猿回し	300
三回忌	277

山菜	251	しゃもじ	261	食物繊維	249
三々九度	287	舎利	278	食糧貯蔵室	262
さんま	267	じゃんけん	298	暑中見舞い	287
三輪車	299	祝儀袋	287	書道	273
		十二支	286	初七日	278
し		十二単	294	除夜	286
ジェットコースター	298	重要文化財	300	除夜の鐘	278
塩辛	252	十両	296	しらみ	269
磁器	275	儒教	278	しりとり	298
色即是空	278	宿泊施設	300	しろあり	269
詩吟	274	殊勲賞	296	白身	252
獅子舞	286	修験道	278	鍼灸	295
四十九日	277	出国カード	300	真空パック	249
自炊	262	出入国管理局	300	新香	259
辞世の句	283	朱肉	290	人工甘味料	249
史跡	300	手裏剣	295	神道	281
しそ	270	周遊観光船	300	神仏混交	281
地蔵	279	春菊	270		
七五三	289	春分	289	**す**	
七福神	282	純文学	283	随筆	283
地鎮祭	289	純米酒	249	水墨画	272
実印	290	将棋	298	すき焼き	256
漆器	275	焼香	279	双六	299
しっくい	292	障子	291	すずめ	266
七宝焼き	275	しょうじょうばえ	269	すずめばち	269
シテ	274	小乗仏教	278	硯	272
地鶏	250	精進料理	259	すだれ	291
しまりす	264	醸造酒	249	砂場	299
注連飾り	286	焼酎	249	滑り台	298
注連縄	282	賞味期限	262	墨	272
霜降り牛肉	256	浄瑠璃	274	墨絵	272
写経	278	鐘楼	299	スルメ	256
尺八	275	精霊流し	288		
シャチ	264	昭和の日	289	**せ**	
しゃちほこ	300	食前酒	249	青磁	275
借景	300	食品宅配サービス	262	成人の日	288
社殿	281	食品添加剤	249	生鮮食品	249
しゃぶしゃぶ	256	植物園	300	蒸籠	262

世界一周旅行	300	大根おろし	259	茶漬け	259
世界文化遺産	300	大豆	271	茶屋	273
脊椎動物	264	大道芸	273	チャンバラ	298
石庭	292	大仏	276	中元	287
赤飯	259	たいやき	254	銚子	261
関脇	296	薪能	274	弔辞	279
節足動物	264	托鉢	279	ちょうちん	290
切腹	282	竹馬	299	ちらし	256
節分	288	竹とんぼ	299	ちりめんじゃこ	252
せみ	269	たけのこ	270	ちんどん屋	275
セリ（歌舞伎）	273	凧揚げ	299		
ぜんざい	254	だしの素	248	**つ**	
千秋楽	296	多神教	282	月見	288
扇子	290	畳	291	佃煮	259
銭湯	294	立会い	296	つくね	252
仙人	282	立ち食いそば屋	262	付け合せ	260
餞別	295	立ち飲み	260	漬け物	252
1000円で食べ放題	262	タツノオトシゴ	267	鼓	275
ぜんまい	270	七夕	287	綱引き	289
千枚漬け	250	だに	269	つまようじ	261
川柳	283	たにし	267	通夜	279
		たぬき	264		
そ		足袋	294	**て**	
草書	273	食べ残し	262	定食	260
草食動物	264	食べ放題のレストラン		手品	299
雑炊	258		262	出初式	286
雑煮	260	玉ぐし料	281	鉄火巻	257
草履	291	他力本願	278	てっさ（ふぐ刺し）	256
即身成仏	278	だるま	275	てるてる坊主	298
そば	255	短歌	284	田楽	274
そば粉	252			伝記	284
そろばん	291	**ち**		電気あんか	291
		竹輪	252	転生	283
た		地酒	249	てんとう虫	269
たい	267	千歳飴	289	天然記念物	300
体育の日	289	地ビール	249	天皇誕生日	289
大鼓	275	ちまき	254		
大黒	282	茶こし器	262		

と

唐辛子	271
陶芸	275
道祖神	282
豆腐	250
灯籠	292
童話	284
とき	266
読経	279
床柱	290
ところてん	253
年越しそば	286
どじょう	267
とそ	286
土葬	279
戸棚	291
徳利	261
土鍋	262
土俵入り	296
留め袖	294
どら焼き	254
鳥居	280
とり貝	267
トロ	256
とろろ	256
とろろ昆布	252
豚汁	256
どんど焼き	286
とんび	266
とんぼ	269

な

長唄	273
なぎなた	295
なぞなぞ	298
名取り	273
七草粥	258
鍋焼きうどん	255

なまこ	266
なます	256
なめくじ	269
奈良漬	252
軟体動物	264

に

仁王	277
にぎりずし	256
肉じゃが	260
肉まん	260
錦	273
錦絵	272
にしん	267
煮干	252
日本髪	295
日本三景	300
にらめっこ	298
人形浄瑠璃	274
人形遣い	274
忍者	295

ぬ

ぬか	252
ぬか漬け	248

ね

ねぎ	270
根付け	291
根回し	282
年中行事	287

の

能	274
熨斗(のし)	291
野点	273
のみ	269
祝詞	280

のれん	291

は

バイキング料理	257
袴	294
履物	294
白菜	271
羽子板	298
箸	262
ハゼ	267
八十八夜	289
はちまき	291
爬虫類	265
パチンコ	298
初釜	273
初日の出	286
発泡酒	249
初詣	286
初夢	286
鼻緒	291
花形	273
花見	287
花道	273
破魔矢	282
囃子	274
ハヤシライス	257
はやぶさ	266
腹芸	283
ばら寿司	256
針供養	288
はりねずみ	264
春雨	252
番傘	292
パン粉	252
反すう動物	264
番付	295
般若	274

ひ

ビー玉	298
日替わりメニュー	260
彼岸	287
ひきがえる	264
引き出物	287
ひき肉	248
ひぐま	264
ビジネスホテル	300
雛人形	287
雛祭	289
火鉢	290
ひばり	266
ヒヒ	264
干物	258
百人一首	299
百年祭	287
冷やし素麺	256
ひょう	264
屏風	273
ひょっとこ	274
ひる	269
琵琶	275

ふ

麩	250
風致地区	300
風鈴	295
舞楽	273
ふきん	262
ふぐ	267
ふぐ刺し	256
福袋	291
福笑い	299
武士道	283
ふすま	291
豚角煮	260
札所	277
仏壇	279
仏滅	279
フナ	267
フライパン	262
ブランコ	298
ぶり	267
振り袖	294
ふるい	262
文化の日	289
文鎮	295
ふんどし	294
文楽	274

へ

弁財天	282
弁当	260

ほ

鳳凰	277
判官びいき	283
法事	279
坊主	276
忘年会	286
ぼうふら	269
ほこら	280
捕食動物	264
菩提寺	279
ほたる	269
哺乳類	265
保養地	300
堀	293
盆	287
盆栽	275
本膳料理	258
煩悩	279

ま

間	283
舞妓	300
前頭	296
回り舞台（歌舞伎）	273
巻き寿司	257
枕草子	284
まげ	295
抹茶	273
まないた	262
招き猫	291
ままごと	298
豆まき	289
まわし	295
漫才	298

み

見合い結婚	286
見得（歌舞伎）	273
三笠	254
巫女	280
神輿	279
水入り	296
水切りボール	262
水引き	287
みそぎ	280
密教	279
三つ葉	270
みつばち	269
みどりの日	289
みのむし	269
みみず	270
宮大工	280
みりん	252
民芸品	300
民宿	301
民謡	275

む

ムササビ	264

無常	283

め

名勝	300
命日	279
メザシ	248
めだか	267
目玉焼き	260

も

猛禽類	265
モーニングサービス	300
木魚	279
木馬	299
もぐら	264
持ち帰り料理	262
持ち帰り用の袋	258
もなか	254
物言い	296
喪服	291
もろみ	250
紋付き	294

や

矢	295
屋形船	300
焼き網	262
焼き芋	259
焼き魚	257
焼き鳥	259
厄年	287
薬味	250
厄除け	282
屋号	273
夜行動物	265
ヤスデ	269
屋台	262, 287
山掛け	256

山伏	277

ゆ

結納	287
幽玄	282
釉薬	275
浴衣	294
雪合戦	299
雪だるま	286
ゆず	270
湯たんぽ	291
湯豆腐	260
百合根	252

よ

洋服ダンス	292
横綱	296
寄せ鍋	258
嫁入り道具	287
寄り切り	296

ら

雷鳥	266
落語	274
落語家	274
らっきょう	270
欄間	292

り

両生類	264
料亭	262
旅程	301
輪廻	279, 282

れ

霊山	279
霊長類	265

冷凍食品	252
礼服	294
冷麺	256
レトルト食品	257

ろ

浪曲	274

わ

わさび	270
綿菓子	253
輪投げ	299
わび	282
わらじ	275
わらび	270

索引

(参考文献)

情報通になるための英語新語・流行語ハンドブック、英語新語研究会編、朝日出版社
最新英語キーワードブック2003-04、小学館辞典編集部編、小学館
ニュース英語のキーフレーズ8000、晴山陽一著、DHC
最新ニュース英語辞典、デイリー・ヨミウリ編、東京堂出版
imidas 2002 別冊付録IT用語/カタカナ・略語辞典、情報通信総合研究所編、集英社
ネットの英語術―インターネットを使いこなすための英語表現ハンドブック、デイビッド・セイン、小松アテナ、エドジェイコブ著、実務教育出版
最新ビジネストレンド英語キーワード辞典、菊池義明著、ピアソン・エデュケーション
工業英語 Technical Terms 7000、日本工業英語協会編
Judy先生の耳から学ぶ工学英語、野口ジュディー、渋谷陽二、杉森直樹著、講談社
1998, 2000, 2001年度国連英検問題集特A級／A級、日本国際連合協会編、講談社
2003年度国連英検問題集特A級／A級、日本国際連合協会編、三修社
連鎖式英単語この方法・この法則、西村喜久著、明日香出版社
化学の不思議がわかる本、満田深雪監修、成美堂出版
医学英語検定試験3・4級教本、日本医学英語教育学会編、メジカルビュー社
合格する！医歯薬への英語、西村真澄著、東京コア
トレンド英語日本図解辞典、Timon Screech, Margaret Elizabeth Price, マーク・大島明著、小学館
和英日本文化表現辞典、研究社辞書編集部編、研究社
日本の観光、山口百々男著、研究社出版
イラスト日本まるごと辞典、インターナショナル・インターンシップ・プログラムス著、講談社インターナショナル
日本文化を英語で紹介する事典、杉浦洋一・John K. Gillespie著、ナツメ社
項目別通訳ガイド事典、山口百々男・小島節子著、ジャパンタイムズ
和英・日本文化辞典、山口百々男・小島節子著、ジャパンタイムズ
HAIKUのすすめ、吉村侑久代・阿部貢著、ジャパンタイムズ
ニッポン不思議発見！―日本文化を英語で語る50の名エッセイ集、日本文化研究所（編集）・松本 道弘（翻訳）、講談社バイリンガル・ブックス
I SEE ALL英語百科事典、堀内克明編、学習研究社
発信型英語世界を読み解くキーワード、植田一三著、ベレ出版

著者略歴

植田一三 (Ichy Ueda)

英語のプロ・達人養成教育学校、Aquaries School of Communication 学長。英語の百科事典を10回以上読破し、辞書数十冊を暗記し、洋画100本以上の全せりふをディクテーションするという「超人的」努力を果たす。ノースウェスタン大学コミュニケーション学部修士課程修了後、テキサス大学スピーチコミュニケーション学部博士課程に留学し、学部生に異文化間コミュニケーションを1年間、パブリックスピーキング、ラップミュージックコミュニケーション、ビジュアルコミュニケーションをそれぞれ半年間指導。Let's enjoy the process!(陽は必ず昇る!)をモットーに、過去23年間に、通信教育受講者を含めて英検1級合格者を1,000人以上、英検1級優秀賞受賞者を17名以上、資格3冠突破者を100名以上、TOEIC満点990点突破者を15名以上、その他アルク翻訳コンクール優勝者や、ハーバード大学、プリンストン大学、UCバークレー、ロンドン大学などをはじめとする英米トップの大学院合格者を50名以上育てる。過去23年間に独自の英語学習教材を100以上開発し、全国出版したベストセラー25冊のうち、5冊は中国、韓国、台湾、マカオ、シンガポールなどアジア5カ国以上で翻訳されている。主な著書に「CD BOOK 日本の地理・歴史の知識と英語を身につける」「発信型英語スーパーレベルリーディング」、「発信型英語スーパーレベルライティング」、「発信型英語スーパーレベル英文法」、「英語で意見を論理的に述べる技術とトレーニング」、「英語スピーキングスキルアップBOOK」、「TOEIC TEST これ1冊で860点突破」、「コンピューター版TOEFL TEST ライティング完全攻略」、「英検1級直前合格対策」などがある。

[連絡先] Aquaries School of Communication
大阪校:〒530-0014 大阪市北区鶴野町4A-709
姫路校:〒670-0053 姫路市南車崎1-1-24
東京校:〒151-0053 渋谷区代々木2-15-12 クランツ南新宿1階
　　　　フリーダイヤル:0120-858-994

CD BOOK 発信型英語(はっしんがたえいご)10000語(ご)レベルスーパーボキャブラリービルディング

2008年11月25日	初版発行
2014年 4月20日	第11刷発行
著者	植田一三(うえだ いちぞう)
カバーデザイン	赤谷　直宣　本文イラスト　　　末吉　陽子

© Ichizo Ueda 2008. Printed in Japan

発行者	内田　眞吾
発行・発売	ベレ出版 〒162-0832 東京都新宿区岩戸町12 レベッカビル TEL (03) 5225-4790 FAX (03) 5225-4795 ホームページ　http://www.beret.co.jp/ 振替 00180-7-104058
印刷	株式会社　文昇堂
製本	根本製本株式会社

落丁本・乱丁本は小社編集部あてにお送りください。送料小社負担にてお取り替えします。

ISBN978-4-86064-211-2 C2082　　　　　　　編集担当　脇山和美

【CD の内容】

- 収録時間：DISC1 72 分 47 秒／DISC2 70 分 55 秒／DISC3 69 分 42 秒
- ナレーション：Howard Colefield　Carolyn Miller　久末絹代
- 収録内容：第 2 章は重要なコロケーション 3 つを収録（英語のみを収録）
  第 3 章、第 5 章は見出しの英語・日本語の順で収録
  第 4 章は見出し語の日本語・英語の順で収録
- 本書の DISC1 と DISC2 はビニールケースに重なって入っています。